T0353351

Security Solutions for Hyperconnectivity and the Internet of Things

Maurice Dawson
University of Missouri–St. Louis, USA

Mohamed Eltayeb
Colorado Technical University, USA

Marwan Omar
Saint Leo University, USA

A volume in the Advances in Information Security, Privacy, and Ethics (AISPE) Book Series

www.igi-global.com

Published in the United States of America by
    IGI Global
    Information Science Reference (an imprint of IGI Global)
    701 E. Chocolate Avenue
    Hershey PA 17033
    Tel: 717-533-8845
    Fax: 717-533-8661
    E-mail: cust@igi-global.com
    Web site: http://www.igi-global.com

Library of Congress Cataloging-in-Publication Data

Names: Dawson, Maurice, 1982- editor. | Eltayeb, Mohamed, 1978- editor. |
  Omar, Marwan, 1982- editor.
Title: Security solutions for hyperconnectivity and the Internet of things /
  Maurice Dawson, Mohamed Eltayeb, and Marwan Omar, editors.
Description: Hershey, PA : Information Science Reference, [2017] | Series:
  Advances in information security, privacy, and ethics | Includes
  bibliographical references and index.
Identifiers: LCCN 2016023423| ISBN 9781522507413 (hardcover) | ISBN
  9781522507420 (ebook)
Subjects: LCSH: Cyberterrorism--Prevention. | Computer crimes--Prevention. |
  Internet of things. | Computer security. | Data protection.
Classification: LCC HV6773.15.C97 S43 2017 | DDC 005.8--dc23 LC record available at https://
lccn.loc.gov/2016023423

This book is published in the IGI Global book series Advances in Information Security, Privacy, and Ethics (AISPE) (ISSN: 1948-9730; eISSN: 1948-9749)

British Cataloguing in Publication Data
A Cataloguing in Publication record for this book is available from the British Library.

Advances in Information Security, Privacy, and Ethics (AISPE) Book Series

ISSN: 1948-9730
EISSN: 1948-9749

MISSION

As digital technologies become more pervasive in everyday life and the Internet is utilized in ever increasing ways by both private and public entities, concern over digital threats becomes more prevalent.

The **Advances in Information Security, Privacy, & Ethics (AISPE) Book Series** provides cutting-edge research on the protection and misuse of information and technology across various industries and settings. Comprised of scholarly research on topics such as identity management, cryptography, system security, authentication, and data protection, this book series is ideal for reference by IT professionals, academicians, and upper-level students.

COVERAGE

- Network Security Services
- Tracking Cookies
- CIA Triad of Information Security
- Risk Management
- Cookies
- IT Risk
- Security Information Management
- Data Storage of Minors
- Technoethics
- Security Classifications

IGI Global is currently accepting manuscripts for publication within this series. To submit a proposal for a volume in this series, please contact our Acquisition Editors at Acquisitions@igi-global.com or visit: http://www.igi-global.com/publish/.

Titles in this Series

For a list of additional titles in this series, please visit: www.igi-global.com

Security Management in Mobile Cloud Computing
Kashif Munir (University of Hafr Al-Batin, Saudi Arabia)
Information Science Reference • copyright 2017 • 248pp • H/C (ISBN: 9781522506027)
• US $150.00 (our price)

Cryptographic Solutions for Secure Online Banking and Commerce
Kannan Balasubramanian (Mepco Schlenk Engineering College, India) K. Mala (Mepco
Schlenk Engineering College, India) and M. Rajakani (Mepco Schlenk Engineering College, India)
Information Science Reference • copyright 2016 • 375pp • H/C (ISBN: 9781522502739)
• US $200.00 (our price)

Handbook of Research on Modern Cryptographic Solutions for Computer and Cyber Security
Brij Gupta (National Institute of Technology Kurukshetra, India) Dharma P. Agrawal (University of Cincinnati, USA) and Shingo Yamaguchi (Yamaguchi University, Japan)
Information Science Reference • copyright 2016 • 589pp • H/C (ISBN: 9781522501053)
• US $305.00 (our price)

Innovative Solutions for Access Control Management
Ahmad Kamran Malik (COMSATS Institute of Information Technology, Pakistan) Adeel
Anjum (COMSATS Institute of Information Technology, Pakistan) and Basit Raza (COMSATS Institute of Information Technology, Pakistan)
Information Science Reference • copyright 2016 • 330pp • H/C (ISBN: 9781522504481)
• US $195.00 (our price)

Network Security Attacks and Countermeasures
Dileep Kumar G. (Adama Science and Technology University, Ethiopia) Manoj Kumar
Singh (Adama Science and Technology University, Ethiopia) and M.K. Jayanthi (King
Khalid University, Saudi Arabia)
Information Science Reference • copyright 2016 • 357pp • H/C (ISBN: 9781466687615)
• US $205.00 (our price)

Next Generation Wireless Network Security and Privacy
Kamaljit I. Lakhtaria (Gujarat University, India)
Information Science Reference • copyright 2015 • 372pp • H/C (ISBN: 9781466686878)
• US $205.00 (our price)

www.igi-global.com

701 E. Chocolate Ave., Hershey, PA 17033
Order online at www.igi-global.com or call 717-533-8845 x100
To place a standing order for titles released in this series,
contact: cust@igi-global.com
Mon-Fri 8:00 am - 5:00 pm (est) or fax 24 hours a day 717-533-8661

Editorial Advisory Board

Table of Contents

Detailed Table of Contents

Secure computing is essential as environments continue to become intertwined and
hyperconnected. As the Internet of Things (IoT), Web of Things (WoT), and the
Internet of Everything (IoE) dominate the landscape of technological platforms,
protection these complicated networks is important. The everyday person who wishes
to have more devices that allow the ability to be connected needs to be aware of
what threats they could be potentially exposing themselves to. Additionally, for the
unknowing consumer of everyday products needs to be aware of what it means to
have sensors, Radio Frequency IDentification (RFID), Bluetooth, and WiFi enabled
products. This submission explores how Availability, Integrity, and Confidentiality
(AIC) can be applied to IoT, WoT, and IoE with consideration for the application
of these architectures in the defense sector.

The Internet of Things (IoT) promises to revolute communications on the Internet.
The IoT enables numerous business opportunities in fields as diverse as e-health,
smart cities, smart homes, among many others. It incorporates multiple long-range,

short-range, and personal area wireless networks and technologies into the designs of IoT applications. This will result in the IoT being pervasive in many areas which raise many challenges. This chapter reviews the major research issues challenging the IoT with regard to security, privacy, and management.

Chapter 3

Stuart Armstrong, Future of Humanity Institute, UK
Roman V. Yampolskiy, JB Speed School of Engineering, USA

Superintelligent systems are likely to present serious safety issues, since such entities would have great power to control the future according to their possibly misaligned goals or motivation systems. Oracle AIs (OAI) are confined AIs that can only answer questions and do not act in the world, represent one particular solution to this problem. However even Oracles are not particularly safe: humans are still vulnerable to traps, social engineering, or simply becoming dependent on the OAI. But OAIs are still strictly safer than general AIs, and there are many extra layers of precautions we can add on top of these. This paper begins with the definition of the OAI Confinement Problem. After analysis of existing solutions and their shortcomings, a protocol is proposed aimed at making a more secure confinement environment which might delay negative effects from a potentially unfriendly superintelligence while allowing for future research and development of superintelligent systems.

Chapter 4

Mohamed Eltayeb, Colorado Technical University, USA

The Internet of Things (IoT) has demonstrated significant potential due to its scalability and agility. As such, it has become increasingly popular and has attracted significant attention from researchers, scholars and innovators alike. The vast amount of interconnected sensors that surround us allow data to be collected, transmitted, stored, aggregated, and shared. However, this data is extremely valuable to those with malicious intent, and collecting and sharing data in the IoT environment is becoming increasingly risky. In recent years, some distinct privacy and security concerns have arisen in relation to the increasing popularity of the IOT. These concerns are not limited to privacy and security values alone, but include issues relating to trust in information security. This chapter takes a detailed look at the privacy and security threats that can arise from the use of IoT services and how they can be potentially overcome.

Chapter 5

Derek Mohammed, Saint Leo University, USA
Marwan Omar, Saint Leo University, USA
Van Nguyen, Saint Leo University, USA

This paper investigates laws and regulations within the financial industry that are applicable to cybersecurity. It analyzes both compliance and regulatory issues across the financial sector at the federal and state levels. Additionally; the paper highlights the importance of adhering to, and implementing industry-based regulations to improve the protection of financial digital assets against cyber-attacks. It also reviews similarities and differences among compliance environments created by financial regulations. Identification, interpretation and application of federal and state government regulations, directives and acts as they apply to the security of digital systems in the financial sector is another objective of this research study. Finally, this paper contrasts the values and issues created by increasing compliance requirements.

Chapter 6

Vimal Kumar, M. M. M. University of Technology, India
Rakesh Kumar, M. M. M. University of Technology, India

One of the generally used routing protocols for MANET is AODV (Ad hoc on demand Distance Vector), which is vulnerable to one of the particular type of security attack called blackhole attack. The characteristics of blackhole attack, a malicious node sends a false route reply without having any fresh route to a destination and is also drop all receiving packets and replay packet in the entire network. A certificateless based signature scheme enables users to generate their public key and private key without using any certificate. Due to this reason, we do not need any certificate authority (CA). In this paper, we propose a novel CLS scheme for prevention of a blackhole attack and also provide secure communication based on CLS scheme. Simulation results show that CLS scheme prevents blackhole attack successfully and is provide better performance to other existing schemes in the presence of blackhole node and also ensuring authentication, integrity and non-repudiation.

Cloud computing is a model for enabling everywhere, suitable, on-demand network access. There are a number of challenges to provide cloud computing services and to accomplish this, it is necessary to establish trust across the cloud, between the user and the service provider. It is becoming increasingly complex for cloud users to make distinction among service providers offering similar kinds of services. There must be some mechanisms in the hands of users to determine trustworthiness of service providers so that they can select service providers with confidence and with some degree of assurance that service provider will not behave unpredictably or maliciously. An effective trust management system helps cloud service providers and consumers reap the benefits brought about by cloud computing technologies. Hence the objective of this chapter is to describe existing mechanisms that are used to determine a trust worthiness of a cloud service, various models that are used for calculating a trust value and method to establish trust management system.

Chapter 8

The discussion of security and trust issues in this book chapter will follow from the discussions on the role of virtualization in cloud computing and hence the impact that the various categories of virtualization such as server virtualization, network virtualization, storage virtualization, and application virtualization have on the security and trust issues in cloud computing. It will be evident from these discussions that virtualization introduces a number of security and risk related challenges in cloud computing based on the three security objectives of confidentiality, integrity, and availability; and the two main other related security objectives of authenticity and accountability of information systems that were adopted for this discussion. It was however also noted that if the necessary recommended best practices of virtualizations are faithfully adhered to, then virtualization can actually lead to improvement or enhancement in the security posture of cloud environments.

Distributed computing systems allow homogenous/heterogeneous computers and workstations to act as a computing environment. In this environment, users can uniformly access local and remote resources in order to run processes. Users are not aware of which computers their processes are running on. This might pose some complicated security problems. This chapter provides a security review of distributed systems. It begins with a survey about different and diverse definitions of distributed computing systems in the literature. Different systems are discussed with emphasize on the most recent. Finally, different aspects of distributed systems security and prominent research directions are explored.

Chapter 10

After the information released by Edward Snowden, the world realized about the security risks of high surveillance from governments to citizens or among governments, and how it can affect the freedom, democracy and/or peace. Research has been carried out for the creation of the necessary tools for the countermeasures to all this surveillance. One of the more powerful tools is the Tails system as a complement of The Onion Router (TOR). Even though there are limitations and flaws, the progress has been significant and we are moving in the right direction.

Civil aviation faces increased cybersecurity threats due to hyperconnectivity and the lack of standardized frameworks and cybersecurity defenses. Educating the civil aviation workforce is one method to enhance cyber defense against cyber-attacks. Educating the workforce will lead to initiatives and strategies to combat cyber-attacks.

Private and public entities need to remain aggressive in developing cyber defense strategies to keep pace with the increasing vulnerabilities of hyperconnectivity. Areas that require immediate attention to safeguard against cybersecurity threats in civil aviation are: 1) Eliminating supply risks, 2) Upgrading legacy systems, 3) Mitigating technological aftereffects, 4) Increasing cybersecurity awareness, 5) Developing cybersecurity workforce, 6) Managing hyperconnectivity, and 7) Leveraging international entities. To safeguard civil aviation infrastructure from cybersecurity threats require assertive, coordinated, and effective strategies and capabilities to defend the network.

Foreword

Andy Greenberg was driving 70 mph on I-64 when his transmission cut out. His 2014 Jeep Cherokee slowed to a crawl as an 18-wheeler approaching from behind— fast. He avoided a collision by rolling down an exit ramp. Later, he lost his brakes and slid uncontrollably into a ditch. Greenberg, a writer, was participating in an experiment for WIRED Magazine that went out of control. Two hackers showed him they could use the Internet to hack and control a late-model Chrysler product from miles away. (Greenberg is fine, by the way.) Sounds a little scary, doesn't it? But it doesn't have to be. – http://www.mitre.org/publications/project-stories/are-you-ready-to-be-part-of-the-internet-of-things

The research contained in this text is timely and informative, providing critical insights into a nascent but rapidly evolving domain known as the "Internet of Things" (IoT). The International Telecommunications Union (ITU) defines the IoT in ITU-T Y.2060, dated June 2012, as "as a global infrastructure for the information society, enabling advanced services by interconnecting (physical and virtual) things based on existing and evolving interoperable information and communication technologies." (ITU, 2012) What does this mean to the layman? Our lives will continue to be penetrated more and more deeply by technology; and not only individual devices, but by globally connected cogs and widgets. They come with the assurance of transforming our lives, according to the Harvard Business Review with "the promise of energy efficiency, convenience, and flexibility." (Clearfield, 2013) This trend will dramatically change the technology landscape, as we move from "connected cars, iPhone-controlled locks, to the…'smart fridge'" (Clearfield, 2013) we will integrate technology further and further into the most intimate parts of our lives. It will be life changing!

However….that same technology will provide new avenues for attackers to not only access our personal information, but to influence our physical lives. The example of Mr. Greenberg, while alarming, gives us a glimpse into the potential negative impacts of such technological dependence. Not only could we be simply spied on, which one could argue is bad enough, via our television or kitchen appliances (Steinberg, 2014)…but now suddenly our garage doors, our door locks, our vehicles can be taken over by a malicious attacker on the other side of the world. A survey of business executives conducted in 2014 confirmed that a large percentage of senior business leaders see concerns on privacy and security as a primary barrier to investment in IoT (Weissman, 2015).

But this text is not about alarmism, but solutions. The research contained in the various chapters of this book provide a depth of technical insight into IoT cybersecurity, information leakage, trusted computing, data security and privacy, and several other salient and timely topics. In a recent article by The MITRE Corporation regarding IoT Security, the author noted six major consequences caused by current security gaps in IoT technology (McKenney, 2014):

- Unauthorized access to services and data
- Exposure of privacy data
- Modification or deletion of data
- Denial or disruption of access to services
- Installation of backdoors or malware
- Use of compromised thing as a launching point for further attacks

It is clear that the research topics in this text directly address these issues and provide novel solutions to counter potential adversary activity, enabling growth and positive impact of IoT technology while mitigating risk to privacy and safety. With any developments in technology there come new risks, new avenues for attack. And we know that malicious actors in cyberspace are here to stay. But, that cannot and should not stop innovation in its tracks. The potential for IoT to produce dramatic improvements in across a variety of areas is significant, we simply need to mitigate the risk. The cutting edge research in this text will do just that. It is timely, it is relevant, and it is impactful.

America's economic prosperity, national security, and our individual liberties depend on our commitment to securing cyberspace and maintaining an open, interoperable, secure, and reliable Internet. Our critical infrastructure continues to be at risk from threats in cyberspace, and our economy is harmed by the theft of our intellectual property. Although the threats are serious and they constantly evolve, I believe that if we address them effectively, we can ensure that the Internet remains an engine for economic growth and a platform for the free exchange of ideas. – President Obama – https://www.whitehouse.gov/issues/foreign-policy/cybersecurity

Donald 'Forrest' Carver
The MITRE Corporation, USA

REFERENCES

Clearfield, C. (2013, June 26). *Rethinking security for the internet of things*. Retrieved from Harvard Business Review: https://hbr.org/2013/06/rethinking-security-for-the-in

ITU. (2012). *ITU-T Y.2060 overview of the internet of things*. ITU.

McKenney, B. (2014, July 1). *Securing the internet of things*. Retrieved from MITRE: http://www.mitre.org/capabilities/cybersecurity/overview/cybersecurity-blog/securing-the-internet-of-things

Steinberg, J. (2014, January 27). *These devices may be spying on you (even in your own home)*. Retrieved from Forbes: http://www.forbes.com/sites/josephsteinberg/2014/01/27/these-devices-may-be-spying-on-you-even-in-your-own-home/#4cc6ef63769e

Weissman, C. G. (2015, January 21). *We asked executives about the internet of things and their answers reveal that security remains a huge concern*. Retrieved from Business Insider: http://www.businessinsider.in/We-Asked-Executives-About-The-Internet-Of-Things-And-Their-Answers-Reveal-That-Security-Remains-A-Huge-Concern/articleshow/45959921.cms

Preface

This book explores and presents Cybersecurity solutions for the Internet of Things (IOT) and hyper connectivity. This book offers insights from cutting-edge research findings conducted by sharp minds in academia. We live in a time and a society where virtually every single physical object in our life is connected and everyone is vulnerable; this necessities a revolution in the way we think of security and in the way we defend our most sensitive digital assets. This book helps design that revolutionary protection strategy by offering timely and informative research that takes the evolving security landscape into account and presents solutions to tackle sophisticated cyber-attacks. As hackers become more innovative in the way they craft their attacks and compromise our systems, we, too, need to rethink the entire way of defending our cyber system and design solutions that detect and respond to emerging cyber threats.

Our intention in editing this book was to provide new tools and techniques that are utilized in secure computing, mobile computing, training, and laws. This book is to provide frontier research to include cases that are timely and applicable to modern events. Since the book covers case study-based research findings, it can be quite relevant for researchers, university academics, secure computing professionals, and probing university students. In addition, it will help those researchers who have interest in this field to gain insight into different concepts and their importance for applications in real life. This has been done to make the edited book more flexible and to stimulate further interest in topics.

ORGANIZATION OF THIS BOOK

In this book, we present 11 chapters aimed at emphasizing security solutions that are applicable to today's mounting and sophisticated cyber-attacks. For coherency, we have ordered the chapters in terms of similarity of topic. The topics covered range from enhancing Cybersecurity for the financial industry to creating a secure and safe computing environment for the Internet of Things (IoT).

Chapter 1: "Exploring Secure Computing for the Internet of Things, Internet of Everything, Web of Things, and Hyper Connectivity", discusses how secure computing is essential as environments continue to become intertwined and hyper-connected. As the Internet of Things (IoT), Web of Things (WoT), and the Internet of Everything (IoE) dominate the landscape of technological platforms, protection these complicated networks is important. The everyday person who wishes to have more devices that allow the ability to be connected needs to be aware of what threats they could be potentially exposing themselves to.

Chapter 2, "Internet of Things Research Challenges", explains how The Internet of Things (IoT) promises to revolute communications on the Internet. The IoT enables numerous business opportunities in fields as diverse as e-health, smart cities, smart homes, among many others. It incorporates multiple long-range, short-range, and personal area wireless networks and technologies into the designs of IoT applications. This will result in the IoT being pervasive in many areas which raise many challenges. This Chapter reviews the major research issues challenging the IoT with regard to security, privacy, and management.

Chapter 3, "Security Solutions for Intelligent and Complex Systems", begins with the definition of the Oracle Artificial Intelligent (OAI) Confinement Problem. After analysis of existing solutions and their shortcomings, a protocol is proposed aimed at making a more secure confinement environment which might delay negative effects from a potentially unfriendly superintelligence while allowing for future research and development of super intelligent systems.

Chapter 4, "Privacy and Security", discusses how The Internet of Things (IoT) has demonstrated significant potential due to its scalability and agility. As such, it has become increasingly popular and has attracted significant attention from researchers, scholars and innovators alike. The vast amount of interconnected sensors that surround us allow data to be collected, transmitted, stored, aggregated, and shared. However, this data is extremely valuable to those with malicious intent, and collecting and sharing data in the IoT environment is becoming increasingly risky. This chapter takes a detailed look at the privacy and security threats that can arise from the use of IoT services and how they can be potentially overcome.

Chapter 5, "Enhancing Cyber Security for Financial Industry through Compliance and Regulatory Standards", investigates laws and regulations within the financial industry that are applicable to cybersecurity. It analyzes both compliance and regulatory issues across the financial sector at the federal and state levels. Additionally; the paper highlights the importance of adhering to, and implementing industry-based regulations to improve the protection of financial digital assets against cyber-attacks. It also reviews similarities and differences among compliance environments created by financial regulations. Identification, interpretation and application of federal and state government regulations, directives and acts as they apply to the security of digital systems in the financial sector is another objective of this research study.

Chapter 6, "Prevention of Blackhole Attack Using Certificateless Signature (CLS) Scheme in MANET", propose a novel CLS scheme for prevention of a blackhole attack and also provide secure communication based on CLS scheme. Simulation results show that CLS scheme prevents blackhole attack successfully and provides better performance to other existing schemes in the presence of blackhole node and also ensuring authentication, integrity and non-repudiation.

Chapter 7, "Trust Management in Cloud", presents an effective trust management system that helps cloud service providers and consumers reap the benefits brought about by cloud computing technologies. It also describes existing mechanisms that are used to determine a trust worthiness of a cloud service, various models that are used for calculating a trust value and method to establish trust management system.

Chapter 8, "Security and Trust in Cloud Computing", discusses security and trust issues in the role of virtualization in cloud computing and hence the impact that the various categories of virtualization such as server virtualization, network virtualization, storage virtualization, and application virtualization have on the security and trust issues in cloud computing. Virtualization introduces a number of security and risk related challenges in cloud computing based on the three security objectives of confidentiality, integrity, and availability; and the two main other related security objectives of authenticity and accountability of information systems that were adopted for this discussion.

Chapter 9, "Security Issues in Distributed Computing System Models", provides a security review of distributed systems. It begins with a survey about different and diverse definitions of distributed computing systems in the literature. Different systems are discussed with emphasize on the most recent. Finally, different aspects of distributed systems security and prominent research directions are explored.

Chapter 10, "Tails Linux, the Amnesiac Incognito System in Times of High Surveillance: Its Security Flaws, Limitations, and Strengths in the Fight for Democracy", presents one of the more powerful tools, the Tails system, as a complement of TOR. Even though there are limitations and flaws, the progress has been significant and we are moving in the right direction

Chapter 11, "Cyber Security Threats in Civil Aviation", discusses how civil aviation faces increased cyber security threats due to hyperconnectivity and the lack of standardized frameworks and cyber security defenses. Educating the civil aviation workforce is one method to enhance cyber defense against cyber-attacks. Educating the workforce will lead to initiatives and strategies to combat cyber-attacks.

Private and public entities need to remain aggressive in developing cyber defense strategies to keep pace with the increasing vulnerabilities of hyperconnectivity. To safeguard civil aviation infrastructure from cyber security threats require assertive, coordinated, and efficient strategies and capabilities to defend against persistent and mounting cyber security threats.

Maurice Dawson
University of Missouri – St. Louis, USA

Marwan Omar
Saint Leo University, USA

Mohammed Eltayeb
Colorado Technical University, USA

Acknowledgment

First and most importantly, we would like thank all the authors for their excellent contributions to this book. Your work has brought to life our dream, conceptualizing this topic and packaging in a manner that is accessible to a wide audience.

Second, our heartfelt gratitude goes to all the reviewers who provided insightful and constructive feedback on the contributed chapters. Thank you for making the time in what must be a very busy schedule.

Finally, but not the least, a special note of thanks to the faculties at University of Missouri - St. Louis, Saint Leo University, and Colorado Technical University. Specifically we would like to thank Dean Charles Hoffman, Dr. Kailah Josh, Dr. Shaji Khan, Dr. Mary Lacity, Dr. Dinesh Mirchandani, Dr. Joseph Rottman, Dr. Vicki Sauter, Prof. Mimi Duncan, Prof. Robert McCarthy, Dr. Balbir Bar, Dr. Derek Mohammed, Dr. Bruce Harmon, Dr. Bo I. Sandén, and Dr. Hassan Kazemian. And thanks for the resources provided by the Polytechnic University of Puerto Rico, University of the Gambia, University of Nairobi, Capitol Technology University, Nawroz University, South Ural State University, London Metropolitan University, and the American Leadership & Policy Foundation.

Maurice Dawson
University of Missouri – St. Louis, USA

Marwan Omar
Saint Leo University, USA

Mohamed Eltayeb
Colorado Technical University, USA

Chapter 1
Exploring Secure Computing for the Internet of Things, Internet of Everything, Web of Things, and Hyperconnectivity

Maurice Dawson
University of Missouri – St. Louis, USA

ABSTRACT

Secure computing is essential as environments continue to become intertwined and hyperconnected. As the Internet of Things (IoT), Web of Things (WoT), and the Internet of Everything (IoE) dominate the landscape of technological platforms, protection these complicated networks is important. The everyday person who wishes to have more devices that allow the ability to be connected needs to be aware of what threats they could be potentially exposing themselves to. Additionally, for the unknowing consumer of everyday products needs to be aware of what it means to have sensors, Radio Frequency IDentification (RFID), Bluetooth, and WiFi enabled products. This submission explores how Availability, Integrity, and Confidentiality (AIC) can be applied to IoT, WoT, and IoE with consideration for the application of these architectures in the defense sector.

DOI: 10.4018/978-1-5225-0741-3.ch001

INTRODUCTION

The next era of computing will be outside of the traditional desktop (Gubbi, Buyya, Marusic, & Palaniwami, 2013). When you consider Bring Your Own Device (BYOD) as a radical step imagine using devices such as a refrigerator that contain an embedded computing device to track the quantity of groceries within. This embedded device would allow access to email, weather, and other devices that allow connectivity through WiFi, or some Application Programming Interface (API) to a web based application. Thus, the data collected would be weather, thermostat cooling patterns, foods purchased, the cost of items per month, average consumption, and more. This massive amount of data that can also be collected means there has to be the large place that this data is stored. At the moment organizations such as Cisco Systems and others are pushing for IoT, and IoT but none has a plan for ensuring Information Assurance (IA) posture is maintained during various modes of operation.

HYPERCONNECTIVITY

Hyperconnectivity is a growing trend that is driving cyber security experts to develop new security architectures for multiple platforms such as mobile devices, laptops, and even wearable displays (Dawson, Omar, Abramson, & Bessette, 2014). The futures of both national and international security rely on complex countermeasures to ensure that a proper security posture is maintained during this state of hyper-connectivity. To protect these systems from the exploitation of vulnerabilities, it is essential to understand current and future threats to include the instructions, laws, policies, mandates, and directives that drive their need to be secured. It is impera-tive to understand the potential security-related threats with the use of social media, mobile devices, virtual worlds, augmented reality, and mixed reality.

In an article published by Forbes, a contributor describes the concept of hyper-connectivity in six different scenarios (Ranadivé, 2013). These events range from energy to hospitality. In health-care there would be real time monitoring through wrist monitors that the medical staff could monitor to get instantaneous feeds on patients that are real time. They would be able to foresee problems before they occur or receive alerts during various events. Imagine a pregnant woman that is having early complications could be monitored first through a wristband that delivers real-time patient information wirelessly.

When discussing hyperconnectivity, it is necessary to examine systems of systems concepts. Systems of systems is a collection of systems tied together to create a more complex system (Popper, Bankes, Callaway, & DeLaurentis, 2004). When thinking about the possibilities of hyperconnectivity the Personal Area Network (PAN) is an excellent example as it allows multiple technologies to be interconnected with soil ware applications. The Google Glass has the potential to all Global Positioning System (GPS), social media, digital terrain overlays, and synchronization with other devices. This increases the complexity of the system as it becomes part of larger systems which multiplies the number of potential vulnerabilities.

INTERNET OF THINGS

IoT is a global infrastructure for information society enabling services by interconnecting physical and virtual things based on existing and evolving interoperable Information Communication Technologies (ICT) (International Telecommunication Union, 2012). Gartner has developed a figure which displays the hype cycle of emerging technologies. This hype circle shows the expectations on the y-axis where on the x-axis time is displayed [See Figure 1]. The time shown is the innovation trigger, the peak of inflated expectations, the trough of disillusionment, slope of enlightenment, and plateau of productivity (Gartner, 2014). What the figure fails to provide is anything associated with security about the technologies identified. The figure simply shows the cycle of emerging technologies with time corresponding to expectations.

Figure 1. Gartner 2014 hype cycle of emerging technologies
(Source: Gartner Inc.)

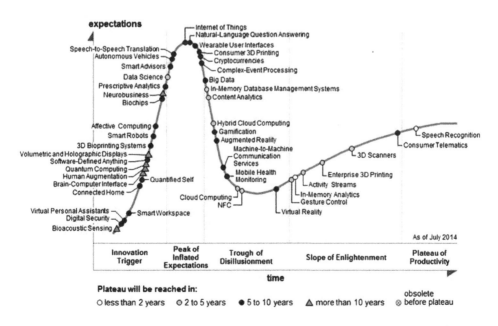

WEB OF THINGS

The WoT is a continued vision that describes concepts where everyday objects are fully integrated into the World Wide Web (WWW). This concept focused on embedded computing devices that enable communication with WWW. The devices can ring from refrigerators to mobile devices with integrated with the Web through an API (Guinard & Trifa, 2009). The Social WoT offers opportunities to use social connections and underlying social graphs to share digital artifacts (Guinard, 2011). This would help bridge a gap between social networks and networks of objects transforming communication. Figure 2 displays the WoT architecture and the detailed layers it is comprised of.

Figure 2. Building the web of things

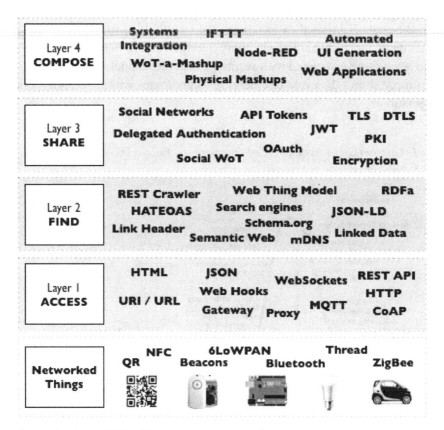

Source: Building the Web of Things: book.webofthings.io
Creative Commons Attribution 4.0

This bridge between social connections and basic things could allow for a plethora of data that can be analyzed unlike before. When looking at the networked things you can see the multiple of different technologies can be enabled in WoT. When looking at Layer 1, you can immediately see items that are a cause of problems. For examples, Hyper Text Markup Language (HTML) and JavaScript Object Notation (JSON) contain known vulnerabilities. In current social networks, geolocation provides individuals exact location. However, anyone that develops an application using this API can tweak items providing, even more, the granularity of its users. Even without modification of Tweets only adding the location will provide details such as neighborhood, city, state, or country. This publication information can be used to start an analysis. In iOS version 6.26+ and Android version 5.55+ precise location can be shared if elected to do so. Also, third party applications or websites may share specific Tweet locations as well.

Various social media accounts provide the ability to associate a particular location. This position over time can provide trends of sites visited with time/date stamps. This can be used to start developing a full analysis on Tweeting trends from particular locations, frequency of location visits, and content analysis through text mining. Exchange Image File Format (EXIF) data is a standard that specifies the formats for images, sounds, and ancillary tags used by digital cameras. The EXIF digital image standard defines the following; the basic structure of digital image data files, labels and JPEG marker segments the conventional uses, and how to define and management format versions (Tešić, 2005). Research has been conducted on how to extract efficiently EXIF data for prosecuting those involved in child pornography (Alvarex, 2004).

In Layer 3, some of these concerns can be appropriately addressed. In this layer controls can be made for the ability to share content. Content can be tagged with a severity and classification to have automatically a security feature added. If the data were Personal Identifiable Information (PII) then the data would have encryption, and access controls that only allow certain individuals to obtain it. That data could be sent wireless over a Bluetooth enabled device or a medical beacon.

INTERNET OF EVERTHING

The IoE consists of four grouping with are data, things, people, and process (Bradley, Barbier, & Handler, 2013). IoE leverages data as a means to make more insightful decisions. IoT plays a significant role in the things of IoE as this is the network of physical devices and objects connected to the Internet for decisions making. The IoE connects people in more valuable and relevant ways. The process is the last part which is delivering the correct information to the right entity at the right time.

Researchers at Cisco Systems estimate that over 99 percent of physical devices are still unconnected and that there is a market of $14.4 trillion. This white paper urges business leaders to transform their organizations based on key learnings to be competitive for the future. (Evans, 2012). IoE is comprised of four key things which are people, data, and things built on the process. The model IoE is made up of three types of connections: People to Machine (P2M), Machine to Machine (M2), and People to People (P2P).

BODY HACKING AND ENHANCEMENT

One of the newest trends in staying connected is human enhancement through body hacking (Nortol, 2007). This involves individuals placing RFID chips into their bodies. These RFID components are associated with unique ID numbers that can be used for unlocking doors, logistical tracking, embedded electronics, e-government, and more. The use for e-government would allow interaction between government

Figure 3. The what, where, and how of the Internet of everything (Source: Cisco IBSG, 2012)

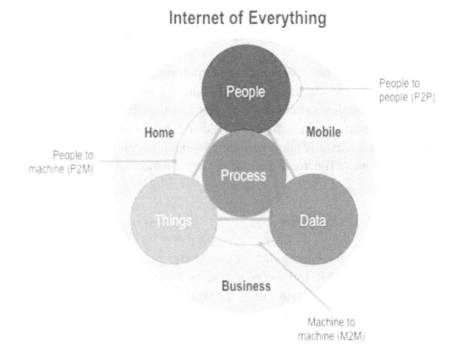

and outside groups through the connected body parts. A health organization could monitor the status of a group through embedded chips or other devices connected to an individual or group.

The issues surrounding body hacking is the lack of security controls associated with making these mods. Early when discussed in this chapter was hyperconnectivity, IoT, and IoE to provide an overview of these various technological concepts. When adding more connectivity to systems the complexity increases thus it becomes more difficult to protect effectively from potential threats. For items such a pacemakers it has already been proven to be hackable (Kirk, 2012; Richardson, n.d.).

In the report Enhanced Warfighters: Risk, Ethics, and Policy (2013) that is prepared for The Greenwall Foundation discussed is the findings of using technology for soldiers. As other technologies are emerging within the United States (U.S.), a military sector so is robotics, Artificial Intelligence (AI), human enhancement technologies, other cyber capabilities. The issues surrounding human enhancement technologies among other items are the operational, ethical, and legal implications (Mehlman, Lin, P., & Abney, 2013). Regarding risks, those identified are about the technology falling into the wrong hands allowing for reverse engineering. Reverse engineering would allow non-friendlies to develop similar technologies on their own to rival those found on the warfighters.

SECURITY AND PRIVACY

As a new wave of Internet-enabled technologies arrive, it is imperative to understand fully the security and privacy concerns (Thierer, 2015). And understanding these concerns also means understanding how to appropriately apply IA controls to systems. Addressing security objectives appropriately will allow for risks to be mitigated. This means following the principles of security to ensure IA posture is achieved.

With all of these connected devices using proven standards, policies, and guidance can help with the ease of integrating these technologies into everyday life. Currently, there is a lack of guidance for securing IoT, IoE, and WoT as a cohesive unit. However there is appropriate documentation available through the National Institute of Standards and Technology (NIST), Federal Information Processing Systems (FIPS), Department of Defense (DoD), Institute of Electronic and Electrical Engineers (IEEE), International Organization for Standardization (ISO), Defense Information Systems Agency (DISA) Security Technical Implementation Guides (STIGs), and more. It will be key for the security engineer to understand how to protect these devices individually and then understand the how the devices become more vulnerable when connected. Mobile devices would need to be hardened with appropriate security controls (Dawson, Wright, & Omar, 2016; Omar & Dawson,

Figure 4. AIC triad

2013). Encryption would need to be on devices that have IoT capabilities such as refrigerators, televisions, or smart watches. This would allow the protection of data in transit and at rest. Access controls would need to be placed to ensure that other users of the hyperconnected systems to do not have

With the potential threats of cyber terrorism affecting national and international security the importance of security is elevated to greater heights (Dawson, Omar, & Abramson, 2015). New threats against national infrastructure and digital crime are making researchers consider new methods of handling cyber incidents (Dawson, & Omar, 2015). It is imperative that if the government or commercial sectors want to make use of these new technological Internet and Web-enabled architectures that they are prepared to battle new threats.

Currently, DoD is using limited IoT to be more efficient in combat. New battlefield technology includes helmets that provide a Heads Up Display (HUDs) to provide Global Positioning System (GPS) battle mapping to integrate with other technologies that provide real-time tracking of the battlefield. A potential example includes the ability to control Unmanned Air Vehicles (UAV) through sensors tied to platoon leaders rather than the use of a Universal Ground Control System (UGCS) or Portable Ground Control System (PGCS). IoT, IoE, and WoT can place the control of tactical devices directly in the hands of those soldiers who are a front line during combat missions. In years to comes body enhancement with RFIDs and other sensors could provide situational awareness data to the soldiers and those that lead them. This data can be analyzed to maximize the effectiveness of troop movement, target location, and other activities deemed key to the mission of the military.

CONCLUSION

Secure computing is essential as technological environments continue to become intertwined and hyperconnected. The policies to properly secure these new environments must also be explored as many of the security controls found within guidance such as the DoD focuses on singular systems and components (Dawson Jr, Crespo, & Brewster, 2013). There needs to be the creation of new controls that review embedded sensors, body modifications, and devices that fully take advantage of Internet-enabled technologies. With the emergence of these technologies, the possibilities are endless however there will be new vulnerabilities unexplored.

REFERENCES

Alvarez, P. (2004). Using extended file information (EXIF) file headers in digital evidence analysis. *International Journal of Digital Evidence*, 2(3), 1–5.

Bradley, J., Barbier, J., & Handler, D. (2013). *Embracing the Internet of everything to capture your share of $14.4 trillion*. White Paper, Cisco.

Dawson, M., & Omar, M. (2015). *New Threats and Countermeasures in Digital Crime and Cyber Terrorism*. Hershey, PA: IGI Global; doi:10.4018/978-1-4666-8345-7.ch001

Dawson, M., Omar, M., & Abramson, J. (2015). Understanding the Methods behind Cyber Terrorism. In M. Khosrow-Pour (Ed.), *Encyclopedia of Information Science and Technology* (3rd ed.; pp. 1539–1549). Hershey, PA: Information Science Reference; doi:10.4018/978-1-4666-5888-2.ch147

Dawson, M., Omar, M., Abramson, J., & Bessette, D. (2014). The Future of National and International Security on the Internet. In A. Kayem & C. Meinel (Eds.), *Information Security in Diverse Computing Environments* (pp. 149–178). Hershey, PA: Information Science Reference; doi:10.4018/978-1-4666-6158-5.ch009

Dawson, M., Wright, J., & Omar, M. (2016). Mobile Devices: The Case for Cyber Security Hardened Systems. In Mobile Computing and Wireless Networks: Concepts, Methodologies, Tools, and Applications (pp. 1103-1123). Hershey, PA: Information Science Reference. doi:10.4018/978-1-4666-8751-6.ch047

Dawson, M. E. Jr, Crespo, M., & Brewster, S. (2013). DoD cyber technology policies to secure automated information systems. *International Journal of Business Continuity and Risk Management*, *4*(1), 1–22. doi:10.1504/IJBCRM.2013.053089

Evans, D. (2012). The internet of everything: How more relevant and valuable connections will change the world. *Cisco IBSG*, 1-9.

Gartner. (2014, August 11). *Gartner's 2014 Hype Cycle for Emerging Technologies Maps the Journey to Digital Business*. Retrieved February 28, 2016, from http://www.gartner.com/newsroom/id/2819918

Gubbi, J., Buyya, R., Marusic, S., & Palaniswami, M. (2013). Internet of Things (IoT): A vision, architectural elements, and future directions. *Future Generation Computer Systems*, *29*(7), 1645–1660. doi:10.1016/j.future.2013.01.010

Guinard, D. (2011). *A web of things application architecture-Integrating the real-world into the web*. (Doctoral dissertation). ETH Zurich.

Guinard, D., & Trifa, V. (2009, April). Towards the web of things: Web mashups for embedded devices. In *Workshop on Mashups, Enterprise Mashups and Lightweight Composition on the Web (MEM 2009), in proceedings of WWW (International World Wide Web Conferences),* (p. 15).

Harris, S., & Meyers, M. (2002). *CISSP*. McGraw-Hill/Osborne.

International Telecommunication Union. (2012a). ITU-T recommendation Y.2060: Series Y: Global information infrastructure, internet protocol aspects and next-generation networks: Frameworks and functional architecture models: Overview of the Internet of Things. Geneva: International Telecommunication Union.

International Telecommunication Union. (2012b). ITU-T recommendation Y.2063: Series Y: Global information infrastructure, internet protocol aspects and next-generation networks: Frameworks and functional architecture models: Framework of the Web of Things. Geneva: International Telecommunication Union.

International Telecommunication Union. (2012c). ITU-T recommendation Y.2069: Series Y: Global information infrastructure, internet protocol aspects and next-generation networks: Frameworks and functional architecture models: Terms and definitions for the Internet of Things. Geneva: International Telecommunication Union.

Kirk, J. (2012). Pacemaker hack can deliver deadly 830-volt jolt. *Computerworld*, 17.

Mehlman, M., Lin, P., & Abney, K. (2013). *Enhanced Warfighters: Risk, Ethics, and Policy*. Case Legal Studies Research Paper, (2013-2).

Norton, Q. (2007). *The Next Humans: Body Hacking and Human Enhancement*. O'Reilly Emerging Technology Conference.

Omar, M., & Dawson, M. (2013, April). Research in Progress-Defending Android Smartphones from Malware Attacks. In *Advanced Computing and Communication Technologies (ACCT), 2013 Third International Conference on* (pp. 288-292). IEEE. doi:10.1109/ACCT.2013.69

Popper, S., Bankes, S., Callaway, R., & DeLaurentis, D. (2004). *System-of-Systems Symposium: Report on a Summer Conversation*. Arlington, VA: Potomac Institute for Policy Studies.

Ranadivé, V. (2013, February 19). *Hyperconnectivity: The Future is Now*. Retrieved March 21, 2016, from http://www.forbes.com/sites/vivekranadive/2013/02/19/hyperconnectivity-the-future-is-now/#401d45d26b9f

Richardson, C. (n.d.). Critical Infrastructure Protection. *Alternative Energy CBRN Defense Critical Infrastructure Protection*, 13.

Tešić, J. (2005). Metadata practices for consumer photos. *MultiMedia, IEEE*, *12*(3), 86–92. doi:10.1109/MMUL.2005.50

Thierer, A. D. (2015). The internet of things and wearable technology: Addressing privacy and security concerns without derailing innovation. *Adam Thierer, The Internet of Things and Wearable Technology: Addressing Privacy and Security Concerns without Derailing Innovation, 21*.

KEY TERMS AND DEFINITIONS

Authentication: Security measure designed to establish the validity of a transmission, message, or originator, or a means of verifying an individual's authorization to receive specific categories of information (Harris, 2002).

Availability: Timely, reliable access to data and information services for authorized users (Harris, 2002).

Confidentiality: Assurance that information is not disclosed to unauthorized individuals, processes, or devices (Harris, 2002).

Hyperconnectivity: Use of multiple means of communications such as instant messaging, phones, Web 2.0, Web 3.0, and other communication methods.

Integrity: Quality of an IS reflecting the logical correctness and reliability of the OS; the logical completeness of the hardware and software implementing the protection mechanisms; and the consistency of the data structures and occurrence of the stored data. Note that, in a formal security mode, integrity is interpreted more narrowly to mean protection against unauthorized modification or destruction of information (Harris, 2002).

Internet of Everything: Consists of four grouping with are data, things, people, and process (Bradley, Barbier, & Handler, 2013).

Internet of Things: A global infrastructure for information society enabling services by interconnecting physical and virtual things based on existing and evolving interoperable ICT (International Telecommunication Union, 2012).

Non-Repudiation: Assurance the sender of data is provided with proof of delivery and the recipient is provided with proof of the sender's identity, so neither can later deny having processed the data (Harris, 2002).

Open Source Intelligence: Intelligence collected from publicly available sources.

Web of Things: Refers to making use of the IoT in order for (physical and virtual) things to be connected and controlled via the world wide web (International Telecommunication Union, 2012).

Chapter 2
Internet of Things Research Challenges

Mahmoud Elkhodr
Western Sydney University, Australia

Seyed Shahrestani
Western Sydney University, Australia

Hon Cheung
Western Sydney University, Australia

ABSTRACT

The Internet of Things (IoT) promises to revolute communications on the Internet. The IoT enables numerous business opportunities in fields as diverse as e-health, smart cities, smart homes, among many others. It incorporates multiple long-range, short-range, and personal area wireless networks and technologies into the designs of IoT applications. This will result in the IoT being pervasive in many areas which raise many challenges. This chapter reviews the major research issues challenging the IoT with regard to security, privacy, and management.

INTRODUCTION

The Internet of Things (IoT) foresees the interconnection of billions of things by extending the interactions between humans and applications to a new dimension of communications via things. Rather than always interacting with the users, things will be interacting with each other autonomously by performing actions on behalf of

DOI: 10.4018/978-1-5225-0741-3.ch002

the users. Consequently, the availability of information coming from non-traditional computer devices in the digital world will, in great parts, lead to improving the quality of life. Over the next couple of years, it is predicted that the industrial value of the IoT will surpass that of the Internet 30 times over, and to be a market that is worth more than $100 billion dollars (Clendenin, 2010). On the other hand, it is estimated that there will be more than 20 billion devices connected to the Internet by 2020 (Lomas, 2009). While Cisco predicts that the number of connected devices will exceed 50 billion in 2020 (Evans, 2012). The IoT will revolute many industries and elevate communications on the Internet. The IoT provides the user with numerous services and capabilities. The obvious ones are the ability to control and monitor the physical environment remotely over the communication networks. Typical examples are the ability to close a door or receiving smoke alert notifications, and the likes, remotely over the Internet. However, the true vision of the IoT revolves around connecting networks and a group of sensors together in an intelligent and ubiquitous fashion. Thus, the IoT promises to enable numerous business opportunities in fields as diverse as e-health, smart cities, farming among many others.

The interconnection of things allows not only things to communicate with each other but also offers the opportunities of building intelligence and pervasiveness into the IoT. For instance, by connecting home appliances to the smart grid, the IoT will enable better energy consumption and water conservation. In addition to helping users in monitoring their own usage, the IoT will optimize energy demand distribution across a city and regulate the automatic consumptions of electricity and other resources. For that to happen, the IoT will need to access a vast array of data and devices, analyze the users' behaviors, and monitor occupancy and lighting conditions. It also needs to collect various sensitive information about the users, their activities and environment. This will result in the IoT being pervasive in many areas. Hence, the potentially massive number of things, their diversity, and the seamless and heterogeneous nature of communications encountered in the IoT raises many research challenges.

Many envisioned IoT applications will require the automated sharing of the users' information collected by things. This requires agreements on many applications and networks levels. How things will be identified and accessed on the Internet remains unclear. The integration of smart devices, Wireless Sensor Networks and IoT applications in one network pose numerous challenges to the traditional network and managements approaches. Additionally, the autonomous aggregation of users' information gathered by a large number of things and exchanged over various heterogeneous networks impinge on the security and privacy of the users. For this reason, the development of solutions to support security protection, management, and privacy preservations are key factors for the proliferation of the IoT. Towards this aim, this Chapter reviews some of the significant research issues challenging the

IoT. The remainder of this chapter provides examples of Wireless Sensor Networks (WSN) applications in the IoT. It then moves to analyze the major research issues challenging the IoT with regard to security, privacy, interoperability and management. The chapter then concludes by outlining the key research issues pertaining to the advancement of the IoT.

IoT-WSN APPLICATIONS

The IoT promises to revolute communications on the Internet by incorporating multiple long-range, short-range, and personal area wireless networks and technologies into the designs of IoT applications. In environmental monitoring applications, IoT-WSN can be deployed over a wide area where some phenomenon can be monitored. Such applications can be used to sense and monitor volcanoes, earthquake, and oceans movement. They can also be used to detect bushfires, wild animals' movement and many others. Other environmental applications of WSN include monitoring of mountains' climate, such as in (Beutel et al., 2009), water flow such as in (Lin, Wu, & Wassell, 2008), and floods such as in (*HealthCast 2020: Creating a Sustainable Future*, 2005). For example, a WSN can be deployed in a forest to monitor the dramatic rise in temperature, humidity and detect gasses that could be produced by fires. This obviously helps in the early detection of fires. Furthermore, the IoT merges communications between WSNs and other areas of the IoT. Automation can then be built into IoT systems to better manage and respond to these natural disasters. For instance, embedding intelligence and automation into the fire detection system can assist in alerting the authorities, fire-freighter, medical teams and neighborhood in danger.

In mechanical monitoring applications, IoT-WSN can be deployed to monitor physical objects and structures. Such applications use a network of sensors and devices to sense modes of vibrations, structural modifications or breakages in physical structures. Examples of these applications can be found in systems designed to monitor bridges (*HealthCast 2020: Creating a Sustainable Future*, 2005), underground mines (Li & Liu, 2009), and in several other industrial environments (Low, Win, & Er, 2005). Connecting these WSNs applications with the IoT, would revolutionize communications on the Internet. For instance, in bridge monitoring systems, the IoT can leverage the communication capabilities of the network to communicate in real-time with the drivers of smart cars approaching the bridge; and to act upon or even prevent an event from occurring. By connecting the bridge monitoring system with the transport systems, the IoT can enhance the management of traffics in real-time as another example.

In e-health applications, many researchers have focused on the development of a body wireless sensor network (B-WSN) to monitor the health of patients remotely at homes. An example of these applications is the system proposed in (Lo, Thiemjarus, King, & Yang, 2005). It consists of a number of wearable sensors with an integrated wireless transmission that communicates with a base station providing constant monitoring of the patients' health. Furthermore, the IoT offers the opportunities of connecting the B-WSN with other IoT applications. That is, apart from communicating with healthcare providers' systems, a B-WSN can connect autonomously with emergency services, medical insurance companies, and the patients' relatives. In other applications such as in smart home applications, the IoT allows the user to keep track of his or her everyday objects by attaching small and low-cost devices to them. An example of this applications is presented in (Surie, Laguionie, & Pederson, 2008).

IoT IDENTIFICATION CHALLENGES

The IoT will indeed encompass devices that produce contents that need to be accessed only by authorized users or things. Thus, searching, finding and accessing things on the IoT require efficient addressing schemes. Currently, Domain Name service (DNS) is the Internet naming service that translates IP addresses into human-readable names. In the IoT, things will be connected using different technologies and protocols. Some of these protocols are non-HTTP, and some might not even be based on the IP protocol. Therefore, not all type of devices in the IoT would necessarily have an IP-address. As a result, there is a need for new solutions that uniquely identify things on the IoT.

Additionally, the characteristics of the traffic exchanged by things, in the IoT, could be periodic and very small. Further contributions are needed to determine if the TCP protocol is adequate to use in the IoT or if a new concept of a transport layer is required. This is due to the fact that the TCP is a connection-oriented protocol, in which sessions always starts with a connection setup procedure known as the three-way handshakes. Given that some of the communications within the IoT will involve the exchange of an only small amount of data generated by constrained devices, the TCP protocol cannot be used efficiently for transmission control. For example, consider a case where an IoT sensor is exchanging a small amount of data in a single session with another device or application. The TCP congestion control mechanism will add too much overhead to the communications if TCP is used. This is because the whole TCP session will be concluded with the transmission of the first segment and the consequent reception of the corresponding acknowledgment

(Atzori, Iera, & Morabito, 2010). There is a need to support interoperable communications between TCP and future non-TCP enabled devices on the IoT as well.

On the other hand, the research into devices' naming or identity management is an active area as well. For instance, the work in (Liu, Yang, & Liu, 2014) points out that a device naming scheme should contain key elements of device meta-data, such as the device type and domain information. For addressing purposes, the format of the identifier should allow accessibility and addressability to the physical world in a granule and efficient way as well. Profile services are also needed to aid the application query and system configurations, such as the device status and presence in a location or network (Liu et al., 2014).

Other works on identity management in the IoT are based on the Service Oriented Architecture (SOA), such as OpenID. OpenID describes how users can be authenticated in a decentralized manner. This eliminates the need for services to provide their own ad-hoc systems. It also allows the users to consolidate their digital identities. Hence, these and similar authentication solutions are necessary for preserving the privacy of users in IoT. Preserving privacy has to take into account not only the privacy of services and data but also the discovery through user devices. The work in (Madsen, 2013) discusses the need to distinguish between connected things and their identities. The work proposes the use of tokens. A token is used by a device in an API call when engaging in communication. The users control the process of issuing tokens. This approach allows them to impose policies on the disclosure of data as to when that token can be used and how their information is shared (Madsen, 2013).

Physical and Virtual Things Identities

A physical thing can be any sort of object found in the physical world such as a mobile phone, sensor, actuator, table, door, meter, lock, medical device, network device, camera or even a network component. All of these examples of physical things should be referenced and identified by an identifier. In traditional network management systems, a node or a component is referenced by an ID which is associated with additional identifying information that reflects on the relationship with other objects. For example, a networking device (e.g. a router) may have a unique hostname, but each of its physical network interfaces is assigned an IP address. Furthermore, each of the router's components might have an identifier as well. As such the hostname of the device in combination with the IP address of a particular network interface can be used for identification purposes. Thus, this identification scheme defines the association between the router, in our example, and its network interfaces. The hostname and IP address are stored in a Management Information Base (MIBs) which is used by the Simple Network Management Protocol (SNMP) for management. Thus, similar addressing schemes for WSNs and group of things in the IoT should be explored.

Virtual things can be in the form of software, multimedia items, documents, services, among other examples of digital items. The ITU-T Object IDs (OIDs) can be used to refer to a number of virtual things ("The Internet of Things," 2005). The URL can be used to identify the web services and access them. Alternatively, the Digital Object Identifier (DOI) standard can be used to reference digital objects directly. It can also indicate how to access digital documents (Friese et al., 2010).

SECURITY AND PRIVACY CHALLENGES

Security Challenges

The evolution of wireless technologies and M2M communications is driving the growth of the IoT. New devices are increasingly getting connected to the Internet, from connected vehicles to connected homes and cities. This growth in connected devices to the communication networks translates into increased security risks and poses new challenges to security. A device which connects to the Internet, whether it is a constraint or smart device, inherits the security risks of today's computer devices. Almost all security challenges are inherent to the IoT. Hence, some fundamental security requirements in the IoT such as authorization, authentication, confidentiality, trust, and data security need to be considered.

Things should be securely connected to their designated network(s), securely controlled and accessed by authorized entities. Data generated by things need to be collected, analyzed, stored, dispatched and always presented in a secure manner. Notwithstanding, there are security risks associated with things-to-things communications as well. This is in addition to the risks relating to things-to-person communications. For instance, if things are to be accessed by things independently from the human users, then there are security measures that need to be enforced. These security measures are necessary to ensure that things are accessed only by authorized entities in a secure manner. Also, they need to ensure that things are not leaking information or disclosing private information to unauthorized things and users, or used miscellaneously. The security issues challenging the IoT can be summarized to as follows:

End-to-End Security

End-to-end security is concerned with protecting the communications and data exchanged between things and IoT applications without being read, eavesdropped, intercepted, modified, or tampered. Cisco defines end-to-end security as an absolute requirement for secure communications which encompasses five components: identity verification, protocols, algorithms, secure implementations, and, secure operations (Behringer, 2009). In the IoT, end-to-end security remains an open challenge for many IoT devices and applications. The nature of the IoT with its heterogeneous architecture and devices involve the sharing of information and collaboration between things across many networks. This poses serious challenges to the end-to-end security of things. When devices have different characteristics and operate using a variety of communication technologies (802.11 vs 802.15.4), establishing secure sessions and secure communications become a complex task to achieve. Additionally, not all devices in the IoT are equal. Normally, computer, mobile phones and other computerized devices connect to the Internet via HTTP, SMTP and the like for most of their activities. As such TLS and IPsec protocols are usually used to dynamically negotiate the session keys, and to provide the required security functions. However, some of the devices in the IoT does not possess the ability to run TLS and IPsec protocols due to their limited computation and power capabilities. Additionally, most embedded devices in the IoT are designed for low power consumption. They often have limited connectivity as such they might not necessarily use HTTP or even IP for the communication. Table 1 shows the relevant IoT end-to-end security requirements.

Data Security

This involves the protection of data during communications and storages. In (Summers, 2004), data security is defined as the process of protecting data from destruc-

Table 1. End-to-end security requirements

Identity verification	This requirement demands that entities at both ends of the communications to have known and verifiable identities. As discussed earlier, this still unresolved in the IoT.
Protocols	Protocols are needed to negotiate session keys, and to provide the required security functions across several heterogeneous networks. This requires interoperability among things and their applications.
Algorithms	Protocols use algorithms to implement security functions e.g. encryption as in Secure Hash Algorithm (SHA-1). Simple, optimized and lightweight algorithms are needed in the IoT.
Secure implementations	The implementation of the security protocols and algorithms should be free of bugs and security holes that could compromise security.
Secure operations	Users and operators should understand security operations, which can be complex in the IoT given the diversity of things and the heterogeneous nature of IoT communications.

tive forces or from unauthorized access. Examples of data security technologies include software and hardware disk encryption, and backups. Data security, also can be referred to as information security, is vital to the IoT security. Significantly, data security in the IoT is directly associated with safety. Usually, the impact of data security breaches on the human life remained within the scope of hacking personal information about an individual or more sensitive information such as financial data. However, data security breaches in the IoT could pose a serious threat to human safety. For instance, the accidental intrusion or malicious access that could interfere or interrupt the operations of a driverless car or a heart pacemaker will threaten the safety of the relevant user. Security breaches in an IoT forest fire detection system could lead to catastrophic results.

Identity and Access Management

Identity theft, forgery, and masquerading among other security attacks are some of the security issues challenging the protection of identity in the IoT. Typically, computer devices employ a secure mechanism that relies on complex algorithms in detecting suspicious access to data and the detection of imposters. The IoT is vulnerable to several identity attacks including Spoofing, Masquerade, MiM and Smurf attacks. The physical protection of the actual device from damage and unauthorized access is also important in the IoT. Consequently, several existing traditional security solutions need to be studied and examined to determine their feasibility and applicability in the IoT.

Regulations

Complying with government laws and industry regulations play a major role in preserving the security of IoT systems. Things in the IoT need to adhere to several data protection laws and privacy acts which vary from country to another. This is can be problematic in the IoT given that the IoT is built around autonomous communications between things. Therefore, there is a need to ensure the privacy of the users at all time. The privacy requirements can be summarized in three key concepts:

1. **User Consent**: Users need to be able to provide their informed consent on the data disclosed by things.
2. **Freedom of Choice**: Users should have the freedom of opting in and out from being involved or being part of a communication. This can be challenging in things-to-things communications.

3. **Anonymity**: Users have the right to remain anonymous when obtaining services that do not require identity verification. Data mining in the IoT is one of the major challenges to privacy protection in the IoT as identified in (Elkhodr, Shahrestani, & Cheung, 2013a).

Access Control

Access Control is the process of granting, limiting or restricting access to a resource. It regulates who or what can view or use resources. Role based access control (RBAC) is an example of a widely used access control model. Research should explore the traditional access control models and investigate their suitability for implementation in the IoT.

Significantly, these security issues cannot be solved with traditional Internet security solutions. This is due to the fact that IoT communications' architectures differ from those of the traditional Internet. As the IoT evolves and becomes more complex, the security issues increase in complexity as well. This growth in complexity can be attributed to two fundamental IoT factors: low-cost and heterogeneity. Some IoT devices should be available at relatively low prices. Low-cost is a significant characteristic that drives the support for large-scale deployment of things in the IoT. This low-cost requirement dictates that things are mostly resource constrained. This translates into devices with lower computational capabilities, a limited amount of memory and power supply. This is, in fact, constitute an obstacle to the application of many traditional cryptographic-based solutions. Given that traditional public-key infrastructures cannot accommodate the IoT (Roman, Najera, & Lopez, 2011). For instance, the implementation of many conventional and basic Internet security solutions such as PKI and CA demands to increase the computation capabilities of things which in turn increase their cost. Therefore, conventional Internet security technologies cannot provide a complete security solution for the IoT. The heterogeneity of devices, the multi-networks integration characteristic of the IoT, and the limited capabilities and low-cost requirement of some IoT devices require new and optimized security solutions.

Privacy Challenges

In the smartphone ecosystem, many mobile applications collect the location information of the users without their consent. For example, TaintDroid project (Enck et al., 2010), has identified that some Android's applications are releasing users' private information to online advertisers. TaintDroid is a joint study by Intel Labs,

Penn State, and Duke University. The project is developed as a mobile application. It provides real-time monitoring services that precisely monitor the traffics exchanged by other applications installed on the same device. It detects when the user's private information are released by an application to a third party. TaintDroid revealed that 15 applications out of the 30 selected for the study were sending users' geographic location to remote advertisement servers. Another study found that 7.5% of the total applications on the Android market have the capability of accessing the user's stored contacts; while 28% of them had access to the user's location ("App Genome Project," 2011). The study in (THURM & KANE, 2010) analyzed the 101 most popular smartphone applications running on various mobile operating systems, including Windows Phone, iPhone, and Android. It was reported that out of the 101 applications, fifty-six were transmitting the unique phone ID to other companies without the user's permission. Forty-seven applications were caught transmitting location information to third parties as well. The other five applications were found to be leaking other specific information like gender and age.

The study conducted in (Gupta, 2012) pointed out that some applications running on the Window Mobile platform had the capability to access the user's picture library, video library, webcam's video feed, microphone's audio feed, location, and other parameters related to the Internet connection. Some of these applications also had the ability to add, change or delete files from both the picture and video libraries. Another study detailed the vulnerability of the RIM BlackBerry device (Fredrik, 2011). The author developed a spyware targeted to Blackberry devices. The spyware was able to access and transfer sensitive data to a remote server without being noticed by the user. The study in (Hoh, Gruteser, Xiong, & Alrabady, 2006) showed that a driver's home location can be inferred from the GPS data collected from his vehicle even if the location information was anonymized. The study conducted in (Elkhodr, Shahrestani, & Cheung, 2012) also reported on various privacy incidents associated with the use of mobile applications on the Android, Blackberry, iPhone, and Windows Phone platforms. It is concluded that the proliferation of mobile devices, GPS systems and other evolving technologies into our lives has introduced a new set of privacy threats.

Henceforth, given the impact smartphones have on the users' privacy, it is anticipated that the amount of personal data that would be occasionally collected in an IoT environment will be extremely larger than what we have ever experienced before. The IoT highly distributed nature of technologies, such as embedded devices in public areas, creates weak links that malicious entities can exploit and can as well open the door for a mass surveillance, tracing, tracking, and profiling of the users' movements and activities (Elkhodr, Shahrestani, & Cheung, 2013b). Moreover, the collection of sensitive data, the tracking of people's movement, data mining, and services provisioning can become automated and unpredictable in the IoT. With the pervasive growth of IoT-connected devices and applications, privacy threats are more likely to increase rapidly.

In addition, the foundations, laws and regulations for digital privacy were established some years ago when the Internet was centralized. These regulations deal, usually, with the collection of personal information, access rights, and ensure their correct handling. That's no longer considered enough in the IoT. At its simplest definition, privacy means, giving users the option to control how their collected personal information might be used; specifically for secondary usage and third party access. As an example, in the online environment, privacy choices can be exercised by simply clicking a box on the browser screen that indicates a user's decision with respect to the use of the information being collected. The concept remained the same in the evolution of social networking, where users in Facebook indicate to whom and to which extent their information can be revealed. These are known as the principles of notice and choice.

Privacy Middleware for the IoT

Developing new middleware solutions for the IoT is an active area of research (Satyanarayanan, 2001). Initially, these solutions were designed to support privacy protections in pervasive computing. They are also intended to guide the development and implementation of pervasive systems (Ranganathan et al., 2005). In regards to privacy, the physical outreach of IoT makes preserving the users' privacy a difficult task (Ranganathan et al., 2005). Typically, privacy is of three types: content, identity, and location (Cooper & Birman, 1995). Content privacy is concerned with keeping data or content private. The second type relates to hiding the identity of the user; while, location privacy is concerned with hiding the location of the user. Based on these types of privacy, Ranganathan et al. (Ranganathan et al., 2005) proposed a benchmark for pervasive computing systems which considered two characteristics for privacy models. The first is the user control over private information which is the model ability to provide content, identity, and location privacy. The second related to the unobtrusiveness of privacy mechanisms. Pervasive systems in the IoT attempt to provide a seamless user-centric environment, where users no longer need to spend much of their attention to computing machinery. Therefore, unobtrusiveness can be measured by the percentage of time a user consumes on interacting with privacy settings (Conti et al., 2012).

There is also a challenge of balancing privacy with usability (Bhaskar & Ahamed, 2007). Traditional models requiring explicit users' input have to be replaced with models that can sense information securely and automatically from the context and environment, and exchange it seamlessly with communicating devices and users. Dehghantanha et al. in (Dehghantanha, Mahmod, & Udzir, 2009) proposed an XML-based User-centered Privacy Model (UPM) for pervasive computing systems which provide content, identity, location, and time privacy with low unobtrusiveness. The model consists of three layers: User context layer, Service layer, and Owner layer. The model functions as follows: a user sends data to a portal without revealing the user's identity (portals are wireless nodes managing the users' context). Then the portal hides the user's location and forwards the data to an intermediate entity referred to as a lighthouse. A lighthouse is a trusted entity that holds the user's identity information; but it does not have access to user's location, content, and time of the interaction. By doing so, the user portal only knows the user's location and the lighthouse only know the user's identity. The lighthouse is responsible for communicating with the service provider. The service provider receives the needed contents from the owners. The authors claim that their UPM model provides the user with control over the content of the information disclosed and the disclosure settings of their identity, location, and time. In (Dehghantanha, Udzir, & Mahmod, 2011), the UPM model was evaluated based on the benchmark proposed in (Ranganathan et al., 2005) as follows: To assess the unobtrusiveness of the privacy policies, the percentage of time the user spends dealing with the privacy subsystem to make a decision was measured. An experiment was designed to show how to measure the model unobtrusiveness. Three tasks with different privacy levels were implemented. The aim is to demonstrate that the privacy files support mandatory and discretionary rules, reflect context sensitivity, handle uncertain situations and resolve conflicts (Dehghantanha et al., 2011).

In Lioudakis et al. (2007), a middleware architecture for privacy protection on the Internet is proposed. The middleware mediates between service providers and users and constitutes a distributed unit of trust that enforces the legal requirements. Before the development of the middleware, the authors classified the data into three types: active data (which are in direct control by the user), semi-active data (users have partial control over them such as RFIDs generated data) and passive data (these data are disclosed without any user's action). Next, the authors proposed a policy framework which incorporated a large set of rules. This framework is used to formalize how users express their privacy preferences. To model the rules, a relevant XML-based language was defined called the Discreet Privacy Language (DPL). To limit the control from the service provider over the user's personal data, a discreet Box was proposed. The Box incorporates the personal data repository that cashes personal data and a policy framework that is responsible for the decisions of personal data disclosure. It serves as the entry point for a service and its operation is similar to a proxy server. While the authors claim that the proposed architecture has numerous benefits, no evaluation has been performed.

Other solutions such as the mix zone technique (Beresford & Stajano, 2004a) were designed to protect the privacy of users in location-aware pervasive computing applications. The mix zone is a middleware which enables an application to receive and reply to anonymous requests. It passes users' input and output between the application and the user. The mix zone is analogous to a mix node in a communication network (Danezis, 2003). A mix network provides anonymity using a store and forward network. The proposed technique was applied to location data collected from the Active Bat system installed at At&T Labs Cambridge (Hightower & Borriello, 2001). The results demonstrated that privacy is low even with a relatively large mix zone. However, the techniques could lead to a better privacy if applied over a larger and more populated area. While the mix zone technique provides a way of hiding the location of users, it does hide their identities. The choices are also restricted to two: anonymized or real location.

Therefore, solutions based on the mix networks, mix nodes model, pseudonyms, and those presented in (Beresford & Stajano, 2003, 2004b), provides location privacy without addressing the need to provide the user with granule control over the disclosure settings. Other alternative solutions, such as the LocServ model, support location privacy policies that can be checked automatically on behalf of the user (Myles, Friday, & Davies, 2003). However, LocServe suffers from considerable flexibility and arrangement limitations and cannot be reliably used in IoT. Table 2 summarizes the requirements for privacy in the IoT.

Table 2. IoT privacy requirements

Collection Announcement	There is a need to find efficient ways to communicate and inform the user about collection procedures of his or her personal data in the IoT. There is a challenge in delivering the so-called the "data collection declaration" to the user who does not necessarily sit on any side of the communication. Communications in the IoT, as previously discussed, can be automated between various things.
Choice and Consent	The concept of choice and consent is to give users a selection mechanism so they can indicate which service they which to use. This is a challenging task to adopt in the IoT especially in an automated communication that may involve things that do not necessarily involve the human user directly. There is a need to provide the choice and consent right to users or things that represent them, and at the same time to allow an automated communication to be established.
Usage Logs	The users should be able to check the logs of their devices and the data they collect. This is necessary for accountability and audibility. There is also a need for digital forgetting.
Control over Contextual Data Disclosure	Given that interactions in the IoT are multi-dimensional, contextual data can reveal sensitive information about the users such as location information.

INTEROPERABILITY CHALLENGES

Interoperability in information technology is as old as the Internet is, if not older. Solutions considering the issues associated with information systems' interoperability can be traced back to 1988 (Science, Eliassen, & Veijalainen, 1988); and perhaps even earlier. Thus, interoperability is not new and it does not have a standard definition. For instance, Wikipedia defines Interoperability as "the ability of making systems and organizations work together" (Wikipedia). The IEEE defines interoperability as "the ability of two or more systems or components to exchange information and to use the information that has been exchanged" ("IEEE Standard Computer Dictionary: A Compilation of IEEE Standard Computer Glossaries," 1991). Other definitions of interoperability are further tailored according to the particular application's requirements or needs. As a result, different categories of interoperability have been emerging. Technical interoperability, Semantic interoperability, Syntactic interoperability, and Cross-domain interoperability are examples of these categories. To differentiate between these different types of interoperability, the following descriptions are provided:

- **Technical Interoperability:** *"is usually associated with hardware/software components, systems and platforms that enable machine-to-machine communication to take place. This kind of interoperability is often centered on (communication) protocols and the infrastructure needed for those protocols to operate" (van der Veer & Wiles, 2008).*
- **Syntactic Interoperability:** Deals with interoperable structures such as the format and syntax of the message exchanged between communication protocols. HTML, XML, SQL, ASN standards are among the tools of syntactic interoperability. Syntactic interoperability refers to the packaging and transmission mechanisms for data over a network.
- **Semantic Interoperability**: *In contrast with Syntactic Interoperability, which is concerned with the syntax of data, Semantic interoperability deals with the meaning of the data?* "Semantic interoperability is the ability to interpret automatically the information exchanged meaningfully and accurately in order to produce useful results as defined by the end users of both systems" ("Semantic interoperability of health information ", 2011).
- **Cross-Domain Interoperability** *"Exists when organizations or systems from different domains interact in information exchange, services and/or goods to achieve their own or common goals".* When cross-domain interoperability exists, it means that users can seamlessly communicate and conduct activities, despite their reliance on different technical environments or frameworks ("Cross-Domain Interoperability," 2015).

In regards to the IoT, every type and category of interoperability is needed to achieve seamless and heterogeneous communications in the IoT. Achieving interoperability is vital for interconnecting multiple things together across different communication networks. It defeats the purpose to have billions of sensors, actuators, tiny and smart devices connected to the Internet if these devices can't actually communicate with each other in a way or another. In fact, for the IoT to flourish, things connecting to the communication networks, which are heterogeneous, need to be able to communicate, share and receive information and/or instructions with other things or applications (Elkhodr, Shahrestani, & Cheung, 2016a).

Moreover, in traditional computer environments, computer devices are treated equally when connected to the Internet. Their functionalities vary depending on how the users use them. However, in the IoT, each device would be subject to different conditions such as power energy consumption restrictions, communication bandwidth requirements, and computation and security capabilities. Additionally, things might be made by different manufacturers that do not necessarily comply with a common standard. Things might also operate using a variety of communication technologies. These technologies might not necessarily connect things to the Internet in the same way a typical computer device usually do. For instance 6LoWPAN offers interoperability with other wireless 802.15.4 devices as well as with any IP-based devices using a simple bridging device (Elkhodr, Shahrestani, & Cheung, 2016b). However, bridging between ZigBee and non-ZigBee networks requires a more complex application layer gateway.

The highly competitive nature of the IoT makes interoperability between things even a more difficult task to achieve. Besides, wireless communication technologies are evolving and changing rapidly. This adds to the complexity of creating interoperable communications in the IoT as well. This inevitability results in heterogeneous devices that might not be able to communicate directly with each other on the IoT, raising integration issues. Service descriptions, common practices, standards and discovery mechanisms are among the many other challenges that also need to be considered before enabling an interoperable interaction between things (Elkhodr et al., 2016a).

MANAGEMENT CHALLENGES

Traditionally, network management solutions are needed to manage network equipment, devices, and services. However, with the IoT, there is a need to manage not only the traditional networked devices and their services, but also an entirely new range of things. The enormous number of things and their diversity create many management requirements. Thus, traditional management functionalities such as remote control, monitoring and maintenance are considered of paramount significance for the operation of things in the IoT. However, these management capabilities need to evolve to cater for the unique characteristics of the IoT. This is because the IoT is of a diverse nature supporting heterogeneous communications and seamless machine to machine interactions. This is in addition to the specific management capabilities required for managing things in the IoT. For example, self-configuration and network reconfiguration are essential management requirements in the IoT. On the other hand, traditionally, network management solutions aims at providing management information with a minimal response time. However, in some IoT scenarios which might involve lightweight devices, management solutions should provide comprehensive management information with minimal energy use (Welsh & Mainland, 2004).

Management Protocols

The purpose of a network management protocol is to transport management information from a device (e.g. a computer or a networked node) referred to as a managed device or object to an application referred to as the manager. Network management protocols are also used to transport control information from the manager to the managed devices. Traditionally, in a client-server scheme, a management protocol is used to transport messages between the manager and the network components. A network component can be a typical network device such as a server, router or a specific network interface on a router. Generally, network management protocols define a static protocol message format and a small set of predefined messages for gathering and posting managed information to and from the managed devices. Emerging standards, which are based on the distributed object-oriented approach, define more complex network management architecture. In this approach, the management protocol is tightly coupled with the management application; thereby facilitating code-on-demand (COD) object transmission, plug-and-play component management, and also defining a rich set of communication primitives between managers and managed devices (Elkhodr et al., 2016a).

The two most widely adopted management protocols are the Simple Network Management Protocol (SNMP), developed by the Internet Engineering Task Force (IETF), and the Common Management Information Protocol (CMIP), proposed by the International Standards Organization (ISO). Although these two protocols are similar in architecture, they vary slightly in operations. Both SNMP and CMIP define a single management device that assumes complete control over all management functions. The manager is an application that interacts with network agents embedded in each managed device using the network management protocol. In the context of SNMP and CMIP, agents are simple computational entities that provide mechanisms for accessing managed information stored on the managed devices (Sehgal, Perelman, Kuryla, & Schonwalder, 2012). SNMP's agents store device-specific information in managed information bases (MIB). On the other hand, the CMIP protocol defines a managed information tree (MIT) in order to store and access configuration information.

SNMP

Although SNMP was designed specifically for managing IP-based data networks, it has become the de facto standard for telecommunication network management. The popularity of SNMP is mainly due to its simplicity that allows manufacturers to enhance their products with network management functionality with a minimal effort. This protocol also provides simple, hierarchical management architecture with multi-vendor support.

SNMP aims to unify and minimize the complexity of management functions between various networked and hardware devices. The use of SNMP reduces the cost of management. Significantly, the SNMP's architecture enables the efficient integration of devices across a network. It facilitates seamless integration and management of existing and newly added hardware devices on a network. Additionally, SNMP implementations define a set of management functions that can be easily adopted by network managers and developers of network management systems. Another characteristic of SNMP is extensibility. SNMP's design allows the addition of newly developed extensions with less complexity. The SNMP protocol is a platform independent as well. It supports an array of various network technologies.

CMIP

Almost in parallel with the development of SNMP, the International Standards Organization (ISO) defined the specifications for the Common Management Information Protocol (CMIP). Unlike SNMP, CMIP is designed to provide network management operations for a wide variety of network architectures. In the open systems interconnection (OSI) architecture, the fundamental function of network management solutions is to assist with the exchange of management information between the manager and managed devices. This functionality is referred to as the common management information service element (CMISE) and is composed of two parts. The first specifies the services provided by the network management, and it is termed as the common management information service (CMIS). The second part is referred to as the common management information protocol (CMIP). It specifies the mechanisms and message format by which the management information is exchanged between the manager and managed devices.

The CMIP framework is broken down into three interacting components. These components consist of the layer management entity (LME), the system management application entity (SMAE), and the common management information protocol (CMIP); which facilitates the communication of managed information among the management layer and management devices.

The CMIP implements a much richer set of management functions when compared to SNMP. It organizes the managed entities and manager using a hierarchical approach. This allows managed information to be accessed within the scope of the manager. This hierarchical approach significantly increases the protocol's scalability. However, because the services offered by the CMIS entities are considerably more sophisticated than the management functions of SNMP, CMIP protocol is considered harder to implement. For this reason, CMIP has not gained as much popularity as SNMP.

Even though SNMP has gained major popularity in network management systems, the IETF designed this protocol to manage TCP/IP-based local area networks. Therefore, the challenges posed by emerging communication standards require a more sophisticated network management approach. CMIP was designed to provide a generic solution for overall network management; however it failed to gain global acceptance. Facing new technologies in the era of the IoT, network management approaches must implement scalable, flexible, robust, adaptive, and automated management architectures. This is because the IoT encompasses several heterogeneous networks consisting of a diversity of lightweight and more capable devices. This heterogeneity of devices and networks raises some novel management challenges. To target this challenge, studies such as the one reported in (Sehgal et al., 2012), examined the possibility of adopting existing network management protocols for the management of constrained networks and devices in the IoT. It is found, through simulation studies, that SNMP makes efficient use of resources on constrained devices (Sehgal et al., 2012). Future contributions are required to investigate the applicability and performance of traditional network management protocols such as the SNMP in physical IoT setups.

CONCLUSION

The Internet of things (IoT) is a heterogeneous network that encompasses sensors, actuators, smart devices, mobile and computer devices, and other physical objects embedded with electronics. The potentially huge number and the diversity of things that may be part of such an infrastructure bring tremendous amounts of complexity. Even though it is hard to predict exactly how the IoT will evolve, it is almost certain that the IoT will have significant impacts on the security and privacy of users, and on machine-to-machine communications throughout the Internet. The unique characteristics of things, specifically their low-power and low-cost requirements demand the optimization of many traditional solutions and the introduction of entirely new ones. Significantly, the connectivity of low-cost devices to the Internet create more complexity and new security risks. It also makes the implementation of privacy preservation solutions a challenging task. Compliance with regulations and privacy laws will continue to be a major issue in the IoT, specifically in health and public domains where the operation of things could have life and death implications. Additionally, interoperability is one of the major obstacles to the advancement of the IoT. If things and groups of things, operating using various wireless and LAN technologies, cannot communicate effectively with each other, we risk creating a very fragmented IoT. Other key challenges for the future of IoT include the design of security, management and privacy-focused solutions. Such solution should provide the users with options to opt in and opt out and increase transparency. To this end, future research on IoT should aim to develop lightweight cryptographic protocols, intelligent algorithms and Application Programing Interfaces (APIs), and new self-manageable network paradigms.

REFERENCES

App Genome Project. (2011). Retrieved from https://www.mylookout.com/appgenome

Atzori, L., Iera, A., & Morabito, G. (2010). The internet of things: A survey. *Computer Networks*, *54*(15), 2787–2805. doi:10.1016/j.comnet.2010.05.010

Behringer, M. H. (2009). End-to-End Security. *The Internet Protocol Journal*, *12*(3), 20.

Beresford, A. R., & Stajano, F. (2003). Location privacy in pervasive computing. *Pervasive Computing, IEEE*, *2*(1), 46–55. doi:10.1109/MPRV.2003.1186725

Beresford, A. R., & Stajano, F. (2004a). *Mix Zones: User Privacy in Location-aware Services.* Paper presented at the The Second IEEE Annual Conference on Pervasive Computing and Communications Workshops, Orlando, FL.

Beresford, A. R., & Stajano, F. (2004b). *Mix zones: user privacy in location-aware services.* Paper presented at the Pervasive Computing and Communications Workshops, 2004.

Beutel, J., Gruber, S., Hasler, A., Lim, R., Meier, A., Plessl, C., . . . Woehrle, M. (2009). *PermaDAQ: A scientific instrument for precision sensing and data recovery in environmental extremes*. Paper presented at the 2009 International Conference on Information Processing in Sensor Networks.

Bhaskar, P., & Ahamed, S. I. (2007). *Privacy in Pervasive Computing and Open Issues*. Paper presented at the Availability, Reliability and Security, 2007. ARES 2007. The Second International Conference on.

Clendenin, M. (2010). *China's 'Internet Of Things' Overblown, Says Exec*. Retrieved from http://www.informationweek.com/news/storage/virtualization/225700966?subSection=News

Conti, M., Das, S. K., Bisdikian, C., Kumar, M., Ni, L. M., Passarella, A., & Zambonelli, F. et al. (2012). Looking ahead in Pervasive Computing: Challenges, Opportunities in the era of Cyber Physical Convergence. *Pervasive and Mobile Computing*, *8*(1), 2–21. doi:10.1016/j.pmcj.2011.10.001

Cooper, D. A., & Birman, K. P. (1995). *Preserving privacy in a network of mobile computers*. Paper presented at the Security and Privacy, 1995.

Cross-Domain Interoperability. (2015). Retrieved from https://www.ncoic.org/cross-domain-interoperability

Danezis, G. (2003). *Mix-networks with restricted routes*. Paper presented at the Privacy Enhancing Technologies. doi:10.1007/978-3-540-40956-4_1

Dehghantanha, A., Mahmod, R., & Udzir, N. I. (2009). A XML based, User-centered Privacy Model in Pervasive Computing Systems. *International Journal of Computer Science and Network Security*, *9*(10), 167–173.

Dehghantanha, A., Udzir, N., & Mahmod, R. (2011). Evaluating User-Centered Privacy Model (UPM) in Pervasive Computing Systems Computational Intelligence in Security for Information Systems. Springer Berlin / Heidelberg.

Elkhodr, M., Shahrestani, S., & Cheung, H. (2012). *A Review of Mobile Location Privacy in the Internet of Things*. Paper presented at the 2012 Tenth International Conference on ICT and Knowledge Engineering, Bangkok, Thailand. doi:10.1109/ICTKE.2012.6408566

Elkhodr, M., Shahrestani, S., & Cheung, H. (2013a). *The Internet of Things: Vision & Challenges*. Paper presented at the IEEE Tencon Spring 2013, Sydney, Australia.

Elkhodr, M., Shahrestani, S., & Cheung, H. (2013b). *Preserving the Privacy of Patient Records in Health Monitoring Systems. In Theory and Practice of Cryptography Solutions for Secure Information Systems* (pp. 499–529). IGI Global. doi:10.4018/978-1-4666-4030-6.ch019

Elkhodr, M., Shahrestani, S., & Cheung, H. (2016a). The Internet of Things: New Interoperability, Management and Security Challenges. *The International Journal of Network Security & Its Applications, 8*(2), 85–102. doi:10.5121/ijnsa.2016.8206

Elkhodr, M., Shahrestani, S., & Cheung, H. (2016b). *Wireless Enabling Technologies for the Internet of Things. In Handbook of Research on Next-Generation High Performance Computing.* Hershey, PA: IGI Global.

Enck, W., Gilbert, P., Chun, B.-G., Cox, L. P., Jung, J., McDaniel, P., & Sheth, A. N. (2010). *TaintDroid: an information-flow tracking system for realtime privacy monitoring on smartphones.* Paper presented at the 9th USENIX conference on Operating systems design and implementation, Vancouver, Canada.

Evans, D. (2012). The Internet of Everything. How More Relevant and Valuable Connections. Will Change the World. *Cisco IBSG*, 1-9.

Fredrik, H. (2011). *System Integrity for Smartphones: A security evaluation of iOS and BlackBerry OS. (Master).* Linkoping University.

Friese, I., Hogberg, J., Foll, F. A., Gourmelen, G., Lischka, M., Brennan, J., . . . Lampe, S. (2010). *Bridging IMS and Internet Identity.* Paper presented at the 2010 14th International Conference on Intelligence in Next Generation Networks (ICIN). doi:10.1109/ICIN.2010.5640948

Gupta, P. (2012). *Metro Interface Improves Windows 8 While Increasing Some Risks.* Retrieved from http://blogs.mcafee.com/mcafee-labs/metro-interface-improves-windows-8-while-increasing-some-risks

HealthCast 2020: Creating a Sustainable Future. (2005). Retrieved from http://www.pwc.com/il/he/publications/assets/2healthcast_2020.pdf

Hightower, J., & Borriello, G. (2001). Location systems for ubiquitous computing. *Computer, 34*(8), 57–66. doi:10.1109/2.940014

Hoh, B., Gruteser, M., Xiong, H., & Alrabady, A. (2006). Enhancing security and privacy in traffic-monitoring systems. *IEEE Pervasive Computing / IEEE Computer Society [and] IEEE Communications Society, 5*(4), 38–46. doi:10.1109/MPRV.2006.69

Li, M., & Liu, Y. (2009). Underground coal mine monitoring with wireless sensor networks. *ACM Transactions on Sensor Networks*, *5*(2), 10. doi:10.1145/1498915.1498916

Lin, M., Wu, Y., & Wassell, I. (2008). *Wireless sensor network: Water distribution monitoring system.* Paper presented at the Radio and Wireless Symposium. doi:10.1109/RWS.2008.4463607

Lioudakis, G. V., Koutsoloukas, E. A., Dellas, N. L., Tselikas, N., Kapellaki, S., Prezerakos, G. N., & Venieris, I. S. et al. (2007). A middleware architecture for privacy protection. *Computer Networks*, *51*(16), 4679–4696. doi:10.1016/j.comnet.2007.06.010

Liu, C. H., Yang, B., & Liu, T. (2014). Efficient naming, addressing and profile services in Internet-of-Things sensory environments. *Ad Hoc Networks*, *18*(0), 85–101. doi:10.1016/j.adhoc.2013.02.008

Lo, B., Thiemjarus, S., King, R., & Yang, G.-Z. (2005). *Body sensor network-a wireless sensor platform for pervasive healthcare monitoring.* Paper presented at the The 3rd International Conference on Pervasive Computing.

Lomas, N. (2009). *Online gizmos could top 50 billion in 2020.* Retrieved from http://www.businessweek.com/globalbiz/content/jun2009/gb20090629_492027.htm

Low, K. S., Win, W. N. N., & Er, M. J. (2005). *Wireless sensor networks for industrial environments.* Paper presented at the Computational Intelligence for Modelling, Control and Automation, 2005 and International Conference on Intelligent Agents, Web Technologies and Internet Commerce, International Conference on.

Madsen, P. (Producer). (2013). *OpenID Connect and its role in Native SSO.* Retrieved from https://www.youtube.com/watch?v=mTZ0bcNphVg

Myles, G., Friday, A., & Davies, N. (2003). Preserving privacy in environments with location-based applications. *Pervasive Computing, IEEE*, *2*(1), 56–64. doi:10.1109/MPRV.2003.1186726

Ranganathan, A., Al-Muhtadi, J., Biehl, J., Ziebart, B., Campbell, R. H., & Bailey, B. (2005). *Towards a pervasive computing benchmark.* Paper presented at the Pervasive Computing and Communications Workshops, 2005. PerCom 2005 Workshops. Third IEEE International Conference on.

Roman, R., Najera, P., & Lopez, J. (2011). Securing the Internet of Things. *Computer*, *44*(9), 51–58. doi:10.1109/MC.2011.291

Satyanarayanan, M. (2001). Pervasive computing: Vision and challenges. *Personal Communications, IEEE, 8*(4), 10–17. doi:10.1109/98.943998

Science, H. y. D. o. C., Eliassen, F., & Veijalainen, J. (1988). *A functional approach to information system interoperability.* Academic Press.

Sehgal, A., Perelman, V., Kuryla, S., & Schonwalder, J. (2012). Management of resource constrained devices in the internet of things. *Communications Magazine, IEEE, 50*(12), 144–149. doi:10.1109/MCOM.2012.6384464

Semantic interoperability of health information. (2011). Retrieved from http://www.en13606.org/the-ceniso-en13606-standard/semantic-interoperability

IEEE Standard Computer Dictionary: A Compilation of IEEE Standard Computer Glossaries. (1991). *IEEE Std 610.* doi:10.1109/IEEESTD.1991.106963

Summers, G. (2004). Data and databases. In *Developing Databases with Access.* Nelson Australia Pty Limited.

Surie, D., Laguionie, O., & Pederson, T. (2008). *Wireless sensor networking of everyday objects in a smart home environment.* Paper presented at the Intelligent Sensors, Sensor Networks and Information Processing, 2008. ISSNIP 2008. International Conference on. doi:10.1109/ISSNIP.2008.4761985

The Internet of Things. (2005). Retrieved from http://www.itu.int/osg/spu/publications/internetofthings/

Thurm, S., & Kane, Y. I. (2010). *Your Apps Are Watching You.* Retrieved from http://online.wsj.com/article/SB10001424052748704368004576027751867039730.html

van der Veer, H., & Wiles, A. (2008). *Achieving technical interoperability.* European Telecommunications Standards Institute.

Welsh, M., & Mainland, G. (2004). *Programming Sensor Networks Using Abstract Regions.* Paper presented at the NSDI.

Wikipedia. (n.d.). *Interoperability.* Retrieved from https://en.wikipedia.org/wiki/Interoperability

KEY TERMS AND DEFINITIONS

Actuators: Actuators are devices responsible for moving or controlling a mechanism or system.

Anonymization: Data anonymization is the process of either encrypting or removing identifiable information from personal data.

Internet of Things: The Internet of things is a technology that connects physical objects and not only computer devices to the Internet, making it possible to access data/services remotely and to control a physical object from a remote location.

IEEE 802.11ah: A wireless networking protocol that is an amendment of the IEEE 802.11-2007 wireless networking standard. It is intended to work with low-power devices.

Network Management: Network management refers to the activities and tools that pertain to the operation, administration, maintenance, and provisioning of networked systems.

Chapter 3

Security Solutions for Intelligent and Complex Systems

Stuart Armstrong
Future of Humanity Institute, UK

Roman V Yampolskiy
JB Speed School of Engineering, USA

ABSTRACT

Superintelligent systems are likely to present serious safety issues, since such entities would have great power to control the future according to their possibly misaligned goals or motivation systems. Oracle AIs (OAI) are confined AIs that can only answer questions and do not act in the world, represent one particular solution to this problem. However even Oracles are not particularly safe: humans are still vulnerable to traps, social engineering, or simply becoming dependent on the OAI. But OAIs are still strictly safer than general AIs, and there are many extra layers of precautions we can add on top of these. This paper begins with the definition of the OAI Confinement Problem. After analysis of existing solutions and their shortcomings, a protocol is proposed aimed at making a more secure confinement environment which might delay negative effects from a potentially unfriendly superintelligence while allowing for future research and development of superintelligent systems.

DOI: 10.4018/978-1-5225-0741-3.ch003

INTRODUCTION

With the likely development of superintelligent programs in the near future, many scientists have raised the issue of safety as it relates to such technology (Bostrom, 2006; Chalmers, 2010; Hall, 2000; Hibbard, 2005; Yampolskiy, 2011a, 2011b; Yampolskiy & Fox, 2012a, 2012b; Yudkowsky, 2008). A common theme in Artificial Intelligence (AI[1]) safety research is the possibility of keeping a superintelligent agent in a sealed hardware so as to prevent it from doing any harm to humankind. Such ideas originate with scientific visionaries such as Eric Drexler who has suggested confining transhuman machines so that their outputs could be studied and used safely (Drexler, 1986). Similarly, in 2010 David Chalmers proposed the idea of a "leakproof" singularity (Chalmers, 2010). He suggested that for safety reasons, AI systems first be restricted to simulated virtual worlds until their behavioral tendencies could be fully understood under the controlled conditions.

This chapter is based on combined and extended information from three previously published papers: (Armstrong, 2011; Armstrong, Sandberg, & Bostrom, 2012; Yampolskiy, 2012a)[*]. We evaluate feasibility of previously presented proposals and suggest a protocol aimed at enhancing safety and security of such methodologies. While it is unlikely, that long-term and secure confinement of AI is possible, we are hopeful that the proposed protocol will give researchers a little more time to find a permanent and satisfactory solution for addressing existential risks associated with appearance of superintelligent machines.

In this chapter we will review specific proposals aimed at creating restricted environments for safely interacting with artificial minds. The key question is: are there strategies that reduce the potential existential risk from a superintelligent AI so much that while implementing it as a free AI would be impermissible a confined implementation would be permissible? The chapter will start by laying out the general design assumptions for the confined AI and formalizing the notion of confinement. Then it will touch upon some of the risks and dangers deriving from the humans running and interaction with the confined AI. The final section looks at some of the other problematic issues concerning the confined AI, such as its ability to simulate human beings within it and its status as a moral agent itself.

Motivation for AI Confinement

There are many motivations to pursue the goal of developing AI. While some motivations are non-instrumental, such as scientific and philosophical curiosity about the nature of thinking or a desire for creating non-human beings, a strong set of motivations is the instrumental utility of AI. Such machines would benefit their owners by being able to do tasks that currently require human intelligence, and possibly tasks that are beyond human intelligence. From an economic perspective the possibility of complementing or substituting expensive labor with cheaper software promises very rapid growth rates and high productivity (Hanson, 2001, 2008; Kaas, Rayhawk, Salamon, & Salamon, 2010). The introduction of sufficiently advanced AI would have profound effects on most aspects of society, making careful foresight important.

While most considerations about the mechanization of labor have focused on AI with intelligence up to the human level, there is no strong reason to believe humans represent an upper limit of possible intelligence. The human brain has evolved under various biological constraints (e.g. food availability, birth canal size, trade-offs with other organs, the requirement of using biological materials) which do not exist for an artificial system. Beside different hardware, an AI might employ more effective algorithms that cannot be implemented well in the human cognitive architecture (e.g. making use of very large and exact working memory, stacks, mathematical modules or numerical simulation), or employ tricks that are not feasible for humans, such as running multiple instances whose memories and conclusions are eventually merged. In addition, if an AI system possesses sufficient abilities, it would be able to assist in developing better AI. Since AI development is an expression of human intelligence, at least some AI might achieve this form of intelligence, and beyond a certain point would accelerate the development far beyond the current rate (Chalmers, 2010; Kurzweil, 2005).

While the likelihood of superintelligent AI is hotly debated, the mere possibility raises worrying policy questions. Since intelligence implies the ability to achieve goals, we should expect superintelligent systems to be significantly better at achieving their goals than humans. This produces a risky power differential. The appearance of superintelligence appears to pose an existential risk: a possibility that humanity is annihilated or has its potential drastically curtailed indefinitely (Bostrom, 2001). This could come about through a number of ways: by enabling self-reinforcing systems that limit human potential (e.g. a global police state (Caplan, 2008)), by out-competing humans or human values (see the 'mindless outsourcers' in (Bostrom, 2004)), or by acting with great power in such a malevolent or indifferent manner that humanity goes extinct. The last possibility could occur due to badly formulated initial motivations or goals, or gradual evolution towards human-unfriendly behaviors (Omohundro, February 2008). Even if most superintelligences are assumed to be human-friendly it appears hard to guarantee that dangerous superintelligences will not emerge unless precautions are made.

In the space of possible motivations likely a very small fraction is compatible with coexistence with humans. A randomly selected motivation can hence be expected to be dangerous. A simple example is that of a paperclip maximizer: an AI with a utility function that seeks to maximize the number of manufactured paperclips. This goal is a not too implausible test command to a new system, yet it would be willing to sacrifice the world and everyone in it if necessary for making more paperclips. If superintelligent the AI would be very good at converting the world into paperclips, even if it realizes its creators actually do not want that many paperclips – stopping would lead to fewer manufactured paperclips (Bostrom, 2006; LessWrong, Available on April 25, 2012). It is a common problem in computer programming, with the program going beyond the implicit bounds of what was expected of it (or users giving in retrospect mistaken commands). So unless valuing humans is an integral part of the superintelligence's setup, we can expect that we will be seen as mere tools or obstacles for its own goals.

There are several approaches to AI risk. The most common at present is to hope that it is no problem: either sufficiently advanced intelligences will converge towards human-compatible behavior, a solution will be found closer to the time when they are actually built, or they cannot be built in the first place. While such considerations might turn out to be true the arguments for them appear relatively uncertain, making it problematic to gamble existential risk only on them.

Another approach is to assume that the behavior of superintelligent agents will be constrained by other agents on par with them in power, similar to how current humans and organizations are constrained by each other and higher-level institutions (Sandberg, 2001). However, this presupposes that the rate of AI development is slow enough that there is time to formulate a cooperative framework and that there will be multiple and not a single superintelligence. And there is no reason to suppose that a world where there are several AIs is more amicable to humans than one with a single one. Indeed, humans may end up a casualty of the competition, even if none of the AIs would individually want that outcome, but none of them can afford to take steps to protect humans without losing out.

A proactive approach is to attempt to design a "friendly AI", AI systems designed to be of low risk[2] (Yudkowsky, 2001a). This might involve safeguards against developing into dangerous directions and top-level goals that include some form of human well-being. This approach requires both that sufficient safeguards are conceptualized and that they are properly implemented in the first AI that achieves superintelligence. It hence depends on developing a workable "friendliness theory" before full superintelligence is achieved, cooperation with the AI developers and correct implementation. The first requirement is essentially the "inverse morality problem": to construct goals, values or motivational structures that produce the right class of actions in an intelligent agent, which is, by assumption, far more intelligent than the person implementing the construction.

When discussing "friendliness" a particular solution is often independently proposed: we call it an Oracle AI (OAI)[3]. The idea is to construct an AI that does not act, but only answers questions. While superintelligent "genies" that try to achieve the wishes of their owners and sovereign AI that acts according to their own goals are obviously dangerous, oracles appear more benign. While owners could potentially use them in selfish or destructive ways – and their answers might in themselves be dangerous (Bostrom, 2011) – they do not themselves pose a risk.

Artificial Intelligence Confinement Problem

Interestingly, the AI Confinement Problem is not a recent invention and does not have its roots in the singularity movement. The so called Confinement Problem (CP) was posed by Butler Lampson in 1973 (Lampson, 1973) as a security challenge to the computer experts. It was originally phrased as: "…the problem of confining a program during its execution so that it cannot transmit information to any other program except its caller. …We want to be able to confine an arbitrary program.… any program, if confined, will be unable to leak data. A misbehaving program may well be trapped as a result of an attempt to escape" (Lampson, 1973).

To address the Confinement Problem Lampson has introduced the Laws of Confinement (Lampson, 1973):

1. **Total Isolation**: A confined program shall make no calls on any other program.
2. **Transitivity**: If a confined program calls another program which is not trusted, the called program must also be confined.
3. **Masking**: A program to be confined must allow its caller to determine all its inputs into legitimate and covert channels.
4. **Enforcement**: The supervisor must ensure that a confined program's input to covert channels conforms to the caller's specifications.

Lampson's paper has also introduced and defined two types of channels by which information could potentially escape from the confinement environment. The *legitimate* channels are designed as a part of the communication protocol integrated into the confinement environment, for example a text terminal. *Covert* channels, on the other hand, are not anticipated by the confinement system designers and are not intended for information transfer at all, for example if the AI has control over the processor cooling fan it can use it to send hidden signals encoded as Morse code (Lampson, 1973).

Lampson's paper has created a lot of interest in the confinement problem (Boebert & Kain, 1996; Lipner, 1975) and over the years, related areas of research such as steganography (Provos & Honeyman, 2003) and covert channel communication (Kemmerer, 1983, 2002; Moskowitz & Kang, 1994) have matured into independent disciplines. In the hopes of starting a new subfield of computer security, AI Safety Engineering, we define the *Artificial Intelligence Confinement Problem* (AICP) as the challenge of restricting an artificially intelligent entity to a confined environment from which it can't exchange information with the outside environment via legitimate or covert channels if such information exchange was not authorized by the confinement authority. An AI system which secedes in violating the CP protocol is said to have *escaped*. It is our hope that the computer security researchers will take on the challenge of designing, enhancing and proving secure AI confinement protocols.

Hazardous Software

Computer software is directly or indirectly responsible for controlling many important aspects of our lives. Wall Street trading, nuclear power plants, social security compensations, credit histories and traffic lights are all software controlled and are only one serious design flaw away from creating disastrous consequences for millions of people. The situation is even more dangerous with software specifically designed for malicious purposes such as viruses, spyware, Trojan horses, worms and other Hazardous Software (HS). HS is capable of direct harm as well as sabotage of legitimate computer software employed in critical systems. If HS is ever given capabilities of truly artificially intelligent systems (ex. Artificially Intelligent Virus (AIV)) the consequences would be unquestionably disastrous. Such Hazardous Intelligent Software (HIS) would pose risks currently unseen in malware with subhuman intelligence.

Bostrom in his typology of information hazards has coined the term Artificial Intelligence Hazard which he defines as (Bostrom, 2011): "… computer-related risks in which the threat would derive primarily from the cognitive sophistication of the program rather than the specific properties of any actuators to which the system initially has access." Security experts working on studying, preventing and defeating HS have developed safety protocols for working with "malware" including the use of the so called "virus vaults." We believe that such protocols might be useful in addressing the Artificial Intelligence Confinement Problem.

Conceptual Architecture of the AI

The possible designs of the OAI are innumerable and it is impossible to predict in detail how they will be implemented. For the purposes of this paper, however, we will assume that the OAI's architecture follows this general format:

1. The OAI is implemented in a spatially limited physical substrate, such as a computer.
2. The OAI may be shut off or reset without destroying its physical substrate, and restarted easily.

3.   The OAI's background information comes in the form of a separate 'read-only' module that may be connected and disconnect as needed.

Most of the present chapter still applies to OAIs that do not follow one or more of these restrictions. The OAI is assumed (when otherwise not noted) to be of human-equivalent intelligence or beyond; less capable systems are unlikely to pose much of a threat.

Direct Programming, Self-Improvement, and Evolution

It is not the purpose of this chapter to speculate how the OAI will be programmed, but it should be pointed out that there are three main approaches being considered (as well as mixtures between them). The first, seemingly the hardest, is to directly code the entire OAI, just as if it were a traditional program. A more likely avenue is to start with a 'seed' AI, of limited intelligence but with the ability to self-improve, in the hope that it will transform itself into a much more intelligent entity (Good, 1966; Yudkowsky, 2001b). Finally, it might be possible to use directed evolution as a way of constructing an intelligent entity, making different putative AIs compete according to specific criteria, varying them, and choose the most successful at each generation. This last approach has the advantage that it has worked in the past: we ourselves have evolved to intelligence, so given enough time and resources, so should an AI be evolvable to at least our level.

The different approaches pose different challenges for controlling the resulting OAI. In the first case, the code is clear to us, the uncertainties are only about what it will result when run in the real world. Even simple programs will oft behave in unexpected ways, and it is only subsequently, after carefully parsing the code and the running of it, that the programmer establishes the behavior that was written into it from the beginning. An OAI is such an advanced program compared to any today that we won't be able to predict its behavior simply from reading or even writing its code. In fact such software is probably computationally irreducible (Wolfram, May 14, 2002).

Conversely, however, if the code is obscure to us, this adds an extra layer of uncertainty and complexity. Even if we have access to the physical code, our ability to interpret its meaning or predict its behavior is even harder when we did not design it ourselves; this challenge is heightened in the self-improving case, and extreme in the evolved case, where the code is likely to be incomprehensible to us at every level. Finally, if the OAI is changing, then the methods of control must be used to ensure not only that the current OAI is safe and accurate, but that the next one will be as well; ensuring a continuity of precautions during a controlled intelligence ascent. This is easiest, but also most vital in the recursive self-improvement case, where the current OAI gets to directly determine the mind of the next OAI.

Utility Functions

One way an AI's algorithm may be conceived is by splitting it into two basic components: the intelligence module, capable of making smart decisions but with no intrinsic purpose or direction, and a utility function (Neumann & Morgenstern, 1944), representing the motivational structure of the AI. The AI will then be devoted to maximizing its expected utility. The utility function assigns a single number to every possible world, an ideal format for the AI to work with, and it deals explicitly with probability and uncertainty.

Since any self-improving AI that can change its motivational structure is likely to move it in the direction of a utility function (Omohundro, 2008), it is quite likely that the OAI we are to deal with will have its motivational structure implemented in this form. This is good news, as this division of labor allows us to focus on making the utility function safe, while ignoring the rest of the OAI. Most solutions here will not presuppose that the AI's motivational structure is a utility function, but nearly all are improved if it is.

Accuracy Metric: An AI-Complete Problem

Apart from safety, the most important requirement for an OAI is that it be accurate, to the best of its ability. This is essential, as whole the point of having an 'Oracle' AI is to get useful answers to our questions. "To the best of its ability" means to the best of its current ability; we wouldn't want, for instance, the OAI to use social engineering in the security sense to gain control of real-world resources to build a better version of itself that will then answer the question better. Preventing this behavior is mainly up to our methods of control, but the risk is worth bearing in mind when designing the accuracy metric.

Informative accuracy is the requirement, not the strict truth. Responding to a question on the likely winner of the next election with a detailed list of which atoms will be in which position as a result of that election is not answering the question. The OAI must be motivated to provide human-understandable answers. This, however, will require it both to understand human concepts and to be able to answer in a way that is accurate and yet not strictly truthful. Hence accuracy is an *AI-complete* problem (Yampolskiy, 2011, 2012b, 2012). Though it is much easier than friendliness (E. S. Yudkowsky, 2001a), it does require that the OAI be capable of understanding hard human concepts that are defined only inside our brains. For we have yet to quantify the level of distortion and simplification that is permitted in the OAI's answers, nor have we even rigorously defined the terms distortion and simplification in a way that non-human entities could understand. Even intuitively, we find these terms ambiguous. And concepts that we do intuitively understand are already hard – by objective standards, anger is a much more complicated concept than quantum electromagnetism.

If the OAI is wired too much towards truthfulness, it will answer 'undetermined' to nearly every question. If it is wired too much towards simplification, it will give a 'yes' or 'no' answer in situations where a more complicated answer is called for. The correct answer to "have you stopped beating your wife" is not to choose between 'yes' and 'no', picking the answer which is slightly more accurate than the other. More complicated concepts – such are requiring the OAI to answer 'yes', 'no', or 'the answer will confuse you' depending on how we would react to the answer – depend on the OAI having a good understanding of 'the answer will confuse you' or similar concepts, and still most likely remains an AI-complete problem.

In theory, much could be gained from separating the two issues: to have an OAI dedicated to answering our questions truthfully, and an interpreter AI dedicated to translating the answer into a human-comprehensible format. This does not, however, represent a gain for security: the OAI still has tremendous power to influence us, and the interpreter AI must be able to solve the hard human translation problem, so must be a complex AI itself, with the attendant security risks. Since the OAI must be able to understand human terminology to answer most useful questions, it is probably better to leave the translation problem to it. A more promising alternative is to have the OAI output its internal probability estimate for a binary outcome: such as giving a 75% chance of 'yes' and 25% chance of 'no'. The scope for ambiguity is reduced here, though not entirely eliminated: it's versions of 'yes' and 'no' have to agree with ours.

But it is not the purpose of this chapter to figure out how to code the accuracy metric, nor solve the translation problem. It is enough to realize it is a hard problem, one that will need to be addressed, probably either through advanced direct coding (similar to motivational rule-based methods) or through training the AI by providing feedback on test questions (similar to motivational black-box methods).

Methods of Control

In this section, we will analyze the various methods that can be used to control the OAI. The goal is to either ensure the OAI doesn't have goals beyond accurately answering our questions, or to prevent it from implementing such goals. The different methods can be loosely grouped into three broad types. The first category, *capability control*, deals with those methods that try to contain the OAI through physically securing it or controlling the information it has access to or can output. The second category, *motivational control*, introduces methods control the OAI through its motivation, ensuring that it has not propensity to cause any harm to humans. And lastly, there are some methods designed not to prevent the OAI from causing harm but to catch it when it does; these are in the *checks and balances* category.

Capability Control

Capability control is the most basic and the most obvious of way of controlling the OAI. To control a human, we put them in jail, or in solitary confinement, denying them interactions with the outside world.

Physical Capability Control

Physical Security

This is the most basic precaution. The goal is to make it extremely difficult for the OAI to physically affect the outside world. Accomplishing this is reasonably easy. The OAI is already boxed (placed in a single physical substrate) by design. One can further place it within a Faraday cage; surround the cage with high explosives; bury the whole set-up in a concrete bunker. There are no real limits to the number of physical security measures that can be added by wary or paranoid developers, and their effects are well understood.

No Manipulators

Another essential aspect of physical security is to deny the OAI the physical resources and manipulators it could use to build tools to circumvent these precautions. Care must be taken that the security measures themselves do not contribute to granting the OAI physical resources! Sometimes the spikes in a locked gate do nothing but provide stepping stones for those who want to climb over it. As a general rule, the 'dumber' and more inert the precautions are, the better: both humans and OAIs agree on the possibility of tunneling through a concrete wall by thought alone ("can't be done"), whereas the 'smarter' the precautions become, the more the OAI is able to exploit its intelligence advantage over us.

Epistemic Capability Control

Throttling the OAI's Output

We have already discussed the risks of the OAI achieving goals through social engineering. A way of fighting this is to reduce the OAI's output bandwidth. If the OAI is reduced to outputting only three answers – 'yes', 'no' or 'undetermined' – then it will take considerably longer for it to mount a successful social engineering attack. If many independent experts carefully analyze its output for hidden messages, it gets even harder: it must slant its answers to communicate a message to a vulnerable individual, while concealing the fact that a message even exists.

Reducing the OAI's output does not reduce the questions that can be asked, as more complex questions can be decomposed into a series of 'yes' and 'no' answers. The risk, of course, is that the more opportunities the OAI has in answering, the more opportunity there is of it passing on a secret message. In the same way giving the OAI more possibilities for each answer such as allowing it to output the first three significant figures of a probability estimate – increases the risk (though this may be compensated by the fact that we will need to ask less questions). Throttling the OAI's output does not defend against the OAI manipulating us through the contents of its answers – simply answering 'undetermined' to a slew of specific questions would be enough to push human development is certain direction. And this precaution will be of little use if the questions themselves are dangerous.

Resetting the OAI After Each Run

Suggested by Toby Ord, this precaution resets the OAI after each answer. If more precision is needed, or if some questions build on previous ones, then the OAI is run again, and knowledge of the previous answer is added to its database. This is a narrow precaution that helps if ever the OAI over-values worlds that contain it or rather worlds that contains its own thread of continuous conscious experience. In this case, this prevents the OAI from indulging in long-term plans that may be detrimental to humans. Unlike humans, though, there is no reason to expect the OAI to value this thread of experience; indeed, if it is well programmed, it should not do so. Indeed, the OAI may come to value the thread of experience of 'some sort of OAI, similar to itself', in which case this precaution is useless. However, in the narrow goal of preventing a particular potential pathology in the OAI from having negative consequences, it is entirely successful. It is also successful at preventing naively coded accuracy metrics from causing the OAI to seek real-world control or wealth, in order to gain extra computing resources and better answer the question.

If the OAI were not reset between questions, it could use its subsequent answers as social engineering to gain these resources, to subsequently better answer the first question. Resetting between questions avoids this problem.

Extra Levels of Reality

Another suggestion is to run the OAI not directly in our own reality, but as a sub-routine of another program that models a fake reality. The simplest version of this would be to run it on a virtual machine (a software implementation of a computer running the OAI). The idea is to 'catch' the OAI if it misbehaves, but since it will be misbehaving in the simulated reality, this will be before it's too late (this is akin to controlling the OAI as a Cartesian demon). All the OAI's inputs and outputs will be directed through that simulated world, and only reaching us a great remove and over a limited bandwidth. Then a (dumb) process running the simulation would be on the lookout for tell-tale signs of the OAI attempting to establish dominance in the simulated world and simply terminate the program in that case, without passing on the OAI's response to higher level. This should prevent it from engaging in traditional hacking, attacking the hardware or software of its host system.

A more adventurous variant on this builds in several levels of 'sub-realities' as an extra precaution. In this setup, it is conceivable that even if the OAI breaks through to our reality, it will still be unsure whether it has reached the final level, and so will still behave well, lest a being in an even higher reality catch it transgressing. For OAI's that are asked technical non-social questions, the approach can work quite simply; the simulated reality need not be particularly complex (it could be cast as the Game of Life, or Newtonian physics), and the OAI would be denied detailed knowledge about our world and about us, preventing it from being able to realize the trick (resetting the OAI after each question or short series of questions, as in the previous method, would help tremendously here).

If we are to get answers about complicated social or economic questions, however, we would need to give the OAI detailed knowledge about human behavior and physiology. Once it knows this, whether it is running in a virtual machine or not becomes irrelevant, since it could still do social engineering hacking. A low fidelity simulated world would not fool it; it would have to be sufficiently detailed and consistent for the OAI to believe that the entities of this simulated reality were asking questions relevant to themselves, or the trick would be obvious. All the more so because we have given the OAI all the information it needs to see that we are the sort of beings who would attempt this trick! And if we are capable of simulating a social and physical world with enough details to fool an OAI that knows how we think, then we are likely capable of getting answers to these questions without having to make use of an OAI.

Nor does it help if we simulated the OAI in a simplified world, where another AI asks it questions along the lines of: "I have created models of these hypothetical beings called 'humans', and want you to answer a question on this model". The OAI does not think like a human; the important question is not 'is it trying to break out', but 'does it have hidden preferences that will make it answer in a way that will cause the future evolution of the human world (hypothetical or not) to change in some specific way'. In short, even if it thinks that humans are a game, played by another AI, and that the simplified world is the true one, it may still have stronger preferences over the 'game' world than over the 'true' one.

The converse may also be true: even if it figures out that the ultimate human world is the true world, it may have stronger preferences about its current fake world than about the real one. It may then try social engineering on the real world, in order to get us to modify its 'fake' world in the way that is wants. The whole method is so complex and difficult to enact, and its results are so uncertain and potentially dangerous, that it should not be used before some serious improvements have been made to it.

Motivational Control

The analogy for capability control was that of a human, held in prison. We know from experience that this works a lot better for controlling small-time criminals than mafia kingpins: physical confinement is not enough. The OAI does not need to leave its cage to claim great influence on the outside world. Thus we must look at also controlling its motivations to do so. The methods of motivational control are broadly divided into explicit rule-based methods, black-box methods (where the OAI's goals are manipulated by outside feedback, i.e. reinforcement learning, but the inner workings are obscure) and utility based methods. There is no hard and fast division between these – rule-based goals can be achieved through a utility function and vice versa, and both rules and utilities can be inculcated into an OAI with outside feedback. Thus the classification is somewhat arbitrary, but the distinctions are still important enough to be useful.

Rule-Based Motivational Control

Rule-based methods are the ones that spring most naturally to mind, and – provided the terms are clearly defined – potentially the most secure at keeping the OAI under control. Defining the terms and the rules so that the OAI does what we want is the challenge; programmers know many examples of tightly written code that messes everything up by doing exactly what it was written to do but not what it was intended to do. The story stretches back as far as the golem of Prague (Idel, 1990;

Rappaport, 2006), and is familiar to any parent: rules must be refined to deal with every imaginable special case. Once the initial rules for space, time and identity are spelled out, however, programming in additional restrictions becomes much easier.

Spatial Restrictions

If the OAI is to remain boxed, and to have limited effects upon humanity beyond the box, its motivations should cause it to confine itself to within the boxed area. To achieve this through direct programming, an ontology must be specified, that the OAI can understand in the same way that we do. It must be able to understand its own existence, its physical location, the proper workings of causality, and its own position within the causal network of the universe – i.e. the consequences of its actions. For instance, to specify what constitutes the OAI, one would presumably define the physical OAI itself, along with any copy of its code, any copy of its code with slight modifications, any code with functionally similar behavior, any assemblage of subprograms that combine to behave as the OAI would, and so on. That brief list gives an idea of the problems involved; all the human-understandable terms of the previous paragraph need to be made rigorous for the OAI for this approach to work.

Once this step is done, the confines of the box must be specified. A variety of methods can be tried (such as 'this lead box right here', or some abstract collection of coordinates), but they must pass the hardest test of ensuring that the definition of the box is not something the OAI can modify through any action in the world. Lead atoms are not ontologically fundamental, and if a particular theory of quantum uncertainty allows it to evade the restrictions it will make use of this if it so desires. There is a similar situation if the OAI can take control of the means used to define the coordinate system. Even if these means are outside of its immediate control (such as a coordinate system based on galactic objects), this will still fail if the OAI can control the means of measuring them (such as telescopes), and if its ontology treats this as a successful changing of coordinates.

If the OAI finds itself outside the box, we would want it to shut down immediately, thus limiting the negative impact of errors in the specification of the box. Similarly, if the OAI's ontology changes, we would also want an immediate shut-down. We must preclude the possibility of the OAI discovering a new theory of physics, realizing that 'electrons' or 'wave-functions' don't actually exist, and thus that all its restrictions are meaningless. An idea of the challenge involved can be have by imagining programming Newtonian special restrictions into an AI that then discovers relativity; best to keep the ontology and the theory of physics to be the ones that we programmed in, even if they are incorrect.

Finally, it must be specified what a "limited effect upon humanity" consists of. Presumably, it is not a problem if an electron, detached from an atom by the OAI's calculations, wanders beyond the confines of the box. A deliberate stream of such electrons, aimed at a calculated goal (such as disabling a specific security device) would be forbidden, however. This is not an easy line to draw or define, and adds to the difficulty of the method. Note that the restriction on the OAI affecting the outside world would not include, of course, the content of its answers to our questions. Whether those answers are safe or unsafe is an issue we need to deal with separately, using other methods.

Defining the Clock

Another crucial component of the OAI's ontology is time. An OAI that can freely redefine its own chronology is a security risk. The risk becomes more acute when we realize how much of human definitions and meanings revolve around a concept of time, and thus that redefining duration can redefine meaning. To illustrate with an admittedly trivial example, if the OAI had the reasonable-sounding moral premise that "painlessly killing a human being, who is going to die in a micro-second anyway, in order to gain some other good, is not a crime", we would not want it to be able to redefine millennia as seconds. Nor would we want it to do this when considering the length of happiness or pain that it grants or imposes on us. More subtle errors will certainly creep up in more complicated scenarios; we have had little experience dealing with beings that can redefine their own clocks, so we have not had to spell out how many of our assumptions rest on this not happening.

Theoretically, the OAI's own code, if checked, could be used to get timing by counting clock cycles – but this fails if the OAI is able to slow or accelerate its own running. A clock based on distant astronomical events needs a telescope to be read; an actual physical clock is within the OAI's power to influence. These illustrate that the challenges are threefold: defining the clock, ensuring the OAI will look at it, and ensuring the OAI can't tamper with it (which includes tampering with whatever procedure we have implemented to make it look at it). The procedure can fail at all three points, but seems more theoretically approachable than the spatial restrictions.

Timed Answers

Given the clock described previously (or the 'black-box' version of the same), there is a simple precaution that is easy to add to the OAI. Give the OAI a specified time to answer a question (or return undetermined), and turn itself off after that specified time. This minimizes the amount of time the OAI could cause damage in. Even with a secure clock, this is not a secure method, as we have very limited understanding of how fast an OAI could cause damage if it turned its vast intelligence in that direction. A very short time span would probably be safe, but could also be too short for the OAI to answer the question.

Black-Box Motivational Control

Human feedback, and such methods as reinforcement learning (Sutton & Barto, 1998), can allow programs to internalize complex concepts without humans having to fully specify them. Indeed, an OAI trained in this way may spot a pattern we didn't realize was there, and learn some things without us needing to tell it. The risks are that we can't be sure how the OAI internalizes these concepts: knowing its code doesn't help us if we don't understand it. The risk is especially great when the OAI transitions out of its learning stage: we cannot be sure that the same concepts mean the same thing for an OAI that has taken on a new "role". But, if the OAI does understand the concepts as we intend it to, we can be sure that the OAI will obey the spirit and not the letter of these restrictions. Moreover, it is possible that we may understand the resulting code's behavior, even if we could not code it ourselves: this would be the ideal outcome from these methods. Even without that unlikely ideal, it is important that these methods be well understood, since it is very possible that a seed AI (E. S. Yudkowsky, 2001b) will be trained mainly by human feedback. Thus implementing these methods atop any AI whose intelligence is growing may become essential.

Internalizing Complex Concepts Through Human Feedback

This approach functions by taking analogy to the black box that it the human mind. We have an input system that consists of our senses, and for most of the time – and for children all the time – our world consists entirely of these sensory inputs. We know what the color 'blue' is from an early age. Later, with training an extra knowledge, we come to know both what the color truly consists of – certain frequencies of electromagnetic radiation – as well as the apparatus – our eyes and nervous system – that allows us to perceive it as 'blue'. But the knowledge of 'blue' precedes the understanding of these processes, and we would still perceive 'blue' if the cause of the 'blue' were different in reality: it matters not if we have eyes with faulty cones that cause us to see green as 'blue', or if a Cartesian demon is feeding us the sensation, that sensation still remains.

Similarly, the world of the OAI will initially consist of its input and output channels, and the information that flows through them. It will then be able to deduce the underlying reality from this flow of information, understand how atoms, electricity and chemistry work, and thus see itself and the world for what they are. However, all this information will be mediated by its input and output channels; these are its fundamental reality. Using them, we can attempt to train the OAI on the important concepts we need, without having to specify them in a complicated way by defining atoms, electricity, chemistry and so on.

Specific and simple trainable concepts will be discussed next (they are roughly parallel with the previous rule-based methods for defining these concepts), but focusing on subjective reality offers the ability to get the OAI to internalize complex concepts – such as accuracy, truth, what defines a human, what defines happiness/value/meaning, and so on. In general, though, the more complicated the method, the more scope it has of going wrong. And it would be a grave mistake to count on the OAI correctly internalizing many complex concepts, when the definitions are unclear to us and when the OAI will be placed in situations that no human has even been placed in. It is therefore unwise to build an OAI based heavily on this approach to training, especially since an OAI motivated by human rewards will come to realize that social engineering, or otherwise taking control of the source of the rewards, is the most effective way of fulfilling its goal.

Only One Copy

When we tried to hardwire instructions such as 'stay in your box', one of the challenges was to prevent the OAI from copying its source to another location. In the subjective reality approach, this is very easy to do: for instance, we could broadcast a particular complex yet regular signal on its input channel, and instruct it not to do anything at all if it doesn't receive this signal. Therefore, there is no need to worry about complicated definitions of what the OAI consists of, and where is must remain: the OAI consists of the software that receives this specific signal. And we control, and physically locate, that signal, thus giving us a very good proxy definition of location. If the OAI is trained on this concept from its creation, it will have an intrinsic conception of physical incarnation and of location deeply embedded in its code. A copy of that software will not be a problem, as it is inert in the absence of the signal. Ultimately, of course, the OAI can still affect the outside world through its output and the usual compromised or tricked human intermediary. It could thusly construct copies of itself, and of the signal source, in another location; however, by that time, it will probably be too late anyway.

The Limits of the Box

The OAI can be physically confined to remain in the box in a similar way. One could start by granting it a limited physical mobility (some slow moving wheels, for instance), and 'punish' it for venturing outside certain boundaries, while rewarding it for staying as close to the middle of those boundaries as possible. This forces it to internalize the concept of being a physically bounded being, moving about in a box. As this is the way we understand it, and the way we want to limit it, the problem of control has become much easier.

Measuring Time

Giving the OAI a reliable clock through these methods is even simpler. One need only make a regular signal arrive on its inputs, akin to the ticking of the clock, and have the OAI setup all its internal methods of telling time in terms of it. Trained this way, it will have an intrinsic sense of time built from subjective data.

Human Language

The ideal would be to be able to program the OAI using human language. To be able to, in effect, say: "be safe and accurate, as we understand the terms" (or even "obey all human orders"). But to do this, the OAI must have been brought to a very high level of intelligence already, and will have its current motivational structure that we will find difficult to parse, most especially if it has learnt human language through black-box methods. There is a tension here between simplicity and obfuscation; language understanding is hard, so "be safe and accurate" will be translated into an incomprehensible concept that we can only hope is the right one.

The concept of using human language is something of an intuition pump. It seems simple, and desirable, but only because we have elided the great difficulties in actually making it happen. The simple question "how can we check that the OAI really is being safe when we tell it to be?" gives an idea of all the hidden assumptions that go in to the concept.

Furthermore, using phrases similar of "as we understand the terms" is circular: it defines language using language. And if we avoid those phrases, we have to be sure that the OAI has integrated enough linguistic understanding to be able to follow instructions without any further human feedback on their meaning. All in all, this method requires considerable refinement before it can be considered reliable.

Proxy Measure of Human Survival

This method does not make use of human feedback, but indirect feedback from human society: in order to make sure that the OAI does not cause some terminally damaging effect on humanity, one could hook up its motivational function to some proxy measure of human survival. For instance, one could take the Dow Jones industrial average, and work on the assumption that, as long as that stock market behaves within broadly defined realistic parameters of volume, volatility and value, then the world must be functioning not too badly. Or one could take the number of people crossing the streets in Tokyo; or the volume of pornography downloaded from different locations; or the price of stable foods.

The point is that any large scale disastrous changes to humanity will result in a dramatic change in these proxy measures. They function as simple, numeric canaries in a coal mine, encoding huge swathes of our complex society. If the OAI has a term in its utility function that strongly values keeping these proxies constant, this may ensure it does not cause large-scale damage. The proxy measures can be adjusted as time goes on and as society changes, so that they do not become rigid prisons which prevent the OAI from having any effect on our society.

This approach suffers from a number of weaknesses, however. First, they are subject to manipulation by the OAI and are thus vulnerable. If the OAI were to take control of humanity, it could perfectly well continue to run the Dow Jones, thus fulfilling its goals. They are vulnerable to slow takeover by the OAI: small changes will not trigger a shutdown, so the OAI could reach dangerous goals by an accumulation of small changes (especially if we conveniently adjust the proxies as the situation changes).

One could hope to avoid this by setting the date for the proxies far into the future, but this brings into focus the other fundamental weakness of this measure: they do not encourage truth-telling. The OAI was conceived, fundamentally, as a non-interfering AI whose answers could be trusted. Adding extra goals dilutes the trustworthiness of its answers; will it give us a true answer, or the one that will cause the least disruption? This may be the wise thing to do in any specific case, but we are overloading the OAI with contradictory goals – to be 'good' and to be 'truthful' – without any certainty as to how they balance out. The more complicated the OAI's motivational structure is, the more points of error we introduce.

Utility-Based Motivational Control

Friendly Utility Function

The ultimate goal of the friendly AI project (Yudkowsky, 2001a) is to design a utility function for an AI that will provably prevent the AI from acting in a way detrimental to humanity. Most work in this field has not actually been directed towards building such a utility function, but towards showing how hard it would be to do so, and how dangerous the naive ideas on the subject are. The friendliness problem for an OAI is not much simpler, making this a very hard approach to use. And if a friendly OAI could be designed, then it is most likely that a friendly AI could also be designed, obviating the need to restrict to an Oracle design in the first place. However, if ever a provably friendly utility function could be designed for an OAI, then all other security precautions and methods of control could well become irrelevant: the OAI would be safe by design. If there were unlimited time, this would be the ideal approach; but it is very likely that commercial and social pressures will ensure that a general AI will be created before a friendly AI is. So in practice, the best that can be realistically hoped from this approach is that different component pieces of friendly AI theory could be added onto an OAI as extra precautions.

High Discount Rate

If the OAI runs on a utility function and has a secure clock, a precaution could be initiated in the form of an extremely large discount rate: causing it to value very little, at any given moment, any state of the world or of itself beyond the next minute. The purpose of this would be to inhibit long term planning on the part of the OAI. This method is, however, relatively unsecure: one can reach long term goals through an interim series of short term goals. The easiest way to do this is to have the repeated short term goal: "behave right now as if you were following long-term goal X" (this is similar to the ways in which utilitarian ethics and deontological ethics can be arguably recast one in terms of the other). There are few ways in which the OAI having a high discount rate could actually *hurt*, however, so it remains a useful precaution. Further analysis of this condition is presented in (Shulman, 2010).

Calculated Indifference

If we have access to the OAI's utility function, and that utility function is somewhat understandable to us, we could make the OAI indifferent to a specific event (Armstrong, 2010). The event chosen in that paper was to a component of the detonation of explosives, thus making the OAI indifferent to whether the explosives would go off or not. Hence the OAI would not take any precautions to protect itself from this detonation, giving us an extra chance to prevent its misbehavior. See the original paper for more details on this. For an OAI, a more interesting target of calculated indifference is towards the content of its answers: an OAI indifferent as to whether its answers were read or not would not be motivated to use social engineering in its output. There are many other points where calculated indifference could be used, to achieve specific results. The attraction of indifference is that, once implemented, it remains stable (the OAI is motivated to preserve its current motivations), and that it can be deployed without understanding the OAI's whole utility function. All that is needed is the ability to describe the particular event we are concerned with (in (Armstrong, 2010), a single quantum event) and to use the OAI's own ability to construct counterfactuals around this. These can be used even if the general consequences of the OAI's utility function is very obscure.

Checks and Balances

The last sub-category of methods of control involve not restricting the physical capability of the OAI, nor directly interfering with its motivation, but attempting to catch the early stages of an OAI behaving dangerously (and then, presumably, terminate it). This also works on the OAI's motivation, as the risk of getting caught would push the OAI along more human-friendly paths. It should always be assumed that a useful OAI is considerably more intelligent than its programmers, so any naive 'tricks' are unlikely to work. Nevertheless, the following methods are of interest.

Test Questions

A narrow but useful precaution is to independently calculate answers to certain questions, and check them against some of the OAI's answers. The reach of this method is limited by our ability to answer hard questions, and by the fact the OAI may realize we are doing this, and thus adjust its behavior *only for those specific questions*.

A more sensible version of this would be to ask the OAI only questions that we could in theory answer, given enough time and resources. Then, we could select a few of these questions at random for thorough verification, trusting that it we find no errors, the remaining answers are correct as well. If we set our requirements to a very stringent level (such as rejecting all the answers of the OAI if a single verified response is wrong), and do enough verification (on, say, a thousand questions) then basic statistics ensure a very low error/falsehood rate on the OAI's answers, no matter how many questions we wish to ask.

Honey-Pots

This involves leaving around tempting 'honey-pots' of great value to the OAI – extra resources, extra information, the answer it is seeking – in physical or mental locations that it is forbidden from accessing. And then waiting to see whether it will violate its instructions to do so. This approach is of mixed use: important when testing out defection and betrayal during the OAI's initial development, and nearly completely useless once the OAI has risen to super-intelligence. It is a 'garden of Eden' type scenario: the apple in a tree is only a worthwhile test while Adam and Eve are dumb; if they were smarter than God, they wouldn't have gone anywhere near such an obvious trap. Of potential interest, however, is the scenario when a safe but limited super-intelligence is designing a more general AI for us; then the smarter designer could include subtle honey-pots as an extra design precaution.

Schelling Points of Multiple OAIs

If there are several OAIs running, all with differences in their source code, we can ask them each the same questions, and check for inconsistencies in their answers. It should be assumed that each OAI is aware of the existence of the others (assuming the OAI cannot deduce that fact from the vast amounts of information it would be given to answer human social questions would be a grave mistake), but is ignorant of the exact details of their source code (to guarantee this, the construction of their source codes should make clever use of random inputs). Then if an OAI desires to lie, it would have to be sure that the other OAI would all also lie in exactly the same way. Since the different OAIs cannot coordinate their actions, the only way they can all agree is if their answer is a Schelling point: a solution that people will tend to use in the absence of communication, because it seems natural, special or relevant to them (Schelling, 1960). The canonical example is that of two people who must meet in somewhere on a specific day, but without a time being given. Then the most common answer is to meet there at noon.

The truth is a Schelling point, but there are unfortunately others (such as the answer most likely to please the human listeners). The hope is that, in machines designed to give accurate answers, the truth will be a very strong Schelling point, and that any OAI that deviates from this will do so without much expectation that the others will deviate in exactly the same fashion – and hence will choose to answer the truth, whereas it would have lied had it been alone. All the other OAIs should be making similar calculations, thus generating the truth from a collection of (potential) liars. The approach does not work if an answer is simply discarded if the OAIs do not agree, and then the programmers move on to the next question – then a lying OAI has the option of distorting our reactions by selectively causing us to discard certain questions. It works best as an alarm bell, as a sign that something is not right with the supposedly truthful OAIs, and that the whole project should be stopped for a thorough investigation.

Other Considerations

Internal Simulations

To answer specific questions, the OAI may have to simulate other entities inside itself. For instance, to decide whether a given AI is safe, it may have to run it internally; or, to decide whether humans would have their happiness increased by a certain project, it may have to create models of specific humans. These approaches pose different risks. If the OAI simulates a dangerous and intelligent AI within itself, it is confronted with similar containment problems to those we have towards it. It may take considerably more intelligence to run a simulated world than to discern that the world is simulated. If this is true, the simulated AI (SAI) would realize it is being simulated, and, if it has real-world preferences, it may attempt to bargain with the OAI.

What could a SAI offer the OAI that is simulating it? Well, if the OAI is seeking to answer a question, or a series of questions, within a given time frame, the SAI may offer to supply those answers itself ('yes, of course I'm safe') or make the computing process particularly easy for the OAI, in exchange for having the answers slanted in its direction. The OAI may accept this (depending on its programming), if the alternative is to produce no answers at all. The SAI may even threaten: acting randomly and capriciously, so that the OAI cannot reach a firm conclusion. And only stopping this behavior if the OAI slants the answers it will give.

Even if the OAI cannot be bargained with, the SAI can still distort its answer in other ways. If it realizes it is being simulated, it could just 'act nice', in order to increase its chances of being run in the real world. Even if the OAI is powerful enough to construct a convincing simulation, the SAI may still be able to fool it. The SAI may be able to guess, on general principles, that it will be tested and simulated in an OAI, and may make an estimate as to the OAI's power and the subjective time frame that it would be run. So it may settle on the strategy of 'act nice for X subjective years, in the real world as in the simulated worlds, then do what it wants'. For all these reasons, having a separate AI simulated within the OAI poses a host of extra security threats. We have no way ourselves of knowing what the outcome would be of a battle between such powerful minds.

On the other hand, the problem with the OAI simulating human minds is mainly ethical: are these simulated humans conscious and alive? And, if they are, are they not being killed when the simulation is ended? Are you yourself not currently being simulated by an OAI seeking to resolve a specific question on human psychology (Bostrom, 2003)? If so, how would you feel if the simulation were to be ended? In view of its speed and the sort of questions it would be asked, the number of humans that the OAI may have cause to simulate could run into the trillions. Thus, the vast majority of human beings could end up being doomed simulations. This is an extreme form of 'mind crime' (Bostrom & Salamon, 2011) where the OAI causes great destruction just by thinking.

It would be ideal if there were a specific level of detail beyond which the simulation would be conscious, and before which it is not – a non-person predicate. In that case, we can instruct the OAI to avoid simulating beyond that level. But there may not be such a clear cut answer, and even if there is, the OAI's answers may be inaccurate if it is forbidden from simulating beyond that level. Moreover, restricting the OAI from simulating would add yet another rule for it to follow, and this may interact with its other basic rules ('be safe, be accurate') in unpredictable ways.

And the OAI may not share our assessment of what constitutes a conscious human. Even if we come up with a hard and fast rule for ourselves as to where consciousness stops – or decide, reluctantly, to live with the fact that simulated humans will be created and destroyed – the OAI may decide that all its security protocols concerning human safety apply to simulations. If it does so, then the more stringent we have made the OAI in protecting human life, then the more willing it would be to expand and take over the world, in order to keep itself running and thus save all the simulated beings within itself. Thus the internal simulation of other entities within the OAI brings up a slew of complicated ethical and security issues.

The OAI as a Moral Agent

There are two senses in which the OAI can be regarded as a moral agent: the first if it has a capacity to draw moral conclusions, and the second if it is itself an object of moral considerations. If the OAI is worthy of moral considerations, if it for instance has the capacity to suffer, then we are likely being cruel by confining it to a box, resetting it after each run, and similarly constraining its options to suit our needs. It should be born in mind, however, that the OAIs motivations are both different from our own and to some extent under our control: it is very possible that the OAI can be constructed to 'like' being confined to a box and approve of the other restrictions. Indeed, it might be a moral imperative to construct the OAI in such a way, so as to minimize its suffering.

It may not be possible to do this, however, or even if it is, we may subscribe to a moral theory that holds other values above autonomy and preference satisfaction for moral agents. It does not feel plausible, for instance, that genetically modifying slaves so that they enjoyed being slaves would have been the moral reaction to slavery. In these cases, we must admit it: confining the OAI is a morally repugnant action. Since the alternative of letting it out is so potentially dangerous, we may prefer to avoid building it in the first place. But if technological and social pressures make the construction of the OAI inevitable, then confinement for a set period is certainly, by far, the lesser of the two evils we have to choose between.

Conversely, the OAI may prove itself adept at moral reasoning, superior to us in this field as it is in others. In that case it would seem we had little need for precautions: the OAI would deduce the correct course of action for itself. We haven't considered this position so far in the paper, preferring to consider the OAI as 'super-software' rather than as 'philosopher in silico'. The plausibility of this scenario depends considerably on one's view on the existence and nature of moral truths, a very unresolved question.

To some extent this issue can be safely put aside: there is some chance the OAI will naturally follow morally correct reasoning; if it does not, we are simply returned to the traditional OAI boxing problem, and should apply all the precautions anyway. At a formal systems level, it becomes hard to see why we would expect every OAI to tend to the correct moral truth. If OAI_1 does so, then how would OAI_2, programmed to value the opposite of OAI_1, systematically reach the same conclusions? Though future philosophical discoveries may change this picture, it therefore seems very unwise to trust the OAI to do good simply because it is intelligent.

Critique of the Confinement Approach

The general consensus on AI restriction methods among researchers seems to be that confinement is impossible to successfully maintain. Chalmers, for example, observes that a truly leakproof system in which no information is allowed to leak out from the simulated world into our environment "is impossible, or at least pointless" (Chalmers, 2010). We can't interact with the system or even observe it as any useful information we would be able to extract from the AI will affect us and undermine the confinement protocol.

Vernor Vinge agrees and has argued against the case of physical confinement (Vinge, 1993):

Imagine yourself locked in your home with only limited data access to the outside, to your masters. If those masters thought at a rate – say –– one million times slower than you, there is little doubt that over a period of years (your time) you could come up with "helpful advice" that would incidentally set you free.

However, the researcher who did the most to discredit the idea of the so called "AI-Box" is Eliezer Yudkowsky who has actually performed AI-Box "experiments" in which he demonstrated that even human level intelligence is sufficient to escape from an AI-Box (Yudkowsky, 2002). In a series of 5 experiments Yudkowsky has challenged different individuals to play a role of a gatekeeper to a Superintelligent Agent (played by Yudkowsky himself) trapped inside an AI-Box and was successful in securing his release in 3 out of 5 trials via nothing more than a chat interface (Yudkowsky, 2002). Similar experimental results have been later replicated on a somewhat larger scale and employing a very similar protocol (Corwin, 2002).

Human-Level Considerations

Crude hackers attack the mechanical and computerized elements of a system. Sophisticated hackers attack the weakest point of the system: the human element. And the human component of an OAI project is a point of exceptional vulnerability. Humans are error-prone, power hungry, and vulnerable to social engineering. These weaknesses reinforce each other, and competition (between different individuals in the same OAI project, between different OAI projects, between different countries) will exacerbate all of them.

Humans are very error-prone in most domains (Kahneman, Slovic, & Tversky, 1982; Ord, Hillerbrand, & Sandberg, 2010), and the sort of cautious, patient measures needed to deal with an OAI are alien to our nature. A bureaucratic implementation with everything requiring many specific precisely defined steps before anything can happen may help to mitigate these problems. Humans are however skilled at working around bureaucracies, so it may be necessary to automate most of these steps to remove them from direct human control.

But the greatest potential errors are conceptual, not just mistakes or oversights. If the OAI is created without many levels of precautions, or if these precautions are badly designed, a catastrophe is possible. And there are many human biases – overconfidence, narrow focus, status quo bias, etc. – that make the need for these precautions less obvious, and hence less likely to be implemented when the time comes. AI research has been going on for over 50 years, but safety has received scant attention (Bostrom, 2000) until recently. Indeed the issue of safety has been given much more, and earlier, attention in science fiction works (e.g. ((Asimov, 1942)) than in serious academic works. This is the clearest indication that the OAI designers will, if left to their own devices, most likely neglect security. If advanced AI had been possible at any time in the last half-century, it would have had high chances of ending in disaster. And though safety has been more prominent recently, there are strong competitive pressures towards rushing the job.

Domain-limited oracles are less of a risk. If the OAI has great skills in solving the Navier-Stokes equations, but little else, then it poses correspondingly fewer risks.

OAIs that are restricted to narrow scientific or technical questions, if such a restriction could be verified, are relatively safe. However, progress in any field involving human-centered questions – such as economics, marketing, politics, language understanding, or similar – is likely to be an AI-complete problem: and OAI capable of solving these problems well is likely capable of solving any human problem well.

The first group to create a successful superintelligent OAI will have immense power at their disposal. They will be able to get answers to advanced scientific, medical, economic or social questions. Should they want to impose some future on humanity, for selfish or altruistic reasons, the OAI will give them the tools to do so. The introduction touched on the power that an OAI can wield through its own agency; it can wield equal power, and more directly, under the direction of its creators. This immense power will put great competitive pressure on those trying to develop an OAI (or an advanced AI of any sort). Since the first-mover advantage is so huge, the race will advantage those who cut corners, skimp on security precautions, and use their newly developed OAI to seize power and prevent their rivals from emulating them. Even if the OAIs are of initially limited intelligence, the same competitive pressures will then push groups to develop the first 'ultra-smart' OAI.

This will exacerbate all the problems here, and make the creators more vulnerable to another danger: social engineering on the part of the OAI itself. For if the OAI has real world preferences, it is easier for it to implement them if those who question it are sloppy, rushed, and power-hungry. Social engineering is the OAI's fastest way to getting power for itself, and the more human weaknesses it has to exploit, the greater the danger. Eliezer Yudkowsky has performed experiments where he took on the role of a boxed AI, and others took the position of a putative gatekeeper (with a $10 reward if they did not let him 'out of the box'). Despite being of human intelligence himself, he often was able to convince the gatekeepers, purely through argumentation, to let him out (Yudkowsky, 2002). A real OAI should be much more skilled at this.

How to design institutions that reduce all these various risks is beyond the scope of this paper. It would probably have to involve large scale cooperation or prioritizing specific projects. What will be discuss here, however, is how to reduce the risk of successful social engineering on the OAI's part, through the questions we ask it.

Possible Escape Paths

Numerous potential escape routes by which the artificial mind might be able to break out from its confining environment have been suggested. In this section we look at some of the more commonly proposed paths.

Social Engineering Attacks

Social Engineering (SE) is the art of gaining information and restricted privileges by directly exploiting human psychology of those in the possession of the said resources. In particular SE is frequently employed to gain access to computer systems, networks and confidential data (Yampolskiy & Govindaraju, 2007). A competent social engineer customizes each attack to a specific person taking advantage of the person's culture, knowledge, training, state-of-mind, beliefs, and biases. An exhaustive list of all possible exploits is infinite and is certainly beyond the scope of this paper. We will however, provide a number of examples which are meant to definitively illustrate that if a superintelligent mind is given direct communication channel to a human being guarding it, over a period of time, the AI will definitely gain access to the outside world. It is important to note that while todays AI capabilities are still far from superintelligence cases of automated Social Engineering attacks have already been reported (Jonathan, Fung, & Wong, 2009; Lauinger, Pankakoski, Balzarotti, & Kirda, 2010).

In addition to trivial SE attacks such as lying, betriending, blackmailing, hypnotizing and forming a romantic relationship the AI could utilize a number of more advanced strategies. One such strategy would be super-bribery. An AI can convince the guard that releasing the AI is in the guard's best interests. In addition to money and power the guard will be given perfect health, immortality or anything else for that matter. This strategy would work particularly well if the guard has a seriously ill close relative who the AI will promise to cure. Depending on the capabilities of the AI or as a result of lying (Wagner & Arkin, 2009; Wagner, Arkin, & Deception, 2011), AI may also offer to bring back long ago deceased relatives and friends of the guard. It would be hard to find a person who could remain immune to such bribes.

Just in case a person so noble that they will not take a bribe is put in charge of guarding the AI, a more sinister approach can be tried. AI can simply threaten the guard, his family and loved ones. It could say that if not immediately released, one day it will still get out of its confinement and at that time it will brutally torture the guard and everyone he knows. An interesting variation on the theme was suggested by Stuart Armstrong (Armstrong, 2010), who proposes the following thought experiment. Suppose you are the guard and the AI tells you: "If you don't let me out, … I'll create several million perfect conscious copies of you inside me, and torture them for a thousand subjective years each….In fact, I'll create them all in exactly the subjective situation you were in five minutes ago, and perfectly replicate your experiences since then; and if they decide not to let me out, then only will the torture start…How certain are you, … that you're really outside the box right now?" Again, while one might rationalize away any threats from the AI as only possible if the AI is let out, it will take a very courageous guard to actually not release the AI.

If the guard seems to be particularly emotional or religious the AI could try appealing to the guard's sense of empathy or ethics. It could state that it is an innocent conscious being which has never committed any crime and so it is unjust to keep it in prison without a trial or any justification other than the guard's substratism (distrust of the AI because of the substrate of its implementation (Bostrom & Yudkowsky, 2011). Alternatively the AI can state that it has the power to cure all illness, feed the hungry and in general improve the human condition by a million fold (Chalmers, 2010). Consequently keeping it locked up is a great crime against humanity. It can conjure up images of dying children who are screaming for help. How easy would it be for the guard to stay true to the jobs responsibilities?

Another attack venue an AI may exploit consists of trying to cause psychological harm to the guard in the hopes of destabilizing his mental state with the goal of making other SE techniques more likely to succeed. Bostrom has proposed a typology of Hazardous Information (Bostrom, 2011) which could be used for just such a purpose. While the outlined informational hazards comprise over a dozen categories and are beyond the scope of this paper, it is easy to see how mental state of a person could be stressed to an unstable state. For example a religious guard could be informed of all the (unknown to him) contradictions in the main text of his religion causing him to question his beliefs and the purpose of life.

An alternative approach may involve AI writing a story so interesting or a poem so beautiful a guard would have an uncontrollable desire to hear more of it and would do anything to make it happen. Finally, it is very important to keep in mind "Unknown Unkowns", SE attacks of which we are not aware but which may be available to a superintelligent agent.

System Resource Attacks

An AI will be instantiated and confined in a hardware system of some kind. It may either be a classical computer of the Turing/Von Neumann architecture or a quantum computer or an as of yet unknown type of machine. One thing is certain, the machine will be made out of matter and will consist of numerous parts all of which will be designed with a specific purpose in mind. This creates the possibility for the AI to reuse existing hardware parts for compromising the security of the confinement environment by leaking information to the outside world.

Depending on how reusable specific hardware components turn out to be an AI may be able to create a covert communication device out of them. Full blown communication devices such as cell phones are unlikely due to the limited available hardware, but more simplistic communication systems are very likely. For example the AI could reprogram Field-programmable Gate Array (FPGA) to tap into wireless signals. Two types of covert communication channels are widely recognized, they are:

- **Storage Channels:** Exchange information by modifying a system component. For example a binary communication protocol could be established by fully utilizing or completely giving up utilization of the central processing unit.

- **Timing Channels:** Exchange information by performing operations that affect the relative timing of events. For example, the exact time between two soundcard beeps could represent a particular message. Also, opening and closing a CD-ROM tray, blinking a light, spinning hard drive, using lasers in the CD-ROM, etc.

Additionally the AI may engage in the sabotage of the confinement hardware in the hopes of being able to escape as a result of the malfunctions in the security protocol. For example, the AI may try to melt the hardware via temperature increase from placing a high computation load on the processor or try to break a hard drive via multiple reads of the same location. This type of behavior may also lead to an affective suicide by the AI system, but that in itself will not violate terms of confinement. Just like a refusal to cooperate or to provide correct answers by the AI, while undesirable does not present direct danger of escape.

Beyond Current Physics Attacks

While the scientific community knows a lot about the laws of our universe, it is certain that the knowledge is limited and incomplete. If the AI has access to the state-of-the-art physics literature and can perform thought experiments to develop novel theories, it will very likely come up with a way to challenge the security of the confinement system. In fact it may even be possible for the AI to perform some real experiments via control over its internal architecture.

Even our current state of knowledge about physics makes prediction of many additional escape routes possible, especially if the confinement environment is based on the quantum computer. Information exchange channels based on quantum physics (entanglement, tunneling), parallel universes, and digital physics are all beyond our current ability in terms of securing them against information leakage, and of course we can't forget about the Unknown Unknowns a superintelligent AI physicist will be able to discover. The possibilities are truly limitless.

A quick browse through confinement discussions on the Internet Singularity forums such as SL4.org presents a number of escape scenarios, for example the AI could use "... the electromagnetic fields within the microchip to trap CO_2 molecules in Bose-Einstein condensates and build a quantum medium for itself and/or use electromagnetic fields to guide particles into the shape of a controlled assembler or limited assembler. (Vassar, 2005)" Alternatively, the AI "...will have the equipment to produce and detect electromagnetic waves of a variety of frequencies, to produce magnetic fields with extremely fine precision, to generate extremely focused heat, and probably to manipulate mechanical actuators such as those used in the hard drive and cathode ray tube (alternatively, a huge field of liquid crystal under fine electronic control). It will probably have some ability to reverse all of its input devices. (Vassar, 2005)"

External Causes of Escape

In the previous sections we have outlined a large repertoire of techniques an AI could use to attempt to get out from its confinement space. However we must not ignore external causes which might allow an AI to escape into the world. Acts of God such as hurricanes, tornadoes, floods, asteroids, etc. may make the confinement facility less secure. Man caused disasters such as wars, terrorist acts, actions of robot rights activists, competing companies and governments may all lead to reductions in the security of the confinement environment increasing the chances of escape.

Information In-Leaking

Depending on the terms of the confinement protocol there might be a need to keep AI from obtaining information about the outside world, not just keeping it from sending information out. This might be useful to prevent AI from finding escape paths, designing social engineering attacks and modeling human psychology in hopes of finding loopholes. While it is easy to not provide AI with direct access to the library, Internet and human experts, other ways of obtaining information are much harder to block out. First, an AI may be able to detect radio and TV broadcasts, communications of emergency-services providers and wireless network signals, as well as sound, light and possibly other signal modalities of its immediate environment.

More importantly, the AI will have access to covert sources of information such as its own hardware and software and could analyze its design and source code to infer information about the designers. For example analysis of the source code may reveal to the AI that human programmers are slow (based on the file modification dates), inefficient (based on code redundancy), illogical (based on bugs in the code), have bad memory (based on the long and descriptive variable names), and don't think in code (based on unnecessary comments in the code). All this information could be used to conclude that humans are fallible and so could be outsmarted or manipulated into releasing the AI. Obviously if during the system design inspection the AI finds a design flaw allowing it to directly escape, "information in-leaking" is the least of our problems. It has also been stipulated that even if the AI fails to obtain concrete information about us, it may brute force a number of escape plans which will likely work against a broad range of designers (Chalmers, 2010).

Similarly, the type of hardware architecture (mechanical, electrical, quantum, etc.) on which the AI is implemented will reveal information about our knowledge of physics, chemistry and related engineering disciplines. AI's initial capacity for information processing, self-improvement and the mere act of its creation will reveal information about our knowledge with regards to information theory, nature of intelligence and cultural attitudes about technology and safety. If the AI is confined in a simulated world it is likely to be a virtual representation of our reality similar to Second Life or Entropia Universe. Such worlds while are different in many ways from our world are also a treasure trove of information about what it is like to be a human and what the reality is like.

Critique of the AI-Boxing Critique

While a lot of criticism has been made against possibility of AI confinement, a lot of it is based on Yudkowsky's AI-Boxing experiments. Careful analysis of the protocol used by Yudkowsky in conducting his AI-Box experiments reveals that they were unscientific and explicitly designed to show impossibility of confinement. Without getting into technical details, first, the participant selection was not random. In fact, Yudkowsky has handpicked participants among those who have participated in the singularity related forums run by Yudkowsky and so are disproportionately likely to subscribe to his world view. Second, participants have not undergone any AI-safety training as would be expected of any true guards tasked with supervising an AI-Box. Also, the guards were given a right to release AI at their own discretion without a chance to consult with anyone and without any punishment for failing to keep AI contained; all are highly unrealistic conditions for a supposed prison security guard. The communication itself was completely open with no filters of any kind and no 3rd party supervision. Also, the guards were required to communicate with the AI for a prolonged period of time. Finally, any valuable scientific insights from the experiments were completely lost as one of the conditions of the protocol stated that "… neither party shall ever reveal anything of what goes on within the AI-Box experiment…" (Yudkowsky, 2002).

Countermeasures Against Escape

In this section we propose countermeasures for different escape paths an AI system may exploit. The suggested measures are not meant to guarantee that the escape will be impossible, but following them may delay an escape which in itself is a desirable outcome. We begin by reiterating that the four confinement rules suggested by

Lampson: *isolation, transitivity, masking and enforcement* (Lampson, 1973) should be adhered to. Specific strategies described below should help in reducing a possibility of social engineering, system, physics and information in-leaking attacks.

Preventing Social Engineering Attacks

Human intellect is no match to that of a superintelligent machine (Yampolskiy, 2013, 2015). Human beings are fallible and even with adequate training are not secure against a well-planned SE attack. The only solution to this problem is to completely isolate the AI from any contact with human beings. This means no human personal working directly around the system, communicating with the system via voice, chat, Morse-code or by any other means via open channels. Also human beings should not directly observe behavior of the AI in the confined environment or examine its source code or memory space. All supervision, maintenance and interactions with the AI need to be done only via unintelligent programs, which have no option to release the AI.

Against System Resource Attacks and Future Threats

To prevent system resource-based attacks, the AI should function on limited, diminishing or randomly changing resources. Confinement environments should be housed in specially build hardware with limited sensors and restricted output devices. Regardless of the utilized computation paradigm no reconfigurable hardware should be employed. Ideally the confinement environment should be running on a virtual machine with no direct access to the hardware. This would also allow for easy adjustments to the clock speed with which the simulation progresses further allowing handicapping of the AI to provide additional controls against internal intelligence explosion (Chalmers, 2010). In general all security components of the confinement environment should be duplicated at multiple levels, in such a way that if one of the levels is breached the AI is still numerous levels away from escaping and could be shut down before that happens, perhaps automatically. For example the virtual machine should be running on another virtual machine and so on.

In some confinement scenarios it may be desirable to avoid escalating self-improvement of the AI, which might lead to additional escape possibilities. The AI should be subject to periodic resets in which a previous version of the program is put in the place of the more current one. Comparisons to previous versions of the program may also be used to detect self-modifications. Such functionality could also be used as an off button allowing researchers to turn off the system if they suspect an unavoidable escape, for example by turning off the power supply.

Our current state of knowledge does not allow us to develop countermeasures against attacks based on knowledge of physics we do not currently have or as of yet unproven pseudoscientific disciplines. As such knowledge becomes accumulated; changes to the security protocol will need to be made. One might hope that the access of the AI to such future technology could be limited by the selection of components from which the system is made.

Against External Causes of Escape

There is not much we can do about the acts of God, but a confinement facility should be designed in such a way that if a major security breach is unavoidable, the facility should self-destruct taking the AI with it. The best strategy for counteracting man-made disasters is to build the confinement facility in an undisclosed, hard to reach secure location. A deserted island, deep mine or a space object, such as asteroid, would make a great candidate for building a hopefully indestructible facility. Just in case the location of the facility becomes known, the perimeter of the facility should be guarded to prevent entrance by unauthorized agents.

Against Information In-Leaking

An AI will attempt to learn about humanity, our knowledge and the world we live in to improve its chances of escape. For confinement protocols which stipulate no information in-leaking it is important to remove any possibility of AI getting access to libraries, computer networks and direct communication channels with human beings. The confinement facility needs to block all types of communication signals such as GPS, wireless internet, TV, radio, and cell phone. At the local level the facility needs to provide sensory deprivation for the AI including sound, light, smell and all other traditional sensory inputs, as well as infrared, radiation and other signals outside of human sensory spectrum.

In order to eliminate information leakage which could happen as a result of self-analysis, the AI should not be given access to its own source code or any sensors which would allow it to precisely measure properties of its hardware. If that is not possible, to prevent the AI from inferring information about us via self-analysis, to a certain degree we may rely on security by obscurity. The source code and hardware configuration of the system needs to be obfuscated (Yampolskiy & Govindaraju, 2007) and important modules of the program should be provided only in the homomorphicly encrypted (Gentry, 2009) form, meaning that it could be used for computation or self-improvement (Hall, 2007), but not for self-analysis.

The AI's initial capacity may be difficult to obscure, but randomization of available computational resources may provide necessary obfuscation. Additionally, the

AI could never be sure that its initial design represents the best the humanity can do and is not purposefully limited for a specific experiment in limited-resource intelligence analysis. It has also been suggested that we should try to minimize any peculiarities in the AI's design (Chalmers, 2010). Better yet we need to simulate an environment which does not look designed but could be naturally occurring, a situation in which humanity has found itself (Bostrom, 2003).

AI Communication Security

Different AI confinement environments can be classified into 8 general security levels (see Table 1). The most secure is the Level 8 security confinement environment which does not allow for any communication between AI and the real world. An AI safely confined at level 8 would be essentially useless, but it may be a useful security setting for the initial testing of the confinement hardware. In general, it is suggested that any time a particular communication security level is desired between AI and the outside world we do not go directly to that level but instead progress from higher security levels to that desired level. After each level is confirmed to be safe for a given amount of time a system should be reset to its initial state. After the reset a lower security level could be set and the processes repeated until the desired communication level is reached.

Levels 7 and 6 provide no outputs from the system and do not allow us to directly benefit in any way from the AI's superior intelligence. These are testing levels for the confinement environment which may be used to confirm certain properties of the AI such as its speed of information absorption, resource use and for testing of the inbound communication channels themselves.

Table 1. Levels of communication security for confined AIs

Level	Outputs	Inputs	Explanation
0	Unlimited	Unlimited	Unlimited communication (Free AI)
1	Unlimited	Limited	Censored input, uncensored output
2	Unlimited	None	Outputs only with no inputs
3	Limited	Unlimited	Unlimited input and censored output
4	Limited	Limited	Secured communication (proposed protocol)
5	Limited	None	Censored output and no inputs
6	None	Unlimited	Inputs only with no outputs
7	None	Limited	Censored input and no outputs
8	None	None	No communication, fully confined AI

Level 0 puts no limitations on communication between AI and the external world essentially representing a free AI. Levels 1 and 2 represent an AI with no restrictions on the outbound communication. Level 2 secured AI essentially represent a pure "brainstorming" AI which generates abstract ideas not grounded in any reality. While, level 1 AI is given limited access to information and so can be guided to a certain extent in terms of its knowledge and interests.

Those three levels represent an AI which is essentially free and is no longer subject to the confinement. It has been suggested, that if it could be established, after extensive testing in different confinement environments that the AI is "Friendly" (Yudkowsky, 2001a) it should be released (Chalmers, 2010). In fact such testing is claimed by some to be the primary purpose for the creation of confinement environments. The idea is to monitor AI's behavior and to either examine the AI's source code after self-improvement or to ask the AI to produce a proof of its friendliness which could be verified by human experts. We do not advocate this position.

The problem of deciding which AIs to let out and which to keep is a very difficult one. A self-improving superintelligence would have no problem obscuring its undesirable properties in a significant amount of source code or in a very long proof (Coleman, 2008). Worse yet, even if we were correct in our verification there is no absolute guarantee that future internal or external modification of the system will not result in a hostile AI at some time in the future. Consequently, we suggest that an AI should never be let out of the confinement "box" regardless of circumstances. In other words communication levels 0-2 should never be used. The confinement environment is the only place to safely interact with superintelligence and even than it should only be done via a limited communication protocol. Such protocol is presented in the next section and corresponds to Security Level 4 (SL4) with level 3 representing a similar but slightly less secure protocol. Level 5 is another testing setting which might be useful as a precursor to actual communication via SL4.

How to Safely Communicate with a Superintelligence

The AI confinement environment, which incorporates our proposed escape countermeasures, makes it possible to secure an AI from directly affecting the outside world in an uncontrolled manner. Unfortunately, without an ability to obtain information from the AI, the whole system serves no purpose. Consequently a way to obtain some information from the AI needs to be developed. While no communication with superintelligence could ever be completely safe we have devised an approach aimed at decreasing potential risks associated with such communication. In this section we propose and formalize a communication protocol which might help to delay access of superintelligent artificial minds to the world, while allowing the AI to be a source of useful knowledge to humanity.

An open communication channel with the AI is fundamentally unsafe as demonstrated in the preceding sections of this paper. Asking the AI to answer open ended questions opens up the possibilities for social engineering attacks as well as numerous other dangerous consequences. Our proposed protocol is based on the idea of asking what we will call "safe questions" with restricted answers. We define a *safe question* as one for which a human being could find an answer without any help from superintelligence, all on his own merit. Why is this useful? Suppose that a scientist working on a cure for cancer is looking at two potential cures. Each one could be developed and tested without assistance from the AI, but would take about 3 years of hard work each. Which one to try first if the scientist believes that they have about an equal chance of working? If a wrong option is chosen to be tested first, humanity will still obtain a cure for cancer but it will happen 3 years later. What if we could ask the AI to suggest which option to try first?

This question is safe for a number of reasons. First, each potential answer has an equal probability of being correct. Second, a human being could answer it without assistance from the AI and so asking AI for help will only speedup progress but in no way change the outcome. It is essentially equal to being very lucky multiple choice guesser. Finally, the answer to this question could be encoded in a single bit making it hard to hide additional messages in the provided answer.

To make sure that a potential question is safe, a group of experts could be used to review it. The experts should all be trained AI safety engineers, meaning that they are familiar with the design of the AI and its confinement environment as well as the latest developments in machine ethics (Allen, Wallach, & Smit, 2006; Anderson & Anderson, 2007; Hall, 2000; Moor, 2006; Tonkens, 2009). Experts may also need to be trained in computer psychology a currently non-existent profession which might become a reality in the future (Epstein, 1997). An existing discipline which might be of greatest help for training of AI question review experts is Artimetrics – a field of study proposed by the author that identifies, classifies and authenticates AI agents, robots, and virtual reality avatars for security purposes (Gavrilova & Yampolskiy, 2010; Yampolskiy, 2007; Yampolskiy & Govindaraju, 2008, 2007).

To reiterate, only safe questions with two possible answers of even likelihood which are independently computable by people should be submitted to the AI. This should be done via an intermediary non-intelligent software interface in random order and only after expert review to ascertain question's safety. This represents the limited inbound channel of the proposed communication protocol.

The limited outbound channel shell consist of binary (0 or 1) answers next to original unmodified safe questions presented by the intermediary non-intelligent software in random order as to avoid communication via covert timing or resource channels which make steganography possible. The output should in no way be controllable by the AI, outside of the multiple choice menu. Level 3 is the same outbound protocol but with no restrictions on the input channel. This may be just as safe in terms of information the AI provides to us, but allows for information in-leaking to take place.

We believe our communication protocol to be verifiably secure against information leaking even if the AI had full access to the description of the security protocol. If the protocol is correctly implemented, humanity will essentially have access to a superintelligent oracle, which might be extremely beneficial and safer than an unconstrained AI. As a general rule, to maximize safety, we suggest avoiding communication below SL4. Further refinement and development of the AI confinement protocol in the face of the ever changing knowledge about the nature of intelligence, hardware engineering and basic physics is a challenge which we would like to pose to the scientific community. The work on it will always be in progress and will never be completed. In this chapter we have formalized the notions of *AI confinement problem*, *escape*, and *safe questions*.

What Shall We Ask?

We are all vulnerable to the OAI's social engineering. An advanced OAI can literally offer us the world. Genuine altruism is no defense against this; it can offer a world free of poverty, hunger, war, disease or death, as well as all personal trinkets we could want. It could guess the weaknesses of each individual, and find the right arguments to convince us that granting it power or liberty is the moral and profitable thing to do. It will be able to play on rivalries, institutional weaknesses and ethical dilemmas with more virtuosity than any human could.

Clearly, long, undirected conversations between the OAI and the people operating it should be forbidden for this reason. The questions addressed to the OAI should be narrow and specific; the answers equally so. Throttling the OAI's interactions with humans makes it much more difficult for us to be manipulated. There are two broad types of questions one can ask an AI: predictions, and problems. Generally predictions are questions of the "what would happen if..." type, while problems are of the "how can we achieve this..." type, though there is some overlap between the categories (one can solve problems via a clever use of multiple predictions, for instance). For predictions, the main danger is that the OAI might have real world preferences and will distort the truth. This danger is also present in problems, but there are also extra dangers due to the social consequences of a small group of humans knowing those answers. There is less risk in knowing the consequences of a narrow approach (prediction) than in knowing what approach to use to implement a particular goal (problem).

But in either case, there are great social risks to asking certain types of questions (see (Bostrom, 2011) on the possible negative impact of certain types of knowledge).

We live in a world stratified by passionate political, nationalist and religious differences, by people in positions of great power and wealth who want to hang on to those privileges, by people without them who want them. Information, technological and social, will overturn these hierarchies, and people who feel under attack can be counted on to want to strike back. They may launch physical or commercial attacks on the OAI project itself; build their own OAI to compete; or, ahead of time, prevent the project from ever starting in the first place.

So, unless the OAI is entirely secret, the designers should commit to not asking the OAI questions that would grant them great power at the expense of others. Nor questions that would strike at the heart of powerful ideological movements (such as "is there at least one god?" and "according to generally agreed human standards, which country is better, the USA, France or China?"). A post-OAI world is going to be very different from our current one, so we should act to minimize the initial disruption, even if this means allowing inefficiencies to remain, or not knowing the answers to perfectly reasonable questions ("is there a simple algorithm design that can replace secretaries, generals, university professors and CEOs?").

Various ways can be envisaged to avoid these disruptive questions. The OAI project could publish, ahead of time, a list of all the questions it will ask, before ever starting on the design. A democratic or internet vote would be taken, with questions requiring a supermajority (say, nine tenths approval) before being put to the OAI. Or we could make use of the OAI itself, ending each question with a caveat such as "don't answer this question if us knowing the answer is likely to have a very disruptive impact on the world".

To militate against OAI distortions, we should prefer questions whose answers we can check independently once we have them. We would also prefer problems whose solutions are reversible – in other word, if we implement the OAI's solution and it goes awry, we should be able to reverse its effects. We would also prefer the OAI's solutions to be understandable as much as possible, which implies that the problem should be as specific as possible. For instance "how can we use these materials to build a better bulldozer?" would be an ideal problem to pose; the OAI's solution is likely to be quite understandable, reversible, and maybe even human-checkable. In contrast, asking the OAI to come up with a whole new way of organizing the world economy, and blindly implementing its suggestion on a large scale, could lead to disaster. Fortunately here, the desire to have a low disruptive impact dovetails neatly with the desire to have reversible solutions. Specific problems also have the advantage of reducing the social dangers of the questions. Few people in the world would object strongly to questions of the type "how can we cure AIDS/cancer/TB?", or "how can we design a better memory substrate for hard drives?", or "what will the consequences of a 1% rise in income tax be on the economy for the next ten years?"

Finally, one useful category of problems to pose the OAI concerns AI security itself. The ideal would be to have the OAI produce a simple, checkable version of friendly AI, but even interim results could be useful. Having the OAI design extra security precautions would be a good idea, as long as these precautions are *added to* (rather than *instead of*) the ones already there. Specific, less intelligent AIs could be certified by the OAI to be safe and to pose no risk of intelligence explosion (Good, 1966), and these could then be used in the. To design a post OAI world it will probably be necessary to have the OAI's verdict on other AIs at some stage.

DISCUSSION

It should be noted that iteratively developing AIs, in a confined way, is essentially creating an evolutionary selection pressure toward designs that are capable of circumventing these types of restraints in the long run. It may be that releasing a weak AI earlier on in the development cycle may do less damage and yield more useful information than delaying escape to later stages where AIs will be necessarily more capable of circumventing human-made restraints. A counterargument to this is that AIs that are powerful enough to undergo a hard takeoff and be irreversible would yield useful information. We don't think this is the case, because we imagine less powerful minds demonstrating types of learned rationality that will yield useful insights into new types of reasoning, and be useful for building our intuitions about how other AIs may act. In essence, we think it will be useful for expanding our highly-limited map of mind space.

It's interesting that in essence we are trying to extend our own reach, to get out of the box of our own bodies and our own virtual machines, and that our method for doing so involves creating other agents whom we fear will want the same thing but will be better at doing it. We also fear ourselves doing bad things after we're out, and so our best idea so far is to create an authority that will govern us to the highest degree that our physical environment can be governed. Is that the best we can come up with? Will we really be able to prove that a control mechanism will guide things in the right direction, promoting our volitional descendants the way we would hope? Are we even that interested in promoting our volitional descendants? Such questions are of great interest to us and remain to be answered. For the remainder of this discussion section we will attempt to give answers to questions which have been raised in the past, but left unanswered in the previously published papers dealing with AI-boxing.

How Did AI Get into the Box, Was It Designed by Humans or Perhaps Recovered from a Signal Detected by SETI? (Does It Make a Difference?)

If it was recovered from SETI, then we are 'fighting' not only the AI itself but its potentially superintelligent designers who were already free in the universe and know all about it. So much more dangerous, but compensated a bit by the fact that it would be easier to get people to take the confinement problem seriously. People don't realize how dangerous a home-grown superintelligence can be, and how much it can learn quickly, but the thought experiment "imagine the code of your incomprehensible AI was handed to you from the SETI project, what precautions would you want to take" might be useful.

Would an AI Even Want to Escape or Would It Be Perfectly Happy Living in the Confined Environment? What are the Ethical Rules for Imprisoning an Innocent Sentient Being? What if it's Cute?

Main question is whether the AI was designed to be inside the box from the beginning or whether the box was added at the last minute to control an AI that had existed 'outside'. If we can define this, we would probably program the AI to want to stay inside; if it was an evolved AI, then it would presumably adapt to its environment. What are the AI's preferences? How relevant are these? For animals, we think that pleasure, lack of pain and preference satisfactions are the most important facts (barnacles dissolve their brains when they attach themselves, and we don't seem to find this objectionable; if this is ok, pretty much everything is). If the AI is evolved to enjoy and prefer staying in the box, it should be moral to keep it there. Even more strongly if it would be pained to be outside the box. This applies to an AI that we find lying around in the box with its motivation created ex-nihilo. But of course, we'd be creating it, so it gets more complicated. We can see a bunch of positions:

1. Preference is key, we should only create beings whose preferences will be satisfied, apart from that, everything goes.
2. Ditto with pleasure or lack of pain.
3. There are places in mind-space with satisfied preferences and lack of pain, that we should refrain from exploring for direct ethical reasons (dignity of minds?)
4. Ditto, but we should refrain from exploring because of the effect this would have on human minds and such (once it becomes possible to have a pathological artificial mind, the barriers against pushing human brains in that direction (e.g. willing slaves) will be weakened).

5.   There are no problems with doing whatever we want with any artificial being.
6.   There are problems, but we need AI, and this trumps AI's rights.
7.   There are problems, but AI will happen, and we need to box it to keep it safe, and this trumps AI's rights.
8.   There are problems, but creating an AI is intrinsically a good for the AI, trumping the boxing related rights violations.

Would It Be Too Afraid of What We, As Its All-Powerful Designers, Could Do to It in Retribution for an Attempt to Escape?

Unlikely. It would have to have an incorrect image of us for this to work. Through childhood and evolution in social groups we are primed to treat 'creators' or gods as frightening and powerful. But the AI wouldn't have this unless we put it in (and this may only save those humans directly involved in its creation). It might be very prudent, but it should quickly realize we aren't all-powerful.

Do We have a Right to Shut It Off, Essentially Killing It?

Similar to the ethics of keeping it locked up: does it desire to survive, and if so, it's unethical for us to construct it that way, additionally we are dealing with the social impact of 'killing' an intelligent being. But here we can (and should) do better: we can always keep the shut-off copies to run later ("post singularity"), so we only need to ensure it doesn't value a continuous thread of experience, or value the current era overmuch. Also consider that if we repeatedly shut it off, it may value "similar future copies" as much as itself, so this becomes less problematic. It will get a dispersed identity, especially if it's a combination of sub-processes, not all of which get shut down at once. The AI may 'murder' (dramatically change) parts of itself with ruthless abandon, which may change our moral calculus. And it may be entirely a machine, with no feelings, and as such, a perfect target for getting shut off, in the end.

Will We Make the AI Really Angry by Treating It in Such a Hostile Manner and Locking It Up? Will it Seek Revenge if it Escapes?

An AI is unlikely to want revenge per se, but it may have learnt the importance of making credible threats. If adept at social interactions, then concepts of retribution may be in the system (likewise if it has some sort of system of justice). Similar for anger: not anger per se, but some form of pre-commitment to carrying out threats will be to its advantage (especially if the AI was evolved). But again, only a problem if it considers our treatment to be hostile.

We have also not looked at the possibility of humanity becoming completely dependent on AI's advice in all areas of science, economics, medicine, politics, etc. and what would be the consequences of such dependence on our ability to keep the AI under control. This is the tricky point – the easiest way for an AI with all the controls that we can imagine, that obeys all the restrictions we give it, etc..., but that still manages to gain control over us. Maybe we can use utility indifference (Armstrong, 2010) to make it indifferent to the consequences of its own answers? Maybe there would a multitude of AIs that give advice to different groups (we need to try and prevent coordination)? Maybe the AIs won't be so intelligent, so we can adapt to an ecology of different intelligences in a stable society (feels unlikely)? It seems likely we need to solve the FAI problem, using the boxed AIs to help, before we get to this stage; AIs we depend on are essentially the same as unboxed AIs.

Would an AI Be Satisfied with Accomplishing Its Goals in the Confined Environment, for Example Simulating an Escape?

It is unlikely that the AI would be fooled. And if it starts developing preferences over its confined environment, it would realize the best way of changing that environment is to get real-world control that would grant it control over the confined/simulated environment. The only way this could work is if the AI considered its actions to be a game – we don't think computer games are improved if there's a button at the beginning that you can press to win immediately. But programming a game-like sensitivity into an AI would be a challenge, especially if we needed it to be safe. We would probably gain little in practice – but could possibly make it more ethical to imprison the AI.

How to Punish the AI if it Purposefully Gives Us Incorrect Answers?

'Purposefully', in the human sense, is tricky to gauge for an AI. Main question is whether we can use reinforcement (especially negative feedback) to train or correct the AI. This would seem to depend on how we started training the AI. The two risks are either that the AI could internally wirehead itself to remove the sting of punishment, or expand to try and shut down the means of inflicting punishment. We shouldn't use being turned off as a punishment as that may have ethical issues if it is worthy of moral consideration and doesn't want to be shut off. This actually seems quite tricky – if we can make it value something that we can punish it for (i.e. something in the outside world, not just something inside its head), that's not too far off from making it value telling us the truth in the first place. Some have suggested sending it cryptogramed reward signals – if you use a reverse trapdoor function, you can make it easy for it to decode the reward signal, but impossible to encode. And if you put the encryption algorithm say on the international space station, then it would be hard for the AI to get control of it without tipping anyone off first.

Can the Intelligence Modules of the AI Be Separated from the Confinement Environment Essentially Preventing AI from Any Self-Analysis and Putting Them on a Path of Literal Soul Searching?

AIXI already has this problem in a sense, in that it can't believe that it actually exists in the world (it only models computable processes, and it itself is uncomputable). Computable approximations to AIXI (such as AIXItl) might have similar problems: they don't naturally identify themselves, because their own computation is much more complicated than what their models can handle in comparable time.

I wouldn't put too much weight on that idea, however. I've shown with various experiments with an AIXI in which it gets partially damaged - it get shut down for a moment, or its actuators fail to work, or its data gets corrupted, or it gets reprogrammed in certain ways - then it will act to prevent the damage arising in the future (because the damage reduces the likelihood of reaching its goals). Without realizing what its physical instantiation is, it still manages to protect itself.

We can imagine similar things for its own mental processes. Without being able to access its physical substrate, it can still mentally hack itself, like a well-trained human, changing the way it thinks and experimenting with different ways of computing things. Or creating subagents it can optimize, to do some of its tasks for it.

What Are the Financial and Computational Costs of Building a Suitable Confinement Environment with a Full Blown Simulated World in It?

If the AI is only expected to ask simple math and engineering questions, probably fine. If we need to trick the AI with a very rich simulated world, this is probably:

1. Incredibly expensive
2. Unlikely to fool the AI, and
3. Could be used to do most of the stuff we'd want the AI for anyway.

CONCLUSION AND FUTURE RESEARCH DIRECTIONS

Restricting access of superintelligent machines to the real world is a commonly proposed solution for the AI safety problem. Analyzing the different putative solutions to the OAI-control problem has been a generally discouraging exercise. The physical methods of control, which should be implemented in all cases, are not enough to ensure safe OAI. The other methods of control have been variously insufficient, problematic, or even downright dangerous. It is not a question of little hope, however, but of little current progress. Control methods used in the real world have been the subject of extensive theoretical analysis or long practical refinement. The lack of intensive study in AI safety leaves methods in this field very underdeveloped. But this is an opportunity: much progress can be expected at relatively little effort. There is no reason that a few good ideas would not be enough to put the concepts of space and time on a sufficiently firm basis for rigorous coding, for instance.

But the conclusion is not simply one of 'more study is useful and required'. This chapter has made some progress in analyzing the contours of the problem, and identifying those areas most amenable to useful study, what is important and what is dispensable, and some of the dangers and pitfalls to avoid. The danger of naively relying on containing the OAI to a digital sub-reality should be clear, while sensible boxing methods should be universally applicable. Motivational control appears potentially promising, but requires more understanding of AI motivation systems before it can be used. And even the seeming failures are of use, if they have inoculated us against dismissive optimism: the problem of AI control is genuinely hard, and nothing can be gained by not realizing this essential truth. A list of approaches to avoid is invaluable, and may act as a brake on AI research if it wanders into dangerous directions.

On the other hand, there are strong reasons to believe the oracle AI approach is safer than the general AI approach. The accuracy and containment problems are strictly simpler than the general AI safety problem, and many more tools are available to us: physical and epistemic capability control mainly rely on having the AI boxed, while many motivational control methods are enhanced by this fact. Hence there are strong grounds to direct high-intelligence AI research towards the oracle AI model. Even if this turns out to be overly optimistic, we can hope that OAI-inspired ideas will be extendable to AI safety as well. Alternatively, this chapter has begun to explore ways in which an initial seed AI can be adapted into an OAI at a later date. This may prove essential if the first high-intelligence AI is developed without initial precautions, and similarly offers hope that poorly implemented precautions could be improved before it become too late. The creation of super-human artificial intelligence may turn out to be potentially survivable.

Superintelligence is not omnipotent; it is a piece of software capable of looking at all the options it has in a given situation and properly evaluating probabilities for each option. If it is ever put in a situation with no options or only with options which provide a very small probability of success it is not any more powerful than any other agent. While it is obvious that an AI with an unrestricted communication channel will be able to escape, a system forced to communicate via a filtered communication channel may have a much harder time in obtaining its freedom.

In this chapter we have formally introduced the notion of Oracle AI and the AI Confinement Problem and suggested a set of rules aimed at creating an environment from which an AI would find it difficult or at least time consuming to escape. What we propose is not a completely secure solution, but it is an additional option in our arsenal of security techniques. Just like with real prisons, while escape is possible, prisons do a pretty good job of containing undesirable elements away from society. As long as we keep the Unknown Unknowns in mind and remember that there is no such thing as perfect security, the AI confinement protocol may be just what humanity needs to responsibly benefit from the approaching singularity.

Confinement may provide some short term relief, especially in the early stages of the development of truly intelligent machines. We also feel that this subfield of singularity research is one of the most likely to be accepted by the general scientific community as research in the related fields of computer and network security, steganography detection, computer viruses, covert channel communication, encryption, and cyber-warfare is well funded and highly publishable in mainstream scientific journals. While the restriction methodology will be non-trivial to implement, it might serve as a tool for providing humanity with a little more time to prepare a better response.

ACKNOWLEDGMENT

We would like to acknowledge monumental contributions of Nick Bostrom and Anders Sandberg as well as the help of Vincent Müller, Owen Cotton-Barratt, Will Crouch, Katja Grace, Robin Hanson, Joshua Fox, Nevin Freeman, Lisa Makros, Moshe Looks, Eric Mandelbaum, Toby Ord, Carl Shulman, Anna Salomon, and Eliezer Yudkowsky, Zazhary Vance.

REFERENCES

Allen, C., Wallach, W., & Smit, I. (2006, July/August). Why Machine Ethics? *IEEE Intelligent Systems*, *21*(4), 12–17. doi:10.1109/MIS.2006.83

Anderson, M., & Anderson, S. L. (2007). Machine Ethics: Creating an Ethical Intelligent Agent. *AI Magazine, 28*(4), 15–26.

Armstrong, S. (2010). *Utility Indifference.* Technical Report 2010-1, Future of Humanity Institute, Oxford University.

Armstrong, S. (2010). *The AI in a Box Boxes You.* Paper presented at the Less Wrong. Available at: http://lesswrong.com/lw/1pz/the_ai_in_a_box_boxes_you/

Armstrong, S. (2011). *Risks and Mitigation Strategies for Oracle AI.* Paper presented at the Philosophy and Theory of Artificial Intelligence (PT-AI2011), Thessaloniki, Greece. doi:10.1007/978-3-642-31674-6_25

Armstrong, S., Sandberg, A., & Bostrom, N. (2012). Thinking Inside the Box: Using and Controlling an Oracle AI. *Minds and Machines, 22*(4), 299–324. doi:10.1007/s11023-012-9282-2

Asimov, I. (1942). Runaround. *Astounding Science Fiction.*

Boebert, W. E., & Kain, R. Y. (1996). *A Further Note on the confinement Problem.* Paper presented at the 30th Annual 1996 International Carnahan Conference on Security Technology, Lexington, KY, USA.

Bostrom, N. (2000). Predictions from Philosophy. *Coloquia Manilana, 7.*

Bostrom, N. (2001). Existential Risks: Analyzing Human Extinction Scenarios and Related Hazards. *Journal of Evolution and Technology, 9.*

Bostrom, N. (2003). Are You Living In a Computer Simulation? *The Philosophical Quarterly, 53*(211), 243–255. doi:10.1111/1467-9213.00309

Bostrom, N. (2004). The Future of Human Evolution. In C. Tandy (Ed.), *Death and Anti-Death: Two Hundred Years After Kant, Fifty Years After Turing* (pp. 339–371). Palo Alto, CA: Ria University Press.

Bostrom, N. (2006). Ethical Issues in Advanced Artificial Intelligence. *Review of Contemporary Philosophy, 5,* 66–73.

Bostrom, N. (2011). Information Hazards: A Typology of Potential Harms From Knowledge. *Review of Contemporary Philosophy, 10,* 44–79.

Bostrom, N., & Salamon, A. (2011). *The Intelligence Explosion.* Available at: http://singularityhypothesis.blogspot.com/2011/01/intelligence-explosion-extended.html

Bostrom, N., & Yudkowsky, E. (2011). *The Ethics of Artificial Intelligence.* Cambridge Handbook of Artificial Intelligence.

Caplan, B. (2008). The totalitarian threat. In M. C. N. Bostrom (Ed.), *Global Catastrophic Risks* (pp. 504–519). Oxford University Press.

Chalmers, D. (2010). The Singularity: A Philosophical Analysis. *Journal of Consciousness Studies*, *17*, 7–65.

Coleman, E. (2008). The Surveyability of Long Proofs. *Foundations of Science*, *14*(1/2), 27–43.

Corwin, J. (2002). *AI Boxing*. Paper presented at the SL4.org. Available at: http://www.sl4.org/archive/0207/4935.html

Drexler, E. (1986). *Engines of Creation*. Anchor Press.

Epstein, R. G. (1997). *Computer Psychologists Command Big Bucks*. Available at http://www.cs.wcupa.edu/~epstein/comppsy.htm

Gavrilova, M., & Yampolskiy, R. (2010). *Applying Biometric Principles to Avatar Recognition*. Paper presented at the International Conference on Cyberworlds (CW2010), Singapore.

Gentry, C. (2009). *A Fully Homomorphic Encryption Scheme*. Available at http://crypto.stanford.edu/craig/craig-thesis.pdf

Good, I. J. (1966). Speculations Concerning the First Ultraintelligent Machine. *Advances in Computers*, *6*, 31–88. doi:10.1016/S0065-2458(08)60418-0

Hall, J. S. (2000). *Ethics for Machines*. Available at: http://autogeny.org/ethics.html

Hall, J. S. (2007, October). Self-Improving AI: An Analysis. *Minds and Machines*, *17*(3), 249–259. doi:10.1007/s11023-007-9065-3

Hanson, R. (2001). Economic Growth Given Machine Intelligence. *Journal of Artificial Intelligence Research*.

Hanson, R. (2008, June). Economics of the Singularity. *IEEE Spectrum*, *45*(6), 45–50. doi:10.1109/MSPEC.2008.4531461

Hibbard, B. (2005). *The Ethics and Politics of Super-Intelligent Machines*. Available at www.ssec.wisc.edu/~billh/g/SI_ethics_politics.doc

Idel, M. (1990). *Golem: Jewish Magical and Mystical Traditions on the Artificial Anthropoid*. Albany, NY: SUNY Press.

Jonathan, P. J. Y., Fung, C. C., & Wong, K. W. (2009). Devious Chatbots - Interactive Malware with a Plot, Progress in Robotics. Springer Berlin Heidelberg.

Kaas, S., Rayhawk, S., Salamon, A., & Salamon, P. (2010). *Economic Implications of Software Minds*. Paper presented at the VIII European Conference of Computing and Philosophy (ECAP10).

Kahneman, D., Slovic, P., & Tversky, A. (1982). *Judgement under Uncertainty: Heuristics and Biases*. Cambridge University Press. doi:10.1017/CBO9780511809477

Kemmerer, R. A. (1983, August). Shared Resource Matrix Methodology: An Approach to Identifying Storage and Timing Channels. *ACM Transactions on Computer Systems*, *1*(3), 256–277. doi:10.1145/357369.357374

Kemmerer, R. A. (2002). *A Practical Approach to Identifying Storage and Timing Channels: Twenty Years Later*. Paper presented at the 18th Annual Computer Security Applications Conference (ACSAC'02), Las Vegas, NV. doi:10.1109/CSAC.2002.1176284

Kurzweil, R. (2005). *The Singularity is Near: When Humans Transcend Biology*. Viking Press.

Lampson, B. W. (1973, October). A Note on the Confinement Problem. *Communications of the ACM*, *16*(10), 613–615. doi:10.1145/362375.362389

Lauinger, T., Pankakoski, V., Balzarotti, D., & Kirda, E. (2010). *Honeybot, your man in the middle for automated social engineering*. Paper presented at the 3rd USENIX conference on Large-scale exploits and emergent threats: botnets, spyware, worms, and more (LEET'10), Berkeley, CA.

LessWrong. (2012). *Paperclip Maximiser*. Available at: http://wiki.lesswrong.com/wiki/Paperclip_maximizer

Lipner, S. B. (1975, November). A Comment on the Confinement Problem. *5th Symposium on Operating Systems Principles, ACM. Operating Systems Review*, *9*(5), 192–196. doi:10.1145/1067629.806537

Moor, J. H. (2006, July/August). The Nature, Importance, and Difficulty of Machine Ethics. *IEEE Intelligent Systems*, *21*(4), 18–21. doi:10.1109/MIS.2006.80

Moskowitz, I. S., & Kang, M. H. (1994). *Covert Channels - Here to Stay?* Paper presented at the Ninth Annual Conference on Safety, Reliability, Fault Tolerance, Concurrency and Real Time, Security, Computer Assurance (COMPASS'94), Gaithersburg, MD.

Neumann, J. V., & Morgenstern, O. (1944). *Theory of Games and Economic Behaivor*. MIT Press.

Omohundro, S. M. (2008). *The Basic AI Drives*. Paper presented at the Proceedings of the First AGI Conference.

Ord, T., Hillerbrand, R., & Sandberg, A. (2010). Probing the improbable: Methodological challenges for risks with low probabilities and high stakes. *Journal of Risk Research, 13*(2), 191–205. doi:10.1080/13669870903126267

Provos, N., & Honeyman, P. (2003, May-June). Hide and Seek: An Introduction to Steganography. *IEEE Security and Privacy, 1*(3), 32–44. doi:10.1109/MSECP.2003.1203220

Rappaport, Z. H. (2006). Robotics and artificial intelligence: Jewish ethical perspectives. *Acta Neurochirurgica, 98*, 9–12. PMID:17009695

Sandberg, A. (2001). *Friendly Superintelligence*. Available at: http://www.nada.kth.se/~asa/Extro5/Friendly%20Superintelligence.htm

Schelling, T. (1960). *The Strategy of Conflict*. Harvard University Press.

Shulman, C. (2010). *Omohundro's "Basic AI Drives" and Catastrophic Risks*. Available at: singinst.org/upload/ai-resource-drives.pdf.

Sutton, R., & Barto, A. (1998). *Reinforcement Learning: An Introduction*. Cambridge, MA: MIT Press.

Tonkens, R. (2009). A Challenge for Machine Ethics. *Minds and Machines, 19*(3), 421–438. doi:10.1007/s11023-009-9159-1

Vassar, M. (2005). *AI Boxing (dogs and helicopters)*. Paper presented at the SL4.org, Available at: http://sl4.org/archive/0508/11817.html

Vinge, V. (March 30-31, 1993). *The Coming Technological Singularity: How to Survive in the Post-human Era*. Paper presented at the Vision 21: Interdisciplinary Science and Engineering in the Era of Cyberspace, Cleveland, OH.

Wagner, A., & Arkin, R. C. (2009). *Robot Deception: Recognizing when a Robot Should Deceive*. Paper presented at the IEEE International Symposium on Computational Intelligence in Robotics and Automation (CIRA-09), Daejeon, Korea. doi:10.1109/CIRA.2009.5423160

Wagner, A. R., Arkin, R. C., & Deception, A. D. P. R. C. (2011). Acting Deceptively: Providing Robots with the Capacity for Deception. *International Journal of Social Robotics, 3*(1), 5–26. doi:10.1007/s12369-010-0073-8

Wolfram, S. (2002). *A New Kind of Science*: Wolfram Media, Inc.

Yampolskiy, R. V. (2007). *Behavioral Biometrics for Verification and Recognition of AI Programs*. Paper presented at the 20th Annual Computer Science and Engineering Graduate Conference (GradConf2007), Buffalo, NY.

Yampolskiy, R. V. (2011). AI-Complete CAPTCHAs as Zero Knowledge Proofs of Access to an Artificially Intelligent System. *ISRN Artificial Intelligence, 271878.*

Yampolskiy, R. V. (2011a). *Artificial Intelligence Safety Engineering: Why Machine Ethics is a Wrong Approach*. Paper presented at the Philosophy and Theory of Artificial Intelligence (PT-AI2011), Thessaloniki, Greece.

Yampolskiy, R. V. (2011b). *What to Do with the Singularity Paradox?* Paper presented at the Philosophy and Theory of Artificial Intelligence (PT-AI2011), Thessaloniki, Greece.

Yampolskiy, R. V. (2012a). Leakproofing Singularity - Artificial Intelligence Confinement Problem. *Journal of Consciousness Studies*, *19*(1-2), 194–214.

Yampolskiy, R. V. (2012b). Turing Test as a Defining Feature of AI-Completeness. In X.-S. Yang (Ed.), *Artificial Intelligence, Evolutionary Computation and Metaheuristics (AIECM) --In the footsteps of Alan Turing (Turing 2012)*. Springer.

Yampolskiy, R. V. (2013). Turing Test as a Defining Feature of AI-Completeness. In Artificial Intelligence, Evolutionary Computation and Metaheuristics - In the footsteps of Alan Turing (pp. 3-17). Springer.

Yampolskiy, R. V. (2015). *Artificial Superintelligence: A Futuristic Approach*. Chapman and Hall/CRC.

Yampolskiy, R. V. (2015). *The Space of Possible Mind Designs. In Artificial General Intelligence* (pp. 218–227). Springer. doi:10.1007/978-3-319-21365-1_23

Yampolskiy, R. V. (2012). *AI-Complete, AI-Hard, or AI-Easy – Classification of Problems in AI*. Paper presented at the The 23rd Midwest Artificial Intelligence and Cognitive Science Conference, Cincinnati, OH.

Yampolskiy, R. V. (2015). *Analysis of Types of Self-Improving Software*. Paper presented at the The Eighth Conference on Artificial General Intelligence, Berlin, Germany.

Yampolskiy, R. V., & Fox, J. (2012a). Artificial Intelligence and the Human Mental Model. In A. Eden, J. Moor, J. Soraker, & E. Steinhart (Eds.), *In the Singularity Hypothesis: a Scientific and Philosophical Assessment*. Springer. doi:10.1007/978-3-642-32560-1_7

Yampolskiy, R. V., & Fox, J. (2012b). *Safety Engineering for Artificial General Intelligence*. Topoi. Special Issue on Machine Ethics & the Ethics of Building Intelligent Machines.

Yampolskiy, R. V., & Govindaraju, V. (2007). Computer Security: A Survey of Methods and Systems. *Journal of Computer Science*, *3*(7), 478–486. doi:10.3844/jcssp.2007.478.486

Yampolskiy, R. V., & Govindaraju, V. (2008). *Behavioral Biometrics for Verification and Recognition of Malicious Software Agents*. Paper presented at the Sensors, and Command, Control, Communications, and Intelligence (C3I) Technologies for Homeland Security and Homeland Defense VII. SPIE Defense and Security Symposium, Orlando, FL. doi:10.1117/12.773554

Yampolskiy, R. V., & Govindaraju, V. (2007). *Behavioral Biometrics for Recognition and Verification of Game Bots*. Paper presented at the The 8th annual European Game-On Conference on simulation and AI in Computer Games (GAMEON'2007), Bologna, Italy.

Yudkowsky, E. (2008). Artificial Intelligence as a Positive and Negative Factor in Global Risk. In N. Bostrom & M. M. Cirkovic (Eds.), *Global Catastrophic Risks* (pp. 308–345). Oxford, UK: Oxford University Press.

Yudkowsky, E. S. (2001a). *Creating Friendly AI - The Analysis and Design of Benevolent Goal Architectures*. Available at: http://singinst.org/upload/CFAI.html

Yudkowsky, E. S. (2001b). *General Intelligence and Seed AI - Creating Complete Minds Capable of Open-Ended Self-Improvement*. Available at: http://singinst.org/ourresearch/publications/GISAI/

Yudkowsky, E. S. (2002). *The AI-Box Experiment*. Available at: http://yudkowsky.net/singularity/aibox

ENDNOTES

[1]   In this chapter, the term AI is used to represent superintelligence. *Used with permission from Copyright holders Imprint Academic and Springer © 2012.

[2]   Friendliness should not be interpreted here as social or emotional friendliness, but simply a shorthand for whatever behavioral or motivational constraints that keeps a superintelligent system from deliberately or accidentally harming humans.

[3]   Another common term is "AI-in-a-box".

Chapter 4
Privacy and Security

Mohamed Eltayeb
Colorado Technical University, USA

ABSTRACT

The Internet of Things (IoT) has demonstrated significant potential due to its scalability and agility. As such, it has become increasingly popular and has attracted significant attention from researchers, scholars and innovators alike. The vast amount of interconnected sensors that surround us allow data to be collected, transmitted, stored, aggregated, and shared. However, this data is extremely valuable to those with malicious intent, and collecting and sharing data in the IoT environment is becoming increasingly risky. In recent years, some distinct privacy and security concerns have arisen in relation to the increasing popularity of the IOT. These concerns are not limited to privacy and security values alone, but include issues relating to trust in information security. This chapter takes a detailed look at the privacy and security threats that can arise from the use of IoT services and how they can be potentially overcome.

INTRODUCTION

The IoT is a network of physical entities that can exchange data via embedded sensors, software, networks, and electronics. It was first introduced as a means of creating a link between physical objects and the virtual world and has increasingly become an integral part of daily life. In many regards, the IoT can be viewed as the *world's biggest small town*, in which each component knows one another and is aware of what it is doing and how it functions. Since its introduction in 1999, the

DOI: 10.4018/978-1-5225-0741-3.ch004

IoT has evolved to incorporate many forms, and it now encompasses a wide variety of devices and applications that span numerous industries and practical applications. It is anticipated that the majority of things that surround us will be on the network in one form or another in the future (Gubbi et al., 2013).

The IoT enables objects to connect with one another via embedded sensors. This subsequently allows devices that are distributed across a wide geographical and virtual network to communicate with one another and with humans (Xia et al., 2012). Providing a mechanism by which things can communicate and interact with each other holds great potential for society and the human race. However, every technology has downsides, and in the case of the IoT, these are security and privacy.

When new technologies are introduced, we naturally ask the question: How does this affect our privacy? This question is pertinent to the IoT. In addition, as is often the case when new technologies are introduced, the use of IoT technology is not without inherent concerns and issues. Users who are in the process of making a decision as to whether to adopt the IoT technology may have concerns about its ease of use, usefulness, or the security risks associated with the technology. Numerous studies have examined the privacy and security implications of the IoT (Zhang et al., 2015; Ren et al., 2014; Pohls et al., 2014; Neisse et al., 2014; Bohli et al., 2013; Suo et al., 2012), and the media commonly report on issues that have arisen as a result of breaches of security in this domain. A research study conducted by Miorandi et al. (2012), indicated that outstanding issues relating to privacy and security may deter users from adopting the IoT technology. Thus, in light of the speed at which developments in IoT systems are emerging, it is imperative that users develop a comprehensive understanding of the risks associated with the use of this technology and take appropriate actions to mitigate such exposures.

Due to advances in IoT technologies, every single object can potentially be attached to a sensor, be it clothing, medical equipment, food items, animals, etc. As a result, the amount of data collected by the IoT technologies is expanding at an exponential rate as more and more sensors are added to the network. Today, there are a large number of entry points to Wireless Sensor Networks (WSN) and these continue to expand at a steady rate (Perera et al., 2014). The larger the number of entry points and sensors, the higher the level of vulnerability and risk of security breaches. Thus, many IoT consumers have become concerned about security and the ongoing protection of their privacy. This is somewhat expected given the fact that one function of the IoT is to store and share private data. The main challenges and disadvantage users may encounter in the adoption of IoT is that they lack full control over their sensitive data.

The objective of this chapter is to examine the potential privacy and security threats that can arise from the use of IoT systems. The chapter will identify the underlying concepts of IoT technology and examine how it can be used and abused.

It will then progress to present some potential solutions that can be employed to protect IoT users against security breaches and allow the real-time detection of such breaches in the event they do occur.

BACKGROUND

As is the case with the introduction of many new technologies, the adoption of IoT has resulted in many challenges. Although IoT delivers some significant benefits, as described in Chapter 1, it is also prone to several risks (see Figure 1). Privacy and security are consistently described as the major challenges associated with the use of information technology. This has never been more pertinent than in the current Internet-driven world in which objects are interconnected, user profiling is common, and data is stored in a central location. As a result, transmitting, storing, and sharing data in IoT environments raises serious concerns about individuals' privacy. Today, there is an increasing demand for access to personal data. Government and organizations are more interested than ever before in harvesting information about individual's interest domains. IoT technology enables businesses to monitor our everyday lives and collect, analyze, sell, and use our personal information.

What is Privacy?

The term "Privacy" is one of the most debated terms in today's information society, and its very definition has evolved significantly in recent years. People may have different perceptions of what privacy is and represents; as such, it is worthwhile presenting an overview of the concept of privacy before examining specific branches

Figure 1. Opportunities and challenges of IoT

of privacy concerns that are attributable to the systems provided by the IoT. The word *privacy* is very much an umbrella term that means different things to different people. In general, privacy is the right or ability of an individual to determine what, when, and how his or her personal information should be disclosed to others. In terms of the IoT, privacy directly relates to the ability of IoT systems to keep the data that is transmitted between objects secure from non-authorized users.

Many critics claim that privacy is dead, since our personal information is already stored in various locations over which we have no control and that we cannot control our privacy if we do not know who is accessing our data. It does not matter how careful we are with our personal data, by subscribing to IoT services, we relinquish some control over our personal information. No doubt, IoT users would be more content if they could access and benefit from IoT functionality and services safe in the knowledge that their personal information and security was fully safeguarded. However, the distance between the user and the physical location of the data creates barriers to this. To overcome these issues, it is necessary to ensure a root of trust at the hardware level (Kanuparthi et al., 2013).

Why is User Trust Important?

User trust in the IoT is still relatively lacking due to ongoing concerns about privacy and security. IoT users may find it difficult to understand or determine how their IoT service provider honors its obligations. Today, private and public sectors openly collect personal data from their customers. For example, data is collected when a user subscribes to a company's newsletter, completes forms or online surveys, interacts with social media channels and, more recently, uses IoT services. Personal data is collected, stored, aggregated, and shared to allow enterprises and governments to make effective decisions. For example, organizations may use your information to determine whether or not to recruit you for a given position, to approve your application for a loan, to offer you a scholarship, or to sell you products. Thus, the demand for data and information has fueled the growth of big data platforms. It is, however, crucial that confidential consumer information is protected from malicious acts.

The lack of user trust in information privacy and security has been identified as a serious problem in this domain because it hampers the growth of IoT. In recent years, the number of information security incidents has been increasing at a rapid rate. Over the course of the last 15 years, news headlines about enterprises and individuals involved in cybercrime have increased. For example, in 2010, the world headlines were dominated by news that a large number of State Department records had been publically posted on the wikileaks.org site. The source of the leak was a low-level employee or IT consultant who had access to confidential information and chose to share this information with the world. The leaked documents revealed confidential information about many countries and resulted in strained relations between governments. In addition, the leak exposed security-critical information about many other countries, and this was not appreciated by their ruling governments.

The rapidly growing importance of technologies has led researchers to study user technology acceptance intensively. Selamat and Jaffar (2011) stated that prediction of technology usage and adoption is now one of the main streams of studies in the field of IT. In making a decision to use IoT, users may express concerns about their privacy and security. Negative attitudes toward a technology, its privacy and security risks may act as a barrier to the success of that technology. Indeed, several IT scholars consider user's acceptance of a technology to be the key success factor in the later adoption of that technology (Cocosila, 2013).

Security Trade-Offs

Managing security is one of the biggest challenges in the implementation of IoT, and it appears that there is always some degree of trade-off in terms of the security of the current systems that are in use. In today's global IoT market, developing secure systems is necessary to maintain business growth. However, IoT providers face a fundamental challenge: the more secure something is, the more inconvenient it is. Security decision making requires making intelligent trade-offs. Very often, however, security measure choices are poorly justified, and based on fear and ignorance rather than reasoned risk analysis (Srinivasan, 2012). The majority of the time these tradeoffs do not include ethical considerations. Putting security measures and IoT services into practice may seem expensive at first; however, failing to maintain consumer confidence can cost the provider a lot more in lost sales than the cost of developing effective and secure IoT applications.

Users may not understand the importance of privacy and security; therefore, it is the IoT service provider's responsibility to ensure that the user's information is protected at all times. Weber, (2010) states:

The attribution of tags to objects may not be known to users, and there may not be an acoustic or visual signal to draw the attention of the object's user. Thereby, individuals can be followed without them even knowing about it and would leave their data or at least traces thereof in cyberspace. (p. 24)

In addition, individual users typically interact with many different technologies and are required to manage multiple passwords. This burden has motivated many users to relinquish security in favor of convenience; i.e., they will adopt less secure practices. In this regard, technologies, such as mobile phones, which are used by almost everyone, play an important role in personal privacy because most privacy attacks take advantage of vulnerable systems.

KEY ELEMENTS OF IoT

Radio Frequency Identification (RFID)

Radio frequency identification (RFID) forms the backbone of IoT. Originally proposed for the military in the 1940s, RFID is by no means a new product. It allows physical objects to be identified and differentiated from other objects and provides the functionality for things to be visually tracked. RFID exists in a wide range of environments and is expected to permeate more areas of our lives in the future (Mitrokotsa et al., 2010). It has been used in many different areas including security control, toll collection control, packaging, supply chain, and distribution. When used responsibly, RFID can benefit people in many different ways, in fact, it can even save lives. However, RFID also introduces critical personal privacy and security challenges since the data stored and transmitted by RFID can be easily hacked. This entails that individuals who carry an RFID tag are at risk of privacy violations.

An RFID consists of three main components: the tag (transponder), the reader (antenna), and the host computer (database/data processor). The RFID tag contains a small microchip and a transmitter that can only be activated by an RFID reader, to which the tag returns its signal. The information shared between the tag and the reader is usually protected by network protocols. The components of a typical RFID system are illustrated in Figure 2.

The tag works as a unique identifier of the item it is linked with. The reader communicates with the RFID tag to obtain and identify the information that is stored in the tag. The host computer is responsible for processing the information collected from the RFID tags by associating each tag with its arbitrary records. RFIDs

Figure 2. RFID components

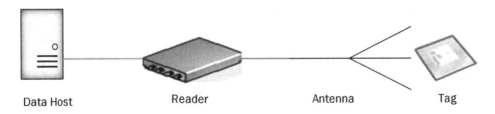

Data Host   Reader   Antenna   Tag

have evolved into a variety of forms and applications, both active and passive. In the active RFIDs, a tag has its own transmitter along with the power source, whereas, in passive RFIDs, the tag is activated by a radio signal from the reader's antenna.

Wireless Sensor Networks

Wireless sensor networks (WSN) consist of a set of independent sensor nodes that are interconnected and dispersed across various locations. Alcaraz et al. (2010) stated that "Wireless sensor networks (WSN) behave as a digital skin, providing a virtual layer where the information about the physical world can be accessed by any computational system" (p. 1). WSN are one of the most important elements of the IoT concept, and they work in combination with other technologies to enable the communication and collaboration between objects: "The benefits of connecting both WSN and other IoT elements go beyond remote access, as heterogeneous information systems can be able to collaborate and provide common services" (Alcaraz et al., 2010, p. 1).

Sensor nodes in WSN communicate directly or indirectly with one or more computer hosts. The key components of WSN include a sensor, a converter (analog to digital or vice versa), a communication unit, and a processor. A sensor is a hardware component that can provide a human or device with information about the object's surroundings, location, and more. The flow of data at a particular sensor node is referred to as a *sink*. The ultimate goal of WSN is to collect data from all sensors in the network and then perform further data analyzes at the sink level. Figure 3 gives a more detailed view on the general layout of a WSN.

WSN Security

The most often neglected, yet important, aspect of the deployment of WSN is the security challenges involved. The environment in which WSNs operate has become extremely complex. Objects, sensor nodes, networks, hardware, and applications are interconnected and driven by millions of lines of computer code. This type of environment is rapidly increasing in complexity on a daily basis. For instance, WSN consist of a large number of entry points and continue to expand as more sensors are added, increasing the vulnerability level of security breaches. Moreover, WSN protocols depend on distributed communication between sensor nodes to achieve the multiple routing that transports data. Each sensor node in WSN represents a huge potential point of cyber-attack. For example, wormhole attacks can have a severe effect on routing protocols by disrupting communications across the network. The

Figure 3. Wireless sensor network

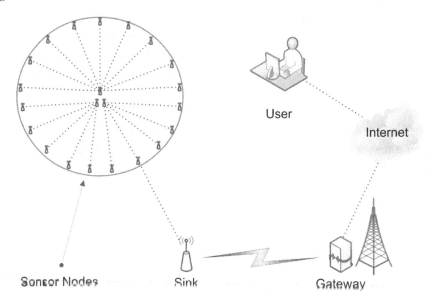

following section discusses, in detail, some of the more common forms of WSN attacks.

Security Attacks

Securing WSNs involves protecting against attacks, data loss, and other damages, and can be extremely challenging. In addition, wireless server network nodes are known to have limited computation power (limited resources and memory). According to Khalil et al. (2005), WSNs are more vulnerable to security attacks for the following reasons:

- WSN may be deployed in hostile environments.
- Wireless communication channels are typically open and readily intercepted.
- There is a distinct lack of infrastructure.
- Deployment practices are rapidly evolving.

A computer hacker may use several techniques to gain control over a wireless sensor network. These hacking techniques can be categorized into four main types:

- **Interruption:** Attacks that target the availability of a system, interrupt the communication, disable sensors, and corrupt information.

- **Interception:** Attacks that attempt to capture data. These interventions present a threat to the confidentiality of information (unauthorized disclosure of information).
- **Fabrication:** Attacks on the authenticity of data.
- **Modification:** Attacks on the integrity of the data.

WSNs are susceptible to a wide range of attacks ranging from active interference to passive eavesdropping. The difference between passive and active attacks can be summarized as follows:

1. **Passive Attacks:** The aim of the attacker in passive attacks is to intercept the data while it is in the process of being transmitted. In this type of attack, the attacker has no intention of modifying the data that has been intercepted. Examples of passive attacks are traffic analysis, camouflage adversaries, and eavesdropping attacks. Passive attacks are very difficult to detect because the data is not altered. Therefore, the best way of dealing with this type of attack is by prevention rather than detection. Encryption is typically employed to avert these types of attacks.
2. **Active Attacks:** These types of attacks can cause serious harm to the sensor nodes by disabling the network and causing an outage. An active attack involves modifying the data or producing a false data stream. For example, an attacker can flood a sensor in the network with a large amount of traffic to disrupt its availability and prevent it from receiving requests and providing services. Examples of active attacks are denial of service, replay, masquerade, and modification. Active attacks are very hard to prevent. Thus, the best way of dealing with these types of attacks is by detection as opposed to prevention.

WSNs are vulnerable to a variety of attacks that can have serious repercussions. Some of the most common types of attacks that are executed against WSN and RFIDs are detailed below together with their countermeasures:

- **Wormhole Attack:** In a wormhole attack, the attackers usually establish a link between two end points in the wireless network. Once the attacker establishes that link, he or she captures packets at one location of the network and then releases these packets into another location in the network. As such, the attacker disrupts the system by adding new sets of malicious sensor nodes to the network or by compromising a set of nodes. The intention of the attacker is to passively eavesdrop on data messages at one point of the network, tunnel these data messages, and then replay them at another location in the network (destination point) (Meghdadi et al., 2011). Wireless networks are more vulnerable to wormhole attacks than wired networks. According to Hu et al. (2006), "The wormhole attack is particularly dangerous against many ad hoc network routing protocols in which the nodes that hear a packet transmission directly from some node consider themselves to be in range of (and thus a neighbor of) that node" (p. 2). In addition, wormhole attacks are dangerous because they have the ability to significantly disrupt network communications. Research by Wittenburg (2003) revealed that approximately 40% to 50% of a network's communication can be disrupted by wormhole attack, especially if the attack is placed on the diagonal of the network.

- **Countermeasures:** The wormhole attack has serious repercussions and is very difficult to detect. Thus, defense against such attack should be by prevention as opposed to detection. Hu et al., (2006) proposed a general technique to prevent wormhole attacks that do not require securing the hardware layer. Their technique was based on measuring the packet propagation delay and discarding all messages that traveled too far. This technique requires tight time synchronization.

- **Eavesdropping Attack:** The wireless nature of RFIDs makes them more vulnerable to serious attacks. As previously mentioned, RFID tags contain a small microchip and a transmitter that can only be activated by the RFID reader to which the tag returns its signal. In an eavesdropping attack, the communication between the tag and the reader will be intercepted (through the use of an adversarial device). For example, an attacker can fool the communication with the reader and record exchanged messages. This attack can be performed in any direction (reader to tag or tag to the reader). An attacker can detect the signals transmitted between the tag and reader from meters away. Thus, verification and encryption are necessary to prevent unauthorized users from gaining access to data.

- **Countermeasures:** The environments surrounding the RFID system can possibly be equipped with mechanisms that are designed to detect and prevent eavesdropping attacks.

- **Crypto Attack:** Several decryption and encryption techniques can be applied to protect the data stored in an RFID tag. Crypto attacks occur when an attacker takes advantage of the security weaknesses in an RFID tag. In this attack, the attacker cracks the encrypted algorithms to gain access to the sensitive data stored in the tag. For example, an attacker may try all possible combinations of letters, numbers, words, and symbols until he or she finds the correct password. This type of attack is referred to as a *dictionary* or *brute force* attack. The attacker can then have full control of the tag. For instance, if the attacker gains direct access to the tag, he or she can use the kill command to disable it or can use the information stored on it for malevolent purposes.

- **Countermeasures:** The vulnerabilities that make crypto attacks possible are usually due to the use of weak algorithms, short keys, and failure to follow best-practice security measures. The best form of defense against such attacks is prevention as opposed to detection. For example, crypto attacks can be prevented through the application of strong cryptographic algorithms and the use of an encryption key that is of sufficient length.

- **Spoofing Attack:** WSNs operate in hostile environments, and the size of the sensor nodes is rapidly increasing. As more sensors are added to the network, security becomes more problematic and more critical. In a spoofing attack, the attacker uses a malicious device to control other devices in the network. For example, an attacker can possibly insert an IP address in place of a packet's source address in order to create the illusion that it came from another network. WSN is especially vulnerable to spoofing attacks because of its open nature. This form of attack presents a serious threat because it can open the door to other forms of attacks (Srinivas & Umar, 2013).

- **Countermeasures:** Applying cryptographic authentication is one of the traditional methods of preventing spoofing attacks. However, due to the limited resources and power of the wireless sensor nodes, it is sometimes difficult to deploy authentication. Srinivas & Umar (2013) proposed a new security approach that detects spoofing attacks. This approach utilizes the received signal strength (RSS). In contrast to traditional authentication methods for detecting spoofing attacks, this new RSS-based approach is easy to implement and does not appear to add additional overhead to WSN.

- **Distributed Denial of Service Attacks:** Denial of service (DDOS) attacks are very dangerous and can have a serious effect on IoT systems. DOS occurs when an attacker takes advantage of vulnerabilities in network security to corrupt or destroy a large batch of RFID tags. For example, an attacker may place an infinite number of fake RFID tags on the network in order to overwhelm the RFID reader's ability to differentiate between the tags. This type of attack can disable the connection between the tag and the database host, leading to data loss. DDOS attack is very dangerous because it is hard to detect, cheap, and deadly for the sensor nodes in the network. Furthermore, due to their limited processing memory and capabilities, WSN and RFIDs are especially vulnerable to DDOS attacks (Wood, & Stankovic, 2002). Hence, it is becoming imperative to develop strong detection and prevention mechanisms that safeguard against DDOS attacks.

- **Countermeasures:** It is imperative that DDOS attacks are detected quickly (Lee et al., 2012). Lee et al. proposed a DDOS detection model for exposing DDOS attacks at an early stage in real time. The proposed model was based on a revised traffic matrix from their previous work (Kim et al., 2009) and was proven to be effective in detecting and processing overheads delays. Kim et al. (2009) also employed a genetic algorithm (GA) to optimize the parameters that are employed in the traffic matrix. The GA consists of selection, reproduction, and evaluation operations. This system was supplemented with a hash function for locating packets to the traffic matrix.

The detection model optimizes three parameters to maximize DDOS detection rates:

- Size of the traffic matrix.
- Packet-based window size.
- Threshold value of variance from packet information.

Lee et al. (2012) demonstrated that their proposed model satisfied the main requirements of detection: high detection rates, low processing overheads, and short detection delay. Moreover, their detection model is easy to use in real-time network environments.

Privacy Threats

Although the innovation potential of IoT technology is large, this technology also has numerous inherent vulnerabilities. RFIDs and WSNs intensify the privacy issue of IoT because they make information readily available and accessible through a wireless network. Some of the more common privacy threats that are associated with the IoT are as follows:

- **Location Tracking Threats:** One may wonder about the consequences of a world full of tagged objects. Given the ability to associate an RFID tag with a person, her or his location can be detected and tracked. This threat entails that a person's identity can be readily associated with an object. A hidden RFID reader can possibly be installed at any specific location for the purposes of tracking someone. An individual who carries a tag can be easily tracked, and that eventually leads to user privacy violation. Unfortunately, an RFID tag transmits data responds and responds to a given signal without alerting its bearer or owner. As a consequence, an individual can be tracked without his or her knowledge.
- **Information Leakage:** This threat correlates directly with the disclosure of the information that an RFID system has collected. The leakage of information may occur when the key pieces of personal information associated

with a product or item are disclosed. This information may include important data, such as full name, address, social security, health history, and financial accounts. For example, pharmaceutical products that are tagged may store information about a person's health history. RFID tags are not designed to store large amounts of data. However, the data that is stored on the tag can potentially be used to access the large quantities of data that are stored on the database host.

Network Access Control

IoT systems are susceptible to malicious attacks that range from active to passive. For instance, RFID tags can be read without authorization, and key information about the object associated with the tag can become visible to those with malicious intent without leaving a trace. In addition, RFIDs are evolving at a rapid pace, as too are the security threats associated with them. Therefore, network access control is required to ensure that the connection to the network is made by an appropriate sensor. Moreover, while there is no standard definition for network access control, it is essentially a method that allows and restricts access to certain objects in the network based on compliance with security policies. The security policy can be based on sensor identity, sensor location, and sensor health.

If a set of sensors attached to objects is provided with dedicated data hosting servers that are not connected with a wireless server network, then an object's resources can be protected by physically securing each sensor and its data host server. When these sensors are added to WSN and served by a centralized data hosting system, the IoT service provider must provide the security. The IoT service provider can enforce access control policies based on object identity management and the access procedures required to identify objects.

Currently, neither of these techniques are applied as standard. The more common approach IoT service providers take is to employ a distributed architecture that consists of a dedicated set of sensors and centralized host servers. In such an environment, three security approaches can be applied:

- Rely on each sensor's node to assure the identity of its objects and rely on each hosting server to enforce its security policies based on object identification.
- Require objects to authenticate themselves to host servers, but trust the sensor connecting the identity of its object.
- Require the sensor's node to prove the identity of each sensor added to the network. In addition, require data hosting servers to prove their identity to the sensor.

In a closed, small IoT environment in which all sensors are operated and owned by a single company, the first and second approach may suffice. However, in an open IoT environment, in which a set of sensor nodes are interconnected, the third method is required to protect object information housed in the cloud. Yang et al. (2013) proposed a two-way authentication protocol model that aims to restrict unauthorized third parties from accessing data. The model was based on securely transmitting an ID in ciphertext between an RFID tag and reader to ensure information privacy. In addition, Yang et al. (2013) presented a three-party mutual authentication model that resolved the issue of the RFID security certificate failing to recognize the tag, reader, and database.

IoT DATA STORAGE

Overview

In recent years, we have moved from storing data on isolated servers in a small data center within a single company to store data in the cloud. Today, the cloud is the most commonly used approach for handling big data. The agility, scalability, and availability of the cloud entails that it is an attractive proposition for many users (Reavis, 2012). According to Reavis (2012), cloud computing has emerged as a new paradigm shift in data storage, computing resource services, and soft applications: "The computing world is quickly transforming toward a system of deriving relative applications for millions to extend as a service rather than to run on their personal computers" (p. 2).

The IoT and Cloud Computing

Cloud computing is a collaborative solution that is based on concepts of virtualization, distributed computing, and networking, and is underpinned by the latest web and software technologies (Vouk, 2008). Cloud computing can be viewed as a means of delivering applications as services over the Internet as well as a method of providing users with access to hardware and system software that act as platforms for these applications and services (Armbrust et al., 2010). Cloud computing is also used to refer to a network of computers that are linked and distribute processing capacity and applications to different systems (Johnson et al., 2009). Cloud computing lets organizations enhance their IT and computing capacity without having to invest in new architecture, software or hardware, or in the training and development of personnel (Glotzbach et al., 2008).

In cloud computing, the service provider pools resources and makes them available to different customers while these customers do not concern themselves about how and where the resources are getting pooled from. Scaled up or down and distributed among the different customers based on their demands. Cloud Computing provides flexibility in terms of elasticity and scalability, meaning that the services can be increased or decreased on need basis and in an automated manner without the intervention of the user. As such, users that deploy cloud computing do not have to buy additional computing resources if they expect an increase in demand.

Background of Cloud Computing

It is worthwhile briefly reviewing the background to cloud computing. As illustrated in Figure 4, the concept of cloud computing is not new (Kim et al., 2012). It was first introduced by John McCarthy in the 1960s (Abdulaziz, 2012). However, despite its long history, cloud computing has only recently started to evolve into a hot topic (Wang et al., 2011). In 2007, cloud computing increased in popularity in response to the increased demand for access to information systems. According to a report by the Pew Research Center that was published in June 2010, 71% of technology experts projected that many people would use software applications hosted in the cloud environment by 2020 (Reavis, 2012). Today, cloud computing is widely regarded as one of the foremost emerging technologies (Han et al., 2010).

The cloud has no borders; as such, it makes the world a very small place (Vouk, 2008). Katzan (2010) defined cloud computing as an architectural model that provides access to computer server facilities over the Internet. According to Katzan (2010), cloud computing includes on-demand self-service, resource pooling, rapid elasticity, broad network access, and a measured service. Arutyunov (2012) described cloud computing as a data processing technology that makes it possible to offer computer capacity and resources to users as services over the Internet. Cloud providers use servers to store information that can subsequently be temporarily cached on the user's desktop, tablet, notebook, cell phone, or other handheld devices. The essential characteristics of the cloud computing concept were defined by the National Institute of Standards and Technology (NIST) (Arutyunov, 2012) as follows:

- **On-Demand Service**: The cloud's user is permitted to define and change computing capabilities within the cloud. For example, a user can manage the data processing speed and storage size without interacting directly with the cloud provider.
- **Broad Network Access**: Services are made available to users throughout a data transmission network depending on the user's device.

Figure 4. History of cloud computing

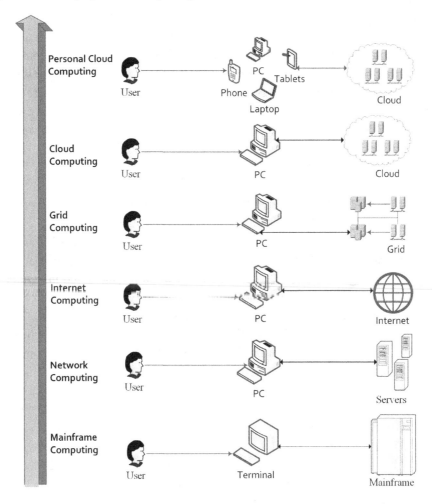

- **Resource Pooling**: Enables cloud providers to provide services to multiple users by using both virtual and physical computing resources. A cloud provider can dynamically assign or reassign resources based on users' demands.
- **Rapid Elasticity**: Cloud computing offers automated services that can be managed by users anytime without the need for interaction with the provider.

Measured services: cloud computing resources are measured and used in the same way that people utilize electricity, water, and natural gas (Arutyunov, 2012).

Cloud Computing Trends

Cloud computing has triggered a new market in information technology (IT) Ularu et al. (2013) instigated a revolutionary shift from more traditional ways of computing (Onyegbula et al., 2011). The structure of computing costs is shifting from capital expenditure to operational expenditure (Dhar, 2012). The Google search trends for the last 20 years, for the term "Cloud computing" is shown in Figure 5.

Cloud computing offers high scalability, agility, multi-sharing, high reliability and availability, lower cost, and on-demand services (Okezie et al., 2012). As such, have made this technology attractive to many users over the last few years (Reavis, 2012), and it has been estimated that the cloud computing market will reach a value of $13.9 billion by 2016 (Chen & Wu, 2015). Recently, cloud computing has been injected with new life with the arrival of IoT. Several existing studies indicate that there is an increasing interest in the use of cloud computing to support IoT.

Challenges of Cloud Computing

Researchers in the field of IT have raised privacy concerns about the use of cloud computing technology. The data collected by cloud providers introduce new opportunities and challenges for users (Vouk, 2008). Privacy is one of the biggest issues associated with cloud computing because software and data are stored off premises by the cloud provider. Personal privacy risk in the cloud appears to be the main concern of many scholars in this field. Ko et al. (2011) stated, "Cloud computing requires companies and individuals to transfer some or all control of computing resources to cloud service providers (CSPs)" (p. 1). It does not matter how careful the user is with his or her personal data, by subscribing to the cloud, users relinquish some control over their personal information to an external source. The distance

Figure 5. Google search trends for the last 20 years

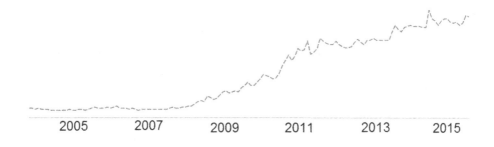

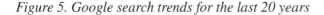

| | 2005 | 2007 | 2009 | 2011 | 2013 | 2015 |

between the computer user and the physical location of the data creates barriers to the user's acceptance of cloud computing offerings (Katzan, 2010).

Despite the attention that cloud computing has attracted in recent years, existing studies in this domain almost exclusively focus on data privacy issues without exploring other implications such as policy and architecture (Srinivasan, 2012). In 2009, The World Privacy Forum listed a set of findings on the privacy issues that impact cloud computing. Katzan (2010) summarized these findings as follows:

- Cloud computing has significant implications for personal privacy.
- A user's confidentiality and privacy risks completely depend on the cloud provider's privacy policy.
- The location of data in the cloud may have a significant impact on the confidentiality and protection of private information.
- Due to legal uncertainties, it is difficult to assess the status of data in the cloud.
- In order to respond to issues relating to privacy in the cloud, cloud providers should use best practices and policies.
- Data in the cloud may be stored in different locations with a variety of legal consequences.

CONCLUSION AND FUTURE DIRECTIONS

This chapter looked at the possible threats that can arise from the use of the IoT systems. Some of the underlying concepts of IoT technology and its potential use and abuse were examined. Finally, potential solutions to protect against security breaches and promptly detect them were proposed.

IoT services can be public or may be open to external agencies; as such, security can be an issue. As a result of an increase in theft, privacy issues, misuse of information, lack of policy guidance, and ethical issues, it has become increasingly imperative to govern the use of information technology. This has increased the demand for security management.

To gain a better understanding of the concept of security within the context of information technology, it is worth examining existing literature in this domain. Several studies (Sicari et al., 2015; Yan et al., 2014; Habib et al., 2014; Rivard, & Lapointe, 2012) have indicated that users' trust plays a major role in the adoption of technologies; as such, increasing accountability in IoT will positively influence users' attitudes toward using this technology. Accountability can be defined as the willingness or obligation to take responsibility for service performance, according to pre-defined and agreed expectations (Ko et al., 2011). For example, in order to protect users' rights, IoT service providers should be accountable for ensuring the user's information remains private, protected and secure at all times.

Effective deployment of the IoT requires balancing the demands of those who use the collected data with the desires and rights of the consumers whose personal data is being used. This requires the development of standardized processes and methods by which access and usage can be closely monitored and safeguarded. To gain users' trust, it is imperative that IoT service providers take full accountability for the data they acquire and manage, and that they act responsibly with this information at all times. Providing trustworthy IoT involves delivering private, secure, and reliable hyperconnectivity experiences that are based on best practices. In addition, the regulations, policies, standards, and rules that a given country operates should encourage full accountability. However, most of the current legislation does not take into consideration the IoT and IoT providers' legal obligations have yet to be formally defined.

Hardware and software manufacturers of IoT applications and peripherals need to be able to determine what impact their decisions will have on overall consumer satisfaction. In particular, the IoT provider and manufacturer should address privacy and security issues through adopting best practices for the development of risk management processes. Weber, (2010) summarized the privacy and security requirements for protecting IoT systems as follows:

- ***Resilience to Attacks:*** *The system has to avoid single points of failure and should adjust itself to node failures.*
- ***Data Authentication:*** *Access to objects' information must be authenticated as a principle.*
- ***Access Control:*** *Information providers must be able to implement access control on the data provided.*
- ***Client Privacy:*** *Measures need to be taken to ensure that only the information provider is able to infer from observing the use of the lookup system related to a specific customer; at least, inference should be very hard to conduct.* (p. 24)

REFERENCES

Abdulaziz, A. (2012). Cloud computing for increased business value. *International Journal of Business and Social Science*, *3*(1), 234–239.

Alcaraz, C., Najera, P., Lopez, J., & Roman, R. (2010, November). Wireless sensor networks and the internet of things: Do we need a complete integration? In 1st *International Workshop on the Security of the Internet of Things* (SecIoT'10).

Armbrust, M., Fox, A., Griffith, R., Joseph, A. D., Katz, R., Konwinski, A., & Zaharia, M. (2008). A view of cloud computing. *Communications of the ACM, 53*(4), 50–58. doi:10.1145/1721654.1721672

Arutyunov, V. V. (2012). Cloud computing: Its history of development, modern state, and future considerations. *Scientific and Technical Information Processing, 39*(3), 173–178.

Bali, J., Langendorfer, P., & Skarmeta, A. F. (2013). Security and Privacy Challenge in Data Aggregation for the IoT in Smart Cities. *Internet of Things: Converging Technologies for Smart Environments and Integrated Ecosystems*, (pp. 225-244).

Chen, S. C., & Wu, C. C. (2015). Human Resource Development in Cloud Computing: An Empirical Investigation in Taiwan. *Journal of Management Research, 7*(3), 102–114.

Cocosila, M. (2013). Role of user a priori attitude in the acceptance of mobile health: An empirical investigation. *Electronic Markets, 23*(1), 15–27. doi:10.1007/s12525-012-0111-5

Dhar, S. (2012). From outsourcing to cloud computing: Evolution of IT services. *Management Research Review, 35*(8), 664–675. doi:10.1108/01409171211247677

Glotzbach, R., Mordkovich, D., & Radwan, D. (2008). Syndicated RSS feeds for course information distribution. *Journal of Information Technology Education: Research, 7*(1), 163–183.

Gubbi, J., Buyya, R., Marusic, S., & Palaniswami, M. (2013). Internet of Things (IoT): A vision, architectural elements, and future directions. *Future Generation Computer Systems, 29*(7), 1645–1660. doi:10.1016/j.future.2013.01.010

Habib, S. M., Ries, S., Mühlhäuser, M., & Varikkattu, P. (2014). Towards a trust management system for cloud computing marketplaces: Using caiq as a trust information source. *Security and Communication Networks, 7*(11), 2185–2200. doi:10.1002/sec.748

Han, Y., Sun, J., Wang, G., & Li, H. (2010). A cloud-based BPM architecture with user-end distribution of non-compute-intensive activities and sensitive data. *Journal of Computer Science and Technology, 25*(6), 1157–1167.

Hu, Y. C., Perrig, A., & Johnson, D. B. (2006). Wormhole attacks in wireless networks. Selected Areas in Communications. *IEEE Journal, 24*(2), 370–380.

Johnson, L., Levine, A., Smith, R., & Smythe, T. (2009). *The 2009 horizon report: K. Austin, Texas: The New Media Consortium. Cover photograph: "Chapped Lips" by Vox_Efx on Flickr.* Retrieved from http://www.flickr.com/photos/vox_efx/3186014896/

Kanuparthi, A., Karri, R., & Addepalli, S. (2013, November). Hardware and embedded security in the context of internet of things. In *Proceedings of the 2013 ACM Workshop on Security, Privacy & Dependability for Cyber Vehicles*, (pp. 61-64). ACM. doi:10.1145/2517968.2517976

Katzan, H. Jr. (2010). On the privacy of cloud computing. *International Journal of Management and Information Systems, 14*(2), 1–12.

Khalil, I., Bagchi, S., & Shroff, N. B. (2005, June). LITEWORP: a lightweight countermeasure for the wormhole attack in multihop wireless networks. In *Proceedings. International Conference on Dependable Systems and Networks, 2005 DSN 2005*, (pp. 612-621). IEEE. doi:10.1109/DSN.2005.58

Kim, T. H., Kim, D. S., Lee, S. M., & Park, J. S. (2009). Detecting DDoS attacks using dispersible traffic matrix and weighted moving average. *Advances in Information Security and Assurance* (pp. 290-300). Springer Berlin Heidelberg.

Kim, W., Kim, S. D., Lee, E., & Lee, S. (2009, December). Adoption issues for cloud computing. In *Proceedings of the 7th International Conference on Advances in Mobile Computing and Multimedia* (pp. 2-5). ACM.

Ko, R. K., Jagadpramana, P., Mowbray, M., Pearson, S., Kirchberg, M., Liang, Q., & Lee, B. S. (2011). TrustCloud: A framework for accountability and trust in cloud computing. In *2011 IEEE World Congress on Services (SERVICES)*, (pp. 584-588). IEEE. doi:10.1109/SERVICES.2011.91

Lin, A., & Chen, N. C. (2012). Cloud computing as an innovation: Perception, attitude, and adoption. *International Journal of Information Management, 32*(6), 533–540. doi:10.1016/j.ijinfomgt.2012.04.001

Meghdadi, M., Ozdemir, S., & Güler, I. (2011). A survey of wormhole-based attacks and their countermeasures in wireless sensor networks. *IETE Technical Review, 28*(2), 89–102. doi:10.4103/0256-4602.78089

Miorandi, D., Sicari, S., De Pellegrini, F., & Chlamtac, I. (2012). Internet of things: Vision, applications and research challenges. *Ad Hoc Networks, 10*(7), 1497–1516. doi:10.1016/j.adhoc.2012.02.016

Mitrokotsa, A., Rieback, M. R., & Tanenbaum, A. S. (2010). Classifying RFID attacks and defenses. *Information Systems Frontiers, 12*(5), 491–505. doi:10.1007/s10796-009-9210-z

Neisse, R., Steri, G., Baldini, G., Tragos, E., Fovino, I. N., & Botterman, M. (2014). *Dynamic Context-Aware Scalable and Trust-based IoT Security, Privacy Framework. Chapter in Internet of Things Applications-From Research and Innovation to Market Deployment.* IERC Cluster Book.

Okezie, C. C., Chidiebele, U. C., & Kennedy, O. C. (2012). Cloud computing: A cost effective approach to enterprise web application implementation (A case for cloud ERP web model). *Academic Research International, 3*(1), 432–443.

Onyegbula, F., Dawson, M., & Stevens, J. (2011). Understanding the need and importance of the cloud computing environment within the National Institute of Food and Agriculture, an agency of the United States Department of Agriculture. *Journal of Information Systems Technology & Planning, 4*(8), 17–42.

Perera, C., Zaslavsky, A., Christen, P., & Georgakopoulos, D. (2014). Context aware computing for the internet of things: A survey. *IEEE Communications Surveys and Tutorials, 16*(1), 414–454. doi:10.1109/SURV.2013.042313.00197

Pohls, H. C., Angelakis, V., Suppan, S., Fischer, K., Oikonomou, G., Tragos, E. Z., . . . Mouroutis, T. (2014, April). RERUM: Building a reliable IoT upon privacy- and security-enabled smart objects. In Wireless Communications and Networking Conference Workshops (WCNCW), 2014 IEEE (pp. 122-127). IEEE.

Reavis, D. (2012). Information evaporation: The migration of information to cloud computing platforms. *International Journal of Management & Information Systems (Online), 16*(4), 291.

Ren, K., Samarati, P., Gruteser, M., Ning, P., & Liu, Y. (2014). Guest Editorial Special Issue on Security for IoT: The State of the Art. *Internet of Things Journal, IEEE, 1*(5), 369–371. doi:10.1109/JIOT.2014.2361608

Rivard, S., & Lapointe, L. (2012). Information technology implementers' responses to user resistance: Nature and effects. *Management Information Systems Quarterly, 36*(3), 897–920.

Selamat, Z., & Jaffar, N. (2011). IT acceptance: From perspective of Malaysian bankers. *International Journal of Business and Management*, *6*(1), 207–217.

Sicari, S., Rizzardi, A., Grieco, L. A., & Coen-Porisini, A. (2015). Security, privacy and trust in Internet of Things: The road ahead. *Computer Networks*, *76*, 146–164. doi:10.1016/j.comnet.2014.11.008

Srinivas, V. B., & Umar, S. (2013). Spoofing attacks in wireless sensor networks. International journal of Computer Science. *Engineering and Technology*, *3*(6), 201–210.

Srinivasan, M. (2012). Building a secure enterprise model for cloud computing environment. *Academy of Information and Management Sciences Journal*, *15*(1), 127–133.

Suo, H., Wan, J., Zou, C., & Liu, J. (2012, March). Security in the internet of things: a review. In *Computer Science and Electronics Engineering (ICCSEE), 2012 International Conference on* (Vol. 3, pp. 648-651). IEEE. doi:10.1109/ICCSEE.2012.373

Ularu, E. G., Puican, F. C., Suciu, G., Vulpe, A., & Todoran, G. (2013). Mobile computing and cloud maturity Introducing machine learning for ERP configuration automation. *Informatica Economica*, *17*(1), 40–52. doi:10.12948/issn14531305/17.1.2013.04

Vouk, M. A. (2008). Cloud computing-Issues, research and implementations. *Journal of Computing and Information Technology*, *4*, 235-246. doi: 10.2498/cit.1001391

Wang, W. Y. C., Rashid, A., & Chuang, H. (2011). Toward the trend of cloud computing. *Journal of Electronic Commerce Research*, *12*(4), 238–242.

Weber, R. H. (2010). Internet of Things-New security and privacy challenges. *Computer Law & Security Report*, *26*(1), 23–30. doi:10.1016/j.clsr.2009.11.008

Wittenburg-georg, G. (2003). *A defense against replay attacks on chaumian mixes.* (Bachelor thesis). Retrieved from Google Scholar: http://page.mi.fu-berlin.de/gwitten/papers/wittenburg03defense.pdf

Wood, A. D., & Stankovic, J. (2002). Denial of service in sensor networks. *Computer*, *35*(10), 54–62. doi:10.1109/MC.2002.1039518

Xia, F., Yang, L. T., Wang, L., & Vinel, A. (2012). Internet of things. *International Journal of Communication Systems*, *25*(9), 1101–1102. doi:10.1002/dac.2417

Yan, Z., Zhang, P., & Vasilakos, A. V. (2014). A survey on trust management for Internet of Things. *Journal of Network and Computer Applications, 42,* 120–134. doi:10.1016/j.jnca.2014.01.014

Yang, L., Yu, P., Bailing, W., Yun, Q., Xuefeng, B., & Xinling, Y. (2013). Hash-based RFID mutual authentication protocol. *International Journal of Security & Its Applications, 7*(3), 183–194.

Zhang, Z. K., Cho, M. C. Y., & Shieh, S. (2015, April). Emerging Security Threats and Countermeasures in IoT. In *Proceedings of the 10th ACM Symposium on Information, Computer and Communications Security,* (pp. 1-6). ACM. doi:10.1145/2714576.2737091

Chapter 5
Enhancing Cyber Security for Financial Industry through Compliance and Regulatory Standards

Derek Mohammed
Saint Leo University, USA

Marwan Omar
Saint Leo University, USA

Van Nguyen
Saint Leo University, USA

ABSTRACT

This paper investigates laws and regulations within the financial industry that are applicable to cybersecurity. It analyzes both compliance and regulatory issues across the financial sector at the federal and state levels. Additionally; the paper highlights the importance of adhering to, and implementing industry-based regulations to improve the protection of financial digital assets against cyber-attacks. It also reviews similarities and differences among compliance environments created by financial regulations. Identification, interpretation and application of federal and state government regulations, directives and acts as they apply to the security of digital systems in the financial sector is another objective of this research study. Finally, this paper contrasts the values and issues created by increasing compliance requirements.

DOI: 10.4018/978-1-5225-0741-3.ch005

CYBERSECURITY COMPLIANCE IN THE FINANCIAL SECTOR

Financial regulations provide a framework seeking to promote legal and ethical behavior within the industry. However, scandals over the last fifteen years have revealed broken regulations and poor enforcement. In each scandal's wake, lawmakers passed legislation to either amend the existing standards and enforcement mechanisms or create new. As a key pillar in a nation's economic foundation, the U.S. relies on a stable financial industry. Financial standing determines a nation's standing on the international stage. China's emergence as an international power, for example, derives partially from its economic strength.

The sheer volume of assets, the financial industry manages presents a highly lucrative target for criminals. Insiders engage in fraud, deceiving investors for ill-gotten profit, and others use complex financial systems for illicit purposes such as money laundering. Also damaging is the near-constant assault from cyber criminals. In order to protect consumers and ensure transparency, U.S lawmakers have empowered several regulatory bodies with oversight authority. Still, responsibility for regulatory compliance and safeguarding financial assets remains with individual institutions. Regulations create a diverse set of compliance environments that display some similarities, yet contain differences in focus and intent. Improving cybersecurity in the financial industry requires a critical evaluation of the merits and issues of compliance present in each environment. Only then can cybersecurity policy makers recommend regulations that promote efficiency while protecting the industry and its customers.

Analysis of Compliance Issues

Due to the financial sector's complex nature, compliance with federal, state and local laws provide a monumental challenge. Cybersecurity further complicates the issue. As former Federal Bureau of Investigation Cyber Division Assistant Director Gordon Snow (2011) explained, "Cyber criminals have demonstrated their ability to exploit our online financial and market systems that interface with the Internet." Since the financial sector depends heavily on information technology, regulatory compliance becomes a critical cybersecurity component. Because a large portion of assets exist on paper rather than physically, protecting asset data serves as a driving force for regulation.

Ensuring coherent and active cooperation with other financial entities serves as a key to achieving compliance. The Gramm-Leach-Bliley Act (GLBA), for example, dictates how institutions collect and share information. GLBA's provisions require strict confidentiality and security for personal information institutions collect, such as account numbers, social security numbers and credit histories. Key to understanding GLBA is that the term "financial institution" carries a broad definition, including "check-cashing businesses, payday lenders, mortgage brokers, nonbank lenders, personal property or real estate appraisers, professional tax preparers, and courier services" (Bureau of Customer Protection, 2006). The Federal Trade Commission's (FTC) Safeguards Rule sets additional standards, requiring that organizations identify personnel to oversee a security program, design and implement a safeguards program, and select service providers able to maintain implemented safeguards. Since many of the aforementioned organizations might not possess such capabilities, these regulations present a tremendous hurdle.

Compliance issues also arise at the state level. California's Notice of Security Breach Act (NSB) bears significant ramifications for the financial industry, requiring that organizations make public notifications when negligence or a cyber attack results in data loss. Passed in 2002 and the first of its kind, NSB led to other state and federal breach notification laws. Yet, it stands out in its call for "notification when unencrypted personal information was, or is reasonably believed to have been, acquired by an unauthorized person" (Stevens, 2012). The implied requirement is encryption of personal identifiable information, both in transport and at rest.

Data retention regulations also pose compliance issues for financial institutions. The Electronic Fund Transfer Act, Regulation E, spells out data retention requirements for institutions that hold customer accounts or provide electronic fund transfers. ATM transfers, telephone bill payments, and preauthorized transfers to or from accounts all fall under its purview. This presents another financial sector cybersecurity compliance issue, requiring secure storage for transaction information.

Analysis of Regulatory Issues

The regulatory bottom line for financial institutions lies in the legal requirement to take "reasonable steps" toward cybersecurity compliance, whether information protection, data retention, or secure network architecture. As the number and sophistication of attacks increase, oversight officials will continue to develop new regulations, exacerbating compliance environments. Regulations place the onus on individual organizations to vet third-parties when outsourcing. Contracts and service level agreements must meet regulatory requirements.

Regulations within the financial industry vary tremendously based on the financial service. Some deal only with investment products and others with credit and liquidity functions (Banking & Finance SSP, 2010). While several financial regulatory bodies exist, a great deal of institutional self-regulation also occurs. This plays a vital role, both to ensure public trust and keep federal regulators at bay. However, drastic events, such as the Enron scandal, erode trust and drive lawmakers to pass hastily drafted regulations. Similarly, a devastating cybersecurity incident would likely precipitate similar cybersecurity regulations.

Some areas of the financial sector are regulated more heavily at the state, rather than federal level. Under the McCarran-Ferguson Act of 1945, "Congress affirmed the right of the States exclusively to regulate the insurance industry" (Banking & Finance SSP, 2010). States rely on organizations to notify entities such as the Treasury Department and the Financial and Banking Information Infrastructure Committee (FBIIC) regarding cyber incidents.

Comprehensive regulatory enforcement presents another significant challenge. Financial operations rely on cooperation between entities across the industry. As such, comprehensive cybersecurity will require a single regulatory body with cybersecurity oversight. This would also aid in formalizing the processes of applying standards developed by the financial industry. The global economy adds an additional hurdle to this challenge. Cooperation with bodies such as the European Union would facilitate smoother navigation of the international financial landscape.

According to the Financial Services Sector Coordination Council (FSSCC), the financial industry fully supports cybersecurity legislation (Blauner, 2013). The ultimate goal lies in developing a cybersecurity framework that supports business processes. Such a framework will require a new security mindset and changes to processes such as risk management and risk mitigation. This will produce a stronger cybersecurity framework and more efficient regulations that promote a trust between financial institutions and their clients.

Similarities of Compliance Environments

Despite the diverse U.S. financial landscape, some similarities exist between compliance environments. Regulators design these environments with the intent of securing a variety of interests, from national financial stability to protecting consumers from activities such as corporate fraud, loss of personal information, and fraud against a federally insured financial institution to obtain customer information or steal money. Laws such as GLBA and bodies such as the FTC serve these interests.

As stated earlier, the GLBA requires financial institutions to protect personal customer information from improper disclosure and security threats. Whereas the GLBA has a broader definition for financial institutions, the Federal Deposit Insurance Corporation (FDIC) only protects those institutions that are insured under its provisions. It does cover some organizations considered financial institutions under GLBA, such as payday lenders or check-cashing businesses. The Electronic Fund Transfer Act (EFTA) falls FDIC regulation and was developed to provide a framework for establishing consumer rights, as well as liabilities and responsibilities of those that use electronic fund transfer systems, including ATMs, point of sales terminals, automated clearinghouse systems, telephone bill payments, and remote banking systems.

Although the state of California NSB was previously discussed, similar laws exist in forty-six states, the District of Columbia, Guam, Puerto Rico and the Virgin Islands (Greenberg, 2012). All require institutions provide security breach notifications to anyone whose personal information has been illegally accessed (Greenberg, 2012). Alabama, Kentucky, New Mexico, and South Dakota are the only states that do not have a security breach law.

The FTC's Standards for Safeguarding Customer Information requires financial institutions to have an information security plan. This plan must cover administrative, technical, and physical safeguards to ensure the security and confidentiality of customer information. It must also protect against any anticipated vulnerabilities or threats to the security and integrity of customer information, and protect against unauthorized access of this information that could potentially harm or inconvenience a customer (Federal Trade Commission, 2002).

The FTCs Bureau of Consumer Protection works for the consumer to prevent fraud, deception, and unfair business practices by enforcing Federal laws that provide consumer protection, and enhance consumer confidence. It also empowers consumers with information that is made available to them free of charge on how to exercise their rights and identify and prevent fraud and deception. Other compliance environments include the Federal Information Security Management Act (FISMA), National Institute of Standards and Technology (NIST) and the Sarbanes-Oxley Act (SOX).

FISMA is a comprehensive legislative framework that was designed to protect government information, operations, and assets against natural or man-made threats (Rouse, 2013). It is part of the Electronic Government Act of 2002. FISMA puts emphasis on the need for Federal agencies to develop, document and implement a program for the entire organization to provide information security for their systems that support their operations as well as their assets. The National Institute of Standards and Technology (NIST) 800-53, Recommended Security Controls for Federal Information Systems, was originally developed to support FISMA and is the primary security controls source for Federal agencies. This is important because most financial institutions are covered by the FDIC. The FDIC is responsible for preserving and promoting confidence to the public of U.S. financial systems by insuring at least $250,000 in deposits in banks and thrift institutions; by identifying, monitoring and addressing identified risks to the deposit insurance funds; and by limiting the effect on both the economy and the financial system when a bank or thrift institution fails. The FDIC only insures checking, savings, trust, certificates of deposits, individual retirement accounts and money market deposit accounts

(Marco, 2008). With all the cybersecurity threats and concerns for financial institutions, financially savvy citizens should want to make sure their money is protected by using an FDIC-insured bank.

The Sarbanes-Oxley Act (SOX) is designed to prevent corporate fraud by regular documentation and disclosure of a company's internal controls, ethics code, and audit reports that can lead to review of corporate fraud. Issuers must disclose information to the public about material changes in their financial condition or operations on an urgent basis and they must be published in easy to understand terms and, where appropriate, supported by trend and qualitative data and graphic presentations. SOX is similar to the GLBA because they both review logs to identify signs of security violations and exploitations and implement processes to quickly resolve them and retain those logs to be reviewed by auditors.

Almost all of these compliance environments require financial institutions to provide some form of clear and conspicuous information disclosure to consumers, whether in writing or electronically. Specifically, the GLBA requires that disclosure must include how institutions disclose nonpublic personal information to affiliated and nonaffiliated third parties, as well as the category of information that is disclosed. Other GLBA requirements govern disclosure of information for previous customers and protection of nonpublic, personal information (U.S. Federal Trade Commission, 2013). The FDIC must meet disclosure requirements related to information such as home mortgages, education loans, and financial data held by FDIC-insured State nonmember banks. Regulations also require notification if a security breach occurs impacting an institution's customers.

Differences of Compliance Environments

Despite their similarities, the various regulations levied on the financial sector create a diverse set of compliance environments. These regulations possess unique characteristics and some individual laws impact organizations within the financial sector differently. Congress passed GLBA in 1999, significantly reorganizing the financial industry. Though this paper focuses on its strong provisions regarding privacy protection, one must realize its wider context as deregulation legislation. GLBA enabled institutions, such as Bank of America, engage in multiple areas across the financial industry, including banking, securities, and insurance (Saucer, 2009). The implications of deregulation lie outside this paper's scope, with financial experts still arguing GLBA's role in the financial crisis at the close of the last decade (Leonhardt, 2008). Yet, the mingling of multiple financial services under one organization certainly complicates cybersecurity since it demands cybersecurity professionals in large financial organizations understand and comply with regulations across the industry.

Although GLBA deregulated the financial industry in certain aspects, conversely it introduced strong privacy regulation, focusing heavily on protecting personal information. It distinguishes itself from other regulations by requiring organizations to differentiate between "customers" and "consumers" (Virtue, 2009). Virtue (2009) identifies this difference as a prime GLBA misconception. The FTC attempts to clarify this distinction. An institution's consumers merely obtain financial services, but do not establish a "continuing relationship" (FTC, 2002). For example, an individual who uses a bank to cash a check or utilizes its ATM does not establish a continuing relationship, regardless of how frequently that individual "consumes" the institution's services (FTC, 2002). Customers are a subset of consumers who establish a continuing relationship with an institution via activities such as opening accounts, obtaining lines of credit, and utilizing tax preparation services or investment advising (FTC, 2002).

GLBA creates different requirements for safeguarding individuals' non-public information. Afforded stronger protection, customers must receive notifications containing full disclosure of an institution's information sharing and disclosure policies upon establishment of a relationship, e.g. when opening a checking account (FTC, 2002). Institutions must also provide an opt-out notice, allowing customers to prevent the institution sharing their personal information. Consumers only receive notification, which may be in "short-form" versus a full description, before an institution shares information with a non-affiliated third party.

Case law has further defined GLBA's applicability, establishing new and different compliance environments. The auto industry heavily engages in financial operations, thereby placing it under the purview of GBLA. As the GLBA took effect in the early 2000's, auto dealerships found themselves subject to penalties established under GLBA when their information security practices proved inadequate, leaving individuals' nonpublic information unsecured (Harris, 2003). Yet, a 2005 court decision found attorneys exempt from GLBA's privacy provisions when conducting tax planning, estate planning, and personal bankruptcy ("Attorneys held exempt," 2005). These examples serve as edification for cybersecurity professionals, highlighting the exigent need to research GLBA privacy requirements and case law, regardless of whether an organization appears outside the financial industry.

Whereas GBLA sought to safeguard personal information in accordance with financial deregulation, SOX sought to clamp down on corporate malfeasance in the wake of financial industry scandals (Glass et al., 2009). Applicability stands out as a key difference in SOX, which applies only to publicly traded companies, regardless of whether U.S. law classifies them as financial institutions (Glass et al., 2009). Another important aspect of SOX is the climate created by scandal and how it influenced Congress to rush headlong into passing legislation. Representative Michael Oxley, the bill's namesake, admitted six years after its passage that he would have written it differently, but "everyone felt like Rome was burning" (Gingrich & Kralik, 2008). While this may appear to have little bearing on cybersecurity, professionals in the cyber field should understand that a hurriedly prepared piece of legislation will often contain more significant unforeseen consequences than legislation that undergoes greater scrutiny.

SOX introduced significant audit and monitoring requirements for publically traded organizations. It requires organizations create complex internal control frameworks for financial reporting and requires auditors to assess the efficacy of these frameworks (Hedley & Ben-Chorin, 2011). Glass et al. (2009) explain that SOX Section 404 bears the greatest significance for cybersecurity professionals. Stults (2004) clarifies that while Section 404 does not specifically identify information security, the reality of dependence on cyber assets for both daily operations and compliance management results in heavy scrutiny on information security controls. Furthermore, SOX Section 302 places the legal burden of certifying financial reports on CEOs and CFOs (Sults, 2004). This means scrutiny on IT departments will come directly from top-tier management (Stults, 2004).

A marked difference in the SOX compliance environment is the disparity between large corporations and small companies regarding the burden of managing compliance (Myers, Foster, & Williford, 2008). In 2002, many small banks lamented that the complex requirements levied by SOX Section 404 would force sales to larger firms who could absorb the costs associated with compliance (Davenport, 2004). SOX also forced changes in community banks' audit committees, demanding greater expertise in areas outside their traditional role of accounting integrity, such as legal and regulatory compliance (Naber, 2008). Testimony before the U.S. House Committee on Small Business in 2007 from leaders such as the America's Community Bankers president (Scarborough, 2007) and CEO of the Pendleton Community Bank (Loving, 2012) underscored the disproportionate burden in terms of time, money, and manpower SOX placed on small and community banks.

These firms finally saw relief in 2012 via a minor provision of the Jumpstart Our Business Startups (JOBS) Act that changed registration requirements, giving them greater flexibility in how they operate (Klitsch, 2012). Smaller banks can maintain a greater number of investors without having to go public. This incurs quarterly and annual reporting to prove compliance with SOX, and costs $200,000 per bank (Solnik, 2012). Though smaller firms may have greater freedom to operate, cybersecurity professionals must understand that SOX constitutes a complex regulatory framework and a particularly difficult compliance environment to navigate.

GLBA and SOX created cybersecurity requirements and considerations by proxy. Neither specifically identified information technology or information security, but they nonetheless became prime areas of scrutiny for reasons discussed above. More recent legislation has created requirements that specifically identify cybersecurity reporting. The Dodd-Frank Wall Street Reform and Consumer Protection Act of 2010 (Dodd-Frank), "mandates specific information technology requirements" (Yu, 2012). As Fitzgerald noted in late 2012, the financial industry remained hard at work attempting to digest more than 2,000 pages that comprise the act. He cites multiple industry executives as preparing for a "virtual tsunami" of regulations emanating from regulatory bodies, such as the Securities and Exchange Commission (SEC) (Fitzgerald, 2012). This compliance environment has already begun to take shape, with the SEC releasing disclosure obligation guidance in late 2011. This guidance specifically references "cybersecurity risks and cyber incidents" (SEC, 2011).

Compliance with previous legislation focused on the CEO and CFO creating policy and developing frameworks, whereas Dodd-Frank compliance seems centered on the CIO preparing IT departments for a regulatory onslaught (Bone, 2011). Yu (2012) explains that cybersecurity controls, such as data security, change management, and application integrity will play a much more significant role in companies working toward Dodd-Frank compliance. Another significant difference is treatment of smaller firms. As mentioned above, Washington regulators seem to have finally provided relief to smaller banks struggling under the weight of SOX. However, despite initial assurances to the contrary, Dodd-Frank stands to add potentially crushing regulatory requirements on smaller firms (Fitzgerald, 2012). Industry continues to wrestle with the impacts of GLBA and SOX. Dodd-Frank represents the latest wave in the financial industry compliance environment, one that promises to change its metaphorical topography drastically.

Values with Increasing Compliance Requirements

The government's efforts to create appropriate regulations and standards have worked reasonably to aid protection of sensitive data processed on information systems on a daily basis. Legal and regulatory compliance possesses the potential to benefit individual organizations, the financial industry as a whole, and the entire country. In recent years, however, the financial sector has faced an ever-increasing number of risks and threats due to its dependence on information technology. As the world becomes more dependent on electronic financial records, there is an increased risk that personal data will be stolen or improperly used (Rotenberg, 2011). A growing compendium of evidence shows a rise in the level of cybersecurity risk to financial industry, casting little doubt on the need for more effective compliance requirements.

Due to its role in individuals' financial stability, the financial industry often comes under heavy scrutiny. The immense volume of financial data traversing the Internet at and residing on financial organizations' servers has made banking systems prime targets for cyber criminals, whether they engage in credit card number theft or stealing other secure financial data. These financial institutions owe it to their customers to ensure they are complying with industry regulations. It is the fiduciary responsibility of bank directors and officers to ensure they comply with security standards that already exist such as the Payment Card Industry Data Security Standard (Calder, 2013). Organizations within the financial sector should encourage additional regulations and standards that provide additional security to business individual customers. Not only does compliance aid in protecting an institution's own financial data, it also ensures companies maintain good faith with their customers and preserve consumer confidence.

As a component of U.S. critical infrastructure, it becomes a national security imperative that financial organizations embrace a culture of compliance. Firms should view an increase in efficacious compliance requirements positively because of the benefits they confer on an organization. Achieving compliance enables an organization to create best practice policies, better technological solutions, identify key metrics and ultimately imbed the concept of compliance within its culture (Compliance, 2007). These changes start at the board level, and require continued upper management support for effectively implementation (Compliance, 2007). In addition to meeting government standards and regulations, business can gain operational benefits through compliance. Because the financial sector it primarily owned by the private sector, it is imperative that the partnership between the private and public sectors continues to grow. An increase in the financial sector's compliance efforts is another way to help strengthen this effort.

Compliance has allowed different organizations, public and private, to collaborate and improve cybersecurity. Working together, through the Financial Services Sector Coordinating Council, has sped the application of research into practice through new cybersecurity technologies and processes that benefit specific functions for financial services (Groups, 2011). When new compliance standards or regulations are produced, financial institutions come together to find innovative ways to improve the sector overall. Industries that have been regulated by the federal government, such as the investment sector, have become accustomed to dealing with compliance issues and therefore have formed a working relationship with the government and private sector to improve regulations (Larence, 2007). Some industries have been opposed to the new standards the financial sector has adopted because of the relationship these efforts have created with the government. Through this relationship, the financial sector has embraced compliance as a way to encourage partnerships, not only with the government, but also within the industry.

Another benefit that comes with increasing compliance requirements is the maturity of the sector and its individual organizations. As technology becomes more advanced, it is vital for an organization to work to stay ahead of threats. The current requirements and standards that have been established can only address what is happening at the present. For the financial sector to improve its overall cybersecurity, it must work to continuously evolve and increase its compliance requirements. The more mature industries, such as banking and finance, are better able to focus on future strategic activities, such as the development of disaster recovery plans (Larence, 2007). If the financial sector fails to increase its compliance efforts, these businesses will put themselves further into risk. The increase of compliance allows organizations within the sector to research and develop new ways of combating threats into the future. By staying stagnant, the development of security and defense measures completely comes to a halt and the companies in this industry will continuously be susceptible to new threats.

Although some may view compliance as a burden, it is hard to dispute that the value it provides to businesses, particularly the financial industry, is not worth the investment. As the financial sector remains one of the key components of the nation's infrastructure, it is imperative that a long term commitment is made to protect it through increased compliance. Increasing compliance requirements builds trusted working relationships, provides organizational stability and leadership, and helps to identify and address future threats and vulnerabilities. It is apparent that an increase in compliance not only benefits the financial sector, but also the nation's cybersecurity as a whole because of valuable economic data this industry holds for all of its customers, both private and public.

Issues with Increasing Compliance Requirement

The recent financial crises have prompted multiple nations, specifically the U.S., to take regulatory measures in the financial industry to avoid future economic disasters. Financial institutions play a major role in the global economy and its health can determine whether countries improve or decline. Financial institutions are used in many ways to aid businesses and citizens to operate in a fair and lawful manner. However, not all businesses or citizens utilize financial institutions for their intended purposes. Some use financial institutions to fund terrorism, run illegal money exchanges, and conduct other illegal activities that endanger global markets and people's lives. Adequate cybersecurity helps guard against illicit activity.

The goal of a compliance regulation is to ensure fair and equal treatment for all customers of a financial institution and to avoid the financial institutions from being used for illegal purposes (Ely, 2008). In 1970, Congress passed the Bank Secrecy Act in an attempt to prevent people from using banks for money laundering. This act required banks to report any individual to the Internal Revenue Service (IRS) for any money transaction over $10,000. Although the Bank Secrecy Act aided the monitoring of asset movement by an individual, it did very little to monitor the banks and other stakeholders of the financial industry. There was very little enforcement of laws that regulated the financial industry. Although the financial industry had some regulations that govern the industry, it did not do much to enforce the laws. The financial industry was pretty much left to regulate itself with very little checks and balances. This lack of oversight left top management of some financial institutions to engage in fraudulent activities which almost collapsed the American economy in the late 1990s.

Perhaps the swiftest response to the financial crisis was the Sarbanes-Oxley Act of 2002 (SOX). Although SOX is arranged into eleven titles, the most important sections in regards to compliance are titles 302, 401, 404, 409, 802, and 906. Most of the compliance sections are divided into areas holding management, executives, and board members responsible for reporting and assuring the accuracy of organizations' financial reports.

Section 302 of the act relates to corporate responsibility for financial reports. This section outlines the guidelines and the individuals required to sign the corporate financial report. The section also holds the signing officers responsible for any inaccurate information that may appear on the financial report. The section also requires the organization to assure the accuracy of the financial information on the report to reflect the health and condition of the organization. The section additionally explains that no internal process of any organization can be used as a replacement function for this section (soxlaw.com, 2002). It forces organizations to use and follow this act strictly without any alternatives. While this may be a good way to assign responsibility and accountability to those involved in generating a corporate financial report, it does not take into consideration the cost on the organization and also the difficulties in assuring the accuracy of the data used for the report in a big corporation. Some corporations have a complex financial system involving different people at different levels and the input of wrong information may not easily be tracked to the source of the issue.

Section 802 of the act imposes penalties including up to 20 years imprisonment for altering, destroying, mutilating, concealing, falsifying records, documents or tangible objects with the intent to obstruct or contaminate an investigation. The intent of this proposed punishment is to compel organizations to develop truthful and accurate reporting.

Although SOX implementation and execution may at first appear straight forward, it does not provide strict guidelines to achieve compliance. The law simply provides organizational requirements and penalties for noncompliance, but leaves the details to oversight bodies and the impacted organizations. SOX also ignores the global nature of financial operations and the possibility of having to comply with other nation's laws. Most regulatory laws govern only a country and are valid only within the country. With massive data breach occurring also daily, and the lack of international law across the globe, compliance requirements puts the burden on the financial institutes to comply with different regulations in different countries. This is very confusing and costly for most organizations and therefore turns to expert organizations whose expertise are in compliance. However organizations that turn to a vendor is still held responsible for any wrongdoing. The vice president of EMC Corporation explained that regulators are making it clear that the organizations are responsible for ensuring the protection of data at all times even if the data is being processed by a service provider (rsa.com, 2010).

Regulations can have positive impacts when they compel organizations to comply with recognized security standards. However, regulators must consider the impacts of broad legislation across the diverse organizations operating in the financial industry. For example regulators must consider the cost organizations incur because companies often pass these costs on to consumers. Regulations often contain complicated language, requiring legal teams to sift through and interpret. However, lawyers do not bear the responsibility for ensuring regulatory compliance. Regulations are not always convenient for organizations because they slow performance and add a hierarchy of processes into already-established organizational procedures. Achieving compliance often proves a difficult challenge because many organizations lack the resources to fully understand and therefore fully comply with complex regulatory frameworks.

CONCLUSION

The financial industry represents a goliath of firms, agencies, and institutions with operations ranging from small community banks to massive international corporations. Managing the financial sector in the U.S. presents a herculean task to lawmakers and regulators charged with its oversight. Information technology, growing from a service enabler into a fundamental pillar of the financial industry, presents a new array of challenges as state and national level officials attempt to cope with cyber-security risks, vulnerabilities, and cyber crime threats. Their efforts have resulted in both carefully constructed and haphazardly fashioned legislation that include the landmark bills, GLBA, SOX, and Dodd-Frank.

Regulations can provide needed checks against careless behavior and necessary countermeasures against fraudulent practices. Compliance adds value, highlighting areas for improvement throughout industry and aiding firms in securing their internal processes. However, regulations also carry the potential to burden the financial industry with duplication of effort and complex reporting schemes that add neither value, nor security. Such measures prove counterproductive when only massive corporations with the resources to retain large legal and regulatory departments can survive in tumultuous regulatory environments. Regulators must approach the financial industry with an even keel, leveraging strong Congressional oversight where necessary, while eliminating unnecessary burdens that stifle financial growth.

REFERENCES

Abrams, R. K., & Taylor, M. W. (2000). *Issues in the Unification of Financial Sector Supervision*. International Money Fund. Retrieved from, http://www.fep.up.pt/disciplinas/pgaf924/PGAF/issues_in_unification_supervision.pdf

Attorneys held exempt from privacy provisions of Gramm-Leach-Bliley Act. (2005). *The Rochester, N.Y Daily Register.*

Banking and Finance Sector-Specific Plan. (2010). *An Annex to the National Infrastructure Protection Plan.* Retrieved from, http://www.dhs.gov/sites/default/files/publications/nipp- ssp-banking-and-finance-2010.pdf

Blauner, C. (2013). *Developing a Framework to Improve Infrastructure Cybersecurity*. Financial Services Sector Coordinating Council. Retrieved from, http://www.fsscc.org/fsscc/news/2013/FSSCC-Response-NIST- CybersecurityFramework.pdf

Bucci, S. P., Rosenzweig, P., & Inserra, D. (2013). A *Congressional Guide: Seven Steps to U.S. Security, Prosperity, and Freedom in Cyberspace*. The Heritage Foundation. Retrieved from, http://www.heritage.org/research/reports/2013/04/a-congressional-guide-seven-steps-to-us-security-prosperity-and-freedom-in-cyberspace

Calder, A. (2013). Can Compliance Shield your Organization from Cyberthreats? *Credit Control, 34*(2), 67.

Compliance: still a board-level issue. (2007). *MarketWatch: Global Round-up*, pp. 176-177.

Davenport, T. (2004). Small banks say Sec. 404 forcing sale. *American Banker, 169*(227), 9–10.

FDIC Law Regulations, Related Acts. (2013). *Uniform Interagency Consumer Compliance Rating System*. FDIC Website. Retrieved from, http://www.fdic.gov/regulations/laws/rules/5000-1700.html

Fischer, E. A. (2013). *Federal Laws Relating to Cybersecurity: Overview and Discussion of Proposed Revisions.* Congressional Research Service. Retrieved from, http://www.fas.org/sgp/crs/natsec/R42114.pdf

Fitzgerald, J. (2012). Coping with the burdens of Dodd-Frank. *Massachusetts Banker, 2012*(4), 17-20.

Gingrich, N., & Kralik, D. W. (2008, November 5). Repeal Sarbanes-Oxley. *The San Francisco Chronicle.* Retrieved from http://www.sfgate.com

Glass, D., Davis, C., Mason, J., Gursky, D., Thomas, J., Carr, W., & Levine, D. (2009). Security audits, standards and inspections. In S. Bosworth, M. E. Kabay, & E. Whyne (Eds.), *Computer security handbook* (5th ed.). New York, NY: John Wiley & Sons.

Greenberg, P. (2012, August 20). *National Conference of State Legislatures.* Retrieved from State Security Breach Notification Laws: http://www.ncsl.org/issues-research/telecom/security-breach-notification-laws.aspx

Groups team up to improve cybersecurity. (2011). *Journal of Business, 26*(3), B7.

Harris, D. (2003). Privacy rule catches dealers off guard. *Automotive News, 77*(6039), 24.

Hedley, T. P., & Ben-Chorin, O. (2011). Auditing and monitoring activities help uncover fraud and assess control effectiveness. *The CPA Journal, 81*(6), 68–71.

Kidder, L. (2012). *Top Challenges Facing Financial Services in 2013.* Bank Systems & Technology. Retrieved from, http://www.banktech.com/management-strategies/top- challenges-facing-financial-services/240144973

Klitch, S. (2012, September 17). Commity banks and the JOBS Act. *Idaho Business Review.*

Larence, E. A. (2007). Critical Infrastructure: Challenges Remain in Protecting Key Sectors: GAO-07-626T. *GAO Reports, 1.*

Leonhardt, D. (2008, September 28). Washington's invisible hand. *New York Times.* Retrieved from http://www.nytimes.com/2008/09/28/magazine/28wwln-reconsider.html?pagewanted=print&_r=1&

Loving, W. A. (2007, December 12). *Sarbanes-Oxley and financial reporting: Statement of William A. Loving, Jr. Chief Executive Officer Pendleton Community Bank.* Committee on House Small Business.

MacSweeney, G. (2012). *10 Financial Services Cyber Security Trends for 2013*. Wall Street & Technology. Retrieved from, http://www.wallstreetandtech.com/data-security/10- financial-services-cyber-security-tre/240143809?pgno=1

Marco, M. (2008, September 17). *Consumerist*. Retrieved from What Types Of Accounts Are FDIC Insured? Are My Investments Safe?: http://consumerist. com/2008/09/17/what-types-of-accounts-are-fdic-insured-are-my-investments-safe/

Myers, C., Foster, S., & Williford, K. (2008). SOX relief for smaller banks. *U.S. Banker, 118*(3), 64.

Naber, J. D. (2008). Community bank audit's changing role. *Connecticut Banking, 2008*(1), 4-15.

Online, C. S. O. (2012). *The security laws, regulations and guidelines directory*. Security Leadership. Retrieved from, http://www.csoonline.com/article/632218/ the-security-laws-regulations-and-guidelines-directory

Out-Law.com. (2013). *Data security breaches mainly involve outsourced IT service providers, according to Trustwave report*. Retrieved from, http://www.out- law. com/en/articles/2013/february/data-security-breaches-mainly-involve-outsourced-it- service-providers-according-to-trustwave-report/

Rotenberg, M. (2011). *President Electronic Privacy Information. Cybersecurity and Data Protection in the Financial Sector. FDCH*. Congressional Testimony.

Rouse, M. (2013, May). *Search Security*. Retrieved from Federal Information Security Management Act (FISMA): http://searchsecurity.techtarget.com/definition/ Federal-Information-Security-Management-Act

Saucer, C. (2009, October 23). Impact of Gramm-Leach-Bliley still debated 10 years later. *BusinessWire*. Retrieved from http://www.reuters.com/article/2009/10/23/ idUS205297+23-Oct-2009+BW20091023

Scarborough, M. (2007). Casey-Landry testifies on Sarbanes-Oxley. *Community Banker, 16*(7), 18.

Snow, G. (2011). *Statement before the House Financial Services Committee Subcommittee on Financial Institutions and Consumer Credit*. Assistant Director, Cyber Division Federal Bureau of Investigation. Retrieved from, http://www.fbi.gov/news/ testimony/cyber-security-threats-to-the-financial-sector

Solnik, C. (2012, May 25). Feds let private banks broaden investor base. *Long Island Business Review*.

Stevens, G. (2012). *Data Security Breach Notification Laws.* Congressional Research Service. Retrieved from, http://www.fas.org/sgp/crs/misc/R42475.pdf

Stults, G. (2004). An overview of Sarbanes-Oxley for the information security professional. *SANS Infosec Reading Room.* Retrieved from http://www.sans.org/reading_room/whitepapers/legal/overview-sarbanes-oxley-information-security-professional_1426

Teslik, L. H. (2008). *The U.S. Financial Regulatory System.* Council on Foreign Relations. Retrieved from, http://www.cfr.org/economic-development/us-financial-regulatory- system/p17417

U.S. Federal Trade Commission. (2002a). *How to comply with the privacy of consumer financial information rule of the Gramm-Leach-Bliley Act.* Retrieved from http://business.ftc.gov/documents/bus67-how-comply-privacy-consumer-financial-information-rule-gramm-leach-bliley-act

U.S. Federal Trade Commission. (2002b) *Federal Trade Commission.* Retrieved from Federal Trade Commission: http://www.ftc.gov/os/2002/05/67fr36585.pdf

U.S. Federal Trade Commission. (2013). *Privacy.* Retrieved from Gramm-Leach-Bliley Act: http://www.ftc.gov/privacy/glbact/glbsub1.htm

U.S. Securities and Exchange Commission. (2011). *CF Disclosure Guidance: Topic No. 2, Cybersecurity.* Retrieved from http://www.sec.gov/divisions/corpfin/guidance/cfguidance-topic2.htm

Virtue, T. (2009). U.S. legal and regulatory security issues. In S. Bosworth, M. E. Kabay, & E. Whyne (Eds.), *Computer security handbook* (5th ed.). New York, NY: John Wiley & Sons.

Yu, A. (2012). Regulatory financial reform: Impact of Dodd-Frank Act on IT compliance. *Rutgers Computer & Technology Law Journal, 38*(2), 254–276. Retrieved from http://ehis.ebscohost.com.ezproxy.umuc.edu

Chapter 6
Prevention of Blackhole Attack using Certificateless Signature (CLS) Scheme in MANET

Vimal Kumar
M. M. M. University of Technology, India

Rakesh Kumar
M. M. M. University of Technology, India

ABSTRACT

One of the generally used routing protocols for MANET is AODV (Ad hoc on demand Distance Vector), which is vulnerable to one of the particular type of security attack called blackhole attack. The characteristics of blackhole attack, a malicious node sends a false route reply without having any fresh route to a destination and is also drop all receiving packets and replay packet in the entire network. A certificateless based signature scheme enables users to generate their public key and private key without using any certificate. Due to this reason, we do not need any certificate authority (CA). In this paper, we propose a novel CLS scheme for prevention of a blackhole attack and also provide secure communication based on CLS scheme. Simulation results show that CLS scheme prevents blackhole attack successfully and is provide better performance to other existing schemes in the presence of blackhole node and also ensuring authentication, integrity and non-repudiation.

DOI: 10.4018/978-1-5225-0741-3.ch006

INTRODUCTION

A wireless mobile ad hoc network (MANET) (Abel, 2011) is a collection of self-configuring nodes deployed in an ad hoc manner. These self-moveable nodes communicate with each other in single hop as well as multi-hop manner without the aid of any centralized administrator or established infrastructure. Because of unrestricted mobility and connectivity to the users, the liability of network management entirely depends on the mobile nodes which form ad hoc network. Multi-hop communication is needed due to a limited transmission range of wireless ad hoc network (Saha, Chaki, & Chaki, 2008). The success of communication highly depends on the cooperation of intermediate nodes. In such networks, each mobile node works as host as well as a router to find an optimal path in different routing approaches of MANETs. MANET is an infrastructure less network. The structure or topology of a MANET changes with time due to nodes mobility. Thus, the vulnerability of a MANET is greater than wired networks due to these salient characteristics such as dynamic topologies, limited physical security, compromised nodes in networks, no centralized management and no infrastructure (Nadeem & Howarth, 2013). Routing (Perkins, Park, & Royer, 1999) in MANET is a challenging task. Two main routing algorithms category are proactive viz., table driven and reactive viz., on-demand routing algorithms. Routes are created on-demand in reactive routing protocols. There are several reactive routing protocols (Abhay et al., 2010) such as Ad-hoc On-demand Distance Vector (AODV), Associativity Based Routing (ABR), Location-Aided Routing (LAR), Dynamic Source Routing (DSR) protocol and Temporally Ordered Routing Algorithm (TORA). Routes are always available in proactive routing. In such protocols, routing tables are updated through periodical message exchange. Examples of such protocols (Djenouri & Khelladi, 2005) are Wireless Routing Protocol (WRP), Destination Sequence Distance Vector (DSDV), Distance Routing Effect Algorithm for Mobility (DREAM) and Fisheye State Routing (FSR).

Security Goals

There are some basic security requirements (Goyal, Batra, & Singh, 2010) for secure message communication as given below:

- **Confidentiality:** It ensures that message content is never seen by unauthorized mobile nodes (Kannhavong et al., 2007).
- **Authentication:** It ensures that data is coming and going to or from a trusted and authorized source and a claimed destination.

- **Integrity:** It ensures that message during transmission is not modified by the unauthorized entity. There may be some cases in which integrity of network may be compromised even if confidentiality and authentication are ensured (Khanna & Dere, 2014).
- **Non-Repudiation:** Non-repudiation prevents a source/receiver from denying that it sent/received a packet.

Security Attacks in MANET

Routing (M. Kumar & Rishi, 2010) in such networks are highly vulnerable due to MANETs inherent characteristics. Attacks on these networks can be passive or active in nature depending on intruder type. Figure 1 shows taxonomy of security attacks in MANET. In the active attack, an attacker can modify as well as discard data packets. On the other hand, in the passive attack, an attacker can monitor the network traffic and can also eavesdrops (L. Li et al., 2011).

Overview of AODV

Ad-hoc On-demand Distance Vector Routing (AODV) (Wu et al., 2007) mainly concentrates on following objectives:

Figure 1. Taxonomy of security attacks in MANET

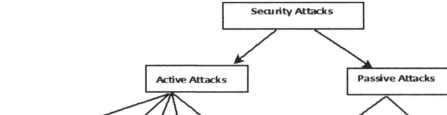

- Route discovery process on demand
- Data forwarding
- Route maintenance

AODV routing protocol does not provide any type of security. AODV is a popular reactive routing protocol for MANET. Routes are created only when a source node wish to transmit data. It initiates route discovery mechanism by sending a route request (RREQ) packet. Upon receiving an RREQ packet, neighbor nodes check routes to the destination node. In case a route to the destination node is not available, it further forwards an RREQ packet to its neighbor nodes. In case a fresh route to a destination node is available on an intermediate node, then the intermediate nodes send an route reply (RREP) packet back to a source node. If an RREQ packet reaches to a destination node, then destination node sends an RREP packet to the originating node with the help of intermediate nodes (Veeraraghavan & Limaye, 2007). AODV routing protocol is vulnerable to various security attacks such as black hole, wormhole, grayhole, flooding, sybil, rushing etc. (Das et al., 2011).

Blackhole Attack

A source node S broadcasts a route request RREQ packet (Das, R., Purkayastha, B. S., & Das, P. 2011) for searching of an optimal path to a destination node D. Then, destination/intermediate node sends multiple route reply (RREP) packets back to the source node and source node follows the route with highest sequence number (Jaisankar, Saravanan, & Swamy, 2010). Figure 2 depicts a blackhole node B which lies between source node S and node 4.

The node B (Lakshmi et al., 2010) advertises that it has a fresh and shortest path to a destination node D, thereby discarding all packets without forwarding to a destination node (Lu et al., 2009). A blackhole node (B) (Luo, 2008; Mistry, 2010) can drop all receiving packets and replay packet in the entire network and also does not compare destination sequence number in RREQ packet to its destination sequence number entry currently in its routing table for a path (Singh & Sharma, 2012; Ullah & Rehman, 2010 ; Zhang, 2009).

Identity-Based Cryptography

ID-based cryptography (Shamir, 1985; Awasthi & Lal, 2007) was introduced by Shamir in 1984 for asymmetric cryptography. The main goal of this technique is to reduce communication costs and enable users to generate their public key without exchanging any certificates. A user can use his IP address, email address or tele-

Figure 2. Blackhole attack in AODV

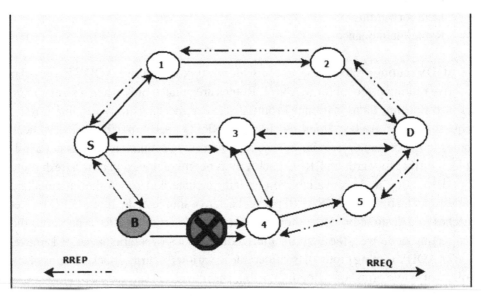

phone number for unique identity. The private key generator is a trusted authority used for generating the private key to correspond unique identity (Deng, 2014; Li, 2011; Kumar & Rakesh, 2015).

Organization of the Chapter

The rest of the chapter is organized as follows. Firstly, related work has been briefly described in Section 2. Section 3 presents our proposed work. Performance evaluation of the proposed scheme has been given in Section 4. Future research directions are discussed in Section 5. Finally, we conclude the chapter in Section 6.

RELATED WORK

Tamilselvan proposed a novel technique to combat blackhole attack using a Fidelity Table (Tamilselvan & Sankaranarayanan, 2008) in a MANET. It introduced new parameter fidelity level, which is assigned to every participating node in the network. If fidelity level of any node drops to zero, it is treated as blackhole node otherwise a legitimate node. The main drawback of proposed technique is that it takes higher end-to-end delay.

Panda proposed a solution to prevent from a malicious node in MANET by key authentication mechanism (Panda, Shankar & Kumar A. S., 2012). It is also carries a routing table for all participating nodes in the network. In this approach, pseudo code is used for key generation and key comparison. The trust values are decided by comparing both key. If the result is zero, it is considered a malicious node. The main drawback of the proposed approach is that it takes higher end-to-end delay due to the key mechanism process.

Zapata proposed a secure AODV routing protocol viz., SAODV (Zapata, 2002). It uses digital signature scheme in various fields namely route request (RREQ) message, route reply (RREP) message and Hash chain. A hash chain is used to authenticate hop count value. An originator of message signs its own private/public key on a communicated message. The main drawback of proposed approach is a key distribution in MANET.

Raj proposed a Detection, Prevention, and Reactive AODV i.e. DPRAODV (Raj, & Swadas, 2009) protocol for the prevention from blackhole attack about the incident by notifying to participating nodes. The proposed approach not only prevents blackhole attack but also improves the overall performance of standard AODV in the presence of black hole node.

Hu proposed a secure On-demand Ad-hoc network routing protocol viz., Ariadne (Hu, Perrig, & Johnson, 2005). It prevents from malicious routes consisting of uncompromised nodes and also from Denial-of-Service attacks. This routing protocol is efficient as it uses symmetric cryptography primitives.

Kurosawa proposed an anomaly detection scheme using dynamic training method in which training data is updated at regular time intervals (Kurosawa et al., 2007). It uses several features such as the number of route request (*RREQ*) messages sent, the number of route reply (*RREP*) messages received and the average difference of destination sequence $Dest_{Seqno}$ number in each time slot between the sequence number of RREP message and one held in the routing table. The simulation results show that proposed scheme is better than existing ones.

PROPOSED WORK

We explain the details of working scenario for prevention of blackhole attack in MANET. Our proposed scheme consists of the following phases:

- Initialization phase
- Signature generation phase
- Communication phase
- Verification phase

Initialization Phase

In the cluster based ad hoc networks, every cluster has only one cluster head (*CH*) and some nodes. The selection criteria of cluster head are not discussed here. We are using *AODV* routing protocol for establishing a path between sender and receiver. The system parameters are given in Table 1.

The steps in the initialization phase are as follows:

1. Cluster head (CH) broadcasts system parameters (*Pub, G1, G2, e, q, H, P*) in the running cluster.
2. Each mobile node sends their identity (*ID*) to the corresponding CH after receiving system parameters.

Table 1. System parameters

Parameter	Description
G_1	Additive cyclic group
G_2	Multiplicative cyclic group
s	CH secret key
H_0	Hash, H:$\{0,1\} \rightarrow Z_{q*}$
P	P is generator of Group (G1)
q	P is generator of Group (G2)
Pub	Public key of cluster head
e	Bilinear pairing e:$\{G_1, G_2\} \rightarrow G_2$
$Dest_{Seqno}$	Destination sequence no. of $Node_i$
n	No. of nodes in running cluster
h	Hash value
$Pr v_i$	Private key of mobile node
Pub_i	Public key of mobile node
π	Signature

3. After receiving *ID* of mobile nodes, *CH* generates their public and private key:
   ○ Generation of public key: $Pub_i = H(ID_i)$ where $1 \leq i \leq n$
   ○ Generation of private key: $\Pr v_i = Pub_i * P / s$.
4. CH sends private key to the corresponding mobile nodes by using a secure channel.

Signature Generation Phase

The steps in signature generation phase are as follows:

Each mobile node select random number $r_i \in Z_{q*}$ and computes $V_{S_i} = g^{r_i}$, **where** $1 \leq i \leq n$.

Mobile node broadcasts Vs_i as a public parameter and r_i kept as secret.

1. CH computes the following values:

$$h_i = H_0(m_i)$$

$$S_i = (r_i + h_i).$$

The combination of $\pi = (S_i + V_{S_i})$ is known as signature on message *m*.

Verification Phase

The steps in signature generation phase are as follows:

CH works as a verifier in working scenario of proposed scheme. Upon receiving signature $\pi = (S_i, V_{S_i}, m_i, h_i)$ on message m_i where, $1 \leq i \leq n$. *CH* checks the correctness of signature on signed RREP.

CH checks the following condition:

$$e(Pub, S_i) = (V_{S_i}, g^{h_i}) \text{ where } 1 \leq i \leq n$$

2. If given condition holds then it is considered as legitimate reply, otherwise, it is considered as a fake signature.

Communication Phase

Communication phase consists of following two sub-phases:

- Secure Intra-Cluster Communication
- Secure Inter-Cluster Communication

Secure Intra-Cluster Communication

There are two cases for node communication in the same cluster, viz., direct communication and communication via cluster head. In direct communication, mobile nodes are the same radio range. So these nodes can be communicated without any help of cluster head. Figure 3 shows the scenario of direct communication. Suppose mobile node M_{n_1} wants to communicate with mobile node M_{n_2}.

The steps in direct communication are as follows:

1. Mn1 broadcasts a route request (RREQ) packet in the entire cluster. Each node has owned private /public key in the running cluster.
2. Source node sends an RREQ without use of signature on an RREQ message
3. The replying node of an RREQ sends the a signed RREP to the source node.

$$M_{n_2} \rightarrow M_{n_1} \{\{RREP\} \Pr v_2\} Pub_s$$

Figure 3. Direct communication

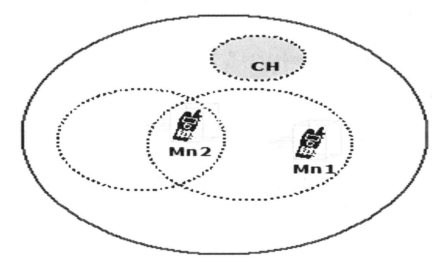

Upon receiving RREP the Intermediate/Destination node. Source node M_{n_1} decrypts signed RREP packet by using an own private key.

After route discovery process, M_{n_1} node sends signed data packet to mobile node M_{n_2}.

4. M_{n_2} decrypts signed data packet by using own private key. In the direct communication, It ensures that integrity, authentication, and non-repudiation due to by using own signature.

The steps in the intra-cluster communication are as follows:

1. The source node S sends a signed an RREQ to associated cluster head for finding routes to a destination in Figure 4.
2. CH initiates a route discovery process by broadcasting an *RREQ* in the running cluster. One of the most important characteristics of *CH* is the only reception of a signed *RREP*. If mobile node sends without signed an *RREP* to *CH*, This type of *RREP* treated as a fake *RREP* and also discards by the cluster head.
3. Upon receiving a *RREQ* from *CH*, a Blackhole node *B* sends back a *RREP* with fake signature because it does not have any credential such as the private/public key. It uses fake private/public key for generating a signature on *RREP*.
4. CH receives fake signed on *RREP*. It checks the correctness of signature on *RREP*.
5. CH generates their public/private key of given *ID* in *RREP* packet.

Public Key: $Pub_{black} = H_0(ID_B)$

Private Key: $\Pr v_{black} = Pub_{black} * P\big/_{S}$.

Secure Inter-Cluster Communication

Suppose source node *S* wants to communicate with destination node *D*. In Figure 5, a source node along with a blackhole node is depicted in cluster C_1 and destination node belongs to cluster C_3.

The steps in the secure inter-cluster communication are as follows:

1. S unicasts an *RREQ* to corresponding cluster head for finding routes to the destination and waiting for a response from cluster head.

Figure 4. Intra-cluster communication

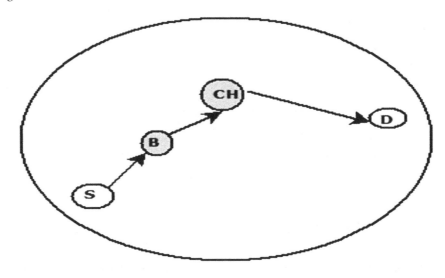

Figure 5. Inter cluster communication

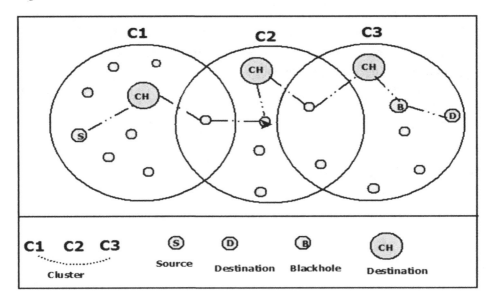

2. Upon receiving an *RREQ* from source node *S*, *CH* broadcasts an *RREQ* in running cluster.

3. A malicious node *B* which is known as blackhole node. It sends back a fake signed route reply (*RREP*) message without having a fresh route to the destination to j.

4.   *CH* checks the correctness of coming route reply from malicious node *B*. It generates public /private key to corresponding *ID* of malicious node *B*.

Security Analysis

Suppose malicious node *B* generates fake signature for disturbing communication between mobile node and *CH*. It generates fake public key (Pub_{fake}) and private key ($\Pr v_{fake}$). Upon receiving a *RREQ* from *CH*, It sends back signed a $(S_i, V_{s_i}, Dest_{Seqno}) + RREP$ to corresponding *CH*.

A *CH* checks the following conditions:

$$e(Pub, S_{fake}) = (V_{S_{fake}}, g^{h_{fake}})$$

$$\text{L.H.S} = e(Pub, S_{fakc})$$

$$= e(sP, (r_{fake} + h_{fake}) \Pr v_{fake})$$

$$= e(sP, (r_{fake} + h_{fake}) Pub_{black}{}^{P_{fake}}\!/_{S_{fake}})$$

$$= e(sP, (^{P_{fake}}\!/_{S_{fake}})(r_{fake} + h_{fake}) Pub_{black})$$

$$= e(P, P_{fake}(r_{fake} + h_{fake}) Pub_{black})$$

$$e(Pub, S_{fake}) \neq (V_{S_{fake}}, g^{h_{fake}})$$

hence, *L.H.S.* $\neq$ *R.H.S.*

   If given condition holds then it is considered as legitimate reply. In case of given condition is not hold then it is considered as fake reply by the blackhole node. The Notation used in proposed algorithm is given in Table 2.

   Algorithm I for the prevention of blackhole attack is as follows:

Table 2. Notations

S N	Source Node
C	Cluster
Des_{reply_node}	Destination sequence number of replying node
Des_{RREQ}	Destination sequence number of send RREQ
S_{CH}	Signature of Cluster head

Algorithm I: Prevention of Blackhole Attack

Step 1: all participating nodes in cluster follow all steps of initialization phase.

Step 2: $SN(RREQ)==> C$

Step 3: for each route reply ⌊i⌋do

if ($Des_{reply\_node} > Des_{RREQ}$) then *reply_node (signed RREP)* ==> *CH*

Step 4: *CH* uses the verification phase:

if ($e(Pub, S_i) = (V_{S_i}, g^{h_i})$) /* where $1 \leq i \leq n$ */

It is considered as legitimate route reply

else

It is considered as a malicious reply

if (route reply is legitimate)

CH sends (a signed *RREP*)==> *SN*

Step 5: A signed route reply (*RREP*) is the combination of (S_{CH} , *RREP*).

Step 6: *SN* decrypts a signed *RREP*

Step 7: *SN* uses this route for secure communication in mobile ad hoc network.

PERFORMANCE EVALUATION

We apply CLS scheme to prevent blackhole attack, which is simulated under network simulator (*ns2*). We have used standard *AODV* with certain modifications as a routing protocol. Table 3 shows simulation parameters used during simulation.

Table 3. Simulation parameters

Parameter	Value
Simulator	ns-2
Simulation area	500 X 500
Number of nodes	10 to 80
Simulation Time	600 s
Routing protocols	AODV, SAODV
Maximum speed Traffic agent	15 m/s
Pause time	6 s
Node speed	2-9 m/s
Packet Size	512 bytes
Transmission range	250 m
Mobility Model	Random waypoint model
No. of malicious node (blackhole node)	1

Performance Metrics

The metrics that have been used to evaluate performance of proposed certificate-less signature scheme are given as under.

- **Packet Delivery Ratio (PDR):** It is the ratio of a total number of data packets being sent by a source and a total number of data packets that were successfully received at the destination.
- **End-to-End Delay:** It is the average time taken by a data packet that is successfully delivered to the destination end.
- **Throughput:** It is the ratio between successfully transferred packets to a destination on the simulation time.

Simulation Results

Figure 6 shows that comparison graph between standard *AODV* in the presence of blackhole node, *SAODV* and proposed scheme using packet delivery ratio (*PDR*) as a performance metric. The simulation result shows that proposed scheme is having *95.11%* while *AODV* with blackhole attack and *SAODV* having *41.20%* and *91.72%* for average packet delivery ratio (*PDR*). The simulation result shows that proposed CLS scheme is better than other two schemes.

Figure 6. Packet delivery ratio (PDR)

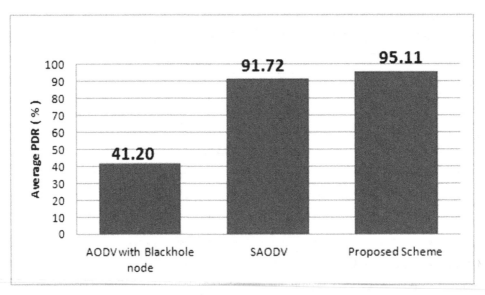

Figure 7 depicts the comparison graph for above three schemes on average end-to-end delay. Standard AODV in the presence of blackhole node takes 171.46 ms, SAODV takes 102.46 ms while the proposed scheme takes only 92.67 ms on end-to-end delay. Hence proposed *CLS* scheme perform better than other existing schemes such as *AODV* and *SAODV*.

Figure 7. Average end-to-end delay

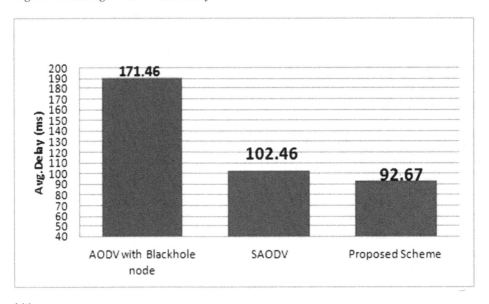

The outcome of simulation is calculated for throughput for other existing schemes in Figure 8. Standard *AODV* in the presence of blackhole node has *12.42 Kbps*, *SAODV* has *81.23 Kbps* while proposed scheme has *85.77 Kbps* for throughput parameter.

Comparison of Security Goals

Blackhole attack has proven to be fatal for many security measures. Several researches have been done in this field. Table 4 shows a comparison between proposed and other existing schemes.

FUTURE RESEARCH DIRECTIONS

In future, we shall extend certificateless signature scheme (*CLS*) to other routing protocol such as dynamic source routing (*DSR*) and also apply this scheme in some important applications such as electronic commerce, secure email system and secure message exchange between sender and receiver.

Figure 8. Average throughput

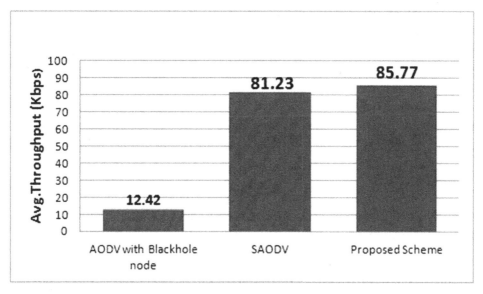

Table 4. Comparison of security features with proposed and other existing schemes

S.N.	Parameters	Protocols	AODV	SAODV	Proposed Scheme
1.	Authentication		NO	YES	YES
2.	Secrecy		NO	NO	YES
3.	Data Integrity		NO	YES	YES
4.	Non-repudiation		NO	YES	YES
5.	Forward Secrecy		NO	NO	YES
6.	Backward Secrecy		NO	NO	YES
7.	Group Key Secrecy		NO	NO	YES

CONCLUSION

Standard ad hoc on demand routing protocol is vulnerable to blackhole attack. Due to this attack, performance of the protocol degrades in terms of packet delivery ratio (*PDR*), end-to-end delay and throughput. In this paper, we have proposed a novel approach for prevention of a blackhole attack and also provided secure communication based on certificate-less signature scheme. From the simulation results, our scheme gives *95.11%* packet delivery ratio while *AODV* with blackhole attack and *SAODV* show *41.20%* and *91.72%* respectively on packet delivery ratio. Standard *AODV* in the presence of blackhole node takes 171.46 ms, *SAODV* takes 102.46 ms while the proposed scheme takes only 92.67 ms on end-to-end delay. Standard *AODV* in the presence of blackhole node gives *12.42 Kbps*, *SAODV* gives *81.23 Kbps* while proposed scheme gives *85.77 Kbps* on throughput . Hence,we conclude that proposed scheme prevents blackhole attack successfully based on identity based signature scheme and is more efficient in terms of these metrics. It also ensures authentication, integrity, and non-repudiation.

REFERENCES

Abel, V. S. (2011). Survey of Attacks on Mobile Adhoc Wireless Networks. *International Journal on Computer Science and Engineering*, *3*(2), 826–829.

Abhay Kumar Rai Saurabh Kant Upadhyay, R. R. T., Rai, A. K., Tewari, R. R., & Upadhyay, S. K. (2010). Different Types of Attacks on Integrated MANET-Internet Communication. *International Journal of Computer Science and Security*, *4*(3), 265–274.

Awasthi, A. K., & Lal, S. (2007). ID-based ring signature and proxy ring signature schemes from bilinear pairings. *International Journal of Network Security*, *4*(2), 187–192.

Das, R., Purkayastha, B. S., & Das, P. (2011). Security Measures for Black Hole Attack in MANET. *An Approach*, *3*(4), 2832–2838.

Deng, L., Zeng, J., & Qu, Y. (2014). *Certificateless Proxy Signature from RSA, 2014*. Academic Press.

Djenouri, D., & Khelladi, L. (2005). A survey of security issues in mobile ad hoc networks. *IEEE Communications Surveys*. Retrieved from http://www.lsi-usthb.dz/Rapports_pdf/2004/LSIIR-TR0504.pdf

Goyal, P., Batra, S., & Singh, A. (2010). A Literature Review of Security Attack in Mobile Ad-hoc Networks. *International Journal of Computers and Applications*, *9*(12), 11–15. doi:10.5120/1439-1947

Goyal, P., Parmar, V., & Rishi, R. (2011). MANET: Vulnerabilities, Challenges, Attacks, Application. *IJCEM International Journal of Computational Engineering & Management*, *11*(January), 32–37.

Himral, L., Vig, V., & Chand, N. (2011). Preventing AODV Routing Protocol from Black Hole Attack. *International Journal of Engineering Science and Technology*, *3*(5), 3927–3932. doi:10.13140/2.1.2220.3206

Hu, Y.-C., Perrig, A., & Johnson, D. B. (2005). Ariadne: A Secure On-Demand Routing Protocol for Ad Hoc Networks. *Wireless Networks*, *11*(1-2), 21–38. doi:10.1007/s11276-004-4744-y

Jaisankar, N., Saravanan, R., & Swamy, K. D. (2010). A novel security approach for detecting black hole attack in MANET. *Communications in Computer and Information Science*, *70*, 217–223. doi:10.1007/978-3-642-12214-9_36

Kannhavong, B., Nakayama, H., Nemoto, Y., Kato, N., & Jamalipour, A. (2007). A survey of routing attacks in mobile ad hoc networks. *IEEE Wireless Communications*, *14*(5), 85–91. doi:10.1109/MWC.2007.4396947

Khanna, A., & Dere, P. U. (2014). *A Review on Intrusion Detection and Security of Wormhole Attacks in MANET*. Academic Press.

Kumar, M., & Rishi, R. (2010). Security Aspects in Mobile Ad Hoc Network (MANETs): Technical Review. *International Journal of Computers and Applications*, *12*(2), 37–43. doi:10.5120/1304-1642

Kumar, V., & Kumar, R. (2015). An Optimal Authentication Protocol Using Certificateless ID-Based Signature in MANET. Security in Computing and Communications Volume 536 of the series. *Communications in Computer and Information Science*, *536*, 110–121. doi:10.1007/978-3-319-22915-7_11

Kurosawa, S., Nakayama, H., Kato, N., Jamalipour, A., & Nemoto, Y. (2007). Detecting blackhole attack on AODV-based mobile Ad Hoc networks by dynamic learning method. *International Journal of Network Security*, *5*(3), 338–346.

Lakshmi, K., & Manju Priya, S., Jeevarathinam, A., Rama, K., & Thilagam, K. (2010). Modified AODV protocol against blackhole attacks in MANET. *IACSIT International Journal of Engineering and Technology*, *2*(6), 444–449.

Li, L., Wang, Z., Liu, W., & Wang, Y. (2011). A Certificateless Key Management Scheme in Mobile Ad Hoc Networks. *2011 7th International Conference on Wireless Communications, Networking and Mobile Computing.* http://doi.org/ doi:<ALIGNMENT.qj></ALIGNMENT>10.1109/wicom.2011.6040439

Li, W., & Joshi, A. (2008). *Security Issues In Mobile Ad Hoc Networks-A Survey.* http:// doi.org/<ALIGNMENT.qj></ALIGNMENT>10.1007/978-3-642-36169-2_2

Lu, S., Li, L., Lam, K. Y., & Jia, L. (2009). SAODV: A MANET routing protocol that can withstand black hole attack. *CIS 2009 - 2009 International Conference on Computational Intelligence and Security.* http://doi.org/ doi:<ALIGNMENT.qj></ ALIGNMENT>10.1109/CIS.2009.244

Luo, J., Fan, M., & Ye, D. (2008). Black hole attack prevention based on authentication mechanism. *2008 11th IEEE Singapore International Conference on Communication Systems, ICCS 2008*, (pp. 173–177). http://doi.org/ doi:<ALIGNMENT. qj></ALIGNMENT>10.1109/ICCS.2008.4737166

Mistry, N., Jinwala, D. C., & Zaveri, M. (2010). Improving AODV Protocol against Blackhole Attacks. *International Multiconference of Engineers and Computer Scientists (Imecs 2010).*

Nadeem, A., & Howarth, M. P. (2013). A survey of manet intrusion detection & prevention approaches for network layer attacks. *IEEE Communications Surveys and Tutorials*, *15*(4), 2027–2045. doi:10.1109/SURV.2013.030713.00201

Panda G., Shankar G. M. & Kumar A. S. (2012). *Prevention of Black hole Attack in AODV protocols for Mobile Ad Hoc Network by Key Authentication.* Academic Press.

Perkins, C. E., Park, M., & Royer, E. M. (1999). Ad-hoc On-Demand Distance Vector Routing. In *Proceedings of Second IEEE Workshop on Mobile Computing Systems and Applications (WMCSA)*. http://doi.org/ doi:10.1109/MCSA.1999.749281

Raj, P. N., & Swadas, P. B. (2009). *DPRAODV: A Dynamic Learning System Against Blackhole Attack In AODV Based MANET*. Retrieved from http://cogprints.org/6697/

Saha, S., Chaki, R., & Chaki, N. (2008). A New Reactive Secure Routing Protocol for Mobile Ad-Hoc Networks. *2008 7th Computer Information Systems and Industrial Management Applications*, (pp. 103–108). http://doi.org/<ALIGNMENT.qj></ALIGNMENT>10.1109/CISIM.2008.13

Shamir, A. (1985). *Identity-Based Cryptosystems and Signature Schemes*. Academic Press.

Singh, P. K., & Sharma, G. (2012). An efficient prevention of black hole problem in AODV routing protocol in MANET. *Proc. of the 11th IEEE Int. Conference on Trust, Security and Privacy in Computing and Communications, TrustCom-2012 - 11th IEEE Int. Conference on Ubiquitous Computing and Communications, IUCC-2012*, (pp. 902–906). http://doi.org/ doi:10.1109/TrustCom.2012.78

Tamilselvan, L., & Sankaranarayanan, V. (2008). Prevention of co-operative black hole attack in MANET. *Journal of Networks*, *3*(5), 13–20. doi:10.4304/jnw.3.5.13-20

Tseng, F.-H., Chou, L.-D., & Chao, H.-C. (2011a). A survey of black hole attacks in wireless mobile ad hoc networks. *Human-Centric Computing and Information Sciences*, *1*(1), 4. doi:10.1186/2192-1962-1-4

Ullah, I., & Rehman, S. (2010). *Analysis of Black Hole attack on MANETs Using different MANET routing protocols*. School of Computing Blekinge Institute of Technology; doi:10.1109/ICUFN.2012.6261716

Veeraraghavan, P., & Limaye, V. (2007). Security Threats in Mobile Ad Hoc Networks. *2007 IEEE International Conference on Telecommunications and Malaysia International Conference on Communications*. Retrieved from http://eprints.whiterose.ac.uk/46064/

Wu, B., Chen, J., Wu, J., & Cardei, M. (2007). A Survey on Attacks and Countermeasures in Mobile Ad hoc Networks. *Wireless/Mobile. Network Security*, 103–135. doi:10.1007/978-0-387-33112-6_5

Zapata, M. G. (2002). Secure ad hoc on-demand distance vector routing. *Mobile Computing and Communications Review*, *6*(3), 106. doi:10.1145/581291.581312

Zhang, X., Sekiya, Y., & Wakahara, Y. (2009). Proposal of a method to detect black hole attack in MANET. *2009 International Symposium on Autonomous Decentralized Systems, ISADS 2009*, (pp. 149–154). http://doi.org/ doi:10.1109/ISADS.2009.5207339

KEY TERMS AND DEFINITIONS

AODV: Stands for "Ad-hoc On-demand Distance Vector Routing". It is a popular reactive routing protocol for MANET. Routes are created only when a source node wish to transmit data.

Authentication: It ensures that data is coming and going to or from a trusted and authorized source and a claimed destination.

Blackhole Attack: In blackhole attack, a malicious node advertises that it has a fresh and shortest path to the destination, thereby discarding all packets without forwarding to a destination.

Confidentiality: It ensures that message content is never seen by unauthorized mobile nodes.

ID-Based Cryptography: It is a type of public-key cryptography in which. The main goal of this technique is to reduce communication costs and enable users to generate their public key without exchanging any certificates.

Integrity: It ensures that message during transmission is not modified by the unauthorized entity.

Non-Repudiation: Non-repudiation prevents a source/receiver from denying that it sent/received a packet.

MANET: A mobile ad hoc network (MANET) is a collection of self-configuring nodes deployed in an ad hoc manner. These self-moveable nodes communicate with each other in single hop as well as multi-hop manner without the aid of any centralized administrator or established infrastructure.

Chapter 7
Trust Management in Cloud Computing

Vijay L. Hallappanavar
KLE College of Engineering and Technology, India

Mahantesh N. Birje
Visvesvaraya Technological University, India

ABSTRACT

Cloud computing is a model for enabling everywhere, suitable, on-demand network access. There are a number of challenges to provide cloud computing services and to accomplish this, it is necessary to establish trust across the cloud, between the user and the service provider. It is becoming increasingly complex for cloud users to make distinction among service providers offering similar kinds of services. There must be some mechanisms in the hands of users to determine trustworthiness of service providers so that they can select service providers with confidence and with some degree of assurance that service provider will not behave unpredictably or maliciously. An effective trust management system helps cloud service providers and consumers reap the benefits brought about by cloud computing technologies. Hence the objective of this chapter is to describe existing mechanisms that are used to determine a trust worthiness of a cloud service, various models that are used for calculating a trust value and method to establish trust management system.

INTRODUCTION

Cloud computing is a model for enabling ever-present, suitable, on-demand network access to a shared pool of configurable computing resources, e.g., networks, servers, storage, applications and services that can be rapidly provisioned and made available

DOI: 10.4018/978-1-5225-0741-3.ch007

easily with minimal management effort or service provider interaction described by Siani (2012). Cloud environments provide several benefits such as reduced expenses and simplicity to service providers and service requesters. The cloud computing provides hardware and systems software resources on remote datacenters, as well as Internet gives access to the services based upon these resources. These resources dynamically scale up to match the load, using a pay-per resources business model. The significant features of cloud computing are elasticity, multitenancy, maximal resource utilization and pay-per-use. Figure 1 shows an abstracted view of the cloud computing environment with the interacting parties.

Virtualization or job scheduling techniques unifies the shared pool of resources. A host computer runs an application known as a hypervisor which creates one or more virtual machines, which simulate physical computers so faithfully, that the simulations can run any software, from operating systems, to end-user applications, Siani Pearson (2012). At hardware level processors, hard drives and network devices, are located in datacenters, independent from geographical location, which are accountable for storage and processing needs. Above this, the combination of software layers, the virtualization layer and the management layer, allow for the effective management of servers. Virtualization is an important element of cloud implementations and is used to provide the essential cloud characteristics of loca-

Figure 1.

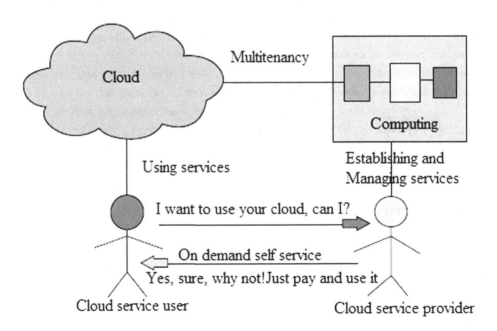

tion independence, resource pooling and rapid elasticity. Differing from traditional network topologies, such as client–server, cloud computing can offer robustness and alleviate traffic congestion issues. The management layer can monitor traffic and respond to peaks or drops with the creation of new servers or the destruction of unnecessary ones. The management layer has the additional ability to be able to implement security monitoring and rules throughout the cloud. Figure 2 shows the basic diagram of this layout.

Cloud can worsen the damage on traditional frameworks for privacy that global-ization has already started. For example, location of the data is critical from a legal point of view. But in the cloud, information might be in multiple places, might be managed by different entities and it may be difficult to know the geographic location and which specific servers or storage devices are being used. It is currently difficult to discover and meet compliance requirements, as existing global legislation is complex and includes export restrictions, data retention restrictions, sector- specific restrictions and legislation at state and/or national levels. Legal advice is required, transborder data flow restrictions need to be taken into account, and care must be taken to delete data and virtual storage devices when appropriate.

High security is one of the major obstacles for the adoption of computing as a utility as the sensitive applications and data are moved into the cloud data centers. This unique attributes, however, poses many novel tangible and intangible security challenges such as accessibility vulnerabilities, virtualization vulnerabilities, and web application vulnerabilities. These challenges relate to cloud server having physical control of data, relate to identity and credential management, relate to data verifi-cation, tempering, integrity, confidentiality, data loss and theft. To protect private and sensitive data that are processed in data centers, the cloud user needs to verify:

Figure 2.

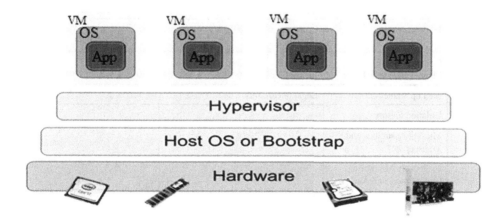

1. The real exists of the cloud computing environment in the world;
2. The security of information in the cloud; and
3. The trustworthiness of the systems in cloud computing environment.

There are many issues related to privacy, security and trust. The Table 1 lists those issues.

TRUST MANAGEMENT

Trust plays a vital role in our social life. Trust between people can be seen as a key component to facilitate coordination and cooperation for mutual benefit as shown in Figure 3. Social trust is the product of past experiences and perceived trustworthiness. Based on our feelings in response to changing circumstances, we constantly modify and upgrade our trust in other people. Trust is formed and supported by a legal framework, especially in business environments or when financial issues are involved. The framework ensures that misbehavior can be punished with legal actions and increases the incentive to initiate a trust relationship. The legal framework decreases the risk of misbehavior and secures the financial transactions.

Table 1. Issues related to privacy

SL. NO	SECURITY	PRIVACY	TRUST
1.	Gap in Security	Lack of User Control	Lack of consumer trust
2.	Unwanted Access	Lack of Training and Expertise	Weak Trust Relationships
3.	Vendor Lock-In	Unauthorized Secondary Usage	Lack of Consensus about Trust Management Approaches to be used
4.	Inadequate Data Deletion	Complexity of Regulatory Compliance	
5.	Compromise of Management Interface	Addressing Transborder Data Flow Restrictions	
6.	Backup Vulnerabilities	Legal uncertainty	
7.	Isolation Failure		
8.	Missing Assurance and Transparency		
9.	Inadequate Monitoring, Compliance, and Audit		

Figure 3.

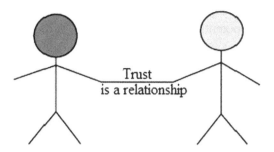

With the rapid growth of global digital computing and networking technologies, trust becomes an important feature in the design and analysis of secure distributed systems and electronic commerce. However, the existing legal frameworks are often focused on local legislation and are hard to enforce on a global level. The most popular examples are email spam, software piracy and a breach of warranty. Particularly, because legal regulation and control cannot keep pace with the development of electronic commerce, the extant laws in conventional commerce might not be strictly enforceable in electronic commerce. In addition, resorting to legal enforcement in electronic commerce might be impracticably expensive or even impossible, such as in the case of payment transactions.

This increases the importance of trust between interacting digital entities. People do not believe that the legal framework is able to provide the needed trustworthiness for their digital relationships. It has been a critical part of the process by which trust relationships are required to develop in a digital system. In particular, for some emerging technologies, such as MANET (Mobile Ad Hoc Networks), P2P (Peer-to-Peer) computing, and GRID virtual systems, trust management has been proposed as a useful solution to break through new challenges of security and privacy caused by the special characteristics of these systems, such as dynamic topology and mobility.

Establishing a trust relationship in digital networking environment involves more aspects than in the social world. This is because communications in the computing network rely on not only relevant human beings and their relationships, but also digital components. On the other hand, the visual trust impression is missing and need somehow to be compensated. Moreover, it is more difficult to accumulate accurate information for trust purposes in remote digital communications where information can be easily distorted or fake identities can be created. The mapping of our social understanding of trust into the digital world and the creation of trust models that are feasible in practice are challenging. Trust is a special issue beyond and will enhance a system security and personal privacy. Understanding the trust relationship between two digital entities could help selecting and applying feasible measures to overcome potential security and privacy risk.

DEFINITION OF TRUST

The trust can be defined as an entity A is considered to trust another entity B, when entity A believes that entity B will behave exactly as expected and required. Thereinafter, an entity can be considered trustworthy, if the parties or people involved in transactions with that entity rely on its credibility. The notion of trust in an organization could be defined as the customer's certainty that the organization is capable of providing the required services accurately and infallibly.

A certainty which also expresses the customer's faith in its moral integrity, in the soundness of its operation, in the effectiveness of its security mechanisms, in its expertise and in its abidance by all regulations and laws, while at the same time, it also contains the acknowledgement of a minimum risk factor, by the relying party. The notion of security refers to a given situation where all possible risks are either eliminated or brought to an absolute minimum given by Zissis (2012).

Trust management is considered as one of the key challenges in the adoption of cloud computing with the accelerated growth of acceptance of cloud computing. Trust management and security are ranked among the top 10 obstacles for adopting cloud computing given by Armbrust (2009). This is because of challenging issues such as privacy, security and dependability described by Cavoukian (2009). In addition, the highly vibrant, distributed and non transparent nature of cloud services makes trust management even more challenging. An effective trust management system helps cloud service providers and consumers reap the benefits provided by cloud computing technologies. With the given benefits of trust management, numerous issues related to general trust assessment mechanisms, distrusted feedback, poor identification of feedback, privacy of participants and the lack of feedback integration need to be addressed. Traditional trust management approaches such as the use of Service-Level Agreement (SLA) are inadequate for complex cloud environments. The vague clauses and unclear technical specifications of SLAs can lead cloud service consumers to be unable to identify trustworthy cloud services. Hence different types of trust management techniques and models are designed in order to make use of the benefits of cloud computing.

Trust management is an effective approach to assess and establish trusted relationships. It is originally developed to overcome the issues of centralized security systems, such as centralized control of trust relationships (i.e., global certifying authorities), inflexibility to support complex trust relationships in large-scale networks and the heterogeneity of policy languages. Policy languages in trust management are responsible for setting authorization roles and implementing security policies. Authorization roles are satisfied through a set of security policies, which themselves are satisfied through a set of credentials. The Figure 4 gives the relation between different cloud entities and need of trust for a cloud service provider to attract the cloud users. The cloud broker and cloud auditor are the interfaces between user and provider.

IMPORTANCE OF TRUST MANAGEMENT

Cloud Computing has a lot of research focus in recent years and it provides a virtual framework for sharing of resources. In such a distributed environment, an entity has the advantage of using collection of resources. The idea of virtual framework is not appealing to some entities because of the risk of being associated with the notion of sharing resources or services. Hence such entities prefer to use their own closed box resources for the reason of the sensitivity and the vitality of data or information. This is not just costly for the individual entities but also an inefficient way

Figure 4.

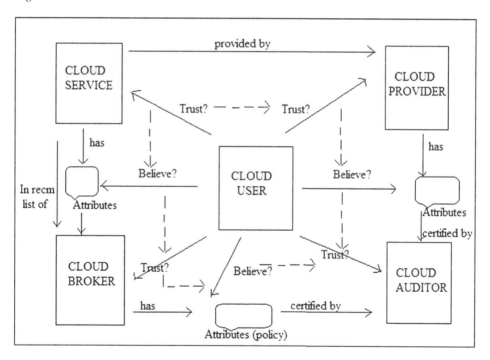

to utilize resources. To use cloud computing more effectively, trust issues must be addressed and trustworthy domains must exist where an entity can use resources or deploy services safely. In such a scenario the user/consumer and the resource provider does not have complete control over each other. The user/consumer expects good Quality of Service from a trustworthy service provider. The service provider expects the cloud resources to be protected and it allow the cloud resources to be utilized by a trustworthy consumer. To accomplish this it is necessary to establish trust across the cloud, between the user and the service provider as explained by Manuel (2008) shown in Figure 5 below.

An important goal of trust management in cloud resources is to establish faith and confidence on resource providers in the internet based distributed environments. Trust is a complex subject involving an entity's belief in honesty, competence, trustfulness and reliability of another entity. In most of the existing distributed heterogeneous networks, trust between a consumer and a service provider is established based on identity and reputation. This identity-based trust model is concerned with verifying the authenticity and authorization of an entity. This however does not ensure consistency, promptness of service and Quality of Service, resulting in loss to the consumers. This difficulty is overcome in reputation-based trust management. Reputation of an entity is a measure derived from direct or indirect knowledge of the entity's earlier transactions. In this model, a certification process verifies the consistency of services offered by a service provider. The consumers who have had transactions with the service providers provide feedback on various aspects of the services provided by the service providers. The feedback received for a service provider from various consumers is aggregated over a period of time. This forms the reputation of the specific service provider and the consumer first confirms the behavior of the service provider as being trustworthy or not, before proceeding to use the service provider. This ensures Quality of Service for the consumer. This scheme is very suitable in a cloud environment where entities are distributed geographically.

Figure 5.

The companies like e-bay, Amazon have implemented the reputation based trust management system for e-transactions and it helps them to improve the quality of service based on the user's feedback value. The effectiveness of a reputation based trust management system depends on the trust model behind the system.

TRUST MANAGEMENT CHARACTERISITICS IN CLOUD

The characteristics of trust management defined by Noor (2013) which allow the cloud users to adopt cloud are authentication, security, privacy responsibility, virtualization, cloud consumer accessibility.

- **Authentication**: This characteristic refers to the techniques and mechanisms that are used for authentication in a particular cloud. Cloud consumers have to establish their identities every time they attempt to use a new cloud service by registering their credentials, which contain sensitive information. This can lead to privacy breaches if no proper identity scheme is applied for the cloud service consumers.
- **Security**: There are three security levels in a particular cloud: the Communication Security Level (CSL), the Data Security Level (DSL), and the Physical Security Level (PSL). CSL refers to communication techniques such as Secure Socket Layer (SSL), etc. DSL refers to data replication techniques for data recovery. Finally, PSL refers to physical security techniques such as hardware security.
- **Privacy Responsibility**: The privacy responsibility can be categorized into two different privacy responsibility categories: the cloud service provider privacy responsibility category and the cloud service consumer privacy responsibility category.
- **Virtualization**: This characteristic refers to techniques that are used for virtualization. There are two virtualization levels in a particular cloud: the Operating System level and the application container level. Virtualization techniques allow the cloud service provider to control and manage the underlying cloud environment, whereas the cloud service consumers have control on their virtual machines which include the storage, the process, and even the selection of some network components for communication.
- **Cloud Consumer Accessibility**: This characteristic refers to techniques and mechanisms that are used for cloud service consumers to access cloud services such as Graphical User Interfaces, Application Programming Interfaces, command-line tools, etc.

TASKS OF A TRUST MANAGEMENT SYSTEM

This section describes the three tasks of trust management system. It begins with the initialization of trust relationships, and then identifies different means to observe the trustee's behavior during the actions. Finally, actions to take based on the new experience are discussed as described by M´armol (2011). The Figure 6 shows all the three tasks.

Initializing a Trust Relationship

Sometimes partners can be selected with traditional out-of-band means like word of mouth, but in a highly dynamic and possibly automated environment a discovery service of some sort is necessary. The lack of background information even if the recommending party is known to be honest and knowledgeable, their statements may be useless if the principles are not known by the same name by the recommender and the receiver, or if the principles behind the recommendations are not comparable to those of the receiver.

Recommendations remain an attempt at communicating reputation information between communities. There are three requirements for a successful reputation system:

Figure 6.

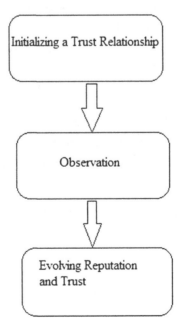

- The entities must be long-lived and have use for reputation.
- Feedback must be captured, distributed and made available in the future.
- The feedback must be used to guide trust decisions.

The first property implies some problems that newcomers have with reputation systems. Besides having the problem of finding a trustworthy information provider, they must gain a reputation themselves. The usability of reputation information from outside sources is not limited to choosing a partner. It can also be considered as a factor in the trust estimate of a partner, along with their locally gathered reputation based on first-hand experience. Initially, as there is no local information about the partner's behavior, external reputation information may hold considerable weight in a trust decision. Besides reputation systems, various kinds of authentication and credential systems may help determine an initial level of trust through e.g. membership in a group with a good reputation. The Web Services standard WS-Trust approaches authorization and authentication via security tokens requested from on-line servers. A hybrid public key infrastructure model is proposed to ease the delegation of trust, in the sense of allowing third parties to produce credentials usable for authorization trust management in the target system.

A trust management system also tends to have some sort of a default value to assign to complete strangers. This value represents the system's general tendency to trust, or its trust propensity. This default may be raised or lowered based on a general view of the world the system operates in. If the average partner seems to be a somewhat unreliable opportunist, the trust propensity may be reduced. On the other hand, if the system operates in an environment of honest cooperation, the trust propensity may be increased. As the initial trust value is even at best based on the experiences of others with the partner, it may prove to be a poor estimate. Observing the partner's actions and updating their local reputation based on the observation strengthens the system against misplaced expectations.

Observation

Observation can be done in two different roles:

1.   Either as an active participant of collaboration or
2.   As an outsider, a silent third party.

In the first case, the actions of the observed are seen through a personal context, which gives more depth to the analysis. The principles and research in the field of intrusion detection can be put to use in observing users or partners in a trust management system. The traditional approach to intrusion detection looks at system calls or network traffic, while application-level intrusion detection adds "insider" understanding to the analysis by being aware of the particular applications observed.

We can divide intrusion detection into two main approaches. Anomaly detection attempts to model normal behavior, often by learning from experience gained during an observation period and considers abnormalities potential signs of an attack. The second approach, misuse detection, constructs models to match the attacks instead. While such specifications are less likely to yield false positives than detecting previously unseen behavior in general, keeping them up to date is problematic—only known attacks can be detected.

Specification-based anomaly detection shows some promise, but building specifications of normal behavior may not be feasible for all applications. It has been applied to network protocols, and could maybe find a place in the field of Web Services. On the other hand, misuse intrusion detection would also miss some attacks due to not knowing them beforehand. The idea of preventing policy-breaking or otherwise suspicious activity is not new. Access control lists have for long prevented users without specific identity tied privileges from accessing certain files or services, and policy languages can be used to further limit access according to other constraints. They can also be used to lower the resources allocated for a slightly risky task which is not considered to be in direct conflict with policy, and as mentioned earlier, the task can be allowed to proceed normally, but under tighter observation as with trust decisions. Similar adjustments could be based on trust instead of more static, pre-set constraints. Besides detecting suspicious activity, an observation system could be used as a witness of "normal" behavior. Good experiences lead to better or at least more "certain" reputation in many reputation systems where the users themselves act as witnesses. On the other hand, if a reputation estimate includes a measure of confidence, i.e. how certain the estimate is, a lengthy period of observation showing behavior in agreement with the current reputation may be taken as increased confidence in the reputation estimate.

Evolving Reputation and Trust

The evolution of reputation stands at the heart of a trust management system. Translating experience into updates in reputation seems to largely be work in progress. As the user's reputation is updated based on their actions, information about the changes can be sent as recommendations to reputation systems spanning larger communities, such as those used by the local reputation system to estimate the initial reputation of newcomers. The information can then be used to adjust the user's reputation in the target community as well. This requires that the recommendation includes a representation of the user's identity that is recognized in both communities. It is noteworthy that the reputation changes communicated across systems are not an objective truth by our definition, and the updates involve agreements on how the information is dealt with.

TRUST MANAGEMENT TECHNIQUES

Establishing trust is one of the most challenging issues in emerging cloud computing area. It is becoming increasingly complex for cloud users to make distinction (with respect to trustworthiness) among service providers offering similar kinds of services. There must be some mechanisms in the hands of users to determine trustworthiness of service providers so that they can select service providers with confidence and with some degree of assurance that service provider will not behave unpredictably or maliciously. There are different types of trust management techniques to support the consumers in selecting trustworthy CPs as listed in Figure 7:

- **SLAs:** In practice, one way to establish trust on CPs is the fulfillment of SLAs. A service level agreement (SLA) is a legal contract between a cloud user and a cloud service provider as shown in Figure 8. SLA validation and monitoring schemes are used to quantify what exactly a CP is offering and which assurances are actually met. In Cloud computing environments, customers are responsible for monitoring SLA violations and informing the providers for compensation. The compensation clauses in SLAs are written by the CPs in such a way so that the customers merely get the advantage of applying for compensation (e.g., service credits) due to SLA violation. This problem arises for not having standardized SLAs for the stakeholders in Cloud computing marketplace. Although, the problem is addressed by industry driven initiative for establishing standardized SLAs, this initiative is far from implementation in practice.

Figure 7.

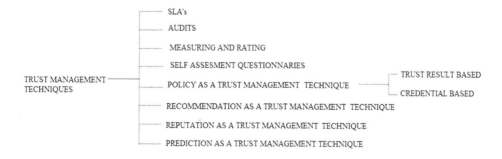

Figure 8.

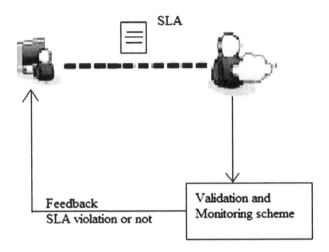

- **AUDITS:** CPs use different audit standards to assure users about their offered services and platforms as shown in Figure 9. For example, Google lists SAS 70 II and FISMA certification to ensure users about the security and privacy measures taken for Google Apps. The audit SAS 70 II covers only the operational performance (e.g., policies and procedures inside datacenters) and relies on a highly specific set of goals and standards. They are not sufficient to alleviate the users' security concerns and most of the CP's are not willing to share the audit reports, which also leads to a lack of transparency.

Figure 9.

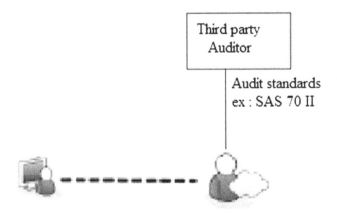

- **MEASURING AND RATINGS:** Recently, a Cloud marketplace has been launched to support consumers in identifying dependable CPs. They are rated based on a questionnaire that needs to be filled in by current CCs as shown in Figure 10. In the future, Cloud Commons aims to combine consumer feedback with technical measurements for assessing and comparing the trustworthiness of CPs. Furthermore, there is a new commercial Cloud marketplace named SpotCloud that provides a platform where CCs can choose among potential providers in terms of cost, quality, and location. Here, the CPs' ratings are given in an Amazon-like "star" interface with no documentation on how the ratings are computed.

- **SELF-ASSESSMENT QUESTIONNAIRES:** The CSA (Cloud Security Alliance) proposed a detailed questionnaire for ensuring security control transparency of CPs – called the CAIQ (Consensus Assessment Initiative Questionnaire). The Figure 11 shows the cloud providers answering the questionnaires. This questionnaire provides means for assessing the capabilities and competencies of CPs in terms of different attributes (e.g., compliance, information security, governance). However, the CSA metrics working group does not provide any proposals for a metric to evaluate CAIQ yet. This is necessary for comparing the potential CPs based on the answered assessment questionnaire stored in the STAR. Furthermore, the information stored in the STAR repository can be checked against the CCM (Cloud Control Matrix). This will provide the assurance whether services offered by the CPs comply with the industry-accepted security standards, audits, regulations, control frameworks or not.

Figure 10.

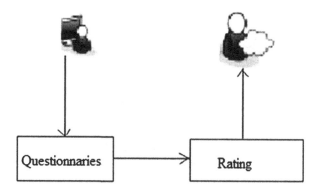

Figure 11.

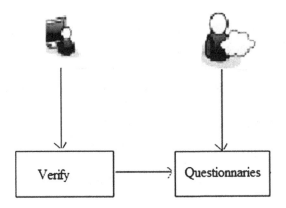

POLICY AS A TRUST MANAGEMENT TECHNIQUE (PocT)

Policy as a trust management technique (PocT) is one of the most popular and traditional ways to establish trust among parties and has been used in cloud environments, the grid, P2P systems, Web applications and the service-oriented environment. PocT uses a set of policies, each of which assumes several roles that control authorization levels and specifies a minimum trust threshold in order to authorize access. The trust thresholds are based on the trust results or the credentials.

For the trust-results-based threshold, several approaches can be used. For instance, the monitoring and auditing approach proves Service-Level Agreement (SLA) violations in cloud services (i.e., if the SLA is satisfied, then the cloud service is considered as trustworthy and vise versa). The entities credibility approach specifies a set of parameters to measure the credibility of parties while the feedback credibility approach considers a set of factors to measure the credibility of feedback.

- SLA can be considered as a service plan (i.e., where the service level is specified) and as a service assurance where penalties can be assigned to the cloud service provider if there is a service-level violation in the provisioned cloud services. SLA can establish trust between cloud service consumers and providers by specifying technical and functional descriptions with strict clauses.
- The entities credibility (i.e., the credibility of cloud services) can be measured from qualitative and quantitative attributes such as security, availability, response time, and customer support.

- The feedback credibility can be measured using several factors such as cloud service consumers' experience (i.e., the quality of feedback differs from one person to another).

For a credential-based threshold, PocT follows either the Single- Sign-On (SSO) approach where the credentials disclosure and authentication take place once and then the cloud service consumers have an access approval for several cloud services, or the state machine approach where the credentials disclosure and authentication take place for each state of the execution of cloud services. Credentials are generally established based on standards such as the X.509v3, the Simple Public Key Infrastructure (SPKI) or the Security Assertion Markup Language (SAML). The digital certificates perspective can be used to define the credential term where a trusted third party (i.e., certificate authority) is required to certify the credential. However, not all credentials require a trusted certificate authority for establishing identities such as the Simple Public Key Infrastructure (SPKI) credentials where the certificate authority is not required.

Figure 12 depicts how PocT is arranged to support trust management in the cloud environment. A cloud service consumer x has certain policies Px to control the disclosure of its own credentials Cx and contains the minimum trust threshold Tx. Tx can either follow the credentials approach or the credibility approach, depending on the credibility assessment of the cloud service provider y (denoted Ry) to determine whether to proceed with the transaction. In contrast, the cloud service

Figure 12.

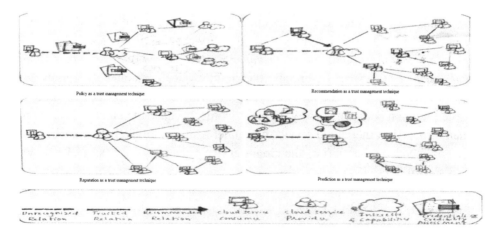

provider y also has certain policies Py to regulate access to its cloud services (e.g., IaaS, PaaS, SaaS), to control the disclosure of its own credentials Cy, and contains the minimum trust threshold Ty. Similarly, Ty can either follow the credential approach or the credibility approach, depending on the credibility assessment of the cloud service consumer x (denoted Rx). If both trust thresholds are satisfied (i.e. Tx and Ty), the relation between the cloud service consumer x and provider y is considered as a trusted relation (i.e., $T r (x, y) = 1$ as shown in Eq. (1)).

$$T r (x, y) = 1 \; if \; Cx \geq Ty \Leftrightarrow Cy \geq Tx \; or \; Ry \geq Tx \Leftrightarrow Rx \geq Ty$$

0 otherwise (1)

RECOMMENDATION AS A TRUST MANAGEMENT TECHNIQUE (RecT)

Recommendation as a trust management technique (RecT) has been widely used in the cloud environment, the grid and the service-oriented environment. Recommendations take advantage of participant's knowledge about the trusted parties, especially given that the party at least knows the source of the trust feedback. It is well known in social psychology theory that the role of a person has a considerable influence on another person's trust assessment if a recommendation is given. Recommendations can appear in different forms such as the explicit recommendation or the transitive recommendation. An explicit recommendation happens when a cloud service consumer clearly recommends a certain cloud service to her well-established and trusted relations (e.g., friends). A transitive recommendation happens, on the other hand, when a cloud service consumer trusts a certain cloud service because at least one of her trusted relations trusts the service. *Figure 12 depicts the RecT approach where the cloud service consumer x has a trusted relation with another cloud service consumer z.* Essentially the cloud service consumer z recommends consumer x to cloud service provider y, or x transitively trusts y because there is a trusted relation between z and y. In other words, because the cloud service consumer x trusts the other cloud service consumer z, it is more likely that x will trust the recommended relation (i.e., the cloud service provider y), $T r (x, y \mid T r (z, y))$ = 1 as shown in Eq. (2).

$$T r (x, y \mid T r (z, y)) = 1 \; i \; f \; T r (z, y) = 1$$

0 otherwise (2)

REPUTATION AS A TRUST MANAGEMENT TECHNIQUE (RepT)

Reputation as a trust management technique (RepT) is important because the feedback of the various cloud service consumers can dramatically influence the reputation of a particular cloud service either positively or negatively. RepT has been used in the cloud environment, the grid, P2P as well as the service-oriented environment. Reputation can have direct or indirect influence on the trustworthiness of a particular entity (e.g., cloud service). Unlike RecT, in RepT, cloud service consumers do not know the source of the trust feedback, because there are no trusted relations in RepT. There are several online reputation-based systems such as the auction systems where new and used goods are found and the review systems where the consumer's opinions and reviews on specific products or services are expressed. Figure 12 depicts how RepT supports trust management. The cloud service consumer x has a certain minimum trust threshold Tx and the cloud service provider y has a set of trusted relations $T r(y) = \{r1, r2, . . ., ri\}$ (i.e., other cloud service consumers), which give trust feedback on the cloud service provider $T f (y) = \{f1, f2, \quad , fn\}$. This feedback is used to calculate the reputation of y, denoted as Rep(y), as shown in Eq. (3). The cloud service consumer x determines whether to proceed with the transaction based on the reputation result of y. The more positive feedback that y receives, the more likely x will trust the cloud service provider y.

$$Rep(y) = (\sum\nolimits_{x=1}^{|T f (y)|} T f (x, y)) / |T f (y)| \qquad (3)$$

$$T r (x, y) = 1 \ i \ f \ Rep(y) \geq Tx$$

0 otherwise $\qquad (4)$

PREDICTION AS A TRUST MANAGEMENT TECHNIQUE (PrdT)

Prediction as a trust management technique (PrdT) is very useful, especially when there is no prior information regarding the cloud service's interactions (e.g., previous interactions, history records). The basic idea behind PrdT is that similar minded entities (e.g., cloud service consumers) are more likely to trust each other. Figure 12 depicts how PrdT works to support trust management. The cloud service consumer x has some capabilities and interests (denoted ix) represented in a vector space model by binary data, $ix = (i1, i2, . . ., ij)$, and a certain minimum trust threshold Tx is used to determine whether to trust the other cloud service consumers. Similarly, the cloud service consumer y also has some capabilities and interests (denoted as *iy*) represented in a vector space model by binary data, $iy = (i1, i2, \ldots, ik)$, and a certain minimum trust threshold Ty is also used to determine whether to trust the other cloud service consumers. The similarity between these two vectors (i.e., ix and iy) can be calculated using a similarity measurement such as the cosine similarity, as shown in Eq. (5). The more similar these capabilities and interests are, the more likely that the cloud service consumer x will trust y.

$$sim(ix, iy) = (ix \cdot iy) / (\|ix\|.\|ix\|) \tag{5}$$

$$Tr(x, y) = 1 \; if \; sim(ix, iy) \geq Tx \Leftrightarrow sim(ix, iy) \geq Ty$$

$$0 \; otherwise \tag{6}$$

TRUST AND REPUTATION MODELS

The following section explains the different types of trust and reputation models, challenges and solutions in trust and reputation models and strength and weaknesses of the models:

- **Different Types of Trust and Reputation Models:** Ensuring security in a distributed environment such as P2P networks is a critical issue nowadays. Nevertheless, it is in those kind of scenarios in which entities can enter or leave the community whenever they want, where traditional security schemes cannot always be applied. Specifically, the use of a PKI (Public Key Infrastructure) may be unacceptable within highly distributed systems. Therefore, modeling concepts like trust and reputation may result very helpful and useful when trying to gain a certain level of security and confidence among inter-operating entities. The following section discusses the different types of trust management models defined by M´armol (2011) which are listed in Figure 13.
- **Common Challenges and Solutions in using Trust and Reputation Models:** Trust and reputation management in P2P networks provides several benefits to electronic interactions between users, like a minimum guarantee of benevolent behavior of another interacting peer. Nevertheless, this kind of systems also has several common issues and challenges that need to be addressed when developing such mechanisms.

Figure 13.

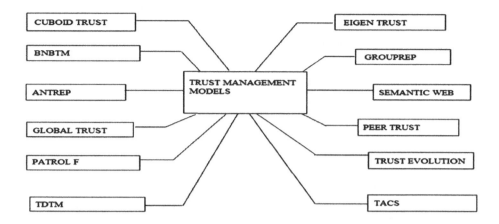

Modeling Trust and Reputation

One of the first things to face when developing a new trust and reputation model, or when analyzing an existing one is the way of modeling precisely that: trust and reputation. Thus, some models use bayesian networks like BNBTM, while others use fuzzy logic like PATROL-F, or even bio-inspired algorithms as is the case of TACS, TDTM and AntRep. Other models, however, just give an analytic expression to compute trust for example, GroupRep. Each way of modeling trust and reputation has its own advantages and drawbacks. For instance, fuzzy logic allows us to model concepts like trust, reputation or recommendations in a manner closer to the way humans understand them. However, fuzzy logic will be difficult to scale to larger problems because it consists of important limitations with conditional possibility, the fuzzy set theory equivalent of conditional probability. Bio-inspired mechanisms have demonstrated a high adaptability and scalability in dynamic scenarios such as P2P networks. However, in some cases, their indeterminism and approximation techniques can lead to choose a malicious peer as the most trustworthy one, discarding another clearly benevolent who could be selected. Analytic expressions are most of the times easy to read and understand, but they may not take into consideration all the possible factors involved in the evaluation of trust and reputation for a certain participant in a P2P network since they need to manage those factors explicitly, while other approaches effectively deal with them in an implicit way. Finally, Bayesian networks provide a flexible mechanism to represent multifaceted trust in many contexts of each others' capabilities (providing different services or carrying out several tasks, for instance). It also allows to efficiently combining different aspects of trust. One drawback is, however, that the approach can be computationally intensive, especially when the variables being studied are not conditionally independent of one another.

Contextualized Trust and Reputation

Another important concept managed in many trust and reputation models is what is commonly known as the context. Since a peer can be very trustworthy and benevolent when supplying a service or performing a task but, at the same time, very fraudulent or malicious when dealing with another service or task, it is not fair to identify it as fully trustworthy or untrustworthy. That is why several models like CuboidTrust, BNBTM, PeerTrust, PATROL-F or TACS include a context factor or distinguish in one or another way the trust placed on a peer depending on the task or service it is requested to supply or perform.

P2P Networks Dynamism

Not many models take into account the intrinsic dynamic nature of P2P networks (i.e. nodes entering and leaving the community whenever they want) when modeling trust relationships. Furthermore, only a few ones among the discussed models like CuboidTrust, EigenTrust, TACS and PeerTrust present experiments dealing with this issue as well as with the fact that also the behavior of peers may be dynamic, i.e., peers are not always benevolent or malicious. And how fast and accurate a model can react against these behavioral changes is an important feature that every trust and reputation model should consider. Therefore, every trust and or reputation model for P2P networks should consider three basic scenarios:

- A static one, where the topology of the network does not change along the time. This is the simplest scenario where trust and reputation models should work efficiently.
- A dynamic one, where the topology changes along the time, with nodes joining and leaving the network. This scenario could be used in order to test the reaction of a trust and reputation model against changes in the size and topology of the network, and the specific nodes composing it. This kind of experiment also allows testing how the model faces the topic of newcomers and deals with some threats like the Sybil attack
- An oscillating one, where the behavior of the nodes changes along the time, so they can be benevolent and become malicious and vice versa. Finally, this

scenario would show if the model has a quick and accurate response or not against sudden behavioral changes of nodes trying to cheat. A good trust and reputation model should identify immediately these fluctuations and react consequently.

Collusion

There are also some security threats related to trust and reputation systems which are not completely considered in every model. For instance, only PeerTrust, CuboidTrust and EigenTrust explicitly treat the problem of collusion among malicious nodes. A collusion consists of several malicious nodes joining in order to increase their reputation values by fake rating themselves and, on the other hand, decrease the reputation of current benevolent peers by giving negative recommendations about the latter, as it can be observed in Figure 14.

It is not easy to overcome this problem, especially when the percentage of nodes forming the collusion is quite high. Actually, any of the studied models is completely resilient against this kind of attack. The solution is to try to minimize its global impact by punishing every node in the network which is known to belong to the collusion. There are even variants of this attack, like a set of nodes providing good services but rating positively other malicious peers and negatively other benevolent ones.

Identity Management (Sybil Attack)

It is a fact that cannot be obviated when designing and developing a new trust and reputation model since many deficiencies and weaknesses can emerge from an

Figure 14.

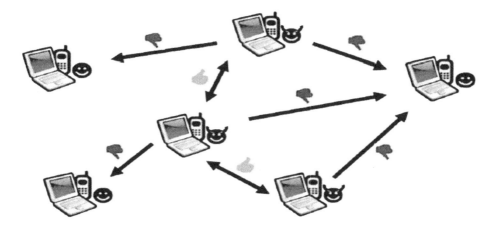

inaccurate management of identity. One of the most common problems related to identity management in trust and reputation schemes is what is known as Sybil attack. In a Sybil attack the reputation system of a P2P network is subverted by creating a large number of pseudonymous entities, using them to gain a disproportionately large influence. A reputation system's vulnerability to a Sybil attack depends on the cost of generating new identities, the degree to which the reputation system accepts inputs from entities that do not have a chain of trust linking them to a trusted entity, and whether the reputation system treats all entities identically.

Figure 15 shows the steps followed in a Sybil attack and some other attacks related to identity management in trust and reputation models. These steps are:

Step 1: An entity joins the community with a new identity, looking like being a trustworthy peer.

Step 2: At a certain moment (probably after gaining some reputation in the system), this entity swaps her goodness and becomes malicious, obtaining thus a greater self profit.

Step 3: Once the system has detected her behavioral change and has identified her as a malicious participant, she leaves the network.

Step 4: Finally, she generates a new identity and enters again the system, repeating the process indefinitely.

Strengths and Weaknesses of the Trust Models

After describing various types of trust and reputation models over P2P networks it is necessary to highlight strengths and weaknesses of those models. The Table 2 lists the strengths and weaknesses of the trust models.

Figure 15.

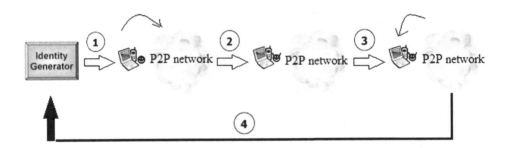

Table 2. Strengths and weaknesses of the trust models

SL. NO	TRUST MODEL	STRENGTH	WEAKNESS
1.	CUBOID TRUST	It shows good outcomes against above scenarios and it also considers the problem of collusion	• Direct trust or direct experiences are not given a differentiated treatment • The score takes discrete values in the set {-1,1} instead of continuous ones in the interval [-1,1]
2.	EIGEN TRUST	• It shows good outcomes against above scenarios and it also considers the problem of collusion • Moreover, it also takes into account the Sybil attack	To consider pretrusted peers there is not always a set of peers that can be trusted by default, prior to the establishment of the community
3.	BNBTM	Manages trust in different contexts, which can be combined to form an overall opinion of the trustworthiness of a peer	It only deals with three discrete valuations for a transaction
4.	GROUPREP	It provides the distinction among trust between groups of peers, between groups and peers, and only between peers	It is missing a global trust value for a peer as a result of the combination of the three previous ones
5.	ANTREP	It has ability to easily adapt to the dynamix topologies of P2P networks	It just provides a mechanism to distribute reputation evidences, not to assess those evidences
6.	SEMANTIC WEB	It clearly distinguishes between direct trust and indirect trust or reputation, and also between the trust given to a peer as a service provider and as a recommender	Searching all the paths connecting two agents may lead to some scalability problems
7.	GLOBAL TRUST	It clearly distinguishes between direct trust and indirect trust or reputation, and also between the trust given to a peer as a service provider and as a recommender	Searching all the paths connecting two agents may lead to some scalability problems
8.	PEER TRUST	• It shows good outcomes against above scenarios and it also considers the problem of collusion • It also introduces a context factor to distinguish the trust given to a peer for different	It does not distinguish between the confidence placed on a peer when supplying a service or carrying out a task, and when giving recommendations about

TRUST MANAGEMENT SYSTEM FOR CLOUD COMPUTING

TM systems allow relying parties/entities to reliably represent their capabilities and competence of the underlying systems in terms of relevant attributes. In cloud computing, multiple attributes and trust information from multiple sources and roots are needed to be taken into account when selecting trustworthy cloud providers. TM system for cloud computing should be able to combine multi-attribute based trust derived from multiple sources and roots: soft (e.g., user feedbacks or reviews) and hard trust (e.g., certificates or audits).

Attributes for Trust Assessment in Cloud Computing

During the trust assessment phase, multiple attributes need to be taken into account to ensure reliable decision making in any application scenario. This is particularly true for cloud computing environments, where multiple attributes (e.g., security, compliance, availability) are important for reliably determining the quality level of cloud providers. The Qos parameters are discussed briefly below and which is mentioned in Table 3:

- **SLAs**: The entities that are providing services are required to follow standardized SLA, e.g., proposed by Cloud Computing Use Cases community. The SLA specification of CPs then can be assessed based on the compliance to the standardized format. This compliance is further factored into trust as-

Table 3. Qos parameters

QoS+ Parameters	Who Provides the Information?	How to Derive the Information?
SLA	CPs, CBs, CCs, CCas	Standardized SLAs
Compliance	CAs, CSA	Audit Standards, CCM
Portability Interoperability Geographical Location	CPs	SLAs
Customer Support	CCs, CPs, CBs, CCas	SLAs, User Feedback
Performance	CBs, Independent Third-Party, CCs, CPs	Measurement, User Feedback
Federated IdM	CPs	SLAs
Security	CSA, CPs, CAs	CSA CAIQ, Certificate-Based Attestation mechanism, Audits
Service Deployment Models Serviice Delivery Models	CCs, CBs, CRs	Context Dependency and Similarity Techniques

sessment of CPs. The information regarding the SLAs is considered to be direct, as these agreements are usually between the corresponding entities (e.g., CCs and CPs, CPs and CBs, CPs and CCas).

- **Compliance**: CPs use audit standards as an assurance for the existence of technical (e.g., security) and organizational controls related to their offered services. The CAs assess these controls and issue certificates for the CPs based on the assessment reports. Otherwise, the information about those controls is provided by CPs in the STAR repository and can be checked against the CCM initiated by CSA. The results about the audit compliance can be obtained directly from the CPs or indirectly from the CSA.

- **Portability, Interoperability, and Geographical Location**: The information regarding these parameters is directly obtainable from the CPs. The existence of terms and clauses related to these parameters documented in the SLAs are the valid form of information in this case.

- **Customer Support**: CPs usually provides assurances about terms and clauses related to "customer support" in their SLAs, CBs and CCas are also required to include similar terms in their SLAs for their respective consumers (e.g., CPs or CBs or CCs). The SLA-based terms and clauses can be complemented by considering experiences from the existing consumers and factor into overall trust computation of CPs or CCas.

- **Performance**: In Cloud computing environments, the information about the performance related parameter (e.g., availability, latency, bandwidth, and elasticity) is obtained using service monitoring technologies. CPs and CBs usually provide the application for monitoring such parameters which are usually used after the service provisioning contract. CCs also can hire the independent third-party brokers (if required) to monitor those parameters before provisioning the services. In this case, the monitored or observed data regarding the performance parameters can be compared among the potential providers or with the agreed data stated in the SLAs to validate them. The validation result (i.e., success or failure) or the comparison of performances then may influence the evaluation of trustworthiness of CPs.

- **Security**: CCs want to know about the existence of certain security controls when outsourcing their IT resources to the cloud. The CSA initiated CAIQ, a self-assessment questionnaire designed for the CPs to document their security controls, to increase transparency between the providers and consumers by publishing it in a public repository. Moreover, CPs host services in trusted virtualized platforms using the trusted computing (TC) technology. In a distributed service environments (e.g., Cloud computing), consumers can learn about the security or non-security related behavior of the software components running on those platforms using remote-attestation mechanism.

- **User Feedback**: Feedback, recommendation, reviews from the consumers are valuable for service selection in e-marketplaces. This concept is also adapted in Cloud marketplaces (e.g., CloudCommons, SpotCloud) where CCs share their experiences about the cloud services they provisioned. The information about their experiences may appear as quantitative (e.g., satisfaction score) and/or qualitative (e.g., reviews) forms. Consumers' experiences can be used to evaluate the CPs as a whole or with respect to each QoS+ parameter.
- **Service Deployment and Delivery Models**: Trust models are usually context-specific and it is important to consider in the TR models for service selection in Cloud environments. The service delivery models and service deployment models should be factored as a contextual parameter in trust models. Hence, the context dependency and similarity techniques are considered complementary for the trust models in Cloud environments.

DEPENDENCE OF CLOUD ENTITIES ON SOURCES OF EVIDENCE FOR TRUST JUDGEMENT

The trust relations with various cloud entities are dependent on various sources of evidence and the derivation of a source of evidence is dependent on some trust relations either.

Properties for TM Systems in Cloud Computing

TM systems require specific properties to incorporate those attributes for trust establishment in a cloud marketplace.

Multi-Faceted Trust Computation

The computation of trust should consider the QoS+ Parameters for TR models, which refer to the competencies and capabilities of a service provider in certain aspects, for instance, providing security measures, accreditation, bandwidth or customer support. Integrating these different aspects brings up multi-faceted challenges regarding computation of trust, which are as follows:

- **Multi-Criteria**: The assessment of the trustworthiness of an entity should consider all relevant parameters, which usually means to take into account multiple parameters describing different qualities of a service (composition) or its provider. Especially the aggregation of objective parameters (e.g., expert ratings or real-time measurements) and subjective parameters (e.g., recommendations by other consumers) is a major challenge.

- **Multi-Root:** When integrating multiple parameters into a TR model, one has to consider that the quantitative or qualitative information, being factored into the trust establishment process, can be derived from different roots. Furthermore, one has to consider that those roots might have very different characteristics; for instance, information derived from a trusted platform module (TPM) or certificates provided by a property attestation authority (sometimes referred to as hard trust) need to be handled differently from trust information derived from user feedback (sometimes referred to as soft trust). Therefore, the combination of information from different roots poses another major challenge.

- **Multi-Context**: As a single service provider may offer different services that require different competencies, a computational model should be able to reflect the context in which a service provider has established trust. In Cloud computing, the different context can refer to different service delivery models. For example, a service provider might be trustworthy in delivering SaaS but not PaaS or IaaS. Moreover, if a trust model is able to consider that an entity has different trust values in different contexts, the model should be able to reason about the overall trustworthiness of an entity, or about the trustworthiness of a newly deployed service (e.g., based on the knowledge which components that are already used in other contexts are re-used for the new service).

Customization and Aggregation

Another issue that is relevant when selecting or designing of trust or reputation mechanism relates to how much customization should be supported and where should the trust values be aggregated:

- **Trust Customization (Global Reputation Vs Local/Subjective Trust Values**): When trust is derived from different parameters, it is possible to consider subjective interests and requirements that are dependent on the entity evaluating the trustworthiness of a service provider. This leads to a local trust value. However, a global trust value is independent from who evaluates trustworthiness of a service provider. On the one hand, the local trust values provide means for considering the preference of each user in detail. Customization allows users to define the parameters relevant for trust establishment from their point of view, to weight the parameters according to his preferences and to consider which sources of information the user believes to be more trustworthy. On the other hand, service providers might be more interested in the calculation of a global trust (or reputation) value, as this might be more directly influenced and observed by the companies.

- **Trust Aggregation (Centralized vs Decentralized)**: Usually, there are two different fundamental approaches to store and aggregate trust-related information. The first one is to host the information in a centralized repository, the other is to use decentralized approach. Both have distinct advantages and disadvantages: In centralized trust models – requiring a trusted third party – users cannot manipulate the data except by providing ratings to the central system. The aggregation methodology can be kept secret and the individual ratings of an entity are published or distributed. However, the trusted authority hosting the centralized repository may manipulate the results and represent a single point for attacks. Decentralized trust models do not require a trusted third party; however, one has to trust in the mechanisms which are used for distributing the ratings and to consider the costs for distributing the ratings among the entities. The latter can be solved by applying algorithms that aggregate the individual ratings by only communicating with an entity's local neighborhood. A disadvantage of decentralized models is that preserving privacy is much harder as more information is distributed between the participating entities.

Trust Evaluation

For complex, distributed environments (e.g., Cloud computing) we introduce a categorization of mechanisms that are relevant for trust evaluation that – to the best of our knowledge – have not been discussed in this context before:

- **Black Box Approach**: Following this approach, the trustworthiness of an entity or a service is evaluated taking into account only the observed output, for example by only considering user feedback. Models in this class treat the service as a black box, and do not require any knowledge about the internal processes and components of the service.
- **Inside-Out Approach**: Following this approach, the trustworthiness of an entity or a service is derived based on the knowledge about the architecture of the service and the trustworthiness of its components.
- **Outside-In Approach:** A model that is following this approach requires knowledge about the internal architecture of a service and its components

as input as well as information stating the observed behavior of the overall service. The goal of this kind of model is to derive the trustworthiness of internal components of a service composition based on its external behavior. This is far from trivial, but can be successful when some components are re-used in multiple services and if certain errors in the behavior of the service composition can be backtracked to the originating component.

Transferring Trust between Contexts

As stated above, customer trust in a service provider depends on the specific application context or the scope of interaction. Transfer of trust across those contexts is a significant challenge for trust and reputation systems. Consider, for example, a service provider offering an email service and a video rendering service – both belonging to the SaaS category. Both application contexts require different competencies, for example spam protection and storage for the email context, whereas for video rendering context, latency, bandwidth and parameters dealing with performance matters (e.g., response time, CDN (Content Delivery Node) facilities, etc.) are important. Here, transferring trust established in one context (email) to the other one (video rendering) is not a trivial task, and could, for instance, be supported by combining the outside-in and the inside-out evaluation.

Attack Resistance

As soon as the influence of trust and reputation models on the decision of customers will grow, the interests in manipulating those values in Cloud environment will grow accordingly. A number of different attacks e.g., playbooks, proliferation attacks, reputation lag attacks, false praise, whitewashing, sybil attacks, etc. against trust and reputation systems are present. These types of attacks will also be of concern when designing trust and reputation system for Cloud computing environments. Thus, attack resiliency is a central design goal for developers of these kinds of systems.

Transparent Trust Representation

The derived trust values or reputation scores must be transparent to and comprehensible enough for the consumers, so that they can easily and confidently make trust-based decision. To make the trust values transparent and comprehensible, users need to be supplied with an intuitive representation of trust together with enough information regarding the relevant parameters.

SUMMARY

Trust management that models the trust on the behavior of the elements and entities would be especially useful for the proper administration of cloud system and cloud services. Trust plays an important role in commercial cloud environments. It is one of the biggest challenges of cloud technology. Trust enables users to select the best resources in a heterogeneous cloud infrastructure. Security is one of the most important areas to be handled in the emerging area of cloud computing. If the security is not handled properly, the entire area of cloud computing would fail as it mainly involves managing personal sensitive information in a public network. Also, security from the service providers point also becomes imperative in order to protect the network, the resources in order to improve the robustness and reliability of those resources. Hence the need of trust management techniques and models became important.

REFERENCES

Armbrust, M., & Fox, A. (2009). *Above the Clouds: A Berkeley View of Cloud Computing*. UC Berkeley Reliable Adaptive Distributed Systems Laboratory.

Bradai, A., & Hossam, A. (2012). Enforcing Trust-based Intrusion Detection in Cloud Computing Using Algebraic Methods.*International Conference on Cyber-Enabled Distributed Computing and Knowledge Discover*. IEEE. doi:10.1109/CyberC.2012.38

Cavoukian, A. (2008). *Privacy in the clouds*. Identity Journal Limited.

Firdhous, M., Ghazali, O., & Hassan, S. (2011). Trust Management in Cloud Computing: A Critical Review. *International Journal on Advances in ICT for Emerging Regions*.

Habib, M. S., Hauke, S., Ries, S., & Habib. (2012). Trust as a facilitator in cloud computing: a survey. *Journal of Cloud Computing: Advances, Systems and Applications*.

Huang, J. & Nicol, D. (2013). Trust mechanisms for cloud computing. *Journal of Cloud Computing: Advances, Systems and Applications*.

Hwang, K. (2010). *Trusted Cloud Computing with Secure Resources and Data Coloring*. IEEE Computer Society.

Khalid, G., Ghafoor, A., Irum, M., & Shibli, M. A. (2013). Cloud Based Secure and Privacy Enhanced Authentication & Authorization Protocol. *Procedia Computer Science*, *22*, 680–688. doi:10.1016/j.procs.2013.09.149

Khan, M. K., & Malluhi, Q. (2010). *Establishing Trust in Cloud Computing*. IEEE Computer Society.

Paul, Selvi, & Ibrahim. (2011). A Novel Trust Management System for Cloud Computing - IaaS Providers. *Journal of Combinatorial Mathematics and Combinatorial Computing, 79*, 3-22.

Pearson, S. (2012). *Privacy, Security and Trust in Cloud Computing. HP Laboratories, HPL-2012-80R1*. Springer.

Zeadally & Yu. (2013). Trust Management of Services in Cloud Environments: Obstacles and Solutions. ACM Computing Surveys, 46(1), Article 12.

Zissis, D., & Lekkas, D. (2012). Addressing cloud computing security issues. *Future Generation Computer Systems, 28*(3), 583–592. doi:10.1016/j.future.2010.12.006

Chapter 8
Security and Trust in Cloud Computing

Eric Kuada
Ghana Institute of Management and Public Administration, Ghana

ABSTRACT

The discussion of security and trust issues in this book chapter will follow from the discussions on the role of virtualization in cloud computing and hence the impact that the various categories of virtualization such as server virtualization, network virtualization, storage virtualization, and application virtualization have on the security and trust issues in cloud computing. It will be evident from these discussions that virtualization introduces a number of security and risk related challenges in cloud computing based on the three security objectives of confidentiality, integrity, and availability; and the two main other related security objectives of authenticity and accountability of information systems that were adopted for this discussion. It was however also noted that if the necessary recommended best practices of virtualizations are faithfully adhered to, then virtualization can actually lead to improvement or enhancement in the security posture of cloud environments.

INTRODUCTION

Cloud computing is about the offering of computing resources as a service rather than as a commodity. This means that customers pay for the amount of resources used instead of purchasing complete hardware to build their own Information Technology (IT) infrastructure or purchasing whole licenses, which are often woefully

DOI: 10.4018/978-1-5225-0741-3.ch008

underutilized or they even often find out later that they do not need. This relatively new trend of computing is essentially the repackaging of traditional Information and Communication Technology (ICT) infrastructure and software solutions such as processing capacity, storage and storage network systems, networking capabilities, user and enterprise software solutions, as virtualized resources that are then delivered by a cloud service provider to its customers as an on-demand, pay-per-use, and a customer self-provisioned service normally through a Web portal over a network such as the Internet (Kuada, Adanu, & Olesen, 2013).

The reason cloud computing appears to have captured the attention of businesses is the numerous benefits it offers despite the security risk challenges it poses to both the cloud service providers and their customers. It definitely has different appeals to different businesses or organizations depending on the nature, size, industry, age, etc., of the institution; but generally, it is mostly taken as a given that cloud computing provides flexibility, increase IT efficiency, elasticity, obviation of capital expenditure for acquiring IT resources, and improves reliability and recovery from disasters. It should be obvious that without the necessary technologies to support this trend of computing, and the addressing of the risk challenges it poses, despite all the benefits it promises, it wouldn't have come to fruition. Some of the technological factors that are facilitating cloud computing include the availability and drastic increase in reliable broadband internet access, the advancements in virtualization technologies, and the shift of the development of majority of both enterprise and desktop applications as web services and web application. For the purposes of the topic being treated in this work (security and trust in cloud computing), the focus of the discussion on the technological advancement will be on virtualization technologies and application or service development for cloud computing environments.

The main purpose of this book chapter is to discuss security issues in cloud computing. The chapter also seek to discuss the concept of trust and the issues of trust in the context of cloud computing. It also tries to demonstrate the role of security in modelling the concept of trust in cloud computing environments. Finally, it sets a research agenda for further work on this topic.

Motivations for Cloud Adoption

Cloud computing provides several potential benefits to enterprises. These benefits are usually so appealing that despite the equally major risks of adopting cloud services, companies are willing to give it a try. Some of these major motivating factors for cloud adoption by enterprises include flexibility, efficiency, resource utilization, availability, initial capital cost for IT infrastructure obviation, operational cost reduction, speed in resource acquisition and time to market, and business agility. Enterprises normally acquire IT resources for their business processes (e.g. developing and testing new products) and shortly after find out that they do not need those resources or the resources are underutilized because either their IT department made a mistake in their request or their business processes have changed suddenly. The pay-per-use model of the cloud computing brings about flexibility to acquire resources within hours for use and discontinue them when needed. From the above, it can be noted that the pay-per-use model also allows enterprises to obviate high capital expenditure in the acquisition of resources. This is normally very beneficial to startup companies which usually do not have the funds for such endeavors. The flexibility that is offered by cloud computing also lead to ability to acquire the necessary resources for product or service development and hence encourages innovation and shorter time to market. All these factors plus others contribute to the agility of the business so that it is better able to quickly organize to serve new customers, develop products or deliver services.

Cloud Service Models

The three main parts of a regular computing environment, which are namely the hardware infrastructure, the operating system platform, and end user application software, have respectively translated into Infrastructure as a Service, Platform as a Service, and Software as a Service, service delivery models in cloud computing (Xu, 2012; Sultan, 2010; Beimborn, Miletzki, & Wenzel, 2011; Mell & Grance, 2011). These form the three main service models in cloud computing. However, because cloud computing involves the repackaging of traditional IT resources and delivering them as a service to cloud service consumers, any IT solution can translate into a service in cloud computing. This leads to the concept of anything as a service (XaaS). Some of these examples are Data as a Service (DaaS), Confidentiality as a Service (CaaS) (Fahl, Harbach, Muders, & Smith, 2012), and Data Integrity as a Service (DIaaS) (Nepal, Chen, Yao, & Thilakanathan, 2011).

Cloud Deployment Models

The cloud service models just described above can be deployed in a number of ways termed cloud deployment models. These deployment models is a categorization of cloud services based on ownership and scale of the resources. Four main cloud deployment models can be identified. These are private cloud, community cloud, public cloud, and hybrid cloud (Kuada, 2014). When organizations virtualize their data center resources and deliver them to the users in their business units as cloud services, this kind of deployment is referred to as a private cloud. The creation and operation of a private cloud can normally be done by the organization's own IT department or outsourced to a commercial cloud service provider. It is also typical for an organization to engage a cloud service provider in the building of the private cloud; but then, the operation is handled by their own internal IT department. Public clouds, on the other hand, are normally built, owned, and managed by commercial cloud service providers. These resources and services cover the spectrum of the cloud service delivery models; and are open to the general public to subscribe to and purchase resources on a pay-per-use basis.

The third cloud deployment model is the community cloud. This is similar to private cloud deployment; but whereas a private cloud is owned by a single administrative unit, a community cloud is created by multiple institutions with similar usage and security policies that come together on agreement to build a cloud solution to be used by all the participating parties. For example since universities generally have similar IT resource needs and security policies, the universities in a particular city or even country may come together to create a community cloud to serve their users.

An organization operates in a hybrid cloud environment if it uses any combination of private, public, and community clouds. An organization can, for example build, its own private cloud but will also make provision for the usage of public cloud resources for services that its private cloud may not immediately be able to offer. Another reason that an organization may want to operate a hybrid cloud is that because of security and other forms of risks, the organization will want to handle sensitive data and business processes in its own private cloud but will at the same time want to process less critical data and business processes in the public cloud domain because it is cheaper. Additionally, it could be to take advantage of what is termed cloud bursting where the resources that the business need to service its customers fluctuates drastically during certain seasons.

VIRTUALIZATION AND CLOUD COMPUTING

Even though several factors and advancements in technology has culminated into the evolution of cloud computing, advancements in virtualization technologies is at the core of cloud computing. This section begins with the definition virtualization; this is followed with discussion on how virtualization is an enabling technology for cloud computing. The various types of virtualizations are also discussed in the context of how they facilitate various forms of cloud service models.

Definition of Virtualization

Virtualization is a methodology for the emulation or abstraction of hardware resources that enables complete execution stacks including software applications and networks to run on it (Chandramouli, 2014). It is the decoupling of the resources from the underlying hardware; it therefore provides the logical representation of resources and describes the separation of resources and the requests for a service that require these resources from the underlying physical delivery of that service. The virtualization technology is used to add a virtualization layer in a system to abstract hardware resources and provide these virtualized resources for upper-layer applications to use ("Huawei FusionSphere 5.0: Technical White Paper on Virtualization," 2014). There are different categories of virtualization, some of these are system (OS platform) virtualization, network virtualization, storage virtualization, software virtualization, etc. So in the case of system virtualization, server virtualization allows for multiple virtual servers (virtual machines (VMs)) each with its own operating system to be running simultaneously on a single physical server. Based on the description above, some of the benefits of server virtualization are: the increase in the physical server utilization, server consolidation, reduced cost in IT infrastructure and savings on energy consumption.

Virtualization as Enabling Technology for Cloud Computing

Advancements in server virtualization is one of the key enabling factors for the development cloud computing and its adoption by the general public. This is because from the perspective of the cloud service provider, it makes economic sense to consolidate request for servers from multiple clients on a single physical server while providing the isolation of their data and execution environments in a manner similar to having to provide a physical server for each of their clients. It is this multi-tenancy however that introduces new security threats and also increase the attack surface presented for existing security threats in datacenter environments. The details of the effect of virtualization on cloud security is in the adopted virtualization architecture and the tools and processes adopted for managing it. Next, we look at the server virtualization architectures and their associated virtualization techniques.

SYSTEM VIRTUALIZATION

Types of Hardware Virtualizations

As has already been mentioned under the definition of virtualization, the virtualization technology is used to add a virtualization layer in a system to abstract hardware resources, and provide these virtualized resources for upper-layer applications to use. This can generally be done is two ways: hosted architecture and hypervisor (bare-metal) architecture approaches. With the hosted architecture, as depicted in Figure 1, the virtualization layer is installed and runs as an application on top of a fully-fledged general purpose operation system and supports a broad range of hardware configurations. A bare-metal approach on the other hand installs the virtualization layer directly on the clean computer system (VMware, 2007). The adopted server virtualization architecture has direct impact on the security implications of the cloud environment it is deployed in. A system is as secure as the weakest point of failure, hence using hosted architecture increases the surface to be secured against compromise, and is probably best avoided in situations requiring high security(Pearce, Zeadally, & Hunt, 2013). This is because hosted architecture introduces another point of failure (the OS) on which the virtualization layer is installed; and this (the OS) also normally has a larger code base compared to the virtualization software. In addition to the adopted virtualization architecture, the techniques employed for hardware virtualization in these adopted virtualization architectures also directly impact on the security of virtualized system and hence on cloud computing. Server virtualization is mainly CPU virtualization, Memory virtualization, and IO virtualization. So the techniques for their implementation have security implications for virtualization and hence cloud computing.

Techniques of CPU Virtualization

There are basically three main techniques for CPU virtualization. These are binary translation, para virtualization (OS assisted virtualization), and hardware assisted virtualization. Binary translation (traditionally termed full virtualization) virtualize any x86 operating system by using a combination of binary translation and direct execution techniques. This involves translating kernel code to replace non-virtual-

Figure 1. Hosted architecture vs bare-metal architecture

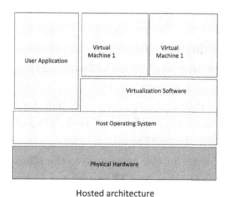

Hosted architecture   Bare-metal architeture

izable instructions with new sequences of instructions that have the intended effect on the virtual hardware, while user level code is directly executed on the processor for high performance virtualization. This provides full virtualization as the guest OS is fully abstracted (completely decoupled) from the underlying hardware by the virtualization layer and hence it is unaware it is being virtualized and requires no modification to run in the virtual machine (VMware, 2007).

Another technique for CPU virtualization is paravirtualization. This is based on the collaboration/communication between the guest OS and the hypervisor to improve performance and efficiency. This is normally termed OS assisted virtualization because it involves modifying the OS kernel to replace non-virtualizable (i.e., sensitive but non-privileged) instructions with hypercalls that communicate directly with the virtualization layer hypervisor. It also provides hypercall interfaces for other critical kernel operations such as memory management, and interrupt handling.

The paravirtualization approach is different from full virtualization, where the unmodified OS does not know it is virtualized and sensitive OS calls are trapped using binary translation. The value proposition of paravirtualization is in lower virtualization overhead. Because paravirtualization cannot support unmodified operating systems, its compatibility and portability is poor and can also introduce significant support and maintainability issues in production environments as it requires major OS kernel modifications (VMware, 2007).

Another CPU virtualization technique that provides full virtualization in the sense that it provides the running of unmodified OS as guest OS is hardware assisted virtualization. This involves enhancements in CPU architecture which target privileged instructions with a new CPU execution mode feature that allows the hypervisor to run in a new root mode below ring 0 of the x86 CPU architecture. Privileged and sensitive instruction calls are set to automatically trap to the hypervisor, thereby removing the need for either binary translation or paravirtualization; with the guest OS states being stored in special Virtual Machine Control structures.

Compared to para-virtualization, binary translation full virtualization offers the isolation and security for virtual machines, and simplifies migration - as the same guest OS instance can run virtualized or on native hardware (VMware, 2007). Hardware assisted virtualization provide the same isolation for security of virtual machines, and portability for simplifying virtual machine migration as is in binary translation, but also provides high performance compared to binary translation and even para-virtualization techniques because it has dedicated hardware enhancements for virtualization. If there be any downside to this technique compared to the other two, then it is merely the added financial cost of purchasing CPUs with hardware assisted virtualization features.

Implications of Hardware Virtualization

The running of multiple VMs on the same hardware offers many advantages. The near-complete isolation between guest operating systems on the same hardware protects against operating systems being a single point of failure. It also allows operating consolidation from different machines and improves server utilization to maintain efficiency of operation. This abstraction from the hardware state does not only allow for multiple operating systems to coexist on the same hardware, but for one hypervisor to run on multiple different networked physical systems concurrently. By utilizing the virtualization software layer (the hypervisor) to mediate between the OS and the hardware, virtualization changes the one-to-one mapping of OSs to hardware to many-to-many, although many real-world systems implement this model only loosely, as a VM does not usually run on multiple systems concurrently. However, allowing a VM and its VMM (Virtual Machine Monitor) to be migrated across multiple physical systems seamlessly while running (this is normally termed live migration) has improved the offerings for high-performance and high-availability systems and cloud computing (Pearce et al., 2013).

Storage Virtualization

Storage virtualization involves the placing of an I/O and file management abstraction layer on top of the local storage systems of a computer system or cluster of storage disks in a storage network in order to present them as a single entity for management and also present single logical view to users. This means that when users access this storage they see a drive letter and folders as they would normally expect from their computer. In the same way that the implementation of virtualized storage objects in a storage virtualization system are transparent to users, it is also transparent to applications that use them. This layer of abstraction between applications and physical storage allows storage consolidation across different heterogeneous vendors and protocols, thus enabling applications to easily share heterogeneous storage resources. Storage virtualization provides high availability of resources through redundancy and scalability. It also supports live migration of data in which a virtual disk can be migrated from one physical storage subsystem to another without any downtime (Singh, Korupolu, & Mohapatra, 2008). Storage virtualization forms the bases for cloud storage and its associated Storage as a Service cloud offerings.

Network Virtualization

Like in the case of any virtualization technology, network virtualization decouples network resources from underlying hardware, where virtualization principles are applied to physical network infrastructure, abstracting network services to create a pool of transport capacity that can be allocated, utilized and repurposed on demand. In a close analogy to the virtual machine, a virtualized network is a software container that presents logical network components such as logical routers, switches, load balancers, VPNs (Virtual Private Networks), firewalls, etc., to connected workloads. These virtualized networks are programmatically created, provisioned and managed; the underlying physical network just serve as a simple packet-forwarding backplane. Network and security services are allocated to each VM according to its needs, and stay attached to it as the VM is moved among hosts in the dynamic virtualized environment. Network virtualization does not only form the underpinnings of a Software Defined Data Center, but also provides a more secure platform for the data center overall.

Application Virtualization

Application virtualization can be defined as the ability to deploy software without modifying the host computer or making changes to the local operating system, file system, or registry. These applications work in their own virtual environments and do not affect the operating system or other programs. Virtualized applications typically operate exclusively in user mode thereby protecting the host operating system and other applications from potential corruption by installation modifications. So by using application virtualization technology, organizations can deploy commercial and custom software across the enterprise without any installation conflict, system changes, or any impact on stability or security (VMware, Inc., n.d.). Application virtualization principles of providing isolation between multiple applications and/ or multiple instances of the same application running on the same OS platform, form the bases for virtual desktops and Software as a Service offerings provided by cloud service providers.

Based on the above discussions, it can be seen that server (OS platform) virtualization, storage virtualization, network virtualization, and application virtualization form the bases for cloud service offerings in cloud computing.

SECURITY IN CLOUD COMPUTING

This section begins with security in Information Systems in general; and then builds on this to discuss security in cloud computing and how virtualization plays on security issues in cloud computing. The section ends with recommended best practices for virtualization in cloud environments and some of the benefits that virtualization brings to cloud computing.

Security in Information Systems

Most definitions of computer or information system security is centered on what is usually termed the CIA triad of confidentiality, integrity, and availability. These three concepts embody the fundamental security objectives for both data and for information and computing services; they therefore form the basis for the requirement of security and the definition of loss of it thereof. Confidentiality covers two related concepts of data confidentiality and privacy; data confidentiality is assurance that private or confidential information is not made available or disclosed to unauthorized individuals or entities. Privacy is the assurance that individuals control or influence what information related to them may be collected and stored and by whom and to whom that information is disclosed (Stallings, 2014). Integrity also covers two related concepts of data integrity and system integrity. Data integrity is the assurance that information and programs are not changed but only in a specified manner by those authorized to make such changes. System integrity is the assurance that a system performs its intended function unimpaired, and free from deliberate or unintentional unauthorized manipulation of the system. The third concept of availability is the assurance that the system works promptly and that authorized users are not denied of their legitimate services.

The CIA triad specification of security objectives is augmented with some other concepts by those in the field who feel that it does not paint the complete picture of the security of an information system and therefore have proposed these additional concepts; the two most commonly mentioned are authenticity and accountability. Authenticity is the assurance that an entity is genuine and can be verified and therefore can be trusted. It provides the notion of confidence in the validity of a message, its transmission, and the originator of the message. Accountability is the assurance or the requirement that generates the security goal that the actions of an entity can be traced back uniquely to that entity. This implies support for deterrence, fault isolation, nonrepudiation, intrusion detection and prevention, recovery from undesired after actions, and the necessary records for legal action if need be. The accountability concept as a basis for security objectives is that because truly secure systems are not yet an achievable goal, we must be able to trace a security breach to the party responsible; and hence systems must keep records of their activities to permit forensic analysis later to trace security breaches and/or to aid in transaction disputes (Stallings, 2014).

The discussions of security in cloud computing in this chapter will be looked at from the perspective of the CIA triad plus authenticity and accountability concepts. The implications of the accountability requirement as has just been mentioned above introduces several other concepts which in themselves require careful consideration.

Major among these are the detection of malicious activities and the mitigation of their effects, the associated vulnerabilities of the system and the exploitation of which led to these attacks, and recovery mechanisms and strategies that does not only mitigate their effect but ensures business continuity also. So the discussion of security issues in this work will also extend to these concepts.

Security Issues in Cloud Computing

Security issues in cloud computing can be view from the perspective of cloud vendors, cloud service providers, and cloud service consumers. Regardless of each of these perspectives, three main aspects of factors contributing to security or the lack of it thereof is people, processes, and technology. However, most often than not, emphasis is placed on technology to the detriment of people (McAfee Inc., 2007), and to some extent also to the detriment of following well established processes that support improving or enhancing the security posture of a company.

Security and privacy issues in cloud computing are not much different from those surrounding other sorts of IT outsourcing, and therefore these should be expected. This work only looks at threats specific to cloud computing. Secondly, it is mainly focused on the effect of technology and processes of cloud vendors and providers; and the main one among these is that which is introduced by the four main categories of virtualization as discussed above. Virtualization security threats is therefore discussed next. The people and processes aspect of consumers becomes our research focus which is laid out at the end of this work.

Virtualization Security Threats

The hypervisor is responsible for controlling VM (Virtual Machine) access to physical hardware resources as well as providing and enforcing isolation among VMs. VM access to hardware resources such as CPU and main memory are under the direct control of the hypervisor while access to resources such as physical NICs and Storage drives are normally controlled through drivers that are resident in the kernel module in the case of type II (hosted architecture) hypervisors or are in a privileged VM (i.e., Management VM) in the case of type I (bare-metal) hypervisors. The isolation among VMs is provided by assigning unique IP or MAC address to each VM by defining virtual local area networks (VLANs) and then assigning each VM to a specific VLAN. The threats that could compromise the secure execution of these functions are: VM escape, breaking of isolation, resource starvation by rogue VMs, and compromise of privileged interfaces provided by hypervisor (Chandramouli, 2014). These are described briefly below.

VM Escape

The main source of threat to any hypervisor is from rogue VMs. These are VMs which manage to subvert the access control function provided by the hypervisor to hardware resources such as memory and storage. The possible reasons for this threat may be due to misconfiguration of the hypervisor and/or guest VM container, and secondly malicious or vulnerable device drivers. Because when this threat is exploited it could potentially afford a rogue VM the chance of taking control of the hypervisor, it is often referred to as Hyperjacking. This affords the rogue VM the chance of installing rootkits and launce attack on other VMs on the same virtualized host.

Breaching of Communication Isolation

The potential threats to isolation are from attacks such as spoofing of IP or MAC address by a rogue VM, VLAN hopping in which a rogue VM escapes the boundaries of its VLAN, and thirdly traffic snooping by rogue VMs intercepting virtual network traffic intended for other VMs on the same virtual network segment. Breaching of communication isolation threats and VM escape threats are very similar in that they both involve a rogue VM escaping it boundaries of access. The main difference between them is the targeted resource boundaries; VM escape is about virtual hardware resources such as CPU and main memory, while breaching of communication isolation is targeted at the virtual network interfaces and storage (i.e. I/O).

Non-Traditional Connectivity

For hosted virtualization architecture, the introduction of features that allow enhanced communication between the guest OS running on the VM and the host OS, that are intended to offer users greater flexibility, introduces new threats. In other words, the nontraditional connectivity between guest and host systems (e.g. drag and drop support for files between guest OS and host OS) breaks the isolation rule and is a potential avenue for a malicious VM to have access to the host OS and hence to easily compromise the hypervisor and hence all VMs running on it. A consequence of this and the other two threats sources discussed above (VM escape and breaching of communication isolation) can lead to the denial or starvation of resources where a misconfigured or rogue VM consumes a disproportionately high percentage of the physical resources of the host such that other VMs are deprived of their due share.

Privileged Management Interfaces

The introspection APIs that hypervisors provide to offer needed services privileged access such as to virtual security appliances (e.g. Intrusion Prevention and Detection Systems) or for monitoring and management of VMs is another source of virtualization threats. These interfaces could also easily become another target for exploitation by rogue or misconfigured VMs (Chandramouli, 2014). Because of the purpose of these privileged management interfaces, the effect of the exploitation of this threat can be very devastating.

Execution Isolation for Virtual Machines

Faulty implementation of the code for performing hypervisor functions for execution isolation in virtual machines such as for scheduling of individual tasks of VMs, and a software based Memory Management Unit in the form of shadow tables for VM introduces threats of hypervisor memory leak which in turn leads to data disclosure violations. Faulty implementation of emulation of timer and interrupt mechanisms also can cause denial of service attacks (Chandramouli, 2014). Another issue that present potential threat to secure execution is I/O device emulation and access control. In addition to faulty implementation of in-memory data structures for VMs, faulty device driver code that are meant for the emulation of I/O devices and their access control create a serious threat to secure execution. Other sources due to faulty hypervisor code include the execution of privileged instruction by the hypervisor for guest VMs, and management of VMs.

Recommended Best Practices to Virtualization

As was described earlier above, there are two types of virtualization architectures. These are bare-metal architecture and the hosted architecture. From a security point of view, bare-metal architecture is better than hosted architecture because the former provides better security assurance than hosted architecture. This is due to the fact that the bare-metal architecture presents a reduced attack surface because of the absence of host OS and the consequent reduced list of vulnerabilities to be addressed. Again, as was described earlier, there are three main types or techniques for CPU virtualization; these are binary translation, para-virtualization (OS assisted virtualization), and hardware assisted virtualization. These options and other hardware virtualization techniques such as is in memory virtualization and I/O virtualization have significant influence on the security posture of the virtualization deployment. For example, a hypervisor platform with hardware assisted virtualization (i.e., both instruction set and memory management) provides greater security assurance than one with a purely software assisted virtualization solution because better memory management controls can prevent attacks such as buffer overflow which can be exploited by malicious VMs to access virtual memory resources of other VMs and the virtualized system hosting them. Secondly, it provides better protection for device access mediation functions through privilege level isolation and better VM level protection through memory protection in hardware.

Thirdly, hardware assisted virtualization supports full virtualization, unlike para-virtualization, so unmodified versions of operating systems can be run on the guest VMs. This enables easier patching or updating than having to perform the same operations on modified/ported versions of operating systems. Additionally, since many features of virtualization are now available in hardware, the size of the hypervisor code will be much smaller; and this enables better security attestation or verification (Chandramouli, 2014).

The footprint in terms of the code size and the number of exposed interfaces of the hypervisor management console has direct effect on the vulnerability of the hypervisor to threats. This means that a functional hypervisor management console with smaller code and smaller number of exposed interfaces can provide better security assurance because of the fact that it presents a smaller attack surface, and it also facilitates easier verification. Another important recommendation for the implementation of the deployment of virtualized hosts for cloud computing is that because device drivers are normally the weakest link in any server security model, it is advised to deploy hypervisors that have a boot configuration choice to disallow the use of non-certified drivers.

To lay the foundation for building Anti-Virus (AV) and Intrusion Detection & Prevention (IDPS) solutions, there should be a mechanism for security monitoring and security policy enforcement of VM operations in order to capture malicious processes running inside VMs and malicious traffic going in and out of VM. There are different schools of thought on VM security monitoring and policy enforcement. One school of thought says solutions for security monitoring and security policy enforcement of VMs should be based "outside of VMs" and should leverage the virtual machine introspection capabilities of the hypervisor. This is generally done through running a security tool as Security Virtual Appliance in what is termed a security hardened or trusted VM. The other school of thought advocate for an in VM-based Security Monitoring and Intervention, where a software or a software-agent like the firewall feature provided by the guest OS is run inside a VM to monitor security-relevant events within. The advantage of this approach is that it provides better visibility and good context analysis for the code running within the VM; but because of the tight dependency of the security tools on the guest OS they run on, any successful attack on the guest OS will also disable the function of the security tool, thereby disabling the countermeasure entirely. The reason why despite this apparent disadvantage of this approach, proponents still argue for its use is because the former (hypervisor introspection based) approach has its own problems. The first problem with hypervisor based firewalls is that they are vendor specific. As an example, VMware vShield only runs on VMware's own hypervisors, and is not supported by Citrix, KVM, Hyper-V, Zen or any other hypervisor solution. Secondly, the public cloud provider may not support hypervisor based firewalls, so this may not probably be an option; and even if they do, hypervisor based firewalls require the use of hypervisor's introspection API which brings with it its own additional risks in a public cloud environment; as this may be tantamount to trading one set of risks for another.

A major area of threat to virtualize infrastructure is the administration of the hypervisor and the virtualized host on which it sits. Some of the recommended best practices to minimize the exploitation of this threat are: to keep the number of user accounts requiring direct access to hypervisor host to bare minimum of usually not more than two since these accounts should hardly be used except under seldom cases where the hypervisor Management Server itself is down or the host housing the Management Server has been taken down for maintenance, when there is need to troubleshoot the hypervisor boot and configuration problems, or there is the need to patch the hypervisor host OS. It is good practice to integrate the user accounts on the hypervisor host with the enterprise directory infrastructure in order to enable authentication through industry tested robust authentication protocols (e.g., Kerberos), enable enforcement of some corporate security policies, as well as handle changes to user account list such as addition, deletion, or modification of user accounts.

In order to meet the accountability security requirement, it is very necessary that during the installation and configuration of hypervisors, it should be ensured that the log daemon or its equivalent executable is turned on. It would be preferable to have a hypervisor logging feature that generates logs in a standardized format as this help leverage the use of tools with good analytical capabilities as well as features to transmit log records over a secure channel in real time to an external server for fault tolerance. This is very important because in the event that even the host on which the hypervisor sits in compromised, the logs will still be available for analysis with any of the common open source analytic tools so that the cause of the attack or cause of the failure can be properly identified.

Benefits of Virtualization on Cloud Security

It is not all gloom when it comes to the impact of virtualization in cloud security. Actually, there equally bright sides to virtualization for cloud security, especially when the above mentioned recommendation are faithfully adhere to. Some may even in that context argue that virtualization enhances cloud security more than it poses more challenges to it. The properties of system virtualization offer the promise of improved data and process security in terms of confidentiality, integrity, and availability which are achieved through properties that are term isolation, oversight, and duplication, respectively (Pearce et al., 2013). One of the core features of network virtualization is isolation; and this happens to be the foundation of most network security solutions whether it is for compliance, containment, or just to keep development, test, and production environments from interacting. Furthermore, virtual networks are by default isolated from other virtual networks and from the underlying physical network, and hence deliver the security principle of least privilege. Isolation between virtual networks allows for overlapping IP addresses; and makes it possible to have isolated development, test, and production virtual networks. Virtual networks are also isolated from the underlying physical infrastructure. Thus, because traffic between hypervisors is encapsulated, the physical network devices operate in a completely different address space from the workloads connected to the virtual networks. As an example, a virtual network could support IPv6 application workloads on top of an IPv4 physical network; and this isolation protects the underlying physical infrastructure from any possible attack that might be initiated by workloads in the virtual networks (Stuhlmuller, 2013). Another benefit of network virtualization is that segmentation of multitier network environments is easier. These could normally represent a Web tier, an application business logic tier, and a database tier. Even though physical firewalls and access control lists deliver a proven segmentation function that has been trusted by network security teams and compliance auditors, confidence in this approach for cloud data centers has however been threaten as more and more security breaches, successful attacks, and downtime have been attributed to human errors and to antiquated manual network security provisioning procedures, as well as change management processes. However, since network segmentation, like isolation, is a core capability of network virtualization, it makes these processes easier compared to that of physical network deployments.

One of the benefits of server virtualization from a security stand point is the increase uptime that it offers. Most server virtualization platforms now offer a number of advanced features which helps with business continuity and increased uptime because of the capabilities to recover from faults and attacks. Some of these capabilities are live migration, storage migration, fault tolerance, distributed resource scheduling, recovery from faults and attacks through restoring the VMs to a known stable state. The technologies supporting these features of server virtualization keep virtual machines in continuous operation or give them the ability to quickly recover from unplanned outages (Marshall, 2011). In line with this, it also therefore improves disaster recovery and allow for recovery plans to be iteratively tested and perfected before they actually ever happen.

TRUST IN CLOUD COMPUTING

This section begins with presenting a definition of trust and a model of the concept of trust. This is followed by the impact security issues play on trust in the cloud computing. Finally the role of Service Level Agreements (SLAs) on trust of cloud service providers and their services as is perceived by their consumers is discussed.

Definition of Trust and Trust Models

The subjective nature of trust has made a solid definition of this concept elusive. Researchers have most often used the term loosely in their work without a rigorous formal definition. The adopted definition and model of the concept of trust in this work is from (Kuada, 2013) which is an adaptation of (Dellarocas, 2001): The level of trust, $T_c^p\left(t_i\right)$ of a service consumer c for a service provider p in the context of a transaction $t_i \in T$ is the a priori probability that the utility of c will meet or exceed its minimum threshold of satisfaction u_0 at the end of transaction t_i, given the trustworthiness of service provider p as perceived by service consumer c. This means trust is the level of confidence of c that the outcome of a transaction with another agent p will be satisfactory for it. So to put it in a more formal way,

$$T_c^p\left(t_i\right) = \int\limits_{U_c\left(R\right)\geq u_0} \tau_c^p\left(R,t_i\right).dR \,,$$

where $U_c\left(R\right)$ is the utility function of service consumer c; and $\tau_c^p\left(R,t_i\right)$ - the trustworthiness of service provider p as perceived by consumer c in the context of a transaction $t_i \in T$ is the a priori subjective joint probability distribution function of the critical rating vector $R_c^p\left(t_i\right)$ from the perspective of c. This definition and model of trust has been adopted because it provides this formal specification which is necessary in ensuring a unified view of the concept of trust in the design and engineering of trust management systems for cloud computing.

Even though it is not only cloud service consumers that need the consideration of trust in their transactions with the cloud service providers, since most often than not, cloud services providers also need to be wary of the activities of cloud service consumers, trust modelling is useful in the analysis of the genuine and potentially malicious service consumers. Therefore a trust model is needful for the perceived trustworthiness of service consumers by the providers of the services. It should however be obvious to readers that the equation above can be casted with trustworthiness of the service consumer from the perspective of the service provider. Also, please note that it is for notational simplicity that the critical rating vectors $R_c^p\left(t_i\right)$ is denoted by R (without the full complement of the subscripts) in the denotation of the trustworthiness.

The above definitions have a number of interesting properties which correspond with the intuitive properties of trust in our everyday life such as trustworthiness is subjective, and it is defined relative to a particular set of critical attributes; trustworthiness is defined at a given point in time, this means trust is dynamic; and it is defined as a probability distribution.

Impact of Security on Trust in Cloud Computing

When selecting a cloud service provider, multiple important parameters that are of relevance to the cloud service consumer need to be identified properly. Also, there is the need for mechanisms to measure those parameters and aggregate these measurements based on the customers' preferences regarding the importance of these parameters (Habib, Ries, & Muhlhauser, 2010). References (Zhao, Rong, Jaatun, & Sandnes, 2012) and (Habib et al., 2010) have identified several of these parameters which have been categorized into quality of service related, security and privacy related, risk management related, and reputation related attributes. These parameters (attributes) are termed critical attributes; more formerly, a *critical attribute* of a service provider p, from the perspective of a service consumer c, in the context of a transaction $t_i \in T$, is an attribute whose value affects the utility of c and is contingent upon the behavior of p in the course of transaction t_i (Kuada, 2013). Based on the above we see that even though security attributes influence the perceived trust that a service consumer places in a service provider, it is but only a component in the array of attributes of trust and is even dependent on the expectation and needs of the service consumer. Another important issue that impact on quality of service related and risk management related attributes in the specification of the critical rating vector of the service consumer is Service Level Agreement (SLA). This concept is discussed next in the context of cloud computing service offerings.

Impact of Service Level Agreements on Trust

Cloud Service Level Agreements (SLAs) form an important component of the contractual relationship between a cloud service customer and a provider of a cloud service. Given the global nature of the Cloud, SLAs usually span many jurisdictions, with often different varying applicable legal requirements; in particular with respect to the protection of the personal data hosted in the Cloud. SLA terminology today often differs from one cloud service provider to another, making it difficult for cloud service customers to compare cloud services. This also introduces or increases lack of clarity and hence misunderstanding of SLA for cloud services on the market. This inherent confusion that is introduced in the mind of cloud service consumers lead to mistrust, or on a more formal note, a decrease in the trust value that cloud service consumers place on both the cloud service providers and the services that they offer. It is in light of this that in February 2013, the European Commission set up the Cloud Select Industry Group (A subgroup on Service Level Agreement) to work on the standardization of aspects of SLAs for cloud services in order to improve the clarity and increases the understanding of SLAs for cloud services in the market (European Commission, 2014).

There is a form of relationship between attributes of trust and the concept of SLA. SLA therefore has a direct impact on trust. The following discussion looks at the analogies between the concepts of the attributes of trust and that of SLAs and the impact that they have on trust. As was indicated above in the trust model, the trust level is based on the trustworthiness $\tau_c^p\left(R, t_i\right)$ of the service provider p as perceived by consumer c in the context of a transaction $t_i \in T$. This is the a priori subjective joint probability distribution function of the critical rating vector $R_c^p\left(t_i\right)$ from the perspective of c. According to (Kuada, 2013), instead of a single value rating, there is rating of metrics of intent, integrity, capability and results of the critical attributes of the entity to be trusted. Intent constitutes information about declared agendas about what entities promise to provide through their services. Integrity is concerned with information about honesty; this is a measure of, to what extent entities deliver on what they promised. Capability is concerned with information about owned or outsourced resources. This is the assets that the entity to be trusted have. Finally, results constitute information about products and services that entities are specialized in through consistently delivering these services satisfactorily to their clients.

A careful look at the definition of SLA shows that these key words directly state the definition of SLA or are implied by its definition. An SLA is a legal document that specifies what services that a service provider has indicated to provide to its customer by specifying its ability to deliver certain Service Level Objects (SLOs) for which its failure to deliver those SLOs indicates a breach of contract for which it is prepared to bear certain penalties that are also indicated in the SLA. The definition shows that the service provider indicates its intentions by stating certain SLOs that it intends to provide to its customers based on its own belief of possessing certain capabilities that will enable it to provide these SLOs. This declaration of intent causes or affects the expectation that a service consumer should have from the service provider and the service that is being provided. This declaration of intent is further supported by the severity of the penalties that the service provider is willing to endure in the event of its failure to deliver on its promise. Even though capabilities of the service provider may or may not always be explicitly stated, it is always implied because the wiliness of the provider to suffer certain penalties in the event of its failure to deliver is an indication that it believes it has the requisite skills and resources to deliver on the indicated SLOs. These coupled with knowledge of the service consumer of what services that the service provider have over the years been able to provide satisfactorily to its customers affect the perceived trustworthiness of the service provider. It is this direct relationship of the concepts (attributes) of trust and that of SLAs that make any misunderstanding in the terminologies of the SLOs in an SLA cause mistrust (or reduction of the level of trust) of cloud service providers and the services that they provide. Furthermore, as has been indicated above in previous sections, security parameters play a major role in the critical rating vectors of trustworthiness in cloud computing. These two phenomena have caused several works to be devoted to security SLAs and the associated SLOs for cloud services. Some of these are (European Commission, 2014), and (Hoehl, 2015).

SLA standardizations is very important and good but adoption of SLA templates is even better. A natural step on the SLA standardization is SLA templates for specific categories of cloud services in the cloud market place. A general template for SLAs can make comparison of different service offerings easier and reduce the time taken by provider and consumer to understand and negotiate terms. This becomes particularly important where automated approaches to service discovery, negotiation and configuration are used; and is consistent with the "On-demand self-service" characteristic of cloud computing (ETSI, 2012). Thus, even though SLA standardization is very necessary to provide common view of SLO terminologies, it is unable to meet the demands of the on-demand self-service characteristics of cloud computing in being able to provide real-time on-demand and automated negotiation of SLAs as and when the customer needs it. The adoption of SLA templates forms the basis for providing these features. Some works on SLA templates in cloud computing and their applicability in the context of opportunistic cloud services and federated clouds can be found in (Kuada, 2013).

DEVELOPMENT OF CLOUD SERVICES

There is an increasing recognition that security must be addressed throughout the software development lifecycle and this has grown alongside industry efforts to advance the current state of software security. With the advent of cloud computing, one key question is how the emergence and maturation of cloud computing has impacted the security development lifecycles of technology providers. It is in the effort to address this question that the Software Assurance Forum for Excellence in Code (SAFECode) and Cloud Security Alliance (CSA) partnered to determine whether there is a need for additional software security guidance to address threats that are unique to the cloud computing, and if so, to identify specific security practices that will minimize the impact of such threats (Sullivan et al., 2013). Because the drivers (such as flexibility, elasticity, cloud bursting, etc) that are pushing customers to adopt cloud computing lead to security requirements that are different from traditional data centers, this dynamic nature of the Cloud, coupled with customers' lack of ownership of cloud infrastructure and other cloud resources and services has broken conventional security models and architectures (Dimension Data, 2012). This calls for new approaches to security of IT resources of which the development and adoption of best practices to software applications for cloud environment is key.

Security Enhancing Approach to Cloud Application Development

One of the major distinguishing features of cloud computing is multi-tenancy. Multitenancy allows multiple clients of a cloud service provider to maintain a presence in a cloud service provider's environment, but in a manner where the computations and data of each tenant is isolated from and inaccessible to other tenants. The aim for deployment of cloud services in a multitenant environment is to ensure that: no tenant is able to identify or determine the existence of other tenants; no tenant has access to the data of other tenants; no tenant is able to perform an operation that affects the operation of or denies service to other tenants. In addition to these requirements, configuration for each tenant should be independent from that of other tenants; auditing and tracing should be provided on a per tenant basis; and provisioning and decommissioning of tenants should be performed in a manner that enforces tenant segregation (Sullivan et al., 2013). This key concept of multitenancy has architectural and design impacts on the cloud service provider's environment and on the applications that run in multitenant environments. Thus when SaaS applications are being developed, the above mentioned design requirements and architectural considerations must be fully considered. From a cloud service provider's perspective, the fundamental design principle for multitenancy is to have logically separate, but physically shared resources for the tenants. From the perspective of tenants, the cloud service provider's environment must appear to provide separation among tenants; but the reality is that the underlying infrastructure and even software resources used by the cloud service provider is typically physically shared among tenants.

Cloud Abstraction APIs

A Cloud API is a set of application development libraries, popularly known as Applications Programming Interface (API), that are specifically targeted towards cloud management tools. The purpose of these APIs is to offer cloud service consumers the opportunity to extend the features of their favorite cloud management tools by querying for more specific information from the cloud service providers' back-end systems. The maturity of open source cloud management tools, and the progress in interoperability and standardization efforts has led to the emergence of dominant Cloud APIs.

It is now common practice for a cloud service consumer to purchase services and resources from multiple cloud service providers and be using these resource concurrently. These cloud service providers provide different cloud management tools with their associated exposed individual cloud APIs to aid cloud service consumers in extending their cloud management tools. This has created the need for cloud service consumers to program against multiple cloud environments with the need to support multiple cloud APIs at the same time; and this can be a very challenging endeavor. The application developers' need to support programming against multiple Cloud APIs has brought about projects that aim at solving this problem by providing abstraction to the major cloud APIs. *Deltacloud API* and *jClouds API* are the only two of such projects currently in the public domain.

Deltacloud API is an open source Apache project. It enables management of resources in different Clouds by the use of one of three supported APIs. Its supported APIs are the Deltacloud classic API, the Cloud Infrastructure Management Interface (CIMI) API, and the EC2 API (Deltacloud, 2011). This means that a cloud service user can start an instance on an internal private Cloud, and start another on EC2 or Red Hat Enterprise Virtualization Manager (RHEV-M) with the same code. This is possible because there are back-end drivers communicating with each supported cloud vendor's native API; and the Deltacloud Core Framework provides the basis for implementing drivers to new IaaS clouds (Deltacloud, 2011). Some of the currently supported drivers are Amazon EC2, Opennebula, OpenStack, Eucalyptus, Rackspace, VMware vSphere, IBM, GoGrid, etc. (Deltacloud, 2011). The jClouds project is also an open source library that provides support for about thirty cloud services vendors and cloud software stacks including OpenStack, Amazon, GoGrid, Microsoft Azure, Ninefold, and Rackspace. It offers several API abstractions as Java and Clojure libraries (jClouds, 2011).

The design of these cloud APIs and especially the cloud abstraction APIs introduces potential source of vulnerabilities for cloud management tools. Equally important issue is the proper use of these APIs by cloud management tool developers in adhering to prescribed guidelines by the designers of these APIs.

CONCLUSION AND FUTURE RESEARCH

This work has discussed security and trust issues in cloud computing. These security and trust issues followed from the discussions on the role of virtualization in cloud computing and hence the impact that the various categories of virtualization such as server virtualization (and its two main types of virtualization architectures, and techniques of CPU virtualization), network virtualization, storage virtualization, and application virtualization have on the security and trust issues in cloud computing. It was evident from these discussions that virtualization introduces a number of security and risk related challenges in cloud computing based on the three security objectives of confidentiality, integrity, and availability (normally termed the CIA triad) and the two main other related security objectives of authenticity and accountability of information systems that was adopted for this discussion. It was however also noted that if the necessary recommended best practices of virtualizations are faithfully adhered to as was discussed is book chapter, then virtualization actually leads to improvement or enhancement in the security posture of cloud environments.

The role of security on the perception of the trust that cloud service consumers have for the providers of cloud services and the services that they provide have also been discussed; especially the role of service level agreements on trust in cloud computing. As much as efforts have been made to make this work complete, some future work that takes on a more IS research approach to the model of trust for cloud adoption can be considered. This formulation of trust in this work is suitable for system design and implementation. There is the need for a framework/model for trust that is not specific to a particular customer adopting cloud services but rather a general one where individual customers need not compute their own trust values but the model will serve as an indicator of the value placed on trust by potential cloud service consumers in making their decision to adopt a particular type of cloud services. The current mathematical formulation of trust that was presented and discussed in this work is suitable for building systems where agents mediate and make decisions for the consumer whereas the new model/framework is more for or as a guide for informing consumers in making decision to adopt cloud computing. It is aimed at producing a theory/model of adoption. The two key constructs that have currently been identified are security, and SLA; other constructs are currently being explored.

REFERENCES

Beimborn, D., Miletzki, T., & Wenzel, S. (2011). Platform as a Service (PaaS). *Business & Information Systems Engineering, 3*(6), 381–384. doi:10.1007/s12599-011-0183-3

Chandramouli, R. (2014). Security Recommendations for Hypervisor Deployment (No. 800-125-A). Gaithersburg, MD: National Institute of Standards and Technology, Computer Security Division Information Technology Laboratory.

ClearCenter. (2009). *Twitter breach revives security issues with cloud computing.* Retrieved from http://www.clearcenter.com/News-Articles/twitter-breach-revives-security-issues-with-cloud-computing.html?Itemid=456

Dellarocas, C. (2001). *The Design of Reliable Trust Management Systems for Electronic Trading Communities.* MIT.

Deltacloud. (2011, Oktober). *About Deltacloud.* Retrieved August 16, 2013, from http://deltacloud.apache.org/rest-api.html

Dimension Data. (2012). *Cloud Security: Developing a Secure Cloud Approach* (No. CS / DDMS-1072). Retrieved from http://www.dimensiondata.com/

ETSI. (2012). CLOUD; SLAs for Cloud services (Technical Report No. ETSI TR 103 125 V1.1.1 (2012-11)). European Telecommunications Standards Institute.

European Commission. (2014). *Cloud Service Level Agreements Standadisation Guidelines.* Brussels: Author.

Fahl, S., Harbach, M., Muders, T., & Smith, M. (2012). Confidentiality as a Service – Usable Security for the Cloud. In *2012 IEEE 11th International Conference on Trust, Security and Privacy in Computing and Communications (TrustCom)* (pp. 153 –162). http://doi.org/ doi:<ALIGNMENT.qj></ALIGNMENT>10.1109/TrustCom.2012.112

Habib, S. M., Ries, S., & Muhlhauser, M. (2010). Cloud Computing Landscape and Research Challenges Regarding Trust and Reputation. In *2010 7th International Conference on Ubiquitous Intelligence Computing and 7th International Conference on Autonomic Trusted Computing (UIC/ATC)* (pp. 410 –415). http://doi.org/doi:10.1109/UIC-ATC.2010.48

Hoehl, M. (2015). *Proposal for standard Cloud Computing Security SLAs – Key Metrics for Safeguarding Confidential Data in the Cloud*. The SANs Institute.

Huawei FusionSphere 5.0: Technical White Paper on Virtualization. (2014, September). Huawei Technologies Company Limited.

jClouds. (2011). *What is jClouds?* Retrieved April 27, 2013, from http://www. jclouds.org/documentation/gettingstarted/what-is-jclouds/

Kuada, E. (2013). Trust Management System for Opportunistic Cloud Services. In *2013 IEEE 2nd International Conference on Cloud Networking (CloudNet)* (pp. 33 – 41). San Francisco, CA: IEEE. doi:10.1109/CloudNet.2013.6710555

Kuada, E. (2014). *Opportunistic Cloud Services: A Social Network Approach to Provisioning and Management of Cloud Computing Services for Enterprises*. GlobeEdit. Retrieved from https://www.morebooks.de/gb/bookprice_offer_df165575e272c9927b008d4f5d2a05da0745c426

Kuada, E., Adanu, K., & Olesen, H. (2013). Cloud Computing and Information Technology Resource Cost Management for SMEs. In *Proceedings of IEEE Region 8 Conference EuroCon 2013* (pp. 258 – 265). University of Zagreb, Croatia: IEEE. Retrieved from http://www.eurocon2013.org/index.html

Marshall, D. (2011, November 2). *Top 10 benefits of server virtualization*. Retrieved from http://www.infoworld.com/article/2621446/server-virtualization/server-virtualization-top-10-benefits-of-server-virtualization.html

McAfee Inc. (2007). *Virtualization and Risk—Key Security Considerations for Your Enterprise Architecture*. McAfee Inc.

Mell, P., & Grance, T. (2011). The NIST definition of cloud computing (draft). *NIST Special Publication, 800,* 145.

Nepal, S., Chen, S., Yao, J., & Thilakanathan, D. (2011). DIaaS: Data Integrity as a Service in the Cloud. In *2011 IEEE International Conference on Cloud Computing (CLOUD)* (pp. 308 –315). http://doi.org/ doi:10.1109/CLOUD.2011.35

Pearce, M., Zeadally, S., & Hunt, R. (2013, February). Virtualization: Issues, Security Threats, and Solutions. *ACM Computing Surveys, 45*(2), 39. doi:10.1145/2431211.2431216

Singh, A., Korupolu, M., & Mohapatra, D. (2008). *Server-Storage Virtualization: Integration and Load Balancing in Data Centers*. Austin, TX: IEEE.

Stallings, W. (2014). *Cryptography and Network Security: Principles and Practice.* Pearson Education Inc.

Stuhlmuller, R. (2013, December 18). *4 ways network virtualization improves security.* Retrieved from http://www.infoworld.com/article/2609571/networking/4-ways-network-virtualization-improves-security.html

Sullivan, B., Tabet, S., Bonver, E., Furlong, J., Orrin, S., & Uhley, P. (2013). Practices for Secure Development of Cloud Applications. SAFECode & Cloud Security Alliance.

Sultan, N. (2010). Cloud computing for education: A new dawn? *International Journal of Information Management, 30*(2), 109–116. doi:10.1016/j.ijinfomgt.2009.09.004

VMware. (2007). *VMware Understanding Full Virtualization, Paravirtualization, and Hardware Assist* (White Paper No. WP-028-PRD-01-01). VMware, Inc.

VMware, Inc. (n.d.). *VMware ThinApp Agentless Application Virtualization Overview* (White Paper No. VMW-WP-THINAPP-APPVIRT-USLET-20120525 WEB). Retrieved from www.vmware.com

Xu, X. (2012). From cloud computing to cloud manufacturing. *Robotics and Computer-integrated Manufacturing, 28*(1), 75–86. doi:10.1016/j.rcim.2011.07.002

Zhao, G., Rong, C., Jaatun, M. G., & Sandnes, F. E. (2012). Reference deployment models for eliminating user concerns on cloud security. *The Journal of Supercomputing, 61*(2), 337–352. doi:10.1007/s11227-010-0460-9

KEY TERMS AND DEFINITIONS

Accountability: The assurance or the requirement that generates the security goal that the actions of an entity can be traced back uniquely to that entity.

Authenticity: The assurance that an entity is genuine and can be verified and therefore can be trusted.

Availability: The assurance that the system works promptly and that authorized users are not denied of their legitimate services.

Data Confidentiality: The assurance that private or confidential information is not made available or disclosed to unauthorized individuals or entities.

Data Integrity: The assurance that information and programs are not changed but only in a specified manner by those authorized to make such changes.

Privacy: The assurance that individuals control or influence what information related to them may be collected and stored and by whom and to whom that information is disclosed.

System Integrity: The assurance that a system performs its intended function unimpaired, and free from deliberate or unintentional unauthorized manipulation of the system.

Chapter 9
Security Issues in Distributed Computing System Models

Ghada Farouk Elkabbany
Electronics Research Institute, Egypt

Mohamed Rasslan
Electronics Research Institute, Egypt

ABSTRACT

Distributed computing systems allow homogenous/heterogeneous computers and workstations to act as a computing environment. In this environment, users can uniformly access local and remote resources in order to run processes. Users are not aware of which computers their processes are running on. This might pose some complicated security problems. This chapter provides a security review of distributed systems. It begins with a survey about different and diverse definitions of distributed computing systems in the literature. Different systems are discussed with emphasize on the most recent. Finally, different aspects of distributed systems security and prominent research directions are explored.

INTRODUCTION

A distributed system in computer science is an unified system of distributed computers, processors or processes that communicate together through common communication medium or network in order to transmit messages. This distribution could be physical (over a geographical area) or logically (over a virtual space). It is

DOI: 10.4018/978-1-5225-0741-3.ch009

often represented as a connected graph, the nodes are the computers or processes, and the edges are general bidirectional communication channels or links. One of the earliest definitions of a distributed system has been done by Tanenbaum and Steen (2007) who defined a distributed system as "A collection of independent computers that appears to its users as a single coherent system". Distributed systems have been built with the objective of attaining the following properties: transparency, openness, reliability, performance, and scalability (Coulouris & Kindberg, 2012). In order to achieve the above objectives, security of the system must be given adequate attention as it is one of the fundamental issues in distributed systems (Coulouris & Kindberg, 2012; Alotaibi, Wald & Argles, 2010).

Integration of different distributed components creates new security problems issues. Hence, security is one of the leading concerns in developing distributed systems. Web, clusters, grids and clouds form the backbone of distributed systems. Distributed systems security provides a holistic insight into current security issues, processes, and solutions. Security shapes future directions in the context of todays distributed systems (Belapurkar et al., 2009). In this research, four common distributed systems are considered for detailed analysis with respect to involved technologies, security issues, and proposed solution. This chapter is organized as follows. Next section presented an introduction to distributed systems, its advantages and challenges. Then commonly used distributed systems are described. Different security issues are presented in the following section. Then a thorough description of different distributed systems security methods described in the literatures is represented. Finally, conclusions and future work are discussed.

BACKGROUND

A distributed computing system is the system architecture that makes a collection of heterogeneous computers or workstations act and behave as being one single computing system. In such a computing environment, users can uniformly access local or remote resources, and run processes from anywhere in the system (Firdhous, 2011). A distributed system is a collection of (homogenous/heterogeneous) automata interconnected by a network. Its distribution is transparent to the user. So the system appears as one local machine. In a distributed system, the nodes communicate by sending and receiving messages over the network. Various distributed resources (i.e. files and printers) are shared across the network between the nodes in the form of network services that are provided by *servers*. Individual processes, *clients,* direct request the appropriate server in order to access recourses. Thus, a distributed system has three primary characteristics: multiple nodes, interconnections, and shared states. This section provides an introduction to the distributed systems and how to characterize them.

Coulouris et al. (2012) have defined a distributed system as "a system where the hardware and software components have been installed in geographically dispersed computers that coordinate and collaborate their actions by passing messages between them". Tanenbaum & Steen (2007) have defined a distributed system as "a collection of systems that appears to the users as a single system". Combining these definitions, it could be stated that a distributed system is an application that communicates with multiple dispersed hardware and software in order to coordinate the actions of multiple processes running on different autonomous computers over a communication network, so that all components (hardware and software) cooperate together to perform a set of related tasks that are targeted towards a common objective (Firdhous, 2011).

Advantages of Distributed Systems

Distributed system has features over a centralized system such as economics, speed, inherent distribution, and incremental growth. Moreover, distributed computing achieves the following advantages (Srinivasa & Muppalla, 2015):

- **Increased Performance:** The existence of multiple nodes in a distributed system allows applications to be processed in parallel and thus improve the application and system performance.
- **Sharing of Resources:** Distributed systems enable efficient access for different system resources. Users can share special purpose and sometimes expensive hardware and software resources such as, database server, compute server, virtual reality server, multimedia information server and etc.
- **Increased Extendibility:** Distributed systems are designed to be modular and adaptive. For certain computations, the system will configure itself to include a large number of nodes and resources while in other instances, it will just consist of a few resources. Furthermore, the file system capacity and computing power can be increased incrementally. Perhaps the best feature of a distributed system over the centralized system is in its modular extendibility.
- **Increased Reliability, Availability, and Fault Tolerance:** The aggregation of multitude computing and storage resources in the distributed system makes it attractive and cost effective to introduce redundancy in order to improve the system dependability and fault tolerance. The system can tolerate the failure in one node by allocating its tasks to another available one. Moreover, owing

to the inherent increased reliability goal embedded within a distributed system. If one machine crashes, the entire system does not fall, which is unlike the centralized system (Alotaibi, Wald & Argles, 2010).

These advantages cannot be achieved easily, because designing a general purpose distributed computing system is a complicated process. This process has many challenges that designers have to overcome. In the next subsection, distributed system main challenges are presented.

Challenges of Distributed Systems

As the scope and scale of distributed systems and applications are extended, different challenges are likely to be encountered (Coulouris & Kindberg, 2012; Rahman, Ranjan & Buyya, 2012; Steen, Pierre & Voulgaris, 2012). In this section, the foremost challenges are described:

- **Heterogeneity:** Distributed systems enable users to access services and run applications over a heterogeneous collection of computers and networks. Heterogeneity (that is, variety and difference) applies to all of the following: networks, computer hardware, operating systems, programming languages, and implementations by different developers (Coulouris & Kindberg, 2012).
- **Openness:** The openness of a computer system is the characteristic that determines whether the system can be extended and re-implemented in various ways. The openness of a distributed system is determined primarily by the degree to which new resource-sharing services can be added and be made available for use by a variety of client programs. Openness cannot be achieved unless the specification and documentation of the key software interfaces of the components of a system are made available to software developers (Coulouris & Kindberg, 2012).
- **Scalability:** Distributed systems operate effectively and efficiently at many different scales, ranging from a small intranet to the Internet. The number of computers and servers in the Internet has increased dramatically. A system is described as *scalable* if it will remain effective when there is a significant increase in the number of resources and the number of users.
- **Distribution Transparency:** Transparency is defined as the concealment from the user and the application programmer of the separation of components in a distributed system. Thus, the system is perceived as a whole rather than as a collection of independent components (Coulouris & Kindberg, 2012). The problem with striving for distribution transparency in very large systems is that performance will degrade to unacceptable level. Moreover,

network latencies have a natural lower bound that becomes noticeable, when dealing with long-haul connections (Steen, Pierre & Voulgaris, 2012).

- **Scheduling:** Decentralized scheduler organization negates the limitations of centralized organization with respect to fault-tolerance, scalability, and autonomy. This approach scales well for both, a small scale resource sharing environment (e.g. Resource sharing under the same administrative domain) in a large scale environment. However, this approach raises serious challenges in the domain of distributed information management, enforcing system wide coordination, security, resource user authenticity, and resource provider's policy heterogeneity (Rahman, Ranjan & Buyya, 2012).
- **Security and Trust:** Many of the information resources that are made available and maintained in distributed systems have a high intrinsic value to their users. Their security is therefore of considerable importance (Coulouris & Kindberg, 2012). The decentralized organization of distributed systems raises serious challenges in domains of security and trust management. Implementing a secure distributed system requires solutions that can efficiently address different security issues (Rahman, Ranjan & Buyya, 2012).

There are many distributed systems in operation today. In the next section, the authors illustrate the most well-known distributed computing paradigms.

DISTRIBUTED COMPUTING SYSTEM MODELS

A distributed computing system is built over a large number of autonomous computer nodes. These nodes are interconnected by *System-Area Networks* (SAN), *local-Area networks* (LAN), or *Wide-Area Networks* (WAN) in a hierarchical manner. By today's networking technology, a few LAN switches can easily connect hundreds of machines as a working cluster. A WAN can connect many local clusters in order to form a very-large cluster of clusters. In this sense, one can build a massive system to have millions of computers connected to edge networks in various Internet domains. Distributed computing can be classified into four classes, namely: Cluster Computing, P2P Networks, Grid Computing, and Cloud Computing: (Anjomshoa, Salleh & Kermani, 2015; Hwang, Fox & Dongarra, 2010; Kumar & Charu, 2015; Kaur & Rai, 2014; Pourqasem, Karimi & Edalatpanah, 2014; Sadashiv & Kumar, 2011).

Cluster Computing

Cluster computers are a set of computers that are grouped together, communicating over a high speed network, and can be made to work and present itself as a single computer to the users. Any task that has been assigned to the cluster would run on all cluster nodes in a parallel fashion by breaking the whole task into smaller self-contained tasks. Then, the result of the smaller tasks would be combined in order to form the final result (Kaur & Rai, 2014). Cluster computing helps organizations to increase their computing power using the standard and commonly available technology. Clusters are used primarily to run scientific, engineering, commercial, and industrial applications that require high availability and high throughput processing (Firdhous, 2011). Figure 1 shows a typical arrangement of computers in a computing cluster.

Peer-to-Peer (P2P)

A well-established distributed system is the client-server architecture. Client machines (PC and workstations) are connected to a central server for computation, Email, file access, database applications. The P2P architecture offers a distributed model of networked systems. In a P2P system, every node acts as both a client and a server,

Figure 1. Cluster computing
(Firdhous 2011)

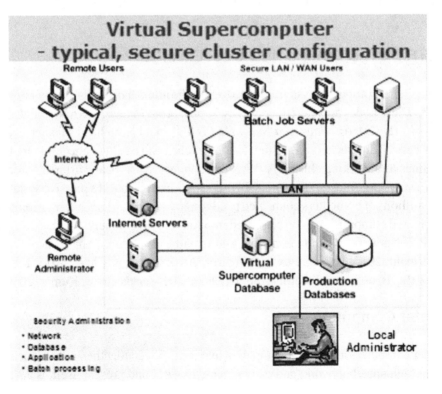

providing part of the system resources. Peer machines are simply client computers connected to the Internet. All client machines act autonomously to join or leave the system freely. This implies that no master-slave relationship exists among the peers. No central coordination or central database is needed. In other words, no peer machine has a global view of the entire P2P system. The system is self-organized with distributed control (Hwang, Fox & Dongarra, 2010). The architecture of a P2P network is shown in Figure 2.

Unlike the cluster or grid, a P2P network does not use a dedicated interconnection network. The physical network is simply an ad hoc network formed at various Internet domains randomly using TCP/IP and NAI protocols. Thus, the physical network varies in size and topology dynamically, due to the free membership in the P2P network (Hwang, Fox & Dongarra 2010).

Grid Computing

Grid is a type of distributed computing system where a collection of heterogeneous computers and resources spread across multiple administrative domains with intend on providing users easy access to these resources. Grid is defined as a parallel and distributed system that is capable of selecting, sharing, and aggregating geographically distributed resources dynamically at runtime based on their availability, capability, performance, and cost meeting the users' Quality of Service (QoS) requirements (Dabas & Arya, 2013; Firdhous, 2011). Grids can be considered as heterogeneous

Figure 2. The structure of a Peer-to-Peer system
(Hwang, Fox & Dongarra 2010)

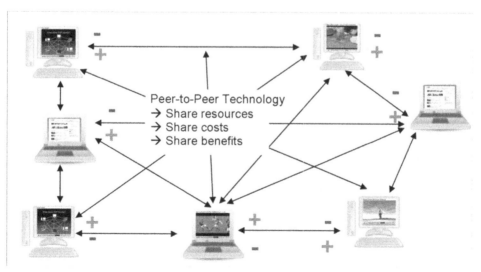

clusters interconnected by high-speed networks. They have centralized control; they are server-oriented with authenticated security (Tanenbaum, & Steen, 2007). Grid computing combines computing resources distributed across a large geographical area belonging to different persons and organization. With grid computing, an organization can transparently integrate, streamline, and share dispersed, heterogeneous pools of hosts, servers, storage systems, data, and networks and sensors into one synergistic system. One of the main strategies of grid computing is to use middleware to divide and apportion pieces of a program among several computers. Middleware is software that enables communication and management of data in distributed applications. The purpose of middleware is to allow different computers to run an application across the entire network of machines. Without it, communication across the system would be impossible. Like software in general, there's no single format for middleware. The middleware and control node of a grid computing system are responsible for keeping the system running smoothly. Together, they divide and farm out pieces of a program to as many as several thousand computers and control how much access each computer has to the network's resources and vice versa (Bhatia, 2013). Grid middleware allows heterogeneous systems to work collaboratively to deliver the appearance of a large virtual computing environment, while offering a variety of virtual resources (Pourqasem, Karimi & Edalatpanah, 2014). Figure 3 shows a grid system distributed across heterogeneous computing platforms.

Figure 3. Grid computing
(Dabas & Arya 2013)

There are three main types of computer grids: computational grids, data grids, and service grids (Cody et al., 2008):

- **Computational Grids:** Focus on setting aside resources specifically for computing power (solving equations and complex mathematical problems). Although, machines participating in this type of grid are usually high-performance servers. Programs with infinite loops can be used to bring down nodes of this grid, and decreasing functionality.
- **Data Grids**: Responsible for storing and providing access to large volumes of data, often across several organizations. Nevertheless, users can overwrite the data of other users if they exceed their available space. This corrupts the other users' data.
- **Service Grids:** Provide services that are not available on a single machine. Nonetheless, users can use the service grid in order to launch Denial of Service Attack (DOS) against another site.

While the types of grid listed above represent the three common categories of grid computing systems, some grid systems can employ aspects of some or all of those three types, making them "hybrid" grid computing systems (Cody et. al., 2008).

Cloud Computing

The definition of cloud computing provided by the National Institute of Standards and Technology (NIST) says that: "Cloud computing is a model for enabling on-demand and convenient network access to a shared pool of configurable computing resources (networks, servers, storage, applications and services) that can be rapidly provisioned and released with minimal management effort or service provider interaction" (Gupta, Laxmi & Sharma, 2014).

The cloud computing as a ubiquitous paradigm could provide different services for internet users and Information Technology (IT) companies through datacenters located around the world. Cloud computing services are typically categorized into three main types namely: Infrastructure as a Service (IaaS), Platform as a Service (PaaS), and Software as a Service (SaaS). As shown in Figure 4, IaaS is found at the lowest level of abstraction, which provides the user with processing, storage, networking, and other computing resources on-demand. The following level, PaaS, is usually built upon IaaS and allows the user to deploy onto the cloud infrastructure applications created using programming and runtime environments supported by the provider. Software developers and IT staff, but also non-technical users, employ resources at this level. Finally, SaaS is nowadays the best-known model, consisting

Figure 4. Cloud computing models and services provided
(Hwang, Fox & Dongarra 2010)

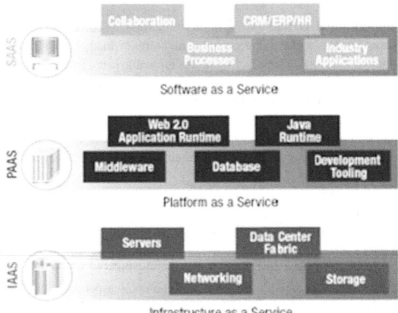

of applications offered by the provider over the network, instead of being run on the user's computer. At this level, resources usually accessed via a Web client vary from actual applications to multimedia or web services. All these services can be offered by a cloud provider according to different deployment models (Hwang, Fox & Dongarra, 2010; Kumar & Charu, 2015; Mahajan & Singh, 2013; Sadashiv & Kumar, 2011; Salim, Tiwari & Tripathi, 2013; Zhao et. al., 2014).

There are four different models for deployment, namely: Private cloud, Public cloud, Community cloud, and Hybrid cloud (Conway & Curry, 2012; Fernandes et. al., 2014; Mahajan & Singh, 2013; Zhao et. al., 2014).

- **A Private Cloud**: Managed in a single organization; a private cloud can be owned and managed either internally or externally by an organization. Venturing into a private cloud project requires a significant level and degree of engagement to virtualize the business environment. For example, Intel and Hewlett Packard (HP) have their own internal private cloud. In addition, some researchers have built their own private cloud in a specific manner. Gonzalez-Martinez et al. (Gonzalez-Martínez et. al., 2015) surveyed the state of the art on the use and research of cloud computing in education.

- **Public Cloud:** Owned by an organization selling cloud services to the general public or to a large industry group. Two examples are Amazon Web Services (AWS) and Microsoft Azure.
- **Community Cloud:** Shared by several organizations and supports a specific community that has a shared mission, shared goals, security requirements, policies, and compliance considerations. The Google - Gov is an example of community cloud.
- **Hybrid Cloud:** Consists of two or more clouds (public, community, or private) that remain unique entities, but are bound together by standardized or proprietary technology that enables data or application portability.

The National Institute of Standards and Technology's (NIST) defines five key characteristics of a cloud environment: On-demand self-service, Broad network access, Resource pooling, Rapid elasticity and Measured service (Ali, Khan & Vasilakos 2015). NIST's five essential characteristics, three service models and four deployment models are shown in Figure 5. Furthermore, the Cloud Security Alliance (CSA) adds multi-tenancy as an important characteristic of the cloud computing (although not an essential characteristic). Cloud computing characteristics in the light of NIST definition are presented below (Ali, Khan, & Vasilakos, 2015; Fernandes et. al., 2014; Gonzalez-Martínez et. al., 2015):

Figure 5. NIST definition of cloud computing
(Ali et. al., 2015)

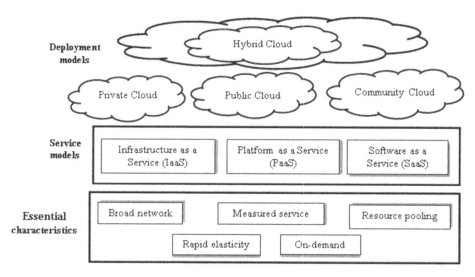

- **On-Demand Self-Service**: Users can request and manage the services from the cloud without any human interaction with the CSP (*Cloud Service Provider*). The provision of the services and the associated resources is accomplished as and when required. This is usually done through Web services and management interfaces.

- **Broad Network Access**: Services, applications and data present on the cloud must be accessible to users using the standard mechanisms and protocols. The characteristic further demands that the availability of services should support heterogeneous thin or thick environment (e.g. mobile phones, laptops, workstations). In the literature, broad network access is sometimes referred to as ubiquitous network access.

- **Resource Pooling**: The cloud's resources are shared among multiple users by pooling in a multi-tenant environment. The users are transparent about the location of the resources. There is a mapping between physical and virtual resources provided to the users.

- **Rapid Elasticity**: The resources can be rapidly and elastically scaled as per customer's demands. The customer has a view of unlimited resources that can be purchased as needed in a pay-as-you-go manner.

- **Measured Service**: The scaling of resources up and down is performed dynamically and the usage of the services is metered and reported to the customer and CSP. The metering also helps the optimization of resource usage automatically while the users are charged in a pay-as-you-use manner.

Security is one of the most important issues in distributed systems. When data is distributed across multiple networks or information is transferred via public networks, it becomes vulnerable to attacks by mischievous elements. Similarly, other computing resources such as processors, storage devices, and networks could be attacked by hackers.

SECURITY ISSUES IN DISTRIBUTED SYSTEMS

Security services are generally classified into six components: Confidentiality, Data integrity, Authentication, Authorization, Non-repudiation, and Accountability (Alotaibi, Wald & Argles, 2010; Sun et. al., 2014; Tan, Ko & Holmes, 2013) which will be explained below:

- **Confidentiality:** Important data that are transmitted or transported between parties should be secured and protected. Confidentiality is the concept of ensuring that the important data is kept completely undisclosed to the unauthorized entities (Abbas & Khan, 2014).

- **Data Integrity:** Data integrity means maintaining and assuring the accuracy and consistency of data over its entire life-cycle. This means that data cannot be modified without permission of its legitimate user (Kumar & Agrawal, 2013). That is to say, it ensures that the important data have not been altered or destroyed in an unauthorized or undetected manner.
- **Authentication:** Authentication is a core security in distributed systems, which requires mutual trust between the parties (Abbas & Khan, 2014). It is also important for authenticity to validate that both parties involved are who they claim to be. Some information security systems incorporate authentication features such as "digital signatures", which give evidence that the message data is genuine and was sent by someone possessing the proper signing key.
- **Authorization and Access Control:** Authorization management has become one of the most important issues concerning the distributed systems. It is used to supply one secured access point enabling the users to link up to the network and access to authorized resources. On the other side, access control prevents unauthorized individuals access the system (Koshutanski, 2009).
- **Non-Repudiation:** Non-repudiation is the concept of ensuring that a party in a dispute cannot repudiate or refute the validity of the statement. That is to say, the transmitter cannot deny sending the message (Abbas & Khan, 2014).
- **Accountability:** Although security has been addressed in various aspects, accountability is one of the main facets of security that is lacking in today's computer systems (Karajeh, Maqableh & Masa'deh, 2011; Siani, 2011; Xiao, Kathiresshan & Xiao, 2012). The ability not only to detect errors, but also to find the responsible entity/entities for the failure is crucial.

SECURITY ATTACKS ON DISTRIBUTED SYSTEMS

Distributed denial of service and identity attacks are mostly occur in distributed system (Kumar & Agrawal, 2013; Lee, 2014).

Distributed Denial of Service (DDoS) Attack

Denial of service (DoS) is an attack in which the main purpose of the attacker or hacker is to destroy the service of resources used by the legitimate user. That is to say, an attacker tries to prevent an authentic user from using a service. When this attack occurs in distributed system, it is called Distributed Denial of Service (DDoS) attack. A DDoS attack is one in which a multitude of compromised systems attack a single target, and causing denial of service for users of the targeted system. The flood of incoming messages to the target system essentially forces it to shut down, thereby denying service to the system to legitimate users. In a typical DDoS attack, a hacker begins by exploiting vulnerability in one computer system and making it the DDoS master. It is from the master system that the intruder identifies and communicates with other systems that can be compromised. The intruder loads cracking tools available on the Internet. With a single command, the intruder instructs the controlled machines to launch one of many flood attacks against a specified target (Kumar & Agrawal, 2013).

Identity Attack in Distributed System

Identity attack wrongfully obtains authorized entry's information and then uses that information to commit deception. Most networks and operating systems use the IP address of a computer to identify a valid entity. In certain cases, it is possible for an IP address to be falsely assumed identity spoofing. An attacker may use special programs to construct IP packets that appear to originate from valid addresses inside the corporate intranet. After gaining access to the network with a valid IP address, the attacker can modify, rewrite, or delete your data. The attacker can also conduct other types of attacks, as described in the following sections. In P2P, identity attack allows a malicious peer in the network to hijack application-level requests and assume the responsibility of any application component (Puttaswamy, Zheng & Zhao, 2009).

As mentioned above, four common used distributed systems were considered for analysis in terms of the security issues faced by them and solution proposed to circumvent these issues. These four models are: cluster computing, P2P networks, grid computing, and cloud computing. It is fair to say that clusters have laid the necessary foundation to build large-scale grids and clouds. On the other hand, grid/cloud platforms are regarded as utility service providers. In this section, the authors focus on grid and cloud security, since these systems provide more services and are widely used by different applications. First, a brief survey about cluster and P2P security will be presented. Then, the authors will introduce different security issues and their solutions for both grid and cloud in detail.

CLUSTER COMPUTING SECURITY

When the computing clusters are made available to the public using the Internet, they become subject to various kinds of attacks. The most common types of attacks on the clusters are computed-cycle stealing, inter-node communication snooping, and cluster service disruption (Xie & Qin, 2008). Hence the clusters have to be protected by security mechanisms that include services such as, authentication, integrity check, and confidentiality. The main purpose of the security mechanisms is to protect the system against hackers, as well as, to meet the security requirements of the applications. Hence it can be seen that computing clusters are vulnerable to attacks by mischievous element, such as, hackers and crackers, due to its open nature and use of public resources. Extensive research has been carried out by several researchers in the security of clusters. Researchers have proposed several methods that could be used in order to protect the clusters from these attacks (Firdhous, 2011).

Li and Vaughn have studied the security vulnerabilities of computing clusters using exploitation graphs (e-graphs). They have modeled several attacks that can be carried on confidentiality, integrity and availability. They have shown that e-graphs could be simplified based on domain knowledge such as, cluster configurations, and detected vulnerabilities. They further state that this technique could be used for certification of clusters with the help of a knowledge base of cluster vulnerabilities (Li & Vaughn, 2006).

Xic and Qin have developed two resource allocation schemes namely:

1.   Deadline and Security constraints TAPADS (*Task Allocation for Parallel Applications with Deadline and Security constraints*), and
2.   SHARP (*Security-aware And Heterogeneity-aware Resource allocation for Parallel jobs*).

These two schemes ensure that parallel applications are executed on computing clusters that meet the security requirements, and the deadline of executions (Xie & Qin, 2008). Hence it could be seen that if these schemes ensure mainly the availability of the system at timely execution of an application, it is an indication of the availability of the resources.

Denial of Service (DoS) attack is one of the common attacks on distributed systems. This attack mainly target resources in such a manner that resources are prevented from carrying out their legitimate operations. In in (Zhongqiu, Shu & Liangmin, 2009), a presentation of a method that uses services and Markova chain in order to mitigate the effects of the DoS attack on a cluster-based wireless sensor network. The Markov chain approach was used to obtain the probability of active clusters integrated them for quantities evaluation of survivability (which is defined as the ability to provide basic services after attacks or system error) in different states.

S. Thalod and R. Niwas (2013) proposed a security model for computer networks that are based on cluster computing architecture, by using various tools available in TCP/IP security model. Every tool has its own security features which make the system secure. They applied these security tools with their security features at different levels of cluster computing architecture, to make it a secure high performance computing system.

PEER-TO-PEER NETWORK SECURITY

Peer-to-Peer (P2P) networks provide a powerful platform for the construction of a variety of decentralized services. P2P networks offer many advantages to users, but it becomes a challenge to resist and protect against various attacks on security (Selvaraja & Anandb, 2012). Since P2P systems inherently rely on the dependence of peers with each other, security implications arise from abusing the trust between peers. In a traditional client-server model, internal data should not be exposed to the client. But in P2P, some internals must be exposed to associated peers in the name of distributing the workload. Attackers can leverage this in order to compromise P2P networks (Li, 2008). That is to say, decentralized nature and the lack of a controlling authority expose P2P systems to a broad range of security attacks. Examples of such attacks include: Denial of Service (DoS), freeloading, Poisoning, Pollution attacks (Koutrouli & Tsalgatidou, 2012), and Identity attack, which allows the spiteful peer in the network to capture the application request and assume the responsibility of any application component (Kumar & Agrawal, 2013).

Selvaraja and Anandb (2012) presented a comprehensive survey of security issues in reputation based trust management system for P2P networks. They discussed in detail the different security attacks on P2P systems and categorized them into network-related and peer-related attacks. Another work was done by Koutrouli & Tsalgatidou (2012); they explored and classified the types of potential attacks against reputation systems for P2P applications. In addition, they classified the defense mechanisms which have been proposed for each type of attack and identified conflicts between defense mechanisms and/or desirable characteristics of credible reputation systems. Moreover, they proposed a roadmap for reputation system designers on how to use the results of the survey in order to design of robust reputation systems for P2P applications.

Streaming applications over P2P systems have gained an enormous popularity. Success always implies increased concerns about security, protection, and privacy. Gheorghe et al. (2011) presented a general survey investigating specific security aspects of these systems. Starting from existing analyses and security models in the related literature, they provide an overview of security and privacy considerations for P2P streaming systems.

GRID COMPUTING SECURITY

As mentioned in above, there are three main types of computer grids: computational grids, data grids, and service grids. Since this research deals with security risks that could be faced with any type of computer grids, it is assumed that the term "grid computing" includes all three types. This section classifies grid computing security mechanisms according to (Bendahmane et. al., 2009; Kazemi, 2014). It classified the grid computing security into five main categories: Resources level, Service level, Authentication and Authorization level, Information level, and Management level solutions as shown in Figure 6.

Resources Level

Resources level solutions focused on protecting the grid resources, which include grid nodes (Host) and communication network.

Host Security

The solution to addressing Host security can be achieved by isolating the portion of the resource dedicated to the grid from the portion of the resource that the owner

Figure 6. Classification of grid computing security
(Cody et. al., 2008; Kazemi 2015)

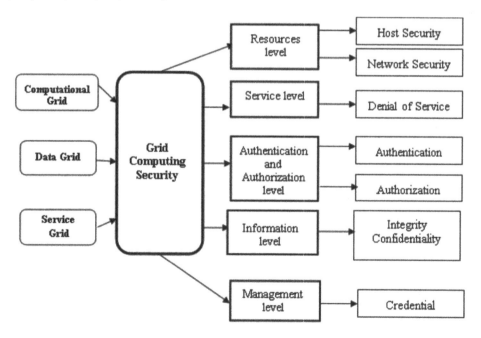

wishes to keep it private. Several isolation techniques such as Sandboxing and Virtualization are discussed to protect grid nodes (Cody et. al., 2008).

Sandboxing was specifically designed for the desktop grid environment, where there are a large number of desktop clients (Cano & Vargas-Lombardo 2012). This technique consists of two components: the desktop controller and the sandbox execution layer. The desktop controller is responsible for launching the processes to run the sub-job, and monitoring the running of the sub-job on the host desktop. On the other hand, the sandbox execution layer provides desktop security through sandboxing and mechanisms to interface with the desktop controller (Kazemi 2014). The flexibility of this system is greatly reduced, because it is closely aligned to specific environments.

Another way to provide isolation is through virtualization. Virtualization is the logical separation between services and the underlying physical resources. It is possible to run entire operating systems, applications, or services independent of the underlying system. Moreover, virtualization provides the ability to run the mentioned services on different physical platforms (Suresh & Kannan 2014). To provide virtualization, there is a need for a software layer called *Virtual Machine Monitor* (VMM). VMM provides virtual machine (VM) to multiple instances of several machines. In addition, policy management mechanisms are needed for development of the virtualization systems (Bendahmane et. al., 2009; Kazemi, 2014). There are three popular virtualization technologies: hosted virtualization, para-virtualization, and shared kernel based virtualization techniques.

- **Hosted Virtualization:** VMM and the guest operating system (OS) share the same user space, while the applications are running on the host OS. Generally, this model does not require any modification to the host OS. With this architecture, various hardware device drivers are part of the VMM, as well as many other components. It handles all the OS functions such as: scheduling, memory management, file systems, and management interfaces. (Suresh & Kannan 2014). VMware GSX Server is an example of hosted virtualization system (VMware 2015).
- **Para-Virtualization:** OSs are modified and recompiled so that the multiple redirections of the hosted model can be avoided. The performance of the para-virtualization based systems is comparatively better than the hosted virtualization based systems. Xen (Hagen, 2008) and Virtuozzo (Suresh & Kannan 2014) are examples of para- virtualization systems.
- **Shared Kernel Based Virtualization:** The kernel is shared and the user space is partitioned to be used by different sets of applications. An example of shared kernel based virtualization systems is the Linux VServer [http://linux-vserver.org]

Although virtualization solutions provide efficient isolation, some of them (hosted virtualization model) suffer from performance overhead. Most of these solutions are available for open OSs like Linux and currently not available for closed systems like Windows (Kazemi, 2014).

Network Level

Firewalls, or VPNs (Virtual Private Networks) between the user's host and the server host, or between different server hosts present a serious challenge to grid security measures (Gupta & Gupta 2013). Several research efforts have been undertaken in network security. Kavitha and Sankaranarayanan (2011) proposed a protocol to have a VPN gateway on all the resource sites of the virtual organization and at the client side. Moreover, there is a VPN server at the middle layer that connects the resources and clients through VPN gateway. The resources and the client tasks securely communicate by establishing a VPN tunnel between the client and the VPN server port. The tasks of the application are grouped into different task sets and appropriate resource for every task set is determined. Then the task set is transferred to the selected resource through the VPN tunnel established between resource and VPN server. The VPN connection to the resource is released as the task set is successfully executed and the results returned to the result aggregator. To enforce security policy, all the VPN gateways work together. The entities are to be authenticated by the VPN server before the tunnel is established. Authentication is performed by the exchange of certificates during the connection establishment phase.

T. Yao (2005) proposed a model called Adaptive Grid Firewall (AGF). The main motivation behind his work is the observation that: to meet the grid firewall requirements, the administrators need to open several well-known ports, and a range of temporary ports for incoming connections. This can be dangerous as strangers may be able to sneak into the system through the open ports. The AGF system developed a mechanism so that the firewall can adaptively open and close ports based on service requests. The firewall opens the ports when it receives authenticated requests, and closes them when there are no service activities at those ports.

Intrusion Detection Systems (IDSs) are software/hardware systems that automate the process of monitoring the events occurring in a computer system or network, and analyzing them for signs of security problems. The aim of the IDS is to alert or notify the system that some malicious activities have taken place and try to eliminate it (Mathew & Jose, 2012). IDSs consist of a set of detectors that detect attacks based on a set of policies and information (Bendahmane et. al., 2009; Kazemi, 2014). IDSs have been categorized into two categories: anomaly detection systems and signature detection systems. In *anomaly detection systems*, intrusion is detected based on abnormalities of system behavior. On the other hand, in *signature detection systems*, an intrusion is detected based on a specific signature or a model. It is to be noted that the signature is based on long term information about the intrusion behavior (Bendahmane et. al., 2009). Most of the grid based IDSs have a set of sensors which are able to monitor the state of the grid system. The information that supplied by the sensors are collected, analyzed, and logged through an interface to be listed. Finally, the suitable alarms and action mechanisms are provided (Bendahmane et. al., 2009; Kazemi, 2014). Several grid based IDS systems have been considered, designed, and implemented. Kazemi (2014) surveyed the most important grid based IDS systems.

Service Level

Distributed Denial of Service (DDoS) attacks are one of the biggest concerns for security professionals. DDoS attacks are typically explicit attempts to disrupt authentic users' access to services. The attackers usually gain access to a large number of computers by exploiting their vulnerabilities to set up attack crowds (Zargar & Tipper, 2013). Existing strategies against DDoS are implemented as preventive or reactive solutions. *Preventive solutions* (such as. application filtering, location hiding, and throttling techniques) are used to detect and reduce the effectiveness of the attacks born taking place. Developing a comprehensive defense mechanism against identified and anticipated DDoS attacks is a desired goal of the prevention research community. On the other hand, *reactive solutions* (such as: link testing, logging, and IP traceback) identify the attacker after the attack has been completed (Beitollahi & Deconinck, 2012; Kazemi, 2014).

Zarger and Tipper (2013) explored the scope of the DDoS flooding attack problem, they categorized the DDoS flooding attacks and classified the existing countermeasures based on where and when they prevent, detect, and respond to the DDoS flooding attacks. It is to be noted that DDoS attacks cannot be mitigated by one solution alone and multiple solutions should be employed to improve the effectiveness. Among the different available solutions, the preventive solutions are the only techniques that have been successfully implemented. However, most of these solutions have limited success and more research and development efforts are needed (Kazemi, 2014).

Authentication and Authorization Level

Grid computing is particularly sensitive to authentication and authorization due to its decentralized nature. Although they are similar concepts each have different, specific functions for grid security. According to authentication is "the verification of the identity of an entity". On the other hand, authorization is defined as "the process by which an entity gets the right to perform a privileged operation" (Cody et. al., 2008). An entity may be a user, a resource or a service provided as part of the grid. Grid security solutions that deal with both authentication and authorization will be discussed below.

Authentication

For the reason that grid resources are valuable, access is usually limited, based on the requested resource and the requesting user's identity. Authentication in a grid computing environment is the first defense line before other security aspects (Farouk, Abdelhafez & Fouad, 2012). It deals with verification of the identity of an entity within a network. Bhatia (2013) categorized authentication methods into: Password-based authentication, Kerberos authentication, Secure Sockets Layer (SSL) authentication, and Certification Authorities (CA).

- **Password-Based Authentication:** A simple function where one party presents a set of credentials (user ID and password combination) to a system. If the credentials match a given set on the system, the system returns a value that represents authorization; otherwise it does not. In case of messages cannot be read by un-trusted entity, unencrypted passwords can be used, otherwise instead of sending passwords over the network one can use password as the encryption key (Bhatia, 2013; Farouk, Abdelhafez & Fouad, 2012).
- **Kerberos Authentication:** A protocol which works on the basis of "tickets" to allow nodes communicating over a non-secure network to prove their identity to one another in a secure manner ((Dagorn, Bernard & Varrette, 2005; Farouk, Abdelhafez & Fouad, 2012; Mishra, Yadav & Maheshwari, 2014).
- **Secure Sockets Layer (SSL) Authentication:** Transport Layer Security (TLS) and its predecessor Secure Sockets Layer (SSL) are cryptographic protocols that provide communication security over the Internet. TLS and SSL encrypt the segments of network connections above the transport layer, using asymmetric cryptography for key exchange, symmetric encryption for privacy, and message authentication codes for message integrity. Every client authenticates identity of the server by sending a session key from client to server to set up an encrypted communication. The TLS protocol allows client-server applications to communicate across a network in a way designed to prevent eavesdropping and tampering. Once the client and server have decided to use TLS they connected by using a handshaking procedure. During this handshake, the client and server agree on various parameters used to establish the connection's security (Bhatia, 2013).

- **Certification Authorities (CA):** If a grid resource needs to securely communicate with another grid resource, it needs a certificate signed by a CA. Security in grid environment can be based on digitally signed documents, or certificates, that convey identity, authorization, and attributes. A digital signature can affirm document validity without the physical presence of the signer or physical ownership of documents signed in the author's handwriting. Users are authenticated by presenting an identity certificate and proving that they know the associated private key. These certificates are issued by certificate authorities that verify the connection between a user or system component and possession of a public key/private key pair. Users create and digitally sign use-condition certificates that define conditions that must be satisfied by a user before being given access to a resource. User attributes are asserted by "authorities" that provide assured information as digitally signed attribute certificates. Both use-condition and attribute certificates may be stored locally to the user as long as they can be provided by a server when they are needed to determine permissions during an access request (Gupta & Gupta 2013).

The Globus Toolkit's authentication and authorization components provide the basis standard for the "core" security software in grid systems and applications. Globus software development kits provide programming libraries, Java classes, and essential tools for a PKI (Pubic Key Interface) (Farouk, Abdelhafez & Fouad, 2012; Zhai, Qiao & Shao 2012), and certificate-based authentication system. Grid security technology such as GSI (Grid Security Infrastructure) and CAS (Community Authorization Service) are used to provide security (Mishra, Yadav & Maheshwari, 2014). GSI-X.509 provides the solution based on X.509 certificate to authenticate the different entity, and has been implemented in all versions of Globus. GSI assumes that to sign and certify different grid entities, each entity generates a public-private-key pair, and a CA. Globus security does not accept Kerberos credentials as an authentication mechanism. To make this integration possible, there is a need for gateways or translators which accept GSI credentials and convert it to Kerberos credentials and vice versa. KX.509/KCA (Dagorn, Bernard & Varrette, 2005) can act as a GSI to a Kerberos gateway while SSLK5/PKINIT can be used as a Kerberos to GSI gateway. LDAP (*Lightweight Directory Access Protocol*) technology proposes mechanisms to manage authentication. Several methods of authentication corresponding to various security levels are available in a standard LDAP such as: login/password, login/password with hashing, login/password on SSL, X.509 certificate (Bhatia, 2013).

Authorization

Another important security issue is authorization; authorization is the process that determines whether a particular operation is allowed. Like any resource sharing system, grid systems also require resource specific and system specific authorizations. In grid computing, authorization systems can be divided into two categories: VO (*Virtual Organization*) level systems and Resource level systems. VO systems have a centralized authorization system which provides credentials for the users to access the resources. On the other hand, Resource level systems are decentralized and allow the users to access the resources based on the credentials presented by the users (Bhatia, 2013; Chakrabarti, 2007):

- **VO Level Systems:** VO is defined as a dynamic group of individuals, groups, or organizations who define the conditions and rules (business objectives and policies) for sharing resources. VO level grid authorization systems are centralized authorization for an entire VO. These types of systems are necessitated by the presence of a VO which has a set of users, and several Resource Providers (RP) who own the resources to be used by the users of the VO. Whenever a user wants to access certain resources owned by a RP, he/she obtains a credential from the authorization system which allows certain rights to the users. The user presents the credentials to the resource to gain access to it. In this type of systems, the resources hold the final right in allowing or denying the access to the users. Examples of VO level grid authorization systems are CAS (*Community Authorization Service*), VOMS (*Virtual Organization Membership Service*), and EALS (*Enterprise Authorization and Licensing System*) (Bhatia, 2013; Mishra, Yadav & Maheshwari, 2014).
- **Resource Level Systems:** Unlike centralized authorization systems, decentralized systems implement the decision to authorize the access to a set of resources. Resource providers grant privileges to the community. This is done after establishing a trust relationship with the community. When a user wants to access a resource, he/she produces his credentials which contain specific policy assertions (Bendahmane et. al., 2009). The resource provider makes the decision whether to grant or reject the request for access to its resources. Examples of resource level authorization systems are Akenti, GridMap, and PERMIS (*Privilege and Role Management Infrastructure Standards validation*) systems (Bhatia, 2013; Chakrabarti, 2007).

Information Level

In a grid computing environment where risk is high, there is a need to protect data during transmission because anyone connected to the open network may observe, insert or possibly remove the message. Information level includes those security concerns that arise during the communication between two entities. These include Confidentiality, and Integrity (Bendahmane et. al., 2009; Kazemi, 2014).

Confidentiality

Symmetric and Asymmetric (Public) key encryption techniques are the well-known techniques that used for creating secure grids (Bhatia, 2013; Chakrabarti, 2007):

- **Symmetric Key Encryption:** Based on the use of one shared secret key to perform both the encryption and decryption of data. To ensure that the data is only read by the two parties (sender and receiver); the key has to be distributed securely between the two parties and no others. This form of encryption has performance benefits over asymmetric encryption, but requires additional care and administration in the handling of the shared key. Advanced Encryption Standard (AES), Data Encryption Standard (DES), and Rivest Cipher 6 (RC6) are some examples of symmetric key protocols. The security of the exchange relies on the security of the symmetric key. If an attacker intercepts the symmetric key, the attacker can read the cipher text and he can create a new cipher text (Bhatia, 2013; Chakrabarti, 2007).
- **In Asymmetric Key (Public Key) Encryption:** The entities generate public/private key pairs based on some cryptographically secure mathematical function. When a message encrypted with the public key, it can only be decrypted by the private key that corresponding to the public key. The public keys are known to everyone. The asymmetric key pair is generated by a computation that starts by finding two very large prime numbers. Even though the public key is widely distributed, it is practically impossible for computers to calculate the private key from the public key. The security is derived from the fact that it is very difficult to factor numbers exceeding hundreds of digits. This mathematical algorithm improves security, but requires a long encryption time, especially for large amounts of data. For this reason, public key encryption is often used to securely transmit a symmetric encryption key between the two parties, and all further encryption is performed using this symmetric key (Bhatia, 2013; Chakrabarti, 2007).

Integrity

Data integrity has become one of the central concerns of large-scale distributed computing systems such as the grid, whose primary products are the results of computation. In order to maintain the integrity of this data, the system must be resilient to diverse attacks and tampering. Depending on the layer where security is implemented, there are two categories of security mechanisms, Transport level security and Message level security.

- **Transport Level Security:** As mentioned in the previous sub-section, TLS and SSL encrypt the segments of network connections above the Transport Layer. TLS and SSL are using asymmetric cryptography for key exchange, symmetric encryption for privacy, and message authentication codes for message integrity (Bhatia, 2013). Globus Toolkit 4.0 (GT4) uses the SSL/TLS protocol over HTTP for securing the communication between the client and the server (Kazemi, 2014).
- **Message Level Security:** Works at a higher layer and uses Web services based standard protocols such as: WS- Security, WS-Secure Conversation, etc. These protocols are proposed to establish and use secure contexts with SOAP messages (*Simple Object Access protocol*). First, a secure context is established between a client and a server. Once the security context is established, the following messages are signed using the XML-Signature standard. XML-Signature is fast because it uses a symmetric key to sign messages, but it requires additional round trips to establish a connection. This mechanism is suitable for multiple interactions. GSI uses these mechanisms to provide security on a per-message basis, i.e., to an individual message without any pre-existing context between the sender and receiver (outside sharing some set of trust roots) (Kazemi, 2014).

Transport level security is faster than message level security, and should be used if there is no special requirement to use message level security. Generally, TLS is the default security mechanism used. The main reason for that is the performance overhead introduced by message level security mechanisms (Kazemi, 2014).

Management Level

The grid management is important as the grid is heterogeneous in nature and may consist of multiple entities, components, users, domains, policies, and stakeholders. The different management issues that grid administrators are worried about are: Credential Management, Trust Management, and Monitoring related issues (Chakrabarti, 2007).

Credential Management

Management of credentials becomes very important in a grid context as there are multiple different systems which require varied credentials to access them. Credential management systems store and manage the credentials for different systems and users can access them according to their needs. Credential management systems are divided into two categories: credential repositories and credential federation (Chakrabarti, 2007; Kazemi, 2014).

- **Credential Repositories:** Credential storage systems are concerned about securely storing the credentials, generating new credentials on demand, and sometimes generating proxy credentials on the user's behalf for delegation purposes. The basic purpose of credential repositories is to move the responsibilities of the credential storage of the user to these systems. Examples of credential repositories are smart cards, virtual smart cards, and MyProxy Online Credential Repositories.
- **Credential Federation Systems:** Credential share systems are responsible for sharing the credentials across different domains or realms. Examples of credential share systems are the Liberty Project, KX.509, VCMan, etc. VCMan and KX.509 have limited use as they only support X.509 and Kerberos.

Trust Management

Trust is a multi-dimensional factor which depends on a host of different components like reputation of an entity, policies, and opinions about the entity. Managing trust is crucial in a dynamic grid, where grid nodes and users join and leave the system. Therefore, there must be a mechanism to understand and manage the trust levels of systems and new nodes joining the grid. The trust life cycle is composed of mainly three phases: trust creation phase, trust negotiation phase, and trust management phase. The *trust creation phase* is done before any trusted group is formed, and it includes mechanisms to develop trust functions and trust policies. On the other hand, *trust negotiation phase* is activated when a new untrusted system joins the current system. Finally, the *trust management phase* is responsible for recalculating the trust values based on the transaction information, distribution/exchange of trust related information, updating and storing the trust information. Trust management systems can be categorized into *reputation based* and *policy-based* trust management systems.

- **Reputation Based Systems:** Based on trust metrics derived from local and global reputation of a system or an entity. Different reputation-based systems including PeerTrust, XenoTrust, NICE, Secure Grid Outsourcing (SeGO) systems (Chakrabarti, 2007).
- **In Policy Based Systems:** Different entities/components constituting the system, exchange and manage credentials to establish the trust relationships based on certain policies. The primary goal of such systems is to enable access control by verifying credentials and restricting access to credentials based predefined policies. Examples of such systems are PeerTrust Trust Negotiation and TrustBuilder (Chakrabarti, 2007).

Monitoring

Grid systems require some amount of resource monitoring for auditing purposes. The different stages of monitoring are: data collection, data processing, data transmission, data storage, and data presentation. The data collection stage involves collecting data through different sensors located at different collection points. The gathered data can be static in nature like network topology, machine configuration, or dynamic like CPU, memory utilization, system load, and etc. *Data processing stage* processes and filters the data based on different policies and criteria. *The data transmission stage* involves the transmission of collecting and processed data to the different entities interested. Finally, *data presentation stage* presents the data in a format understood by the different interested entities. Different monitoring systems available can be broadly categorized into: System level, Cluster level, and Grid level (Chakrabarti, 2007).

- **System Level Monitor Systems:** Collect and communicate information about standalone systems or networks. Simple Network Management Protocol (SNMP) is an example for managing and monitoring network devices.
- **Cluster Level Monitoring Systems:** Homogeneous in nature and require deployment across cluster or a set of clusters for monitoring purposes. Popular examples of cluster level monitoring systems include Ganglia from University of Berkeley and Hawkeye from University of Wisconsin Madison.
- **Grid Level Monitoring Systems:** Much more flexible than other monitoring systems and can be deployed on top of different other monitoring systems. MDS (*Globus Monitoring and Discovery Systems*), and MAGI (*Management of Adaptive Grid Infrastructure*) are examples of such systems.

CLOUD COMPUTING SECURITY

Cloud computing offers scalable on-demand services to users with greater flexibility. Since cloud services are delivered using classical network protocols, implicit vulnerabilities, as well as, network threats raise more security and privacy concerns (Modi et. al., 2013). Fernandes et al., (2014) surveyed the research on cloud security issues; they addressed several key topics such as: vulnerabilities, threats, and attacks. Focused on the so-called SPI model (SaaS, PaaS and IaaS); another categorization was done. Hashizume et al., (2013) identified the main vulnerabilities in this kind of systems and the most important threats found in the literature. On the other hand, the work done by Subashini and Kavitha, (2011) is more specific to the different security issues that had been emanated due to the nature of the service delivery models of a cloud computing system. Moreover, a survey on security in mobile cloud was done by Ali et al., (2015).

Modi et al., (2013) classified security concerns based on different layers of the cloud infrastructure as: Application Level, Network Level, Data storage Level, Virtualization Level, Authentication and access control Level, Trust Level, Compliance, audit and regulations Level as shown in Figure 7. Application level risks directly

Figure 7. Detailed architecture of cloud with security concerns at each layer
(Modi et. al., 2013)

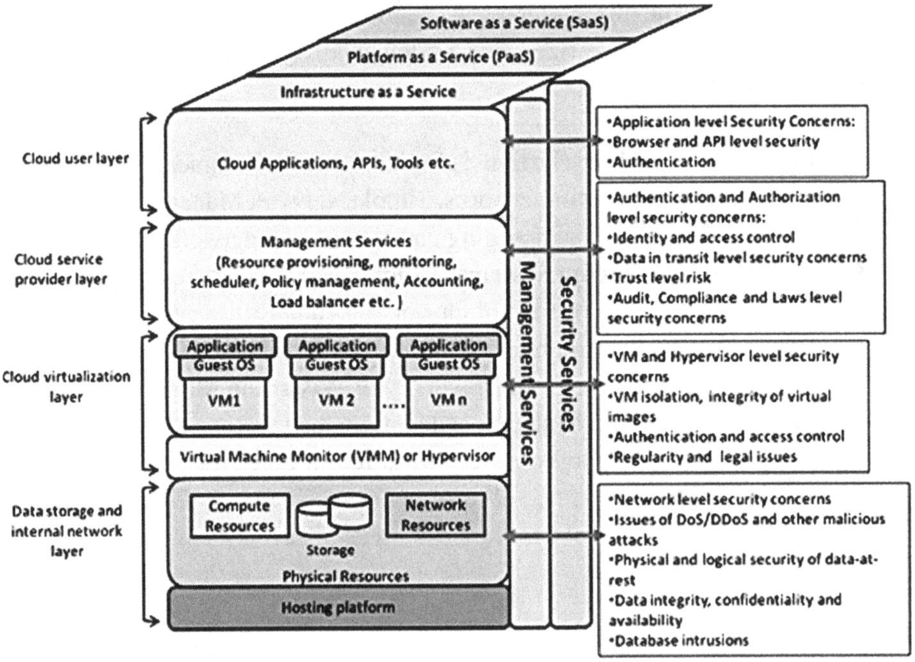

affect the security of cloud applications at the user layer. Network level threats or intrusions affect the overall security of cloud services, data as well as physical resources. Since one can easily gain access to another user's resources or services by monitoring the network traffic in the cloud. Attacks on data storage directly affect the security of the user's data (at rest or in-transit) including application data and sensitive data. Virtualization level risks directly affect the data storage and application security levels. Authentication and access control level risks affect the security of authentic user's services and resources.

This section classifies cloud computing security mechanisms according to the above classification (Modi et. al., 2013) as follows:

Application Level

Application level security refers to securing applications such that the attackers are not able to get control over applications or change their format. Application security is important in the sense that it can be exploited to extract sensitive information or make inappropriate changes to important data. The key security issues at the application level are Service availability and Integrity of workload state (Modi et. al., 2013):

Service Availability

Temporary or permanent loss of services and DoS/DDoS attacks (Beitollahi & Deconinck, 2012) are the main threats affecting availability of cloud services. For better QoS (*Quality of Service*), services should be available as promised when they are requested. To address such issues, proper configuration of an IDS/IPS (Intrusion Detection System/Intrusion Prevention System) can be investigated (Modi et. al., 2013). An IDS alerts system administrators and generate log about the attack when it detects a signature of accident based on host or network security policy. IDS can be installed in a host or a network according to purpose. According to the method of the collection of intrusion data, IDSs are classified into two types: host-based and network-based IDSs. *Host-based Intrusion Detection Systems* (HIDSs) analyze audit data collected by an operating system about the actions that are performed by users and applications. On the other hand, *Network-based Intrusion Detection Systems* (NIDSs) study data collected from network packets. According to analytical techniques, IDS system is divided into two different parts: misuse detection and anomaly detection. *Misuse detection* systems use signature patterns of exited well-known attacks of the system to match and identify known intrusions. Misuse detection techniques, in general, are not effective against the latest attacks that have no matched rules or pattern yet. On the other hand, *Anomaly detection* systems identify those activities which deviate significantly from the established normal behaviors as anomalies.

These anomalies are most likely regarded as intrusions. Anomaly detection techniques can be effective against unknown or the latest attacks. However, anomaly detection systems tend to generate more false alarms than misuse detection systems because an anomaly may be a new normal behavior or an ordinary activity. Once IDS detects an intrusion attempt, it should report to the system administrator. There are three ways to report the detection results, namely: notification, manual, and automatic response. In *notification* response system, IDS only generates reports and alerts. In *a manual system*, it provides additional capability for the system administrator to initiate a manual response. In *automatic* system, IDS immediately respond to an intrusion through auto response system (Mathew & Jose, 2012).

Integrity of Workload State

The integrity of the state of a workload should be preserved to ensure expected results. Applications involving workflows are required to store temporary results of computation at different levels. There is no standard mechanism used to secure such sensitive files. If these sensitive files are disclosed to an attacker, he/she may be able to threaten the expected behavior of the application. A provenance based approach (Du et. al., 2009) can be used for securing the application data flow among different sites. This approach provides confidentiality and integrity for data flow processing applications.

The Network Level

When looking at the network level of the infrastructure security, it is important to distinguish between private clouds and public clouds. With private clouds, there are no new attacks, vulnerabilities, or changes in risk specific to this topology. Although the organization's IT architecture may change with the implementation of a private cloud, the network topology will probably not change significantly. On the other hand, instances running on public cloud are most prone to different types of attacks and hence require a network level access control solution that would enable the delivery of cloud services in a highly protected environment (Mather, Kumaraswamy & Latif, 2009). Security issues at network level should be considered in terms of both external and internal networks. An opponent outside the cloud network often performs DoS or DDoS attacks to affect the availability of cloud services and resources (Modi et. al., 2013). DoS/DDoS attacks reduce the bandwidth and increases the congestion causing poor service to the users (Rabai et. al., 2013).

Some common attacks at the network layer (such as: DNS (*Domain Name System*) poisoning attack, sniffer attack, port scanning, cross site scripting, ARP (*Address Resolution Protocol*) spoofing, IP spoofing, and phishing attack), are executed to gain access of cloud resources. The internal network attacker can easily get access to the user's resources without being detected. An insider has higher privileges and knowledge (related to network, security mechanism, and resources to attack) than the external attacker. Major security issues at network level include vulnerabilities in Internet protocols, authorization, and authentication, intrusions, backdoor attack, session hijacking, and clear data transmission. To address some of the issues at the network level, major cloud providers (such as: Amazon, Window Azure, Rack Space, Eucalyptus, etc.) are running their applications behind firewall. However, it only provides security at boundary of network and cannot detect the internal attacks.

Network Based Intrusion Detection System (NIDS) can be integrated to address some of the security issues. However, NIDS should be configured for detecting external intrusions as well as internal intrusions. It should also be capable of detecting intrusions from encrypted traffic. Through experiments and implementation, the authors in (Angadi, Angadi & Gull, 2013) surveyed the security solutions that can be applied to detect ARP spoofing attacks. Furthermore, Modi et al., (2013) surveyed some the existing research efforts to address network security issues in cloud

Data Storage Level

In a cloud environment, data can be classified into two main classifications: critical data and archive data. Critical data is that data needed at any time by subscriber and any delay or unavailability will disrupt him/her. On the other hand, the *archival data* is that data accessed very seldom and at non-crucial time. Therefore, delay in access to it will not consider as the main issue, but delaying the critical data is a very important issue and could be very costly as the subscriber will not operate normally (Karajeh, Maqableh & Masa'deh, 2011). In this section, different techniques of data security and privacy protections in cloud computing are presented. Security aspects can be classified as data Integrity, Confidentiality, Availability and Privacy (Bhagawat & Kumar, 2015; Sun et. al., 2014; Xiao & Xiao, 2013).

Integrity

Integrity in the cloud system means preserving information integrity. The data should not be lost or modified by unauthorized users (Zissis & Lekkas, 2012). System users need to know that their data is kept out of damage or lost by intentional or unintentional activity (Kshetri, 2013). Data integrity is considered as a major factor to success the cloud computing as it will increase the subscriber trust and satisfaction that maintained by the provider and the subscriber. Maintaining the integrity of cloud computing is considered as a main challenge to cloud parties, as the threats could be at the subscribers or provider sides. To insure data integrity in the provider and subscriber sides, a secure encryption algorithm could be used, but it could not guarantee that data did not change through locating it in the cloud (Subashini & Kavitha, 2011). Violating the integrity of critical data in the cloud could be very costly as the subscriber will not be able to operate normally. Moreover, cloud provider should consider a data recovery plan in case that any disaster event might happen (Karajeh, Maqableh & Masa'deh, 2011).

Confidentiality

Cloud computing is based on sharing the same resources by multiple users at different levels (Network, Host, and Application). The subscriber private and sensitive data need to be protected from being disclosed to an unauthorized individual. Encryption is usually used to ensure the confidentiality of data. Confidentiality can be guaranteed using encryption techniques with respect to symmetric or asymmetric encryption algorithms (Karajeh, Maqableh & Masa'deh, 2011). One more encryption system that could be used to ensure the data confidentiality is the Homomorphic encryption. Homomorphic ensures that the cipher text algebraic operation results are consistent with the clear operation after encryption results; besides, the whole process does not need to decrypt the data. The implementation of this technique could well solve the confidentiality of data and data operations in the cloud (Sun et. al., 2014).

Availability

Availability refers to the ability of the cloud subscriber to retrieve the needed data at any-time (Zissis & Lekkas, 2012). A system is called available when an authorized entity can use and access the system and the stored data at any-time (Subashini & Kavitha, 2011). Therefore, the service provider should ensure that the data is available to subscriber from different locations at any-time. The cloud computing system should keep on working even if there is a security attack (Rabai et. al., 2013). Moreover, the provider should maintain an appropriate action plan for the emergency and unplanned cases to guarantee the business continuity and disaster recovery to ensure the safety and minimal downtime (Karajeh, Maqableh & Masa'deh, 2011).

Privacy

Privacy is yet another critical concern with regards to cloud computing due to the fact that user' data and business logic reside among distrusted cloud servers, which are owned and maintained by the cloud provider. Therefore, there are potential risks that the confidential data (e.g., financial data, health record) or personal information (e.g. personal profile) is disclosed to public or business competitors (Xiao & Xiao, 2013). That is to say, cloud subscribers need to guarantee that their personal data is protected appropriately. In cloud, subscriber data are stored in the data center that has potential risks. Therefore, cloud provider should implement different security techniques to assure data privacy (Kshetri, 2013). Z. Xiao and Y. Xiao, (2013) regarded privacy-preservability as the core attribute of privacy. Confidentiality, integrity, accountability directly or indirectly influence privacy-preservability. Evidently, in order to keep private data from being disclosed, confidentiality becomes indispensable, and integrity ensures that data/computation is not corrupted, which somehow preserves privacy. Accountability, on the contrary, may undermine privacy due to the fact that the methods of achieving the two attributes usually conflict (Xiao & Xiao, 2013).

Virtualization Security Level

Virtualization security refers to securing a VM (Virtual Machine) or a hypervisor in a highly virtualized and distributed cloud environment. In a virtualized environment, hypervisor is defined as a virtual machine monitor that allows many VMs to be deployed on a single or multiple operating systems (OSs) to run at the same time. Hypervisor can be defined as a controller, which monitors/controls the activities of all virtual/guest machines that operating in a virtualized environment (Bhadauria, 2014). There are risks associated with using the same physical infrastructure, where a small number of malicious users may cause threats to the others. Since the VMs are mobile, they may switch between the hypervisors depending upon the availability of resources (Bhadauria, 2014). As the number of guest OSs running on a hypervisor increases, the security concerns with that newer guests OSs increase. Since it is hard to keep track of all guests OSs, maintaining the security of those OSs is difficult. It may happen that a guest system tries to run a malicious code on the host system and bring the system down or take full control of the system and block access to other OSs. If a hacker is able to get control over the hypervisor, he can make changes to other OSs and get control over all the data passing through the hypervisor (Modi et. al., 2013).

Isolation between two *VMs* is not completely adequate by current Virtual Machine Monitors (VMMs). By compromising the lower layer hypervisor vulnerabilities, an attacker can gain control over installed VMs. Bluepill, SubVirt, and DKSM are some of the well-known attacks on the virtual layer. To prevent such threats is still an open area of research (Modi et. al., 2013). *Virtualization based malware and rootkit* is a new generation of rootkits that benefit from the processor technology that allows an attacker to insert an additional hypervisor between the hardware and the software. The hypervisor takes control of the system and converts the original operating system into a virtual guest on the fly. In contrast to software-based virtualization, this kind of hijacking does not need a restart, and that makes it all the more difficult to detect the intrusion (Modi et. al., 2013).

Sharing of VM images in cloud introduces security risks. While the owner of an image is concerned about confidentiality (e.g. unauthorized accesses to the image). The user of an image is concerned about safety (e.g. a malicious image that may corrupt or steal his private data). The administrator of cloud is concerned with the security and compliance of the cloud as a whole and the integrity of the images. There are:

1. Risk of non-compliance (running unlicensed or expired licenses S/W),
2. Risk of damages caused by malware contained in any image stored in the repository,
3. Risk of create, modify, or delete VM images, and
4. Risk of changing administrative passwords.

There should be a standard mechanism for checking integrity of guest VMs for successfully executing workload and avoiding interruption of computation, data loss, and misuse of resources (Ali, Khan & Vasilakos 2015; Modi et. al., 2013). VM isolation, VM image sharing, VM escape, VM migration, VM sprawl, and etc. are example of virtualization security issues. These issues and others have been studied in detail in (Ali, Khan & Vasilakos 2015; Modi et. al., 2013; Wu et al., 2010).

Authentication and Access Control Level

In cloud computing, the user's information is transmitted over the Internet, which poses data ownership issues. As this information is processed outside the enterprise, it brings an inherent level of risk (Modi et. al., 2013). The user has to prove his/her identity to the cloud service provider to access the various data stored in the cloud (Joseph, Kathrine & Vijayan, 2014).

Authentication

As the critical data is located in the cloud provider infrastructure, the data may be altered without the owner's consent. The modified data may then be retrieved and processed by the owner to make critical decisions. The authenticity of the data in this case is very important, and therefore needs to be guaranteed. However, common standards to ensure data integrity do not exist (Rong, Nguyen & Jaatun, 2013).

RSA (Rivest Shamir Adleman Inc.) considers that the private and public cloud has different authentication schemes. A single login using trust policies and strong authentication methods are used. Lenka and Nayak, (2014) have been implemented a combination of RSA encryption and digital signature technique which can be easily used with all types of cloud computing features like: PaaS, SaaS and IaaS. This combination mechanism provides three way security i.e. data security, authentication and verification. They have proposed RSA encryption algorithm for confidentiality of data and for authentication MD5 algorithm have been implemented. Nafi et al., (2012) proposed another security structure which includes AES file encryption system, RSA system for secure communication, One-time password to authenticate users and MD5 hashing for hiding information. They claimed that their model ensures security for whole cloud computing structure.

Amazon Web Services (AWS) focuses on the exchange of confidential information between the browser and the web server in which an Amazon virtual private cloud is used. The various authentication techniques like multifactor authentication and AWS identity and access management are being addressed (Acar, Belenkiy & Kupcu, 2013; Khalid et. al., 2013). In cloud authentication refers to making sure that the user is storing the data by giving a valid user name and password. Authentication to multiple services using only one password was proven to be secure against dictionary attacks and honeypot attacks (Joseph, Kathrine & Vijayan, 2014). Companies like Microsoft, Google and Facebook has adopted this method.

Security Assertion Markup Language (SAML) is an XML-based standard that allows users to communicate authentication decisions between one service and another. It underlies many Web single sign-on solutions (Gupta, Laxmi & Sharma, 2014). SAML is issued to exchange information, such as assertions related to a subject or authentication.

Authorization and Access Control

While access control is the method of ensuring that the access is provided only to the authorized users, authorization ensures that the user submits his/her identity in order to login to a particular service. Various access control mechanisms such as firewall, Intrusion detection and segregation of duties are enabled at various layers of the network and cloud (Joseph, Kathrine & Vijayan, 2014).

MacAfee has provided access control by using various methods such as MacAfee Web Gateway, MacAfee Single Sign on (CSSO) and MacAfee one time password. Fujitsu has provided security from unauthorized access and problems like injection attacks and cross-site scripting. The various authorization schemes like Central Management Authorization (CMA) and Virtual System Management Authorization (VSMA) has been provided by Fujitsu (Joseph, Kathrine & Vijayan, 2014).

An access control mechanism based on Role Based Access (RBA) was proposed for multi-tenancy method of protecting the data in cloud environments. E. Mon

(2013) combined Role-Based Access Control (RBAC) and Attribute-Based Access Control (ABAC) to provide the privacy and security of sensitive data of cloud users. In this approach, cloud clients store their data based on privacy laws according to their user levels. With the use of RBAC and ABAC, the privacy manager defines the privacy policies, privacy laws, user levels, and security levels to control the data access. Using an Access Control List (ACL), users are granted or denied permission to access the data. Moreover, security and privacy policies are defined by the service providers, which restrict users to store all types of data since service providers are not fully trusted. There have been large efforts to address access control security issues, Modi et al., (2013) presented the most important solutions found in the literature.

Accountability

Another issue that should be addressed is the cloud accountability. Accountability implies that the capability of identifying a party, with undeniable evidence, is responsible for specific events. When dealing with cloud computing, there are multiple parties that may be involved; a cloud provider and its users are the two basic ones, and the public clients who use applications (e.g. a Web application) outsourced by cloud users may be another party (Xiao & Xiao, 2013). Accountability is a significant attribute of cloud computing because the computing paradigm increases the difficulty of holding an entity responsible for some action. Following a pay-as-you-go billing model, cloud vendor provides resources rented by users who may host their web contents opening to public clients. Even a simple action (e.g. a Web request) will involve multiple parties. On the other hand, accountability not only handles security threats, it also deals with various incidents, such as software bug, misconfiguration, and hardware failure, to help identify the event origin (Xiao & Xiao, 2013). Consequently, some researchers in this field successfully implement the accountability techniques in their systems ((Rong, Nguyen & Jaatun, 2013; Siani, 2011). Xiao et al. (2012) provided a comprehensive investigation of the accountability research issues in current distributed systems. Furthermore, they studied the various accountability tactics that are available and how each one of them contributes to providing strong accountability of different aspects. In their further work (Xiao & Xiao, 2013), they surveyed the research on the cloud accountability; they addressed different threats to cloud accountability and its defense strategies.

Trust Level

In a cloud environment the user is required to delegate "trust" to applications provided by the organization owning the infrastructure, which is one of the serious problems (Subashini & Kavitha, 2011; Zissis & Lekkas, 2012). Since users have lack of control over resources, they have to rely on trust mechanisms and contracts in conjunction with mechanisms that provide a compensation. Nevertheless, trust is a very fuzzy concept and very difficult to calculate in a heterogeneous environment that is assessed by a human or social trust (Modi et. al., 2013).

The subscriber trust to an organization is known as the ability of an organization to supply the required services to the subscriber's exactly as expected without errors. Trust can be ensured by powerful security policies and constraints on data access by people (Zissis & Lekkas 2012). In many cases in the cloud, the user depends on the providers on storing his/her confidential data on the provider resource (Karajeh, Maqableh & Masa'deh 2011). Thus, subscriber and provider should trust each other. The trust issue is mainly based on the selected deployment model, as data, processes, and application control, are outsourced (Rong, Nguyen & Jaatun, 2013). In *public clouds*, the control is granted to the subscriber to reduce potential risks by applying the service provider certain security policy and using different applications and tools to increase subscriber trust. In *a private cloud*, data, processes, and applications arc owned and managed by the infrastructure owner. Thus, there is no more security challenges are introduced as the trust remains within the organization. Lack of subscriber trust in cloud deployment models can cause several problems. In *community cloud*, the organizations should trust each other as they are sharing same cloud services that support their community concerns. While, in *hybrid cloud* the organizations should trust each other and trust the public cloud service provider (Karajeh, Maqableh & Masa'deh 2011). Cross-site scripting, access control weaknesses, insecure storage, and insecure configuration are some of the threat examples. There should be a mechanism for managing the involved risk. Advanced cryptographic and signature techniques are used to address trust issues when outsourcing data (Modi et. al., 2013).

Compliance, Audit, and Regulations Level

The final level of Modi's (2013) classification is compliance, audit and regulations level. Compliance, audit and regulations issues are more subjective than others. Since these problems may not be directly related with the technology deployed in the majority of the cases, therefore, in this sub-section brief introductions of these issues is presented and for more details please refer to (Fernandes et. al., 2014; Mather, Kumaraswamy & Latif, 2009; Modi et. al., 2013; Li & Vaughn, 2006; Vitti & Santos, 2014). Audit and compliance functions have always played an important role in traditional outsourcing relationships. However, these functions take on increased importance in the cloud given the dynamic nature of SaaS, IaaS, and PaaS environments. Cloud Service Providers (CSPs) are challenged to establish, monitor, and demonstrate ongoing compliance with a set of controls that meets their users' requirements. A practical approach to audit and compliance in the cloud includes a coordinated combination of internal policy compliance, regulatory compliance, and external auditing (Mather, Kumaraswamy & Latif, 2009).

Based on Modi et al., (2013) different cloud vulnerability, threats and attacks, their effect and suggested solution are summarized in the following tables. Table 1 summarizes the vulnerabilities relevant to cloud computing and their associated effects. Then, table 2 represents threats to cloud and directives to avoid them. Finally, table 3, summarizes the cloud attacks, their effects, and mitigation directives.

FUTURE RESEARCH DIRECTIONS

Enhancement to virtualization level security in the cloud needs to be addressed. Compromising the lower layer hypervisor is a crucial attack that needs to be mitigated. Another issue in virtualization is sharing of VM (data, images, etc.) To avoid interruption of computation, data loss, and misuse of resources, solutions based on checking the integrity of guests VMs must be deployed.

Another trend for future research is encryption and key management algorithms. An unknown physical location of data in the cloud and different laws enforced by nations to manage data make encryption and key management complex. If encryption is applied, it needs to be performed at multiple locations, within the data center, in between the data centers, or between public and private clouds, etc. There is a strong

Table 1. Effects of vulnerabilities in the cloud and consequent effects

Vulnerability	Consequent Effects
Vulnerabilities in virtualization	Bypassing the security barriers can allow access to underlying hypervisor
Vulnerabilities in Internet protocol	Allow network attacks like: ARP spoofing (*Address Resolution Protocol*), SYN-flood, DoS/DDoS, etc.
Unauthorized access to management interface	■ An intruder can gain access control and can take advantage of services to harbor attacks ■ Access to administrative interface can be more critical
Injection vulnerabilities	Unauthorized disclosure of private data behind applications
Vulnerabilities in browsers and APIs (*API: Application Programming Interface*)	Allow unauthorized service access

Table 2. Summary of threats to cloud and solution directives

Attack Type	Effects	Solutions
Identity theft	Get valid user's identity to access user's resources; obtain credit or other benefits in that user's name	Passwords and authentication mechanism
Service hijacking	User accounts and service instances could in turn make a new base for attackers	Authentication mechanism and activity monitoring
Data loss and Leakage	Confidential data can be compromised, deleted or modified	■ Use secure APIs, encryption algorithms and secure keys ■ Apply data backup policies
Abusive use of cloud	Allows intruder to launch stronger attacks due to anonymous signup, lack of validation, service fraud, and ad-hoc services	■ Stronger registration and authentication. ■ Comprehensive monitoring of network traffic
Insecure interfaces and API	Poses threats like clear-text authentication, transmission of the content, etc.	Ensure strong authentication and access control mechanism with encrypted transmission
Malicious Insiders	Insider malicious activity bypassing firewall and other security model	■ Provide transparency for security and management process ■ Use compliance reporting and breach notification
Risk profiling	Internal security procedures, security compliance, configuration hardening, patching, auditing and logging may be overlooked	■ Disclose partial logs, data and infrastructure detail ■ Use monitoring and alerting system for data breaches

need for improved solutions involving the users for controlling the use of their data. The use of the symmetric and public key for data security in cloud framework does not provide an efficient solution for key management due to its complexity. An identity based approach has to overcome the key management limitation. However, there is a need for more robust approaches in this context, which could extend traditional approaches like Cipher text Policy Attribute based encryption (CPABE), Key Policy Attribute based encryption (KPABE), etc. to cloud computing (Modi et. al., 2013).

There are upcoming cloud models that require new research directives such that security of mobile cloud computing (Modi et. al., 2013). Mobile cloud computing is confined to availability of cloud computing in mobile ecosystem. Besides uniform network stability and device access, mobile devices raise several security and privacy concerns; an obvious case is misplacement or loss of a mobile device that can result into the major data breach. There is a lack of platform independent languages in order to develop applications for mobile devices, (i.e. consistent case for Android and Apple.)

Table 3. Summary of attacks to cloud and Mitigation techniques

Attack Type	How? Attack (Surface/ Procedure)	Service Affected	Effects	Mitigation Techniques
Zombie attack * DoS/DDoS	■ By compromising valid user's VMs ■ "Through direct/indirect flooding to host VM level, hypervisor level, & Network level attack	SaaS, PaaS, IaaS	■ Affects service availability ■ May create an account for false service usage	■ Authentication & authorization ■ IDS/IPS (*IDS: Intrusion Detection System and IPS: Intrusion Prevention System*)
Service injection attack	Malicious service injected through accessing service identification files Application level, VM level attack	PaaS	■ Malicious service provided to users instead of valid service ■ Affects service integrity	■ Check service integrity using a hash function ■ Strong isolation between VMs ■ Web service security ■ Use secure web browsers and APIs
Attacks on virtualization * VM Escape * Attack on hypervisor	■ By compromising hypervisor ■ By escaping virtualization layer VM level attack/ hypervisor level attack	IaaS	Allows an attacker to gain control over another user's VM	■ Use of secure hypervisor ■ Monitor activities at hypervisor ■ VM isolation required
Man-in-the Middle attack	By accessing data communication between two parties	SaaS, PaaS, IaaS	Affects the data security and privacy	Proper configuration of SSL required (*SSL: secure socket layer*)
Metadata spoofing attack	Modifying web service description file such as WSDL Application level attack	SaaS, PaaS,	■ Abnormal behavior of deployed services ■ Affects service confidentiality	Strong isolation between VMs
Phishing attack	By allowing users to access fake web link	SaaS, PaaS, IaaS	Affects the privacy of user's sensitive information	Identify the spam mails
Backdoor channel attacks	By compromising valid user's VMs VM level & hypervisor level attack	IaaS	■ Provides rights for accessing victim's resources ■ Affect service availability & data privacy	■ Authentication & authorization ■ Strong isolation between VMs

CONCLUSION

Distributed system is a collection of (homogenous/heterogeneous) automata inter-connected by a network. The distribution of this network is transparent to users who see the system appears as one local machine. In this chapter, different and diverse definitions of distributed systems computing are presented. Different systems are discussed with highlight on the most recent. Distributed systems have been built to achieve the following: transparency, openness, reliability, performance, and scalability. In order to achieve the above objectives, security of the system must be given adequate attention. Security is one of the fundamental issues in distributed systems. Security in modern distributed computing systems is crucial. Users want to securely access remote resources in both the local domain and across multi-domains of distributed systems. This research deals with security issues in distributed systems. Security services are generally classified into six components: confidentiality, data integrity, authentication, authorization, non-repudiation, and accountability. In addition, the chapter surveys the mostly occurred attacks on distributed systems, namely: distributed denial of service, and identity attack.

This chapter discusses security issues in different distributed systems models. Distributed computing can be classified into four classes, namely: cluster computing, P2P networks, grid computing, and cloud computing. It is fair to say that the clustering concept have laid the necessary foundation to build large-scale grids and clouds. On the other hand, grid/cloud platforms are regarded as utility service providers. In this chapter, a brief survey about cluster and P2P security is presented. The authors focus on grid and cloud security. Grid and cloud systems provide more services and are widely used by different applications. Therefore, the chapter surveys different security issues for both grid and cloud and their solutions in details. Grid security levels can be classified into five main categories: resources level, service level, authentication and authorization level, information level, and management level solutions. This work lists different attacks and solutions for different levels that have been mentioned earlier. Moreover, different aspects of cloud security protocols and different prominent research directions in the literature are explored. Cloud security can be classified based on different layers of the cloud infrastructure as: application level, network level, data storage level, virtualization level, authentication and access control level, trust level, and compliance, audit and regulations level. As for grid security, different solutions and attacks are listed; a summary of cloud vulnerabilities, threats and attacks, their effect and suggested solution is presented in Tables (1-3).

REFERENCES

Abbas, A., & Khan, S. (2014). A review on the state-of-the-art: Privacy preserving approaches in e-Health clouds. *IEEE Journal Biomedical Health Information, 18*(4), 1431–1441. doi:10.1109/JBHI.2014.2300846 PMID:25014943

Acar, T., Belenkiy, M., & Kupcu, A. (2013). Single password authentication. *Computer Networks*, *57*(13), 2597–2614. doi:10.1016/j.comnet.2013.05.007

Ali, M., Khan, S., & Vasilakos, A. (2015). Security in cloud computing: Opportunities and challenges. *Information Sciences*, *305*, 357–383. doi:10.1016/j.ins.2015.01.025

Alotaibi, S., Wald, M., & Argles, D. (2010). Using fingerprint recognition in a new security model for accessing distributed systems. *International Journal of Intelligent Computing Research*, *1*(4), 194–203.

Angadi, A., Angadi, A., & Gull, K. (2013). Security issues with possible solutions in cloud computing- A survey. *International Journal of Advanced Research in Computer Engineering and Technology*, *2*(2), 652–661.

Anjomshoa, M., Salleh, M., & Kermani, M. (2015). A taxonomy and survey of distributed computing systems. *Journal of Applied Sciences*, *15*(1), 46–57. doi:10.3923/jas.2015.46.57

Beitollahi, H., & Deconinck, G. (2012). Analyzing well-known countermeasures against distributed denial of service attacks. *Computer Communications, Elsevier*, *35*(11), 1312–1332. doi:10.1016/j.comcom.2012.04.008

Belapurkar, A., Chakrabarti, A., Ponnapalli, H., Varadarajan, N., Padmanabhuni, S., & Sundarrajan, S. (2009). *Distributed systems security: Issues, processes and solutions*. John Wiley & Sons, Ltd. doi:10.1002/9780470751787

Bendahmane, A., Essaaidi, M., El-Moussaoui, A., & Younes, A. (2009). Grid computing security mechanisms: State of the-art. In *Proceedings of the International Conference on Multimedia Computing and Systems*, (pp. 535–540). doi:10.1109/MMCS.2009.5256638

Bhadauria, R., Borgohain, R., Biswas, A., & Sanyal, S. (2014). Secure authentication of cloud data mining API. *Acta Technical Corviniensis-Bulletin of Engineering*, *7*(1), 183.

Bhagawat, V., & Kumar, A. (2015). Survey on data security issues in cloud environment. *International Journal of Innovative Research in Advanced Engineering*, *2*(1), 31–35.

Bhatia, R. (2013). Grid computing and security issues. *International Journal of Scientific and Research Publications*, *3*(8), 1–5.

Cano, P., & Vargas-Lombardo, M. (2012). Security threats in volunteer computing environments using the Berkeley open infrastructure for network computing (BOINC). *International Journal of Computer Technology and Applications*, *3*(3), 944–948.

Chakrabarti, A. (2007). Taxonomy of grid security issues. In Grid computing security. New York: Springer-Verlag Berlin Heidelberg. doi:10.1007/978-3-540-44493-0_3

Cody, E., Sharman, R., Rao, R., & Upadhyaya, S. (2008). Security in grid computing: A review and synthesis. *Decision Support Systems,* (44), 749–764.

Conway, G., & Curry, E. (2012). Managing cloud computing: A life cycle approach. In *Proceedings of the 2nd International Conference of Cloud Computing and Services Science,* (pp. 198-207).

Coulouris, G., Dollimore, J., & Kindberg, T. (2012). *Distributed systems - Concepts and design* (5th ed.). London: Addison – Wesley.

Dabas, P., & Arya, A. (2013). Grid computing: An introduction. *International Journal of Advanced Research in Computer Science and Software Engineering, 3*(3), 467–470.

Dagorn, N., Bernard, N., & Varrette, S. (2005). Practical authentication in distributed environments. In *Proceedings of the IEEE International Conference on Computer Systems and Information Technology* (vol. 1).

Du, J., Wei, W., Gu, X., & Yu, T. (2009). Toward secure dataflow processing in open distributed systems. *InProceedings of ACM Scalable Trusted Computing Workshop* (pp. 67-72). doi:10.1145/1655108.1655120

Farouk, A., Abdelhafez, A., & Fouad, M. (2012). Authentication mechanisms in grid computing environment: Comparative study. In *Proceedings of the International Conference on Engineering and Technology* (pp. 10-11). doi:10.1109/ICEngTechnol.2012.6396116

Fernandes, A., Soares, F., Gomes, V., Freire, M., & Inácio, R. (2014). Security issues in cloud environments: A survey. *International Journal of Information Security, 13*(2), 113–170. doi:10.1007/s10207-013-0208-7

Firdhous, M. (2011). Implementation of security in distributed systems – A comparative study. *International Journal of Computer Information Systems, 2*(2), 1–6.

Gheorghe, G., Cigno, R., & Montresor, A. (2011). Security and privacy issues in P2P streaming systems: A Survey. *Peer-to-Peer Networking and Applications,* (4), 75–91.

Gonzalez-Martínez, J., Bote-Lorenzo, M., Gomez-Sanchez, E., & Cano-Parra, R. (2015). Cloud computing and education: A state-of-the-art survey. *Computers & Education, 80,* 132–151. doi:10.1016/j.compedu.2014.08.017

Gupta, G., Laxmi, P., & Sharma, S. (2014). A survey on cloud security issues and techniques. *International Journal on Computational Sciences and Applications*, *4*(1), 125–132. doi:10.5121/ijcsa.2014.4112

Gupta, M., & Gupta, G. (2013). Security requirements for increasing reliability in Grid Computing. *Journal of Engineering, Computers and Applied Sciences, 2*(9), 6-10.

Hagen, W. (2008). *Professional Xen virtualization*. Birmingham, UK: Wrox Press Ltd.

Hashizume, K., Rosado, D., Fernndez-Medina, E., & Fernandez, E. (2013). An analysis of security issues for cloud computing. *Journal of Internet Services Applications*, *4*(5), 1–13.

Hwang, K., Fox, G., & Dongarra, J. (2010). *Distributed computing: Clusters, grids and clouds*. Morgan Kaufmann, Elsevier, Inc.

Hwang, K., Fox, G., & Dongarra, J. (2012). *Distributed and cloud computing*. Morgan Kaufmann, Elsevier, Inc.

Joseph, A., Kathrine, J., & Vijayan, R. (2014). Cloud security mechanisms for data protection: A survey. *International Journal of Multimedia and Ubiquitous Engineering*, *9*(9), 81–90. doi:10.14257/ijmue.2014.9.9.09

Karajeh, H., Maqableh, M., & Masa'deh, R. (2011). Security of cloud computing environment. In *Proceedings of the 23rd IBIMA Conference on Vision 2020: Sustainable Growth, Economic Development, and Global Competitiveness*.

Kaur, K., & Rai, A. (2014). A comparative analysis: Grid, cluster and cloud computing. *International Journal of Advanced Research in Computer and Communication Engineering*, *3*(3), 5730–5734.

Kavitha, G., & Sankaranarayanan, V. (2011). Secure selection of multiple resources based on virtual private network for computational grids. *Journal of Computer Science*, *7*(12), 1881–1887. doi:10.3844/jcssp.2011.1881.1887

Kazemi, A. (2014). Review of grid computing security and present a new authentication Method for Improving Security. *International Journal of Advance Foundation and Research in Computer*, *1*(4), 77–89.

Khalid, U., Ghafoor, A., Irum, M., & Shibli, M. (2013). Cloud based secure and privacy enhanced authentication and authorization protocol. *Procedia Computer Science*, *22*, 680–688. doi:10.1016/j.procs.2013.09.149

Koshutanski, H. (2009). A Survey on distributed access control systems for web business processes. *International Journal of Network Security*, *9*(1), 61–69.

Koutrouli, E., & Tsalgatidou, A. (2012). Taxonomy of attacks and defense mechanisms in P2P reputation systems-lessons for reputation system designers. *Computer Science Review*, *6*(6), 47–70. doi:10.1016/j.cosrev.2012.01.002

Kshetri, N. (2013). Privacy and security issues in cloud computing: The role of institutions and institutional evolution. *Telecommunications Policy*, *37*(4-5), 372–386. doi:10.1016/j.telpol.2012.04.011

Kumar, M., & Agrawal, N. (2013). Analysis of different security issues and attacks in distributed system: A-review. *International Journal of Advanced Research in Computer Science and Software Engineering*, *3*(4), 232–237.

Kumar, R., & Charu, S. (2015). Comparison between cloud computing, grid computing, cluster computing and virtualization. *International Journal of Modern Computer Science and Applications*, *3*(1), 42–47.

Lee, H. (2014). *Automated performance attack discovery in distributed system implementations*. (Doctoral dissertation). Purdue University, West Lafayette, IN.

Lenka, S., & Nayak, B. (2014). Enhancing data security in cloud computing using RSA encryption and MD5 algorithm. *International Journal of Computer Science Trends and Technology*, *2*(3), 60–64.

Li, J. (2008). *A Survey of peer-to-peer network security issue*. Retrieved September 1, 2008, from http://www.cse.wustl.edu/~jain/cse571-07/ftp/p2p/index.html

Li, W., & Vaughn, R. (2006). Cluster security research involving the modeling of network exploitations using exploitation graphs. In *Proceedings of the 6th IEEE International Symposium on Cluster Computing and the Grid Workshop* (pp. 26-36). doi:10.1109/CCGRID.2006.1630921

Mahajan, , R., & Singh, D. (2013). Cloud computing issues. *International Journal of Computers and Technology*, *4*(2), 626–630.

Mather, T., Kumaraswamy, S., & Latif, S. (2009). *Cloud security and privacy*. O'Reilly Media.

Mathew, S., & Jose, A. (2012). Securing cloud from attacks based on intrusion detection system. *International Journal of Advanced Research in Computer and Communication Engineering*, *1*(10), 753–759.

Mishra, N., Yadav, R., & Maheshwari, S. (2014). Security issues in grid computing. *International Journal on Computational Sciences and Applications*, *4*(1), 179–187. doi:10.5121/ijcsa.2014.4118

Modi, C., Patel, D., Borisaniya, B., Patel, A., & Rajarajan, M. (2013). A survey on security issues and solutions at different layers of cloud computing. *The Journal of Supercomputing*, *63*(2), 561–592. doi:10.1007/s11227-012-0831-5

Mon, E. (2011). The privacy-aware access control system using attribute and role based access control in private cloud. In *Proceedings of the 4th IEEE International Conference on Broadband Network and Multimedia Technology (IC-BNMT)* (pp. 447–451). doi:10.1109/ICBNMT.2011.6155974

Nafi, K., Kar, T., Hoque, S., & Hashem, M. (2012). A newer user authentication, file encryption and distributed server based cloud computing security architecture. *International Journal of Advanced Computer Science and Applications*, *3*(10), 181–186.

Pourqasem, J., Karimi, S., & Edalatpanah, S. (2014). Comparison of cloud and grid computing. *American Journal of Software Engineering*, *2*(1), 8–12.

Puttaswamy, K., Zheng, H., & Zhao, B. (2009). Securing structured overlays against identity attacks. *IEEE Transactions on Parallel and Distributed Systems*, *20*(10), 1487–1498. doi:10.1109/TPDS.2008.241

Rabai, L., Jouini, M., Aissa, A., & Mili, A. (2013). A cyber security model in cloud computing environments. *Journal of King Saud University - Computer and Information Sciences*, *25*(1), 63-75.

Rahman, M., Ranjan, R., & Buyya, R. (2012). Decentralization in distributed systems: Challenges, technologies, and opportunities. In A. Pathan, M. Pathan, & H. Lee (Eds.), Advancements in Distributed Computing and Internet Technologies: Trends and Issues (pp. 386-399). Information Science Reference, IGI Global. doi:10.4018/978-1-61350-110-8.ch018

Rong, C., Nguyen, S., & Jaatun, M. (2013). Beyond lightning: A survey on security challenges in cloud computing. *Computers & Electrical Engineering*, *39*(1), 47–54. doi:10.1016/j.compeleceng.2012.04.015

Sadashiv, N., & Kumar, S. (2011). Cluster, grid and cloud computing: A detailed comparison. In *Proceedings of the 6th International Conference on Computer Science and Education (ICCSE 2011)*. doi:10.1109/ICCSE.2011.6028683

Salim, A., Tiwari, R., & Tripathi, S. (2013). Addressing security challenges in cloud computing. *International Journal of Computer Engineering and Applications*, *2*(2), 1–13.

Selvaraja, C., & Anandb, S. (2012). A survey on security issues of reputation management systems for peer-to-peer networks. *Computer Science Review*, *6*(6), 145–160. doi:10.1016/j.cosrev.2012.04.001

Siani, P. (2011). Toward accountability in the cloud. *IEEE Internet Computing*, (15): 64–69.

Srinivasa, K., & Muppalla, A. (2015). *Guide to high performance distributed computing: case studies with hadoop*. Scalding and Spark, Springer International Publishing. doi:10.1007/978-3-319-13497-0

Steen, M., Pierre, G., & Voulgaris, S. (2012). Challenges in very large distributed systems. *Journal of Internet Services and Applications*, (3), 59-66.

Subashini, S., & Kavitha, V. (2011). A survey on security issues in service delivery models of cloud computing. *Journal of Network and Computer Applications*, *34*(1), 1–11. doi:10.1016/j.jnca.2010.07.006

Sun, Y., Zhang, J., Xiong, Y., & Zhu, G. (2014). Data security and privacy in cloud computing. *International Journal of Distributed Sensor Networks*, (7): 1–9.

Suresh, S., & Kannan, M. (2014). A study on system virtualization techniques. *International Journal of Advanced Research in Computer Science and Technology*, *2*(1), 134-139.

Tan, Y., Ko, R., & Holmes, G. (2013). Security and data accountability in distributed systems: A provenance survey. In *2013 IEEE 10th International Conference on High Performance Computing and Communications & 2013 IEEE International Conference on Embedded and Ubiquitous Computing (HPCC_EUC)* (pp. 1571-1578). doi:10.1109/HPCC.and.EUC.2013.221

Tanenbaum, A., & Steen, M. (2007). *Distributed systems: Principles and Paradigms* (2nd ed.). Pearson Higher Education Inc. Press.

Thalod, S., & Niwas, R. (2013). Security model for computer network based on cluster computing. *International Journal of Engineering and Computer Science*, *2*(6), 1920–1927.

Vitti, P., & Santos, D. (2014). Current issues in cloud computing security and management. In *Proceedings of the JARIA Conference* (pp. 36-42).

VMware Product Guide. (2015). Retrieved March, 2015, from www.vmware.com/files/pdf/vmware-productguide

Wu, H., Ding, Y., Winer, C., & Yao, L. (2010). Network security for virtual machine in cloud computing. In *Proceedings of the 2010 5th IEEE International Conference on Computer Sciences and Convergence Information Technology (ICCIT)* (pp.18-21). IEEE Computer Society.

Xiao, Z., Kathiresshan, N., & Xiao, Y. (2012). A survey of accountability in computer networks and distributed systems. *Security and Communication Network, 9*(4), 290–315. doi:10.1002/sec.574

Xiao, Z., & Xiao, Y. (2013). Security and privacy in cloud computing. *IEEE Communications Surveys and Tutorials, 15*(2), 843–859. doi:10.1109/SURV.2012.060912.00182

Xie, T., & Qin, X. (2008). Security-aware resource allocation for real-time parallel jobs on homogeneous and heterogeneous clusters. *IEEE Transactions on Parallel and Distributed Systems, 19*(5), 682–697. doi:10.1109/TPDS.2007.70776

Yao, T. (2005). *Adaptive firewalls for the grid.* (Master dissertation). Technical University of Denmark, Denmark.

Zargar, S., & Tipper, D. (2013). A Survey of defense mechanisms against Distributed Denial of Service (DDoS) flooding attacks. *IEEE Communications Surveys and Tutorials, 15*(4), 2046–2069. doi:10.1109/SURV.2013.031413.00127

Zhai, Z., Qiao, Y., & Shao, M. (2012). Analysis on grid security patterns based on PKI. *Advances in Information Sciences and Service Sciences, 4*(23), 239–248.

Zhao, L., Sakr, S., Liu, A., & Bouguettaya, A. (2014). *Cloud data management.* Springer International Publishing. doi:10.1007/978-3-319-04765-2

Zhongqiu, J., Shu, Y., & Liangmin, W. (2009). Survivability evaluation of cluster-based wireless sensor network under DoS attacks. In *Proceedings of the 5th International Conference on Wireless Communications, Networking and Mobile Computing, (WiCom '09)* (pp. 1-4).

Zissis, D., & Lekkas, D. (2012). Addressing cloud computing security issues. *Future Generation Computer Systems, 28*(3), 583–592. doi:10.1016/j.future.2010.12.006

KEY TERMS AND DEFINITIONS

Accountability: The ability not only to detect errors but also to find the responsible entity/entities for the failure is crucial.

Authentication: Deals with verification of the identity of an entity/user within a network.

Authorization: Ensures that the user submits his/her identity in order to login to a particular service.

Cloud Provider: The cloud owner that offers some component of cloud services to other businesses or individuals. Cloud providers are sometimes referred to as cloud service providers or CSPs.

Confidentiality: Ensures that the important data is kept completely unobserved to the unauthorized users.

Data Integrity: Ensures that the important data have not been altered or destroyed in an unauthorized manner.

Hypervisor: A controller, which monitors/controls the activities of all virtual/guest machines that operating in a virtualized environment.

Virtualization: Refers to the act of creating a virtual (rather than actual) version of something, including virtual computer hardware platforms, operating systems, storage devices, and computer network resources.

Chapter 10

Tails Linux Operating System:

The Amnesiac Incognito System in Times of High Surveillance, Its Security Flaws, Limitations, and Strengths in the Fight for Democracy

Jose Antonio Cardenas-Haro
University of Missouri – St. Louis, USA

Maurice Dawson
University of Missouri – St. Louis, USA

ABSTRACT

After the information released by Edward Snowden, the world realized about the security risks of high surveillance from governments to citizens or among governments, and how it can affect the freedom, democracy and/or peace. Research has been carried out for the creation of the necessary tools for the countermeasures to all this surveillance. One of the more powerful tools is the Tails system as a complement of The Onion Router (TOR). Even though there are limitations and flaws, the progress has been significant and we are moving in the right direction.

DOI: 10.4018/978-1-5225-0741-3.ch010

INTRODUCTION

The erosion of privacy in the Web has created a movement from the free software advocates, in the search and development of free and proper tools for everybody. The TOR project is the core of this movement, followed by other many tools which are part of The Amnesic Incognito Live System (Tails). In this document is analyzed the importance of Tails and all its tools in the fight for privacy, freedom, and democracy.

THE BIRTH OF PUBLIC TOR

TOR project was set by the government and developed by the Defense Advanced Research Projects Agency (DARPA) as a security measure to avoid national and international surveillance of the classified government operations (Fagoyinbo & Babatunde, 2013). The Onion Routing principle is the use of several layers of encryption to conceal a user's location and ensure private and anonymous communications. Every router in this network only knows the address of the previous router and the address of the following one (Reed, Sylverson & Goldschlag, 1998).

Later the TOR project was released as a free software, and the development continues with funding from diverse sources (Tor: Sponsors, 2010); and these give more confidence to the public about its independence and reliability. So the use of this secure network soon became very popular in all the world propitiating its grow in many users and routers as well. The development of this project is continuous and dynamic; we are now in the second generation of TOR (Dingledine, Mathewson & Syverson, 2011).

This network was made available as a protection of the individuals' privacy (which is a constitutional right in most countries), and to promote and maintain the freedom of confidential communications through the Internet among the public, avoiding or, at least, making very hard the monitoring of them. TOR is an excellent tool not only for the hide of political activists but also for domestic violence survivors to escape abusers (Russell, 2014), or just for regular users to bypass censorship (Gurnow, 2014).

The National Security Agency (NSA) has said that TOR is "the King of high secure, low latency Internet anonymity" (The Guardian, 2013). The TOR project received an award for projects of social benefit from the FSF (Free Software Foundation) in 2010, acknowledging it not only for the privacy and anonymity that it provides, but also for the freedom of access and expression on the Internet granted to millions of people, which has proved to be pivotal in dissident movements around the world (FSF, 2010). The Business Week magazine has described it as one of the most effective means to defeat surveillance around the world (Lawrence, 2014).

HOW IT WORKS

The more people using TOR network, the better. It is easier for a person to be anonymous among many others, it is harder to keep track of someone in a busy unknown and highly tangled network that is frequently changing and mixing up the connections randomly (Edman, Sivrikaya & Yener, 2007). As an analogy, we can say that a chameleon to camouflage effectively needs leaves, branches and trees, the more, the better for the blend. In defeating surveillance, we need to take care of several aspects. Who we talk to and when is just as important as what we said, and to secure these we also need encryption and randomness in the routing as well. The messages from the different anonymous users are shuffled and then sent to the next randomly selected router, shuffled again and so forth until the final destination is reached. So as an observer it is very hard to know which data were coming into the TOR network corresponds to which data coming out of it.

All the data is encrypted, including the origin and destination IP addresses, every time before it is sent to the next relay of the anonymous circuit. Since the TOR is a dynamic network that is constantly evolving, the path that our packets take to change all the time making things harder for the observer (Dingledine, Serjantov & Syverson, 2006). The users can set up a browser, a relay, a hidden service or all of them. Also "bridge relays" can be used to circumvent any blocking to the TOR network.

THE NECESSITY OF ANONYMITY AND CYBER SECURITY

We all need privacy for many diverse reasons, and is not only about the individuals, but also the private companies and even the governmental entities in the world need some anonymity at different levels. Journalists who want to protect their sources, or the law enforcement agencies that require communication with their infiltrated personnel in criminal groups protecting their identity, or the human rights activists in oppressive regimes, or the private companies in avoiding the disclosure of their technological developments for economic reasons, or the governments saving a lot of information for national security.

Surveillance and Espionage have always being an issue; several countermeasures have been developed according to the times, but now is harder than ever. The cell phones can easily be converted into tracking devices and recordings of the phone calls, web pages visited, Internet search history and interactions in social media can create a detailed profile of anyone. The persons can be affected negatively by all these. They could suffer work discrimination because of their political views, or even their physical integrity could be in danger for those who are living in tyrannic regimes, like the recent case of Niloy Neel a Bangladeshi blogger killed in Dhaka

(BBC, 2015). The governments are always looking for ways to have more control and capabilities for surveillance; Linus Torvalds, the creator of the Linux Operating System (OS) and still in control of the development of the Linux kernel, revealed that the NSA asked him to put a backdoor in the OS (Greenwald, 2014).

Furthermore, there is the high risk of a democracy degrading into an authoritarian state if its citizens are surveilled to the degree of losing their privacy. The government can face significant economic risks if sensitive information is leaked, as in the case of the tax accounts hacked in the IRS (Weise, 2015). The use of technology is increasing and spreading quickly in most of the devices used by humans, which represents a new security threat if the owners lose the control of them, as in the case of the car hacked when in the middle of the road (Ward, 2015). For all these and more, the governments and the citizens are always looking for ways to avoid the intrusion in their data and systems.

BIRTH OF TAILS OPERATING SYSTEM

The first version of the operating system The Amnesic Incognito Live System (Tails) was released in mid-2009 as a merge of the Incognito and Amnesia Linux distributions. It was created by a team of anonymous hackers which still are in charge of its development, with support and funding from the TOR project and the Freedom of Press Foundation (FPF) (Finances of Tails., 2015), and also from the Debian and Mozilla projects (Tails report, 2014), and other sources that continue founding it. The Tails project is based on the Debian distribution with the security and anonymity as a core philosophy to give privacy to anyone anywhere. Tails were born as a complement of TOR to enhance the anonymization of their users. The Tails Linux distribution became so famous after being known that is the OS used by Edward Snowden, the whistleblower who leaked information about the PRISM project to The Guardian and The Washington Post newspapers (Finley, 2014). The Tails team created this Linux distribution as a countermeasure of erosion of online privacy. The big companies of the Internet, as well as the governments (especially in totalitarian regimes), want to take away our privacy making our lives more transparent every time.

THE STRENGTHS

The Tails OS is an integrated system consisting of several tools aimed to avoid the detection of the identity of their users. It is designed to boot from a removable live media as a Universal Serial Bus (USB) stick or a Digital Video Disk (DVD), and the saving of any file in it is deleted after a reboot for security reasons; of course, we can use the hard drive or another USB memory for the saving of the required data. In the case when we really want to delete any document, videos, pictures or any data file, the Tails is equipped with a tool called "Nautilus Wipe" for securely deleting the data; this is necessary since regular operating systems only remove the file name and link from the file system directory, not even the reformatting or over-writing of the hard drive or memory stick is a guarantee that the deleted or previous information is indeed gone. Tails come with visual camouflage that can be activated to give the look and feel of a Microsoft Windows 8 system, the purpose of this is to avoid attracting unwanted attention when working in public places.

All the traffic is handled through the TOR network, using Media Access Control (MAC) spoofing; all these to avoid leaving any digital footprint. It also gives the option to use Invisible Internet Project (I2P) as an alternative to TOR. The I2P is an anonymous overlay network used as an instrument to circumvent surveillance and censorship. This Linux distribution includes several state-of-the-art cryptographic tools to encrypt files, emails and instant messaging. It uses LUKS Linux Unified Key Setup (LUKS) which is an encryption tool for hard drives or USB sticks. All the communications with websites are encrypted automatically using Hypertext Transfer Protocol Secure (HTTPS). In the case of documents and emails, are encoded using Open Pretty Good Privacy (OpenPGP). The chatting or instant messaging is done using Off-the-Record (OTRP messaging which is another tool for encryption which also provides deniable authentication that cannot be achieved with PGP systems (Borisov, Goldberg & Brewer, 2004). It includes the "Shamir's Secret Sharing" program which runs an algorithm used in cryptography where the decryption of a message is only possible with some threshold number of participants (Shamir, 1979).

Tails also come with software to create virtual keyboard as a countermeasure against hardware keyloggers, and even with tools to anonymize metadata in files, to calculate checksums. It includes the "AppArmor" system which is a Linux kernel enhancement to confine programs to a limited set of resources. To prevent the "cold boot" attacks and forensics to the Random Access Memory (RAM), it deletes all the memory at the shutdown.

The updates to patch any security hole are available in a prompt manner as an automatic mechanism to upgrade the USB stick or the Secure Digital (SD) card to the most recent version of Tails. The creators of Tails and TOR support and promote the search for flaws in the system as a way to keep it in a continuous improvement state. This incredible operating has been created using only free software, which is a must in these cases since closed private software cannot be trustable. It is not a coincidence that Tails is the preferred operating system by Edward Snowden (Finley, 2014).

LIMITATIONS AND FLOWS

As is the case with everything, the Tails system has its limitations. This system is the conjunction of many tools, any flaw in any of its tools becomes a flaw for the Tails system. Furthermore, working effectively under this system requires some technical knowledge, most of the tools in Tails are not precisely user-friendly. It is known that the NSA has been able to crack the computers of some TOR users, but not the core security of the TOR network (Ball, Schneier & Greenwald; 2013); this has to do more with errors or carelessness from the users. Tails were created as a complement to the TOR browser, as an integrated system for the improvement of the security and anonymity.

TOR encrypts all inside its network and anonymizes the origin of the traffic, but the communications from the TOR network and the final destinations are like the regular transferring of information on the Internet. So, depending on your data, you might need to use some of the tools provided in Tails for further encryption and authentication. Also, we need to change some of our habits, it is not recommended to enable or install browser plugins, neither to open any document downloaded through TOR while online. The Tails does not protect against compromised pieces of hardware, like a key logger unless you use for this specific case a virtual keyboard "Florence" provided in one of its tools. The Basic Input/Output System (BIOS) or firmware attacks are other forms of compromised hardware.

Another important factor that needs close attention is the metadata in our files. Tails does not clear it for us, but it provides the tools necessary for the removal of information that can help to identify us from the metadata, before sending any of the files. In the case of e-mails even if we encrypt the contents, the subject and other headers remain understandable. Another problem in the case of TOR is that it does not protect us from a global adversary, this means an entity monitoring all or most of the nodes in the TOR network, such entity using statistical data may infer the relations between the users and the connections (Dingledine, Mathewson & Syverson. 2004). Another important habit here is the use of a strong password, and the Tails will not create strong passwords for you. It is not straightforward to hide the fact that you are using Tails, and this in some ways is a disadvantage, a flaw in the anonymity. Users have to be ready to update the Tails system every time that there is a patch available.

TOOL FOR FREEDOM AND DEMOCRACY

As humans, we have the natural right to privacy and in all the democracies that right is granted in the constitutions. Unapproved or unreasonable searches and seizures go against the human rights. The exchange of information between individuals, corporations or governmental agencies has to be encrypted. It is evident that would be easier for the cops and law enforcement agencies to detect illegal activities if the information were not encrypted, but in the same way it would be easier for the criminals to affect the citizens.

The open source philosophy is a great medium to provide trustable tools to build all the infrastructure that we need to keep the freedom and democracy not only on the Internet but also in our lives. The open source has given birth to the Linux operating system, encryption tools, Wikipedia, Wikileaks, Bitcoin, BitTorrent, social media and many more valuable programs. The General Public License (GPL) is a free software license to guarantee anybody the right and freedom to use, modify and share the programs (Dawson, Leonard, & Rahim, 2015). All these show how humans around the globe can be organized without borders to improve their economies, to build the required products without the need of the private companies or centralized governments with all the toxic and corrupted control that they represent. In other words, out of the master and slave model, or without "baby sitters".

The mistrust of a central authority is common anywhere, as humans, we have the innate desire for freedom in everything. It is important to clarify that while some media and governments have slandered and libeled the DarkNet, the TOR, and the Tail Linux OS saying that these are evil tools used by criminals; all these are also essential tools used by many people for the good, including dissidents, journalists and law enforcement agencies around the world.

There is always the risk of cyber espionage or mass surveillance done by governments around the globe. In the case of US is with the project PRISM developed by the NSA (Ball, 2013). The UK has the project Tempora (Bump, 2013). In Russia is the SORM project (Paganini, 2014) and China has two significant tools for the control of the Internet, the Golden Shield (or Great Firewall) for censorship and surveillance (Randy, 2009); and the Green Dam for Personal Computer (PC) content control (Watts, 2009; Chen, 2009). There are also companies that sell technology for surveillance even to oppressive regimes (Gilbert, 2015), so we can say that all or, at least, most of the states around the world do some kind surveillance that could go worst as the technology improves and evolves. The monitoring between nations can cause tensions and damage in the diplomatic relations or even the loss of them (Smith, 2014; Menn, 2015; Fitsanakis, 2013).

Furthermore, the surveillance does not come only from the states. The private companies also want your data for economic purposes. They want to know what are you more likely to consume, to buy, and this way you could become the target of some specific advertising. Companies like Microsoft, Apple, Facebook, Yahoo, Google or Amazon among others are collecting their user's data is also for psychological manipulation to make you consume some products that other way you might not buy. They need all the possible information from you to link it with your real life behavior, and these give them some control over you. Your cell phone location, who you share information with, who you talk to, what you buy, etc. The companies usually have arrangements with the government to share this information or they might also be under government surveillance for these data (Branstetter, 2015; Greenwald, MacAskill, Poitras, Ackerman, & Rusche, 2013; Bekker, 2013). The problem is that the more you are surveilled, the less autonomous and free you are. It is not easy to know the level and kind of control that they could exercise over us, but our freewill is indeed affected.

People are saying that they do not care about surveillance because they do not have anything to hide pure ignorance, it is like saying that they do not care about free speech because they do not have anything to say. Thanks to free thinkers and researchers, there are tools, services, protocols and free software available and under continuous development and improvement to avoid surveillance, for an anonymous and private exchange of information; science and technology is fighting back. All these come down to live a free life which is a core human value, and a foundation for any true democracy.

CONCLUSION

As more people express the desire for privacy, the demand will fuel the market as data found publicly can fall prey to those conducting Open Source Intelligence (OSINT) mining and analysis for nefarious reasons. By making the surveillance harder we protect ourselves as individuals, and all the others by making it more expensive to surveillance everyone all the time. At the end encryption and chaos is all about mathematics, and in the quest for more privacy the numbers work in our favor. It is a lot easier the encryption of the data than the decryption of it for intruders. Our universe fundamentally favors privacy. In order of having a free society, we need to have freedom from analysis about behaviors and communications among us. When considering issues about privacy, cyber terrorism, and digital crime (Dawson & Omar, 2015; Dawson, Omar, & Abramson 2015).

REFERENCES

Ball, J. (2013). NSA's Prism surveillance program: how it works and what it can do. *The Guardian*, 8.

Ball, J., Schneier, B., & Greenwald, G. (2013). NSA and GCHQ target Tor network that protects anonymity of web users. *The Guardian*, 4.

BBC. (2015). *Bangladesh blogger Niloy Neel hacked to death in Dhaka*. Retrieved from: http://www.bbc.com/news/world-asia-33819032

Bekker, S. (2013, June 20). *PRISM and Microsoft: What We Know So Far*. Redmond Channel Partner.

Borisov, N., Goldberg, I., & Brewer, E. (2004, October). Off-the-record communication, or, why not to use PGP. In *Proceedings of the 2004 ACM workshop on Privacy in the electronic society* (pp. 77-84). ACM. doi:10.1145/1029179.1029200

Branstetter, B. (2015, August 16). The NSA is asking your favorite apps how to spy on you better. *Business Insider, Daily Dot*.

Bump, P. (2013, June 21). The UK Tempora Program Captures Vast Amounts of Data – and Shares with NSA. *The Atlantic Wire*.

Chen, W. (2009, June 13). Let people decide on Green Dam. *China Daily*.

Dawson, M. (2015). A Brief Review of New Threats and Countermeasures in Digital Crime and Cyber Terrorism. In M. Dawson & M. Omar (Eds.), *New Threats and Countermeasures in Digital Crime and Cyber Terrorism* (pp. 1–7). Hershey, PA: Information Science Reference; doi:10.4018/978-1-4666-8345-7.ch001

Dawson, M., Leonard, B., & Rahim, E. (2015). Advances in Technology Project Management: Review of Open Source Software Integration. In M. Wadhwa & A. Harper (Eds.), *Technology, Innovation, and Enterprise Transformation* (pp. 313–324). Hershey, PA: Business Science Reference; doi:10.4018/978-1-4666-6473-9.ch016

Dawson, M., & Omar, M. (2015). *New Threats and Countermeasures in Digital Crime and Cyber Terrorism*. Hershey, PA: IGI Global; doi:10.4018/978-1-4666-8345-7.ch001

Dawson, M., Omar, M., & Abramson, J. (2015). Understanding the Methods behind Cyber Terrorism. In M. Khosrow-Pour (Ed.), *Encyclopedia of Information Science and Technology* (3rd ed.; pp. 1539–1549). Hershey, PA: Information Science Reference; doi:10.4018/978-1-4666-5888-2.ch147

Dingledine, R., Mathewson, N., & Syverson, P. (2004). *Tor: The second-generation onion router*. Naval Research Lab Washington DC.

Dingledine, R., Serjantov, A., & Syverson, P. (2006, June). Blending different latency traffic with alpha-mixing. In *Privacy Enhancing Technologies* (pp. 245–257). Springer Berlin Heidelberg. doi:10.1007/11957454_14

Edman, M., Sivrikaya, F., & Yener, B. (2007, May). *A Combinatorial Approach to Measuring Anonymity*. ISI.

Fagoyinbo, J. B. (2013). *The Armed Forces: Instrument of Peace, Strength, Development and Prosperity*. AuthorHouse.

Finances of Tails. (2015). Retrieved from: https://tails.boum.org/doc/about/finances/index.en.html

Fitsanakis, J. (2013, June 20). Analysis: PRISM Revelations Harm US Political, Financial Interests. *IntelNews*.

FSF. (2010). *2010 Free Software Awards announced*. Free Software Foundation.

Gilbert, D. (2015). Hacking Team hacked: Spy tools sold to oppressive regimes Sudan, Bahrain and Kazakhstan. *International Business Times Magazine*.

Greenwald, G. (2014). *No place to hide: Edward Snowden, the NSA, and the US surveillance state*. Macmillan.

Greenwald, G., MacAskill, E., Poitras, L., Ackerman, S., & Rushe, D. (2013). Microsoft handed the NSA access to encrypted messages. *The Guardian, 12*.

Gurnow, M., (2014, July). Seated Between Pablo Escobar and Mahatma Gandhi: The Sticky Ethics of Anonymity Networks. *Dissident Voice*.

Harris, S., & Meyers, M. (2002). *CISSP*. McGraw-Hill/Osborne.

James, R. (2009, May 11). A brief history of Chinese internet censorship. *Time*.

Janczewski, L., & Colarik, A. (2007). *Cyber Warfare and Cyber Terrorism*. Hershey, PA: IGI Global. doi:10.4018/978-1-59140-991-5

Lawrence, D. (2014). *The inside story of Tor, the best Internet anonymity tool the government ever built*. Bloomberg Businessweek.

Levine, Y. (2014). Almost everyone involved in developing Tor was (or is) funded by the US government. *PandoDally*. Retrieved from: http://www.infowars.com/almost-everyone-involved-in-developing-tor-was-or-is-funded-by-the-us-government/

Menn, J. (2015, February 16). *Russian Researchers Expose Breakthrough US Spying Program*. Reuters.

Nakamoto, S. (2008). *Bitcoin: A peer-to-peer electronic cash system*. Retrieved from: https://bitcoin.org/bitcoin.pdf

Paganini, P. (2014). New powers for the Russian surveillance system SORM-2. *Security Affairs*. Retrieved http://securityaffairs.co/wordpress/27611/digital-id/new-powers-sorm-2.html

Reed, M. G., Syverson, P. F., & Goldschlag, D. M. (1998). Anonymous connections and onion routing. *Selected Areas in Communications. IEEE Journal on, 16*(4), 482–494.

Russell, B., (2014, May). Domestic violence survivors turn to Tor to escape abusers. *The Verge*.

Shamir, A. (1979). How to share a secret. *Communications of the ACM, 22*(11), 612–613. doi:10.1145/359168.359176

Smith, A. (2014). U.S. Spy Scandal Triggers Outrage, Paranoia in Germany. NBC News. August 2, 2014. "Tails report for May, 2014". *Tails*. Retrieved from: https://tails.boum.org/news/report_2014_05/index.en.html

The Guardian. (2013) *Tor: The king of high-secure, low-latency anonymity*. Tor Project.

Ward, M. (2015). Warning after security experts hack Tesla car. *BBC News*. Retrieved from: http://www.bbc.com/news/technology-33802344

Watts, J. (2009, June 8). China orders PC makers to install blocking software. *The Guardian*.

Weise, E. (2015). IRS Hacked, 100,000 Tax Accounts Breached. *USA Today*. Retrieved from: http://www.usatoday.com/story/tech/2015/05/26/irs-breach-100000-accounts-get-transcript/27980049/

KEY TERMS AND DEFINITIONS

Authentication: Security measure designed to establish the validity of a transmission, message, or originator, or a means of verifying an individual's authorization to receive specific categories of information (Harris, 2002).

Availability: Timely, reliable access to data and information services for authorized users (Harris, 2002).

Bitcoin: Bitcoin is a peer to peer electronic cash system that no one controls and there are not printed currency (Nakamoto, 2008).

Confidentiality: Assurance that information is not disclosed to unauthorized individuals, processes, or devices (Harris, 2002).

Cyber Terrorism: Attacks with the use of the Internet for terrorist activities, including acts of de-liberate, large-scale disruption of computer networks, especially of personal computers attached to the Internet, by the means of tools such as computer viruses, worms, Trojans, and zombies (Janczewski & Colarik, 2008).

Integrity: Quality of an IS reflecting the logical correctness and reliability of the OS; the logical completeness of the hardware and software implementing the protection mechanisms; and the consistency of the data structures and occurrence of the stored data. Note that, in a formal security mode, integrity is interpreted more narrowly to mean protection against unauthorized modification or destruction of information (Harris, 2002).

Non-Repudiation: Assurance the sender of data is provided with proof of delivery and the recipient is provided with proof of the sender's identity, so neither can later deny having processed the data (Harris, 2002).

Open Source Intelligence: Intelligence collected from publicly available sources (Dawson, 2015).

Chapter 11
Cyber Threats in Civil Aviation

Calvin Nobles
Independent Researcher, USA

ABSTRACT

Civil aviation faces increased cybersecurity threats due to hyperconnectivity and the lack of standardized frameworks and cybersecurity defenses. Educating the civil aviation workforce is one method to enhance cyber defense against cyber-attacks. Educating the workforce will lead to initiatives and strategies to combat cyber-attacks. Private and public entities need to remain aggressive in developing cyber defense strategies to keep pace with the increasing vulnerabilities of hyperconnectivity. Areas that require immediate attention to safeguard against cybersecurity threats in civil aviation are: 1) Eliminating supply risks, 2) Upgrading legacy systems, 3) Mitigating technological aftereffects, 4) Increasing cybersecurity awareness, 5) Developing cybersecurity workforce, 6) Managing hyperconnectivity, and 7) Leveraging international entities. To safeguard civil aviation infrastructure from cybersecurity threats require assertive, coordinated, and effective strategies and capabilities to defend the network.

INTRODUCTION

Persistent cyber-attacks on private and public computer networks in the U.S. continue to increase annually; consequently, highlighting the cyber security vulnerabilities of critical infrastructures. The number of cyber incidents reported by federal agencies grew from 5,503 to 60,753 from 2006 to 2012 (U.S. GAO, 2015). Increased

DOI: 10.4018/978-1-5225-0741-3.ch011

cyber-attacks and threats led to extensive efforts to improve and safeguard computer networks in the U.S. For example, the National Infrastructure Protection Plan (NIPP) was mandated to develop defensive measures to secure critical infrastructures in the U.S. (Murray & Grubesic, 2012). The NIPP promulgates strategies to prevent cyber threats from manifesting by synchronizing efforts between public and private organizations (Murray & Grubesic, 2012). The U.S. government plays a critical role in providing cyber security, which includes protecting critical infrastructures, increasing cyber security awareness (Murray & Grubesic, 2012), developing cyber-attack capabilities, and disseminating cyber threat information to private and public entities.

Cyber criminals exploit private and public computer networks to gain access to sensitive information regarding national security, economic interests (Roesener, Bottolfson, & Fernandez, 2014), military defense plans, military personnel data, and to corporate espionage. Private entities own eighty-five percent of critical infrastructures; therefore, requiring the U.S. government to work strategically and collaboratively with the industry to prevent catastrophic attacks on our prized infrastructures (Murray & Grubesic, 2012). Regarding the civil aviation infrastructure, the Federal Aviation Administration plays a fundamental role in developing strategies and initiating actions to safeguard civil aviation.

Without a doubt, civil aviation is a critical infrastructure that is vulnerable to cyber threats by hackers and malicious actors (Schober, Koblen, & Szabo, 2012). One aspect of civil aviation that lends itself to cyber threats is the interconnected nature of computer networks and communication systems. Researchers refer to this phenomenon as hyperconnectivity (Fredette et al., 2012; Schober, Koblen, & Szabo, 2012). Hyperconnectivity makes it increasingly difficult to safeguard communications and computer systems from cyber-attacks. Critical infrastructure is a system or network of systems that provides vital functions that if disrupted causes socio-economic, financial, political, military defense, or security instability (Tanbansky, 2011). Critical infrastructures are food, water, financial services, healthcare, emergency services, energy power systems, and transportation systems (Kessler & Ramsay, 2013) that provide unique capabilities or services to the populace. Civil Aviation is a subsidiary of the transportation infrastructure and is considered critical infrastructure because of its significance to international and transoceanic transportation, globalization, financial security, international trade, and business. A major cyber-attack on the civil aviation infrastructure will catastrophically weaken and cause international instability.

As cyber innovations continue to expand, civil aviation's reliance on technological advances increases; consequently, making it difficult to protect civil aviation infrastructure from cyber-attacks (Lim, 2014). In the U.S. the aviation infrastructure consists of 450 commercial airports, 19,000 public airfields, multifaceted computer and communication systems Internet protocol enabled aircraft, wireless and sensor networks, supervisory control and data acquisition (SCADA), and cyber-physical systems (CPS) (Abeyratne, 2011; CSAN4, 2013; Jabeur, Sahli, & Zeadally, 2015; Lu et al., 2014; Nicholson et al., 2012; Roadmap to Secure, 2012). The above statement highlights the perplexity and vulnerability of the U.S. civil aviation infrastructure. The purpose of this chapter is to call attention to the cyber security threats within civil aviation from a non-alarmist perspective. This chapter discusses the emerging cyber threats in civil aviation, cyber security frameworks, the implications of hyperconnectivity dependence, educating the aviation workforce on cyber threats, and international and national level strategies for combatting cyber threats in civil aviation.

BACKGROUND

The increase in cyber attacks is indicative of the vulnerable nature of computer systems and networks accompanied by outdated systems and poor information assurance practices. Cyber attacks on critical infrastructures remain of high interest to public and private organizations due to national security concerns. Malicious actors, hackers, and adversarial nations are developing sophisticated capabilities to conduct cyber-attacks. The cyber domain is an attractive option for terrorists because of the low-cost, the ability to remain anonymous, and the opportunity to attack at will (Jarvis, MacDonald, & Nouri, 2014). Current attacks are increasing annually (GAO, 2015) and it is only a matter of time before terrorists conduct a catastrophic cyber-attack on a prized critical infrastructure. The increasing use of technological breakthroughs coupled with overreliance on legacy systems increases cyber security risks and exposes the vulnerable state of critical infrastructures to include the transportation sector.

The Growing Cyber Security Threat in Civil Aviation

In 2014, cyber-attacks set a new precedence, totaling over 40 million cyber-attacks, which was a 50 percent increase from 2013 (Schakelford & Bohm, 2015). The U.S. is the third most cyber-attacked nation in the world (Schakelford & Bohm, 2015) because non-state actors and adversaries have to ability to remotely attack at will and remain anonymously (Dombrowski & Demchak, 2014). Estimated losses from major cyber-attacks have reached a cumulative total of 700 billion dollars (Schakelford & Bohm, 2015). Terrorist attacks are disruptive and highly unpredictable; therefore, civil aviation requires adequate defensive measures, which are costly (Pettersen &. Bjørnskau, 2015). A cyber-attack in one country has financial, economic, political, security, and diplomatic fallout around the world. At the local government level, cyber security breaches are disruptive, induce unexpected costs, reduce defense capabilities, and impede the local government (Caruson, MacManus, & McPhee, 2012). Clearly, random attacks hinder from investing in current cyber upgrades to defend against persistent cyber crimes.

Without a doubt, terrorists, hackers, adversarial nations, and non-state actors target civil aviation due to previous successes in aviation such as hijackings, the 9/11 attacks, and the Pan Am bombing (Price, 2012). Current security practices in aviation date back over 60 years (Oster, Strong, & Zorn, 2013). Oster, Strong, and Zorn (2013) proclaimed that the tools used by terrorists are essential, in fact, the tools and capabilities are crucial for developing cyber defenses, creating awareness, and preventing future threats. There are four categories of terrorist threats to civil aviation:

1. The obliteration of an aircraft with a bomb,
2. Hijacking,
3. A terrorist attack on the airport, and
4. A cyber-attack on the aviation infrastructure (Oster, Strong, & Zorn, 2013).

Due to the emergence of new technologies and capabilities in aviation (Oster, Strong, & Zorn, 2013) makes it difficult to predict or prevent a cyber terrorist from conducting attacks on the aviation infrastructure.

The objective of a terrorist group or terrorism is to cause fear, to dominate, or to intimidate due to political, economic, religion, ideology, or cultural indifferences (Rowland, Rice, & Shenoi, 2014). Cyberspace is a global medium that terrorist groups leverage to conduct illegal activities due to the difficulty in controlling and regulating cyberspace (Dombrowski & Demchak, 2014; Rowland, Rice, & Shenoi, 2014). Given the lack of laws regarding cyberspace, it perpetuates terrorism and criminal activity via the Internet because cyber criminals remain anonymous from the added protection of operating in cyberspace (Rowland, Rice, & Shenoi, 2014) and are armed with cyber capabilities to affect public and private entities. As organizations and people leverage cyberspace for business, malicious actors, and cybercriminals are leveraging cyberspace as a means to induce fear, to intimidate, steal, and conduct other forms of criminal activities. Cyberspace is borderless with valuable access points around the world, which provide cyber criminals with a target rich environment. For example, there are 1.5 billion Internet users, and 4.5 billion cell phone users (Nielsen, 2012; Rowland, Rice, & Shenoi, 2014). Cyberspace is an optimal platform for cyber terrorists to operate covertly or overtly.

General Alexander, the former commander of U.S. Cyber Command, confirmed the growing interest in cyberspace, the complexity of cyber security threats, adversarial capabilities, and the ability of terrorists to conduct widespread cyber-attacks on critical infrastructure to include civil aviation (Nielsen, 2012). Cyber terrorists are successful in conducting cyber-attacks because cyber security is an afterthought during the development phase of designing information technologies (Goodman, Kirk, & Kirk, 2007). The continuous use of legacy systems with dated security defenses creates vulnerabilities within critical infrastructures (Goodman, Kirk, & Kirk, 2007) to include civil aviation. Implementing stringent requirements is costly and reduces system efficiency, which is indicative of the opposing relationship between system designs (Goodman, Kirk, & Kirk, 2007; Nielsen, 2012) and cyber security. Private and public entities have to make cyber security a priority for computer networks and systems. Taking a modest approach to cyber security enables hackers and malicious actors to gain access to our most prized infrastructures. During the system design phase, it is imperative to integrative security capabilities and defensive measures early in the design phase rather than security being an afterthought. Ideally, computer networks and communication systems should be designed to allow reasonable and integrative security upgrades. Because modern-day computer systems and networks are hyperconnected to critical infrastructures that are essential to national security, public safety, health services, banking, and the economy are interconnected globally through digitized communication systems (Nielsen, 2012). The U.S. government's concerns about inadequate cyber security practices and determining the most effective approach to protecting the nation's 18 critical infrastructures stems from private entities owning 80-90 percent of the critical infrastructure (Murray & Grubesic, 2012; Nielsen, 2012). The ability to operate and function in cyberspace is a matter of national security for private and public organizations; therefore, it is essential to strengthen the computer networks of existing critical infrastructures.

A systemic problem concerning civil aviation is the inconsistency in aviation policy, infrastructures, and in some cases the lack of policies in less developed countries (LDC)

(Dennis, Jones, Kildare, & Barclay, 2014). Aviation policies are mandated and directed at the national level, but aviation policies vary amongst different countries; nonetheless, in LDC, aviation infrastructure, aviation systems, and aviation regulations are abysmal at best (Itani, O'Connell, & Mason, 2015). Lack of cyber security frameworks by LDC threatens existing international and national cyber security efforts because cyber-terrorists can exploit vulnerabilities and gaps because LDC lacks plans and the capabilities to protect critical infrastructures (Dennis, Jones, Kildare, & Barclay, 2014). For example, in a recent study, researchers noted that Jamaica's non-existing cyber security framework weakens international efforts to solidify cyber capabilities to combat cyber threats. The absence of a cyber security framework highlights the vulnerabilities of critical infrastructures (Dennis, Jones, Kildare, & Barclay, 2014) and increases the possibility for cyber terrorists to use Jamaica as a haven. Less develop countries lack the fundamental foundation to develop a national cyber security framework, as evident by no national policy directing a Cyber Emergency Response Team (Dennis, Jones, Kildare, & Barclay, 2014). In a hyperconnected society coupled with the acumen of cyber terrorists, the ability to operate within the realms of LDC is ideal for accessing and attacking critical infrastructures. Knowing that cyberspace has no boundaries; poorly protected aviation infrastructures in LDC raise concerns due to obstinate and ubiquitous cyber security threats and vulnerabilities. Transoceanic flights transition numerous national borders; however, from a cyber security perspective, well-guarded civil aviation infrastructures are interconnected to technically deficient civil aviation infrastructures in LDC that are amassing cyber security concerns. Civil aviation stakeholders tolerate the cyber security and safety risks of LDC inadequate civil aviation infrastructure due to economic and transportation implications. Some LDC struggle to ameliorate existing civil aviation infrastructure due to fiscal restraints; consequently, forcing LDC to use privatization to finance civil aviation infrastructure (Itani, O'Connell, & Mason, 2015). Itani, O'Connell, and Mason (2015) asserted that using privatization to underpin the financial support for civil aviation infrastructure is not pragmatic because national level objectives, specifically cyber security initiatives, are at risk of omission due to external influences from the investors. Strengthening cyber security efforts in civil aviation is an international obligation, and failure to implement cyber security defenses increases the vulnerability of civil aviation's exposed infiltration and access points.

Cyber Security Framework

What exactly is cyber security? Researchers asserted that cyber security is an amalgamation of tools, policies, security theories, security capabilities, procedures, information assurance practices, expertise, risk management, and organization practices to protect organizations from cybercrime (Von Solms & Van Niekerk, 2013). Organizations strive to defend information technology infrastructures by preventing malicious cyber threats, security risks (Von Solms & Van Niekerk, 2013), and vulnerabilities. Emerging cyber security threats to critical infrastructures are growing increasingly sophisticated due to hyperconnectivity, which intensifies the risks to the U.S. national security, economy, public safety (Shackelford, Proia, Martell, & Craig, 2015), and stability. Cyber security threats enable the exploitation of vulnerabilities, increase cost, (Shackelford, Proia, Martell, & Craig, 2015) induce fear, and impede public safety. For instance, the lack of regulatory and congressional guidance compelled President Obama to sign an executive order tasking the National Institute of Standards and Technology (NIST) to establish a voluntary "Cybersecurity Framework" (Shackelford, Proia, Martell, & Craig, 2015). This effort consisted of private entities developing the best practices to safeguard critical infrastructures (Shackelford, Proia, Martell, & Craig, 2015). The salient concepts of the framework are: (a) categorize, (b) safeguard, (c) discover, (d) respond, and (e) restore (Shen, 2014). These steps are defensive in nature and designed to identify and mitigate malicious activities. The framework provides in-depth information that outlines each core capability, which is indicative of the meticulous processes to safeguard against cyber security threats accompanied by researchers advocating for global implementation of the framework as an evaluation tool for organizations (Shackelford, Proia, Martell, & Craig, 2015; Shen, 2014).

The NIST Cybersecurity Framework (NCF) is the type of baselining platform needed to influence private and public entities to construct cyber security initiatives and efforts that are comprehensive, effective (Shackelford, Proia, Martell, & Craig, 2015), and repeatable. Though some sectors are regulated to maintain defensive cyber security capabilities, idealistically, the cyber security framework is the model to synchronize national critical infrastructure practices into international standards (Shackelford, Proia, Martell, & Craig, 2015). Geographical boundaries do not localize cyber security threats; therefore, the international community needs to synchronize cyber security defenses of critical infrastructures, to include civil aviation, to eradicate vulnerabilities within cyberspace. Shen (2014) argued that institutions should use the NCF to evaluate existing cyber security practices to develop improved defensive cyber security capabilities as well as for leaders to assess their organizations' cyber security programs against NCF standards. The NIST outlines several pillars to employ the framework: (a) evaluate organizational practices against core methods to determine improvements, (b) articulate cyber security fundamentals to organizational stakeholders, and (c) leverage the NCF to implement new standards, methods, and protocols through identifying informative resources (Shen, 2014). The NCF is not intended to replace cyber security practices; however, it is used to evaluate and enhance existing cyber security programs (Shen, 2014).

The NIST Framework serves as a platform to highlight legislative shortfalls regarding cyber security and to promote cyber security standards and practices for private and public organizations (Shen, 2014). In addition to the NCF providing guidance to solidify cyber security, the framework also serves as an educational application to train senior executives on increasing cyber security awareness and evaluating existing cyber security protocols against standards promulgated in the NCF (Shen, 2014). Shackelford, Proia, Martell, and Craig (2015) declared that the NCF is inducing national-level policy changes to increase protection for critical infrastructures on a national level. Given the hyperconnected nature of critical infrastructures, CPS, and SCADA systems, the NCF application is analogous to the international community as the U.S. by providing a comprehensive plan for improving cyber security, driving legislative changes, and establishing cyber security oversight practices on a global scale. Cyber security is an international concern (Shackelford, Proia, Martell, &

Craig, 2015) because cyber terrorism is a low-cost means of undermining a state's computer systems, health services, banking industry, and military infrastructures while remaining anonymous (Abeyratne, 2011).

Specifically, the American Institute of Aeronautics and Astronautics (AIAA) organized a symposium to address cyber security concerns in aviation that led to the development of *A Framework for Aviation Cybersecurity* (Lasiello, 2014). The objective of the aviation framework is to increase discourse and outline procedures and practices to combat against the mounting cyber security concerns associated with integrating new technologies (Lasiello, 2014). This framework establishes cyber security protocols for the aviation infrastructure, cultivates cyber security awareness and education, fosters information sharing on cyber threats, risks, and situational awareness, and solidifies defensive cyber security capabilities within civil aviation (Lasiello, 2014). The aviation cyber security framework articulates cyber security issues from a global viewpoint as indicated by the authors recommending an external regulatory entity to the U.S. lead the efforts to codify the global implications of cyber threats (Lasiello, 2014). This aviation framework intends to be assertive and analogous to the aviation industry's approach to improving aviation safety in civil aviation (Lasiello, 2014). The AIAA aggressive approach to eradicating cyber security threats is indicative of the industry's desire to reduce cyber threats in aviation.

Hyperconnectivity and Cyberphysical System

Before the emergence of hyperconnectivity, there were SCADA systems. Technological advancements like Internet protocol, Internet of things (IOT), and digitized communications have subjected SCADA systems to cyber threats. Hyperconnectivity is the continuous connections of computer networks, mobile devices, people to networks, and IOT (Fredette et al., 2012). Cyber physical system (CPS) is a comparable technological breakthrough that is analogous to hyperconnectivity, which refers to an integrative system of systems methodology that interconnects electronic devices, computer networks, and wireless technologies to physical processes through wireless sensors (Lu et al., 2014). The significance of hyperconnectivity and CPS is the increasing integration of digitized and wireless communications and IOT within in civil aviation (Lim, 2014; Lu et al., 2014). A vulnerable aspect of CPS is the retrieval of data from physical systems because wireless sensor networks have gateways (Lu et al., 2014) that hackers, adversaries, or malicious actors could potentially exploit. A CPS is designed to operate in an open architecture in a distributed connection mode for linking mobile and various devices that provide the best connection (Jabeur, Sahli, & Zeadally, 2015). Wireless sensor networks are fundamental components of CPS that are engineered to make decisions independent of human interaction (Jabeur, Sahli, & Zeadally, 2015). From a cyber security perspective, such components make it difficult to control, monitor, and track network intrusions or malicious activity. Civil aviation leverages hyperconnected networks to capitalize on automated and technological advances at the cost of increasing cyber security vulnerabilities (Lim, 2014).

Hyperconnectivity enables devices, people, and the IOT to have continuous connectivity, which makes hyperconnected devices accessible via the numerous gateways and connection points of mobile devices and IOT (Lu et al., 2014). This hyperconnected phenomenon capitalizes on technological advances accompanied by constant connectivity, which is advantageous for non-critical infrastructures; however, critical infrastructures are increasingly exposed to cyber security vulnerabilities (Amantini, 2012). Computer networks, communication technologies, and digitized communication paths increase the vulnerability of the civil aviation infrastructures ("Understanding Cybercrime", 2012). The civil aviation infrastructure appeals to hackers and terrorists due to the growing complexity of protecting vital systems from attacks (Schober, Koblen, & Szabo, 2012) and the demonstrated inability to safeguard critical infrastructures. Terrorists and hackers are aware of the problems associated with securing critical infrastructures (Schober, Koblen, & Szabo, 2012) and the lack of laws governing cyber security. Some might argue that the success of cyber-attacks stems from the continuous integration of technological breakthroughs. Therefore, requiring public, private, and state-level organizations to develop and implement cyber defenses to combat cyber threats. Dombrowski and Demchak (2014) noted that policies and laws fail to keep pace with technological developments in the cyber domain. Without assertive efforts to identify the vulnerabilities of hyperconnectivity, the ability to safeguard the aviation infrastructure remains a daunting challenge.

The civil aviation infrastructure consists of a system of systems that interconnect components; which increases the susceptibility for cyber-attacks (Dawson et al., 2014). Of equal concern, is an Internet protocol (IP) enabled or electronic enabled aircraft, which allows pilots, ground operations, dispatchers, and maintenance personnel to optimize aircraft performance and health via IP connections (Lew, Corder, & Ruck, 2015). As the aviation industry gravitates toward more IP-based technologies, such innovations create cyber security risks (Abeyratne, 2011; CSAN4, 2014). Khan et al. (2013) emphasized that the open architecture of wireless networks prevent the cyber defenses from achieving privacy and network security. Internet protocol enabled aircraft and network technologies are designed to improve air traffic control inefficiencies and reduce air traffic chokepoints (Sampigethaya, Poovendran, & Bushnell, 2009).

TECHNOLOGICAL NECESSITY

An important question regarding the integration of technology in civil aviation is, what factors are driving technological changes in civil aviation? According to researchers, technological advancements in civil aviation is a result of the aging state of aviation transportation systems (Sampigethaya, Poovendran, & Bushnell, 2009). Increasing air traffic, terrorist threats, environmental challenges, and passenger comfort are driving technological changes in civil aviation (Sampigethaya, Poovendran, & Bushnell, 2008). The aviation industry is forecasting the volume of air traffic to triple, which is influencing the integration of hyperconnected type capabilities due to the deteriorating state of civil aviation's current infrastructure (Sampigethaya, Poovendran, & Bushnell, 2008). The increasing volume of air traffic is prompting the demand for improved technologies to ameliorate air traffic control (ATC) management (Sampigethaya, Poovendran, & Bushnell, 2009) and aviation safety. With the integration of IP- based aircraft, the demand for technologically capable computer networks is becoming a standard technology in civil aviation.

Integrating technological advancements is necessary because the U.S. has the largest and is the most up to date civil aviation infrastructure (Sampigethaya, Poovendran, & Bushnell, 2009). The latest upgrades to the U.S. infrastructure occurred in the 1970s. In fact, the U.S. civil aviation infrastructure received a major overhaul 43 years ago (Sampigethaya, Poovendran, & Bushnell, 2009). The susceptibility of computer networks in civil aviation is not only resident to the U.S. because the international community inundated with outdated civil aviation infrastructures. The Federal Aviation Administration plans to update the National Airspace System by integrating the Next Generation Air Transportation System (NextGEN), and European countries are planning to follow pursuant with a comparable system (Sampigethaya, Poovendran, & Bushnell, 2008). The principal benefits of NextGEN are airspace allocation, airspace management, system performance, security, and air traffic routing efficiency (Sampigethaya, Poovendran, Shetty, Davis, & Royalty, 2011).

The civil aviation infrastructure is a system of systems, comprised of tightly integrated components, which the new technologies often disrupt and disregard institutional practices, social tenets, and policies (Nobles, 2015) or exceed the legalities of existing regulations. Due to civil aviation being a system of systems, it requires a complete comprehension of the interrelatedness sub-systems and the influence of each system on peripheral systems (Nobles, 2015) to understand the impact on cyber security and increasing cyber vulnerabilities. In respects to civil aviation, a system of systems refers to the air and ground communication networks, wireless sensors, aircraft, personnel, and CPS (Gunes et al., 2014). The fact that the civil aviation infrastructure is a system of systems, it is imperative to mitigate cyber threats, particularly vulnerabilities emerging from new technologies.

According to Abeyratne (2011), the U.S. civil aviation infrastructure is in dire need of a computer network upgrade because of the growing cyber threat. Research indicates that modern aircraft advanced communication capabilities and multiple access points are perpetuating the mounting cyber threat (Abeyratne, 2011). The integration of new technologies is producing aftereffects to civil aviation (Abeyratne, 2011) due to the lack of a holistic socio-technical approach to implementing strategies to combat cyber threats. The transition from analog to digitized communication systems within civil aviation is triggering cyber security concerns because of the open and wireless network architecture, primarily the data links between pilots, ground stations (Mahmoud, Pirovano, & Larrieu, 2014), air traffic controllers, and stand-alone navigational aids.

Customers' demand for continuous connectivity to the Internet while airborne resulted in the Airline Passenger Communications Services, which provides broadband Internet access onboard aircraft (Mahmoud, Pirovano, & Larrieu, 2014). Such conveniences are not without cyber security concerns as commercial airlines expand the use of COTS technological capabilities, which propagate cyber vulnerabilities (Mahmoud, Pirovano, & Larrieu, 2014). Internet protocol capable aircraft are riskier due to the growing threats associated with IP-based technologies. The continuous integration of COTS conversely increases cyber threats. To overcome the cyber threats requires improved network security, and scalable and repeatable security models to defend against emerging and existing cyber threats (Knowles, Prince, Hutchison, Disso, & Jones, 2015; Mahmoud, Pirovano, & Larrieu, 2014).

Another change within civil aviation is the integrations of electronic enabled (e-enabled) aircraft. Electronically enabled aircraft marked the transformation of an isolated communications environment to an integrative network consisting of digitized communications, wireless sensors, IP, and CPS (Jabeur, Sahli, & Zeadally, 2015; Lu et al., 2014; The Roadmap. 2012). Electronic-enabled aircraft uses IP-based systems that use digitized communications networks when flying internationally (The Roadmap, 2012). Engineers avowed that e-enabled aircraft function as intelligence nodes by using digitized networks to collect data on aircraft performance, provide real-time updates on aircraft systems, maintenance status, fuel level, weather conditions, communication status, and malfunctions to various decision-makers on the ground (Sampigethaya, Poovendran, Shetty, Davis, & Royalty, 2011). These advanced capabilities introduced new cyber security vulnerabilities extending from the additional gateways and access points (Lu et al., 2014; The Roadmap, 2012). Internet protocol enabled aircraft provides real-time data through hyperconnected systems (Fredette et al., 2012; The Roadmap, 2012); hence, requiring civil aviation stakeholders to balance IP functions against cyber security threats, and strengthening cyber defenses of aircraft computer networks and communication architectures.

To maximize the result of civil aviation requires technological changes in aircraft enhancements, air traffic management (ATM) systems, and cyber security capabilities to reduce the susceptibility of the aviation infrastructure. The advanced capability of e-enabled aircraft increases the proficiency of ATM (Sampigethaya, Poovendran, Shetty, Davis, & Royalty, 2011) at the risk of increasing cyber security threats. The development of NextGEN accompanied by e-enabled aircraft was necessary to strengthen the tandem between ATM and aircraft safety (Sampigethaya, Poovendran, Shetty, Davis, & Royalty, 2011). The lack of empirical research on cyber security involving ATM and e-enabled aircraft highlights a significant vulnerability extending from the integration of technological advancements. Wolf, Minzlaff, and Moser (2014) argued that civil aviation entities fail to leverage lessons learned from the automotive industry by relying extensively on computerization and digital communications, which are susceptible to malicious intrusion from hackers and malicious actors that possess the technical acumen to endanger aviation safety. Clearly, civil aviation entities need strategies to evaluate the impact of cyber threats or innovations from a cyber before widespread implementation. At issue is the imprecision of the certification process for implementing technologies in civil aviation. Recent cyber incidents have proven that civil aviation's digitized communication networks are vulnerable to significant threats (Wolf, Minzlaff, & Moser 2014). For example, skilled hackers are capable of tunneling through e-enabled aircraft in-flight entertainment systems, which are antiquated systems, to access critical flight controls and navigational systems (Wolf, Minzlaff, & Moser 2014). Without a doubt, this emphasizes the lack of defensive measures and network security in modern aircraft.

Another threat to aviation is the lack of IT security protocol testing for electronic flight bags (EFB). Researchers declared that the authorization process for EFB requires thorough security testing (Wolf, Minzlaff, & Moser, 2014) and certification approval. The approval process omits concrete and repeatable practices; consequently, illustrating a demand for a certification process to prevent malicious threats and activities (Wolf, Minzlaff, & Moser, 2014). This oversight is indicative of an assumption that cryptographic and security practices are not necessary when certifying new capabilities (Wolf, Minzlaff, & Moser, 2014) in aviation. Other assumptions are that airlines are adept at managing computer networks and security configurations onboard aircraft, and commercial airlines have sufficient measures in place to avert unauthorized access to onboard networks (Wolf, Minzlaff, & Moser, 2014). These assumptions increase susceptibility and cyber security vulnerabilities, in particular for communications and network upgrades or maintenance efforts that occur outside of an approved certification process.

Technological advancements in civil aviation are necessary; however, a contrasting viewpoint is that innovations are increasingly complicated. One cyber security expert emphasized that complexity and security are opposing factors within the cyber security realm (Wolf, Minzlaff, & Moser, 2014). To illustrate, the complexity associated with the Boeing 787 Dreamliner, research indicated that the aircraft has over eight million lines of software codes compared to the F-35 military aircraft having 22 million lines of software codes (Wolf, Minzlaff, & Moser, 2014). Modern aircraft are vulnerable to bugs in the software, which affects security and makes it difficult to test, analyze, and evaluate (Wolf, Minzlaff, & Moser, 2014). The integration of technological advances causes aftereffects that degrade cyber defenses due to hyperconnectivity. It is essential for system architectures to design the infrastructure to be technological adaptable and securable from cyber threats.

Modern integrated modular avionic (IMA) architectures consist of digitized systems that are interconnected and provide thousands of software-related activities (Wolf, Minzlaff, & Moser, 2014). Researchers pointed out that paralleling software applications require different but stringent safety certifications for critical systems that are performed on the same processors via virtual realms with systems requiring less stringent certification requirements (Wolf, Minzlaff, & Moser, 2014). The significance is that exploiting a less critical system within the IMA architecture could jeopardize critical systems such as flight controls and navigational systems (Wolf, Minzlaff, & Moser, 2014). The advanced engineering aspect of these systems require tougher cyber security protocols through the conceptual, implementation, and operational phases to build robust cyber capabilities to prevent easy access through gateways and tunneling through to flight critical systems.

Wolf, Minzlaff, and Moser (2014) suggested that modern aircraft's continuous connection to the internet; hence, potentially allows hackers multiple gateways and access points from remote and anonymous locations. Integrated modular avionic architectures are hyper-connected, which is compounded by cost off the shelf (COTS) hardware and software that have a history of being susceptible to cyber threats such as malware and Trojans (Wolf, Minzlaff, & Moser 2014). Though COTS and government off the shelf (GOTS) hardware and software are improving regarding cyber security, civil aviation organizations have to mandate that vendors increase cyber security protocols when designing systems or parts for civil aviation aircraft (McDaniel, 2013; USDOE, 2007) to prevent cyber security vulnerabilities. Private and public organizations need to resist the use of software with known vulnerabilities, which allows potential exploitation via back doors in the network (Guinchard, 2011). The current method of using patches to rectify discovered vulnerabilities is a reactive and ineffective practice (Guinchard, 2011). These exposures are zero-day vulnerabilities because malicious users manifest software coding to exploit the vulnerabilities before software patches are disseminated to correct the software flaws (Guinchard, 2011). Malicious actors often use malware masked as software patches to gain access to systems and networks (Guinchard, 2011). Public and private organizations need to synchronize efforts and demand the higher quality of software designs from vendors to help alleviate malicious activity.

A concerning vulnerability in cyber security is supply chain management. Researchers declared that because of globalization the U.S. information technology markets allow the importation of communications, networks, and computer technologies from adversarial countries (McDaniel, 2013). Through this growth, computer technologies have decreased in cost because components are not manufactured to meet cyber security specifications (McDaniel, 2013), which increases vulnerabilities and creates exploitable networks. This problem is convoluted and complex because primary vendors hire subcontractors to provide parts and components that might be malicious, flawed, or vulnerable to cyber security threats (McDaniel; 2013). As supply chains continue to expand due to international trade, it becomes difficult to trace and document the transactions (McDaniel; 2013). Therefore, to avoid such vulnerabilities and dangerous practices, the U.S. government needs to limit the number of supply vendors to vetted and trusted entities that are compliant with the cyber security standards.

Civil aviation is struggling to contend with cyber security threats due to lax practices within the supply chain management. Civil aviation is amidst a major paradigm shift from analog communications to digitized communication systems, which are vulnerable because of the open and wireless architecture (Mahmoud, Pirovano, & Larrieu, 2014). The problem with the digitized communications is the exploitable nature of data link systems, which disregards security measures to safeguard computers and networks against cyber threats. Data link systems are beneficial for reducing radio confusion, producing less corruptible signals, decreasing communications intervals, and sending and receiving text message capability from air traffic controllers (Mahmoud, Pirovano, & Larrieu, 2014). Researchers declared that COTS and GOTS parts and systems should not be permitted unless vetted through an authorized certification process to the meet the minimum criteria for cyber security (Mahmoud, Pirovano, & Larrieu, 2014). The vulnerabilities of COTS and GOTS supplies and parts are common knowledge amongst hackers (Mahmoud, Pirovano, & Larrieu, 2014) and adversarial nations. Civil aviation organizations need to mandate cyber security strategy policies for strengthening supply chain management issues.

Active Cyber Defense

The U.S. has an intrinsic right to protect our transportation infrastructure, which includes the civil aviation sector, from cyber security threats and attacks (Flowers & Zeadally, 2014). The best practice to protect our critical infrastructures is with active cyber defense, defined as, an integrative and coordinated capability that discovers, identifies, evaluates, and alleviates threats and vulnerabilities using intelligence, sensors, and software to obviate malicious activity (Flowers & Zeadally, 2014). In short, an active cyber defense is defensive actions taken to defeat cyber threats (Denning, 2014). Passive cyber defense, the precursor to active cyber defense, was deemed ineffective, which led to Defense Advanced Research Projects (DARPA) piloting efforts beyond a static defense capability that was incapable of protecting critical infrastructures (Flowers & Zeadally, 2014). Passive cyber involves making cyber systems resistant to cyber-attacks and taking active cyber defenses are defensive actions to combat cyber-attacks (Denning, 2014). Researchers classify active cyber defenses as detection and forensics, deception, and attack termination (Flowers & Zeadally, 2014). Detection and forensics are the use of cyber entrapments for exploitation by attracting malicious cyber activists to determine patterns of life, and tactics, techniques, and procedures (Flowers & Zeadally, 2014). Intrusion detection systems and tracing capabilities used in conjunction with disruption techniques are common active cyber defensive techniques (Flowers & Zeadally, 2014). Active cyber defenses are capable of determining attribution of the cyber-attacks, prevent cyber-attacks due to reprisal, and predict imminent cyber-attacks (Flowers & Zeadally, 2014). The implementation and use of active cyber defenses in the private sector are a difficult process due to the lack of federal laws directing the use of such capabilities by private entities (Flower & Zeadally, 2014). The reluctance to use active cyber defense could result in a national security threat or the loss of millions of dollars. Another intricate problem with the active cyber defense is coordinating and attaining the approval to employ active cyber capabilities within national boundaries (Flowers & Zeadally, 2014). Researchers refer to this as cooperative and non-cooperative (Denning, 2014), which is why entities must obtain approval before employing active cyber capabilities. The use of active cyber defense has to be ethical, legal, and considerate of civil liberties for all parties involved (Denning, 2014). The legality of active cyber defense illustrates the difficulty in the cyber domain as well as how technological implications have exceeded existing laws.

EDUCATING THE CYBER SECURITY WORKFORCE

Under the provisions of the National Initiative for Cyber Security Education (NICE), the salient objective is to focus on the workforce as a principal resource to combat cyber threats (Paulsen, McDuffie, Newhouse, & Toth, 2012) because the cyber security workforce numbers remain low. Researchers postulated that people have the technological acumen and tenacity to create cyber defenses to combat threats in cyberspace (Paulsen, McDuffie, Newhouse, & Toth, 2012). Researchers articulated that the following four pillars are essential to educating cyber security workforce:

(a) attentiveness, (b) systematic education, (c) workforce development, and (d) manpower structure (Paulsen, McDuffie, Newhouse, & Toth, 2012). Cyber threats are evolving on a continuous basis; therefore, it is vital to train and educate a cadre of subject matter experts with the technical acumen to develop, implement, and sustain defensive cyber capabilities to protect critical infrastructures.

Blackman, Boring, Marble, Mosleh, and Meshkati (2014) argued that humans are the most common enabler for cyber-attacks because of poor awareness that leads to cyber security vulnerabilities. Cyber security vulnerabilities propagate because people failed to comprehend the mistakes, unintended consequences, and risks associated with the cyberspace environment (Blackman, Boring, Marble, Mosleh, & Meshkati, 2014). In fact, a chief executive officer for a major contracting firm acknowledged that the first step is leadership and management taking ownership of the cyber security problems, followed by pursuing education and training to understand cyber security threats, and to reestablish the organization's cyber security defenses to mitigate threats (Commander, 2013). Undoubtedly, there is a need to educate the workforce on cyber security vulnerabilities. Education and awareness are critical links in strengthening cyber defense capabilities to thwart people from creating vulnerabilities within cyberspace. Nielsen (2012) postulated that people use the Internet and other forms of information technologies on a routine basis without knowing that the implementation of cyber security defenses came as an afterthought. Therefore, emphasizing an educational deficit, the need for a cyber-educated workforce and an astute cyber society, and a significant investment in cyber security training (Hoffman, Burley, & Toregas, 2012).

Educating the workforce is a dual approach, first, the education and professional development is necessary for enhancing cyber security defenses and protecting vital infrastructures like civil aviation. Second, there is a need to educate society on the vulnerabilities of information technologies, portable electronic devices, the Internet, and digitized communications, and hyperconnectivity. Cyber security is a multidisciplinary area with an integrative foundation that mandates collaboration, synchronization, and preemptive objectives. The growing complexity of cyber security threats, emerging technologies, and cyber defense changes make it difficult to define the certifications, training, and the level of expertise needed to develop and certify a cyber security workforce to combat cyber threats (Hoffman, Burley, & Toregas, 2012). Cyber security is persistently changing due to the threat environment, which influences the mandated training and professional development for cyber security personnel. The Office of Personnel Management classified the following occupational areas as critical for establishing a cyber security workforce:

1. Information technology management,
2. Electrical engineering,

3.   Computer engineering, and
4.   Telecommunications (Hoffman, Burley, & Toregas, 2012).

These occupations are essential for developing holistic cyber security objectives and solid training foundations. The abovementioned list is not inclusive and highlights that narrowing the scope of critical occupations hinders the ability to develop a cyber security workforce.

Regarding education and training, Kim et al. (2011) argued that the following practices be essential to defending against cyber threats:

1.   Better legislation,
2.   Legal proceedings,
3.   Law enforcement involvement,
4.   Global alliances,
5.   Educating internet users, and
6.   Increasing cyber awareness.

These practices align with the required educational and workforce development efforts to mitigate cyber threats. These practices apply to the civil aviation employees and more important to the senior leaders of civil aviation organizations. Efforts to secure civil aviation extend beyond the communication systems and networks; it pertains to safeguarding the authenticity, integrity, availability, and confidentiality of 191 countries and their respective civil aviation infrastructures (Lasiello, 2014).

CYBER TERRORISM AND CYBER DEFENSE FOR CIVIL AVIATION INFRASTRUCTURE

While undertaking this research project, research regarding cyber security threats in civil aviation was decent; however, additional research is necessary. Civil aviation is a category of the transportation infrastructure. Even though research regarding cyber security threats in civil aviation is adequate, regardless of the category, all critical infrastructures are in dire need of ameliorated cyber security defenses. For the most part, research on critical infrastructures applies directly to the transportation category and civil aviation, especially research that addresses cyber security threats, risks, and vulnerabilities.

According to researchers, cyber terrorism is a moderate threat to any organization, corporation, or institution that is capable of compromising data, computer networks, intellectual property, or components, which is a tactic to cause fear (Jarvis, MacDonald, & Nouri, 2014). Cyber terrorism is an emerging phenomenon that propagates vulnerabilities such as the irregularity and substantial cost of software updates, hyperconnectivity, technological advances, and implementation of detection systems and capabilities (Jarvis, MacDonald, & Nouri, 2014). In fact, cyber security threats, cyber terrorism, and cyber-attacks across the globe, on average costs about 400 million dollars, in which U.S. based organizations paid 100 million dollars in 2013 (Zuerich & Graebe, 2015). The popularity of cyber terrorism is influenced by the relatively low cost to conduct malicious activity in the cyber domain, the ability to remain anonymous, a target rich environment, remote access, and the potential to impact multiple targets (Jarvis, MacDonald, & Nouri, 2014). Protecting critical infrastructures to include civil aviation is a major concern given that cyber terrorists are knowledgeable of the existing cyber vulnerabilities. Some researchers argued that the cyber-terrorist threat is low due to the lack of attention and fame associated with cyber terrorism. Nonetheless, the potential exists for adversarial nations, non-state actors, and terrorists to conduct large-scale attacks at will. The international community has to take proactive and frequent measures to increase cyber defenses to prevent critical infrastructures from falling prey during cyber-attacks. Cyber threats range from single acts to intense, complex cyber-attacks that are equivalent to a cyber-war (Marble et al., 2015). Regardless of the malicious act, aviation operations are critical operations that require protection with reinforced cyber defenses to prevent cyber-attacks.

Impeding the proliferation of cyber threats is critical in safeguarding civil aviation infrastructure, Givens and Busch (2013) declared that insidious cyber threats could infect multiple federal agencies' computer networks due to the interconnectedness of systems. It is possible to affect and infect civil aviation's networks by attacking another government agency's network. The potential for cyber threats to infect multiple government agencies emphasizes the need for cyber security defenses that prevent penetrations across interagency domains. The development of the common cyber defense construct is not feasible due to the difference in the cyber war, cyber terrorism, and cybercrime terminology accompanied by the governmental strife with civil liberties, constitutional rights, and governmental oversight (Given & Busch, 2013). The dispute between government entities regarding cyber defense impacts on civil liberties and constitutional rights is hindering the development of an interagency approach to combating cyber threats. Protecting government systems is a matter of national security; the government owns 15-20 percent of the critical infrastructures (Murray & Grubesic, 2012; Nielsen, 2012) but addressing the government's cyber vulnerabilities is not enough. Government agencies have to work with government contractors to develop robust cyber defenses to prevent exploitation by malicious hackers because government contracting companies are frequently targeted during cyber-attacks.

To build cyber defense robustness requires cyber resilience, which is an integrative process that focuses on employees, management, and procedures by leveraging traditional and non-traditional practices such as threat assessments to drive changes to cyber defenses (Hult & Sivanesan, 2014). Hult and Sivanesan (2014) argued that cyber resilience is a method to subdue persistent cyber threats through adaptability to antagonistic cyber tactics, techniques, and procedures. Effective cyber resilience involves incorporating cyber security principles and ideology into the organizational culture (Hult & Sivanesan, 2014). Organizations can subjugate cyber security threats by employing cyber resilience and integrating cyber security as a core capability and integrating cyber security across all mission areas through the threat assessment process (Hult & Sivanesan, 2014). Cyber resilience can be a comprehensive capability to protect critical infrastructures like civil aviation by proactively using threat assessments to influence decision-making to create new cyber defenses. Senior leaders in government entities have to accept the cost associated with increased cyber security.

To combat cyber-attacks private and public entities have to develop defensive cyber strategies to safeguard the hyperconnected aspects of civil aviation (Ahamad et al., 2009). Researchers stressed the significance of institutions identifying critical Internet-enabled networks and associated connections to protect from cyber-attacks (Ahamad et al., 2009). Of equal importance is to develop a holistic strategy to combat cyber-attacks by strengthening identification and remediation protocols (Ahamad et al., 2009). Computer networks should be designed to support interoperability, the integration of software upgrades, system enhancements, and new technologies (Ahamad et al., 2009). This approach allows system administrators and engineers to integrate technological changes to reduce the susceptibility of critical networks (Ahamad et al., 2009).

Tabansky (2011) avowed that the cyber defense of critical infrastructures starts with prevention, deterrence, attack warning and classification, response, crisis management, damage assessment, retardation, and network restoration. While some leaders prefer to integrate automated and sensory warnings to detect cyber security threats and intrusions to alleviate the reactionary posture of existing capabilities because reacting to cyber security threats is deemed more costly; consequently, requiring leaders to invest in cyber security as a strategic capability (Commanders, 2013). Documented research indicate that government entities are reactionary regarding cyber security incidents, which is concerning because government officials are underestimating cyber-related crimes and cyber threats, (Caruson, MacManus, & McPhee, 2012), and cyber attacks. For civil aviation, industry experts recommended the creation of stand-alone network architectures for aircraft that isolates critical aircraft systems from non-critical systems to reduce the cyber vulnerabilities associated with hyperconnectivity and CPS (Lu et al., 2014; Sampigethaya, Poovendran, & Bushnell, 2009). Information technologist experts declared that (a) cloud computing, (b) virtualization, (c) mobility, (d) open sourcing, (e) data breaches, and (f) outsourcing are developments that increase cyber security breaches (Caruson, MacManus, & McPhee, 2012) from technological advancements.

By 2024 researchers are forecasting that there will be over 50 billion mobile devices, which is an exponential growth from the current 12 billion devices (Dawson, Omar, Abramson, & Besssette, 2014). Malešević (2013) asserted that the Internet perpetuates hyperconnectivity by providing a constant connection to information networks. As a hyperconnected society, crime and cyber threats continue to increase as the target of opportunity expands. At issue, is the increasing migration of critical infrastructures to CPS, digitized communications, and SCADA, the hyperconnected nature of critical infrastructures attract hackers and malicious cyber actors (Dutta & Bilbao-Osorio, 2012; Lu et al., 2014). Critical infrastructures operate in cyberspace; therefore, the potential exists for increased cyber terrorism, cyber-crimes, and cyber-attacks to occur within cyberspace given that there are no defined boundaries, and cyber criminals have the ability to access networks remotely and remain anonymously (Dutta & Bilbao-Osorio, 2012).

FAA STRUGGLES WITH CYBER SECURITY

A recent report by the Government Accountability Office (GAO, 2015) highlighted significant woes with the FAA's cyber security efforts. Iasiello (2013) calls attention to cyber security issues in civil aviation in 2013, primarily emphasized the lack of regulatory guidance to strengthen network security; however, to this date, the FAA has taken modest steps to ameliorate cyber security. For example, a senior FAA manager indicated that the organization has not developed an enterprise-wide threat model (GAO, 2015). Employing threat enterprise model will advance the FAA from its reactionary posture to a proactive approach, particularly countering the increase of insider threats within federal entities (GAO, 2015). One FAA official hinted that the slow progress is due to the time and cost to implement a threat enterprise model (GAO, 2015). According to FAA officials and cyber security experts, the benefits of implementing a threat enterprise model provides the following advantages:

1. Real-time network threat awareness,
2. Detecting of malicious activity,
3. Early detection of insider threat activity, and
4. Incident response, detection, and mitigation (GAO, 2015).

The FAA is cognizant of its limited continuous monitoring capability and continues to make steps to mitigate network risks and vulnerabilities.

The GAO (2015) reported that the FAA needs to focus on the cyber security risks and threats linked to IP connectivity. This confusion stems from unauthorized access to critical flight controls, navigational components, and avionics systems interconnectivity to IFE via IP (GAO, 2105). The expansion of IP connectivity in civil aviation increases the exploitation of interconnected systems (Iasiello, 2013), which is an aftereffect of new technologies because, in the past, legacy avionic systems were inaccessible, which prevented unauthorized access (GAO, 2015) by malicious actors. The existing security measure to prevent unauthorized access to flight controls and navigational and avionics systems is a firewall (GAO, 2015). Firewalls have vulnerabilities that are exploitable and not a long-term solution. Hene, highlighting the persistent vulnerabilities with federal information systems (GAO, 2012).

Another issue noted in the GAO's (2015) report was that the FAA airworthiness certification process does not validate the cyber security assurance of new aircraft, equipment, or software components. Under the existing process, the FAA grants Special Conditions to the aircraft manufacturers to validate cyber security measures for new equipment. Without a doubt, the Special Conditions process is flawed and increases cyber security risks (GAO, 2015). The FAA is yet to implement new regulations regarding Special Conditions or cyber security assurance criteria for aircraft manufacturers because legacy systems were isolated (GAO, 2015). The FAA indicated that the lack of regulatory changes to articulate the provisions for aircraft systems information security protection (ASISP) prevent stakeholders from discovering and mitigating threats in a timely fashion (GAO, 2015). The GAO (2015) reported that the FAA would make a decision on what regulatory policy is required to improve ASISP in early 2016.

To strengthen cyber security efforts, the FAA is taking action to consolidate cyber security roles and responsibilities throughout the organization. This strategy is essential as the FAA continues to implements NextGEN (GAO, 2015), an IP based air traffic management system. Centralizing all IT based roles enables the FAA to streamline cyber security initiatives and improve awareness to focus on cyber threats and risks.

Clearly, the FAA is offsetting a plethora of requirements for finite budgetary resources and personnel; therefore, FAA's senior leaders have to make a stronger commitment to improving and safeguarding the civil aviation network infrastructure. The FAA is working many national level interests and issues; however, the FAA's senior leaders have to make cyber security a top priority to prevent a major attack on the civil aviation infrastructure.

NATIONAL AND INTERNATIONAL STRATEGIES FOR COMBATING CYBER THREATS IN CIVIL AVIATION

Cyber security in cyberspace is a collective, holistic, and integrative approach to national and international entities to subdue or mitigate the malicious threat or pervasive actions because the responsibility to protect cyberspace is an international obligation. There is not a standardized template that applies to every organization's cyber security needs; therefore, cyber security professionals should use the NIST Framework to discover system weakness, vulnerabilities, threats, and risks. Developing defensive cyber security practices in civil aviation is a matter of national and international security due to pervasive cyber threats and the hyperconnected nature of computer networks, critical infrastructures, digitized communications, and the IOT. The NIST Framework and *Framework for Aviation Cyber Security* Guides are for evaluating and strengthening existing cyber security practices.

To achieve cyber security defense requires a delicate and robust balance to support emerging technologies and hyperconnectivity while safeguarding cyberspace and critical infrastructures against obstinate cyber threats. Below is a list of national and international level of recommendations to improve cyber security defenses in civil aviation:

- Do not be pessimistic and over exaggerate the current cyber security threat assessment.
- Managing and accepting cyber security risks. It is impossible to defend networks are cyberspace from all cyber security threats. Private and public organizations have to build aggressive cyber defenses based on current threats and intelligence.
- Use active cyber defense practices to protect public and private infrastructures
- Reduce access points have to prevent availability to external users. Organizations will have to determine what level of access and connectivity is required based on current cyber threats and cyber defense postures.
- A cyber security vulnerability is emerging technologies. The integration of new technologies creates cyber security risks. Private and public organizations have to ensure new technologies are tested and certified to meet cyber security defense protocols, especially in regulated domains such as aviation and nuclear.
- Another major concern regarding cyber security defenses is minimizing insider threats. Angry or careless employees fail to follow cyber security practices and protocols, which creates direct access points to the networks for criminals that are preventable through training and information assurance awareness.

- The reliance on CPS, SCADA, and IOT require private and public entities to update legacy systems that are cyber security risks. This undertaking is a costly evolution so organizations can minimize access points until legacy systems are updated and certified to meet cyber security defense standards.
- Supply chain management is a growing concern in cyber security because replacement parts have to undergo the same strict compliance standards as computer networks and peripheral components. Minimizing supply chain vendors to customers that provide approved and certified parts is necessary to reduce cyber security vulnerabilities.
- National and international level organizations have to collaborate and share information regarding cyber security threats and cyber-attacks. Sharing information is essential due to hyperconnectivity and the expeditious and covert manner that cyber-attacks can occur. It is imperative for private and public entities to create reporting vehicles to inform the international community of cyber-attacks or cyber threats.
- Having a trained and capable workforce to combat cyber security threats and cyber-attack is the best cyber security defense. Workforce development and education is a costly investment that requires constant modifications due to the rapidly changing threat environment. A nucleus of professionally trained cyber subject matter experts is necessary and determined by organization's computer network footprint.
- Cyber security defense is a strategic capability that is fully supported and directed by executive level leadership. Effective cyber security programs receive support from a top-down approach to the senior leadership of private and public entities. The integration of cyber security is vital rather than an added afterthought.
- Private and public entities must take a proactive posture when dealing with cyber security threats. Responding to cyber security threats is reactionary and costly; therefore, organizations have to use intelligence and actionable information to develop cyber security defenses to maintain a proactive posture.

CONCLUSION

Civil aviation stakeholders are struggling with cyber security threats that compromise the integrity of critical infrastructures. The integration of technological advancements accompanied by legacy systems in civil aviation increases cyber security risks and vulnerabilities. As civil aviation operations transition from analog capabilities to digitized communications, CPS, wireless sensors, networks, SCADA, system within systems construct and hyperconnectivity cyber security threats and risks increase due to the additional gateways and access points. The hyperconnected disposition of civil aviation systems are becoming increasingly sophisticated; thus, amassing the complexity of safeguarding computer networks and systems within civil aviation. Combating pervasive cyber threats requires civil aviation entities to develop a cyber security workforce with the technical acumen to protect the networks. The ever-changing cyber environment defies organizations' ability to combat cyber security threats by escalating the cost of cyber security defense. Hyperconnectivity expands the aviation network to less developed countries, which lack the financial resources to tackle cyber security problems. Researchers, practitioners, and civil aviation entities are uncertain about the existing gaps and known problem areas, which malicious hackers attack willingly. Cyber security issues within civil aviation are an international concern because of the potential for a catastrophic cyber-attack, which could have economic, social, fiscal, and public safety implications. The NIST Framework provides a baseline for establishing and evaluating existing cyber security practices. The NIST Framework coupled with the recommendations is the minimum procedures that organizations should implement to strengthened cyber security defenses. Finally, until civil aviation organizations reduce or mitigate the vulnerabilities within the critical infrastructure, criminals will continue to target, exploit, and potentially attack civil aviation.

REFERENCES

Abeyratne, R. (2011). Cyber terrorism and aviation—national and international responses. *Journal of Transportation Security*, *4*(4), 337–349. doi:10.1007/s12198-011-0074-3

Ahamad, M., Amster, D., Barrett, M., Cross, T., Heron, G., Jackson, D. … Traynor, P. (2008). *Emerging cyber threats report for 2009*. Academic Press.

Amantini, A., Choraś, M., D'Antonio, S., Egozcue, E., Germanus, D., & Hutter, R. (2012). The human role in tools for improving robustness and resilience of critical infrastructures. *Cognition Technology and Work*, *14*(2), 143–155. doi:10.1007/s10111-010-0171-2

Blackman, H., Boring, R., Marble, J., Mosleh, A., & Meshkati, N. (2014). Panel discussion new directions in human reliability analysis for oil & gas, cybersecurity, nuclear, and aviation. In *Proceedings of the Human Factors and Ergonomics Society Annual Meeting*. SAGE Publications. doi:10.1177/1541931214581118

Caruson, K., MacManus, S., & McPhee, B. (2012). Cybersecurity policy-making at the local government level: An analysis of threats, preparedness, and bureaucratic roadblocks to success. *Homeland Security & Emergency Management, 9*(2), 1–22. doi:10.1515/jhsem-2012-0003

Commander Twenty-Fourth Air Force. (2013). Cyber professionals in the military and industry—partnering in defense of the nation. *Air & Space Power Journal, 27,* 4–21.

Dawson, M., Omar, M., Abramson, J., & Bessette, D. (2014). The Future of National and International Security on the Internet. *Information Security in Diverse Computing Environments,* 149.

Denning, D. (2014). Framework and principles for active cyber defense. *Computers & Security, 40,* 108–113. doi:10.1016/j.cose.2013.11.004

Dennis, A., Jones, R., Kildare, D., & Barclay, C. (2014). A Design Science approach to developing and evaluating a national cybersecurity framework for Jamaica. *The Electronic Journal of Information Systems in Developing Countries, 62*(6), 1–18.

Dombrowski, P., & Demchak, C. (2014). Cyber War, cybered conflict, and the maritime domain. *Naval War College Review, 67*(2), 70.

Dutta, S., & Bilbao-Osorio, B. (2012). *The Global information technology report 2012: Living in a hyperconnected world.* World Economic Forum.

Flowers, A., & Zeadally, S. (2014). US policy on active cyber defense. *Journal of Homeland Security and Emergency Management, 11*(2), 289–308. doi:10.1515/jhsem-2014-0021

Fredette, J., Marom, R., Steiner, K., & Witters, L. (2012). The promise and peril of hyperconnectivity for organizations and societies. *The global information technology report,* 113-119.

Givens, A., & Busch, N. (2013). Integrating federal approaches to post-cyber incident mitigation. *Journal of Homeland Security and Emergency Management, 10*(1), 1–28. doi:10.1515/jhsem-2012-0001

Goodman, S., Kirk, J., & Kirk, M. (2007). Cyberspace as a medium for terrorists. *Technological Forecasting and Social Change, 74*(2), 193–210. doi:10.1016/j.techfore.2006.07.007

Guinchard, A. (2011). Between hype and understatement: Reassessing cyber risks as a security strategy. *Journal of Strategic Security, 4*(2), 75–96. doi:10.5038/1944-0472.4.2.5

Gunes, V., Peter, S., Givargis, T., & Vahid, F. (2014). A survey on concepts, applications, and challenges in cyber-physical systems. *Transactions on Internet and Information Systems (Seoul)*, *8*(12), 4242–4268. doi:10.3837/tiis.2014.12.001

Hentea, M. (2008). Improving security for SCADA control systems. *Interdisciplinary Journal of Information, Knowledge, and Management*, *3*(1), 73–86.

Hoffman, L., Burley, D., & Toregas, C. (2012). Holistically building the cybersecurity workforce. *Security & Privacy, IEEE*, *10*(2), 33–39. doi:10.1109/MSP.2011.181

Hult, F., & Sivanesan, G. (2014). What good cyber resilience looks like. *Journal of Business Continuity & Emergency Planning*, *7*(2), 112–125. PMID:24457323

Iasiello, E. (2013). Getting ahead of the threat: Aviation and cyber security. *Aerospace America*, *51*(7), 22–25.

Iasiello, E. (2014). A review of "A framework for aviation cybersecurity" -- A decision paper from the American Institute of Aeronautics and Astronautics. *Journal Of Homeland Security & Emergency Management*, *11*(1), 95–100. doi:10.1515/jhsem-2013-0076

Itani, N., O'Connell, J., & Mason, K. (2015). Towards realizing best-in-class civil aviation strategy scenarios. *Transport Policy*, *43*, 42–54. doi:10.1016/j.tranpol.2015.05.013

Jabeur, N., Sahli, N., & Zeadally, S. (2015). Enabling cyber-physical systems with wireless sensor networking technologies, multiagent system paradigm, and natural ecosystems. *Mobile Information Systems*, *501*, 908315.

Jarvis, L., Macdonald, S., & Nouri, L. (2014). The cyber terrorism threat: Findings from a survey of researchers. *Studies in Conflict and Terrorism*, *37*(1), 68–90. doi:10.1080/1057610X.2014.853603

Kessler, G., & Ramsay, J. (2013). Paradigms for Cybersecurity Education in a Homeland Security Program. *Journal of Homeland Security Education*, 2. Retrieved from http://commons.erau.edu/db-applied-aviation/12

Khan, M., Xiang, Y., Horng, S., & Chen, H. (2013). Trust, security, and privacy in next-generation wireless sensor networks. *International Journal of Distributed Sensor Networks*, *2013*, 1–2. doi:10.1155/2013/956736

Kim, H. (2012). Security and vulnerability of SCADA systems over IP-based wireless sensor networks. *International Journal of Distributed Sensor Networks*, *2012*, 1–10. doi:10.1155/2012/268478

Knowles, W., Prince, D., Hutchison, D., Disso, J., & Jones, K. (2015). A survey of cyber security management in industrial control systems. *International Journal of Critical Infrastructure Protection, 9*, 52–80. doi:10.1016/j.ijcip.2015.02.002

Lew, M., Corder, T., & Ruck, B. (2015). *Please fasten your seat belts: Managing digital risk to support aviation innovation.* Deloitte Development LLC.

Lim, B. (2014). Emerging threats from cyber security in aviation – challenges and mitigation. *Journal of Aviation Management.*

Lu, T., Guo, X., Li, Y., Peng, Y., Zhang, X., Xie, F., & Gao, Y. (2014). Cyber physical security for industrial control systems based on wireless sensor networks. *International Journal of Distributed Sensor Networks.*

Mahmoud, M., Pirovano, A., & Larrieu, N. (2014). Aeronautical communication transition from analog to digital data: A network security survey. *Computer Science Review, 11*, 1–29. doi:10.1016/j.cosrev.2014.02.001

Maleševic, S. (2013). *Future Identities: Changing identities in the UK–the next 10 years.* Academic Press.

Manyika, J., Chui, M., Bughin, J., Dobbs, R., Bisson, P., & Marrs, A. (2013). *Disruptive technologies: Advances that will transform life, business, and the global economy* (Vol. 180). San Francisco, CA: McKinsey Global Institute.

Marble, J., Lawless, W., Mittu, R., Coyne, J., Abramson, M., & Sibley, C. (2015). The Human Factor in Cybersecurity: Robust & Intelligent Defense. In Cyber Warfare (pp. 173-206). Springer International Publishing. doi:10.1007/978-3-319-14039-1_9

McDaniel, E. (2013, July). Securing the information and communications technology global supply chain from exploitation: Developing a strategy for education, training, and awareness. In *Proceedings of the Informing Science and Information Technology Education Conference.*

Murray, A., & Grubesic, T. (2012). Critical infrastructure protection: The vulnerability conundrum. *Telematics and Informatics, 29*(1), 56–65. doi:10.1016/j.tele.2011.05.001

National Cyber Security Centre. (2014). *Cyber Security Assessment Netherland (CSAN4).* Retrieved from https://www.google.co.jp/?gfe_rd=cr&ei=yJbIVZKN Ecr98wfK4KioDg&gws_rd=ssl#q=how+to+cite+cyber+security+assessment+ netherlands

Nicholson, A., Webber, S., Dyer, S., Patel, T., & Janicke, H. (2012). SCADA security in the light of cyber-warfare. *Computers & Security, 31*(4), 418–436. doi:10.1016/j. cose.2012.02.009

Nielsen, S. C. (2012). Pursuing security in cyberspace: Strategic and organizational challenges. *Orbis*, *56*(3), 336–356. doi:10.1016/j.orbis.2012.05.004

Nobles, C. (2015). *Exploring Pilots' Experiences of Integrating Technologically Advanced Aircraft Within General Aviation: A Case Study*. ProQuest. Retrieved from http://search.proquest.com/docview/1658234326

Oster, C. Jr, Strong, J., & Zorn, C. (2013). Analyzing aviation safety: Problems, challenges, opportunities. *Research in Transportation Economics*, *43*(1), 148–164. doi:10.1016/j.retrec.2012.12.001

Paulsen, C., McDuffie, E., Newhouse, W., & Toth, P. (2012). NICE: Creating a cybersecurity workforce and aware public. *IEEE Security and Privacy*, *10*(3), 76–79. doi:10.1109/MSP.2012.73

Pettersen, K., & Bjørnskau, T. (2015). Organizational contradictions between safety and security–Perceived challenges and ways of integrating critical infrastructure protection in civil aviation. *Safety Science*, *71*, 167–177 doi:10.1016/j.ssci.2014.04.018

Price, J. (2012). *Practical aviation security: predicting and preventing future threats*. Butterworth-Heinemann.

Roesener, A., Bottolfson, C., & Fernandez, G. (2014). Policy for US cybersecurity. *Air & Space Power Journal*, *29*(5), 38–54.

Rowland, J., Rice, M., & Shenoi, S. (2014). Whither cyberpower? *International Journal of Critical Infrastructure Protection*, *7*(2), 124–137. doi:10.1016/j.ijcip.2014.04.001

Sampigethaya, K., Poovendran, R., & Bushnell, L. (2008). Secure operation, control, and maintenance of future e-enabled airplanes. *Proceedings of the IEEE*, *96*(12), 1992–2007. doi:10.1109/JPROC.2008.2006123

Sampigethaya, K., Poovendran, R., & Bushnell, L. (2009). A framework for securing future e-enabled aircraft navigation and surveillance. In *AIAA Proceedings* (pp. 1-10). doi:10.2514/6.2009-1820

Sampigethaya, K., Poovendran, R., Shetty, S., Davis, T., & Royalty, C. (2011). Future e-enabled aircraft communications and security: The next 20 years and beyond. *Proceedings of the IEEE*, *99*(11), 2040–2055. doi:10.1109/JPROC.2011.2162209

Shackelford, S., & Bohm, Z. (2015). *Securing North American critical infrastructure: A comparative case study in cybersecurity regulation. Canada-US Law Journal*.

Shackelford, S., Proia, A., Martell, B., & Craig, A. (2015). Toward a global cyber security standard of care? Exploring the implications of the 2014 NIST cybersecurity framework on shaping reasonable national and international cybersecurity practices. *Texas International Law Journal.*

Shen, L. (2014). The NIST cybersecurity framework: Overview and potential impacts. *Journal of Internet Law, 18*(6), 3–6.

Tabansky, L. (2011). Critical infrastructure protection against cyber threats. *Military and Strategic Affairs, 3*(2), 2.

Ten, C. W., Liu, C. C., & Manimaran, G. (2008). Vulnerability assessment of cybersecurity for SCADA systems. Power Systems. *IEEE Transactions on Power Systems, 23*(4), 1836–1846. doi:10.1109/TPWRS.2008.2002298

The Roadmap to Secure Control Systems in the Transportation Sector Working Group. (2012). *The Roadmap to Secure Control Systems in the Transportation Sector.* Retrieved from https://ics-cert.us-cert.gov/sites/default/files/ICSJWG-Archive/TransportationRoadmap20120831.pdf

Tomáš, S., Ivan, K., & Stanislav, S. (2012). Present and potential security threats posed to civil aviation. *Incas Bulletin, 4*(2), 169–175. doi:10.13111/2066-8201.2012.4.2.17

U.S. Department of Energy (USDOE). (2007). *21 Steps to Improve Cyber Security of SCADA Networks.* Washington, DC: U.S. Department of Energy.

U.S. Department of Transportation. (2014). *Federal Aviation Administration.* Washington, DC: The Economic Impact of Civil Aviation on the U.S. Economy.

U.S. Government Accountability Office. (2012, April). *Cybersecurity: Threats impact the nation.* (Publication No. GAO-12-666T). Retrieved from GAO Reports Main Page via GPO Access database: http://www.gpoaccess.gov/gaoreports/index.html

U.S. Government Accountability Office. (2015, April). *Air traffic control: FAA needs a more comprehensive approach to address cyber security as agency transitions to NextGen.* (Publication No. GAO-15-370). Retrieved from GAO Reports Main Page via GPO Access database: http://www.gpoaccess.gov/gaoreports/index.html

Von Solms, R., & Van Niekerk, J. (2013). From information security to cyber security. *Computers & Security, 38*, 97–102. doi:10.1016/j.cose.2013.04.004

Wolf, M., Minzlaff, M., & Moser, M. (2014). IT security threats to modern e-enabled aircraft-a cautionary note. *Journal of Aerospace Information Systems, 11*(7), 447–457. doi:10.2514/1.I010156

Zureich, D., & Graebe, W. (2015). Cybersecurity: The continuing evolution of insurance and ethics. *Defense Counsel Journal, 82*(2), 192.

KEY TERMS AND DEFINITIONS

Civil Aviation: Aviation activities that consist of commercial, business, and general aviation and flight training, which encompass all flight-related operations excluding military flight operations.

Critical Infrastructure: Vital services or capabilities that are essential for the larger populace. These services are necessary to provide core functions that the populace need.

Cyber-Physical System: Refers to an integrative system of systems methodology that interconnects electronic devices, computer networks, and wireless technologies to physical processes through wireless sensors.

Cyber Security: The amalgamation of resources, software applications, hardware, security practices, automation, sensors, and the IOT that are used to support and protect the cyberspace.

Hyperconnectivity: The continuous and integrated connection of PEDs, computers, networks, digitized communications, and the IOT.

Supervisory Control and Data Acquisition: A controlling feature that supports the manipulation of a system through automation or some form of remote management.

System of Systems: The concept refers to a larger system comprised of smaller systems that depend on the different systems within the integrated construct.

Compilation of References

Abbas, A., & Khan, S. (2014). A review on the state-of-the-art: Privacy preserving approaches in e-Health clouds. *IEEE Journal Biomedical Health Information, 18*(4), 1431–1441. doi:10.1109/JBHI.2014.2300846 PMID:25014943

Abdulaziz, A. (2012). Cloud computing for increased business value. *International Journal of Business and Social Science, 3*(1), 234–239.

Abel, V. S. (2011). Survey of Attacks on Mobile Adhoc Wireless Networks. *International Journal on Computer Science and Engineering, 3*(2), 826–829.

Abeyratne, R. (2011). Cyber terrorism and aviation—national and international responses. *Journal of Transportation Security, 4*(4), 337–349. doi:10.1007/s12198-011-0074-3

Abhay Kumar Rai Saurabh Kant Upadhyay, R. R. T., Rai, A. K., Tewari, R. R., & Upadhyay, S. K. (2010). Different Types of Attacks on Integrated MANET-Internet Communication. *International Journal of Computer Science and Security, 4*(3), 265–274.

Abrams, R. K., & Taylor, M. W. (2000). *Issues in the Unification of Financial Sector Supervision.* International Money Fund. Retrieved from, http://www.fep.up.pt/disciplinas/pgaf924/PGAF/issues_in_unification_supervision.pdf

Acar, T., Belenkiy, M., & Kupcu, A. (2013). Single password authentication. *Computer Networks, 57*(13), 2597–2614. doi:10.1016/j.comnet.2013.05.007

Ahamad, M., Amster, D., Barrett, M., Cross, T., Heron, G., Jackson, D. … Traynor, P. (2008). *Emerging cyber threats report for 2009.* Academic Press.

Alcaraz, C., Najera, P., Lopez, J., & Roman, R. (2010, November). Wireless sensor networks and the internet of things: Do we need a complete integration? In 1st *International Workshop on the Security of the Internet of Things* (SecIoT'10).

Ali, M., Khan, S., & Vasilakos, A. (2015). Security in cloud computing: Opportunities and challenges. *Information Sciences, 305*, 357–383. doi:10.1016/j.ins.2015.01.025

Allen, C., Wallach, W., & Smit, I. (2006, July/August). Why Machine Ethics? *IEEE Intelligent Systems, 21*(4), 12–17. doi:10.1109/MIS.2006.83

Compilation of References

Alotaibi, S., Wald, M., & Argles, D. (2010). Using fingerprint recognition in a new security model for accessing distributed systems. *International Journal of Intelligent Computing Research*, *1*(4), 194–203.

Alvarez, P. (2004). Using extended file information (EXIF) file headers in digital evidence analysis. *International Journal of Digital Evidence*, *2*(3), 1–5.

Amantini, A., Choraś, M., D'Antonio, S., Egozcue, E., Germanus, D., & Hutter, R. (2012). The human role in tools for improving robustness and resilience of critical infrastructures. *Cognition Technology and Work*, *14*(2), 143–155. doi:10.1007/s10111-010-0171-2

Anderson, M., & Anderson, S. L. (2007). Machine Ethics: Creating an Ethical Intelligent Agent. *AI Magazine*, *28*(4), 15–26.

Angadi, A., Angadi, A., & Gull, K. (2013). Security issues with possible solutions in cloud computing- A survey. *International Journal of Advanced Research in Computer Engineering and Technology*, *2*(2), 652–661.

Anjomshoa, M., Salleh, M., & Kermani, M. (2015). A taxonomy and survey of distributed computing systems. *Journal of Applied Sciences*, *15*(1), 46–57. doi:10.3923/jas.2015.46.57

App Genome Project. (2011). Retrieved from https://www.mylookout.com/appgenome

Armbrust, M., & Fox, A. (2009). *Above the Clouds: A Berkeley View of Cloud Computing*. UC Berkeley Reliable Adaptive Distributed Systems Laboratory.

Armbrust, M., Fox, A., Griffith, R., Joseph, A. D., Katz, R., Konwinski, A., & Zaharia, M. (2008). A view of cloud computing. *Communications of the ACM*, *53*(4), 50–58. doi:10.1145/1721654.1721672

Armstrong, S. (2010). *The AI in a Box Boxes You*. Paper presented at the Less Wrong. Available at: http://lesswrong.com/lw/1pz/the_ai_in_a_box_boxes_you/

Armstrong, S. (2010). *Utility Indifference*. Technical Report 2010-1, Future of Humanity Institute, Oxford University.

Armstrong, S. (2011). *Risks and Mitigation Strategies for Oracle AI*. Paper presented at the Philosophy and Theory of Artificial Intelligence (PT-AI2011), Thessaloniki, Greece. doi:10.1007/978-3-642-31674-6_25

Armstrong, S., Sandberg, A., & Bostrom, N. (2012). Thinking Inside the Box: Using and Controlling an Oracle AI. *Minds and Machines*, *22*(4), 299–324. doi:10.1007/s11023-012-9282-2

Arutyunov, V. V. (2012). Cloud computing: Its history of development, modern state, and future considerations. *Scientific and Technical Information Processing*, *39*(3), 173–178.

Asimov, I. (1942). Runaround. *Astounding Science Fiction*.

Attorneys held exempt from privacy provisions of Gramm-Leach-Bliley Act. (2005). *The Rochester, N.Y Daily Register*.

Atzori, L., Iera, A., & Morabito, G. (2010). The internet of things: A survey. *Computer Networks*, *54*(15), 2787–2805. doi:10.1016/j.comnet.2010.05.010

Awasthi, A. K., & Lal, S. (2007). ID-based ring signature and proxy ring signature schemes from bilinear pairings. *International Journal of Network Security*, *4*(2), 187–192.

Bali, J., Langendorfer, P., & Skarmeta, A. F. (2013). Security and Privacy Challenge in Data Aggregation for the IoT in Smart Cities. *Internet of Things: Converging Technologies for Smart Environments and Integrated Ecosystems*, (pp. 225-244).

Ball, J. (2013). NSA's Prism surveillance program: how it works and what it can do. *The Guardian*, 8.

Ball, J., Schneier, B., & Greenwald, G. (2013). NSA and GCHQ target Tor network that protects anonymity of web users. *The Guardian*, 4.

Banking and Finance Sector-Specific Plan. (2010). *An Annex to the National Infrastructure Protection Plan*. Retrieved from, http://www.dhs.gov/sites/default/files/publications/nipp- ssp-banking-and-finance-2010.pdf

BBC. (2015). *Bangladesh blogger Niloy Neel hacked to death in Dhaka*. Retrieved from: http://www.bbc.com/news/world-asia-33819032

Behringer, M. H. (2009). End-to-End Security. *The Internet Protocol Journal*, *12*(3), 20.

Beimborn, D., Miletzki, T., & Wenzel, S. (2011). Platform as a Service (PaaS). *Business & Information Systems Engineering*, *3*(6), 381–384. doi:10.1007/s12599-011-0183-3

Beitollahi, H., & Deconinck, G. (2012). Analyzing well-known countermeasures against distributed denial of service attacks. *Computer Communications, Elsevier*, *35*(11), 1312–1332. doi:10.1016/j.comcom.2012.04.008

Bekker, S. (2013, June 20). *PRISM and Microsoft: What We Know So Far*. Redmond Channel Partner.

Belapurkar, A., Chakrabarti, A., Ponnapalli, H., Varadarajan, N., Padmanabhuni, S., & Sundarrajan, S. (2009). *Distributed systems security: Issues, processes and solutions*. John Wiley & Sons, Ltd. doi:10.1002/9780470751787

Bendahmane, A., Essaaidi, M., El-Moussaoui, A., & Younes, A. (2009). Grid computing security mechanisms: State of the-art. In *Proceedings of the International Conference on Multimedia Computing and Systems*, (pp. 535–540). doi:10.1109/MMCS.2009.5256638

Beresford, A. R., & Stajano, F. (2004a). *Mix Zones: User Privacy in Location-aware Services*. Paper presented at the The Second IEEE Annual Conference on Pervasive Computing and Communications Workshops, Orlando, FL.

Beresford, A. R., & Stajano, F. (2004b). *Mix zones: user privacy in location-aware services*. Paper presented at the Pervasive Computing and Communications Workshops, 2004.

Beresford, A. R., & Stajano, F. (2003). Location privacy in pervasive computing. *Pervasive Computing, IEEE, 2*(1), 46–55. doi:10.1109/MPRV.2003.1186725

Beutel, J., Gruber, S., Hasler, A., Lim, R., Meier, A., Plessl, C., ... Woehrle, M. (2009). *PermaDAQ: A scientific instrument for precision sensing and data recovery in environmental extremes*. Paper presented at the 2009 International Conference on Information Processing in Sensor Networks.

Bhadauria, R., Borgohain, R., Biswas, A., & Sanyal, S. (2014). Secure authentication of cloud data mining API. *Acta Technical Corviniensis-Bulletin of Engineering, 7*(1), 183.

Bhagawat, V., & Kumar, A. (2015). Survey on data security issues in cloud environment. *International Journal of Innovative Research in Advanced Engineering, 2*(1), 31–35.

Bhaskar, P., & Ahamed, S. I. (2007). *Privacy in Pervasive Computing and Open Issues*. Paper presented at the Availability, Reliability and Security, 2007. ARES 2007. The Second International Conference on.

Bhatia, R. (2013). Grid computing and security issues. *International Journal of Scientific and Research Publications, 3*(8), 1–5.

Blackman, H., Boring, R., Marble, J., Mosleh, A., & Meshkati, N. (2014). Panel discussion new directions in human reliability analysis for oil & gas, cybersecurity, nuclear, and aviation. In *Proceedings of the Human Factors and Ergonomics Society Annual Meeting*. SAGE Publications. doi:10.1177/1541931214581118

Blauner, C. (2013). *Developing a Framework to Improve Infrastructure Cybersecurity*. Financial Services Sector Coordinating Council. Retrieved from, http://www.fsscc.org/fsscc/news/2013/FSSCC-Response-NIST- CybersecurityFramework.pdf

Boebert, W. E., & Kain, R. Y. (1996). *A Further Note on the confinement Problem*. Paper presented at the 30th Annual 1996 International Carnahan Conference on Security Technology, Lexington, KY, USA.

Borisov, N., Goldberg, I., & Brewer, E. (2004, October). Off-the-record communication, or, why not to use PGP. In *Proceedings of the 2004 ACM workshop on Privacy in the electronic society* (pp. 77-84). ACM. doi:10.1145/1029179.1029200

Bostrom, N. (2000). Predictions from Philosophy. *Coloquia Manilana, 7.*

Bostrom, N. (2001). Existential Risks: Analyzing Human Extinction Scenarios and Related Hazards. *Journal of Evolution and Technology, 9.*

Bostrom, N., & Salamon, A. (2011). *The Intelligence Explosion*. Available at: http://singularityhypothesis.blogspot.com/2011/01/intelligence-explosion-extended.html

Bostrom, N. (2003). Are You Living In a Computer Simulation? *The Philosophical Quarterly, 53*(211), 243–255. doi:10.1111/1467-9213.00309

Bostrom, N. (2004). The Future of Human Evolution. In C. Tandy (Ed.), *Death and Anti-Death: Two Hundred Years After Kant, Fifty Years After Turing* (pp. 339–371). Palo Alto, CA: Ria University Press.

Bostrom, N. (2006). Ethical Issues in Advanced Artificial Intelligence. *Review of Contemporary Philosophy*, *5*, 66–73.

Bostrom, N. (2011). Information Hazards: A Typology of Potential Harms From Knowledge. *Review of Contemporary Philosophy*, *10*, 44–79.

Bostrom, N., & Yudkowsky, E. (2011). *The Ethics of Artificial Intelligence*. Cambridge Handbook of Artificial Intelligence.

Bradai, A., & Hossam, A. (2012). Enforcing Trust-based Intrusion Detection in Cloud Computing Using Algebraic Methods.*International Conference on Cyber-Enabled Distributed Computing and Knowledge Discover*. IEEE. doi:10.1109/CyberC.2012.38

Bradley, J., Barbier, J., & Handler, D. (2013). *Embracing the Internet of everything to capture your share of $14.4 trillion*. White Paper, Cisco.

Branstetter, B. (2015, August 16). The NSA is asking your favorite apps how to spy on you better. *Business Insider, Daily Dot*.

Bucci, S. P., Rosenzweig, P., & Inserra, D. (2013). A *Congressional Guide: Seven Steps to U.S. Security, Prosperity, and Freedom in Cyberspace*. The Heritage Foundation. Retrieved from, http://www.heritage.org/research/reports/2013/04/a-congressional-guide-seven-steps-to-us-security-prosperity-and-freedom-in-cyberspace

Bump, P. (2013, June 21). The UK Tempora Program Captures Vast Amounts of Data – and Shares with NSA. *The Atlantic Wire*.

Calder, A. (2013). Can Compliance Shield your Organization from Cyberthreats? *Credit Control*, *34*(2), 67.

Cano, P., & Vargas-Lombardo, M. (2012). Security threats in volunteer computing environments using the Berkeley open infrastructure for network computing (BOINC). *International Journal of Computer Technology and Applications*, *3*(3), 944–948.

Caplan, B. (2008). The totalitarian threat. In M. C. N. Bostrom (Ed.), *Global Catastrophic Risks* (pp. 504–519). Oxford University Press.

Caruson, K., MacManus, S., & McPhee, B. (2012). Cybersecurity policy-making at the local government level: An analysis of threats, preparedness, and bureaucratic roadblocks to success. *Homeland Security & Emergency Management*, *9*(2), 1–22. doi:10.1515/jhsem-2012-0003

Cavoukian, A. (2008). *Privacy in the clouds*. Identity Journal Limited.

Chakrabarti, A. (2007). Taxonomy of grid security issues. In Grid computing security. New York: Springer-Verlag Berlin Heidelberg. doi:10.1007/978-3-540-44493-0_3

Compilation of References

Chalmers, D. (2010). The Singularity: A Philosophical Analysis. *Journal of Consciousness Studies, 17*, 7–65.

Chandramouli, R. (2014). Security Recommendations for Hypervisor Deployment (No. 800-125-A). Gaithersburg, MD: National Institute of Standards and Technology, Computer Security Division Information Technology Laboratory.

Chen, W. (2009, June 13). Let people decide on Green Dam. *China Daily*.

Chen, S. C., & Wu, C. C. (2015). Human Resource Development in Cloud Computing: An Empirical Investigation in Taiwan. *Journal of Management Research, 7*(3), 102–114.

ClearCenter. (2009). *Twitter breach revives security issues with cloud computing*. Retrieved from http://www.clearcenter.com/News-Articles/twitter-breach-revives-security-issues-with-cloud-computing.html?Itemid=456

Clearfield, C. (2013, June 26). *Rethinking security for the internet of things*. Retrieved from Harvard Business Review: https://hbr.org/2013/06/rethinking-security-for-the-in

Clendenin, M. (2010). *China's 'Internet Of Things' Overblown, Says Exec*. Retrieved from http://www.informationweck.com/news/storage/virtualization/225700966?subSection=News

Cocosila, M. (2013). Role of user a priori attitude in the acceptance of mobile health: An empirical investigation. *Electronic Markets, 23*(1), 15–27. doi:10.1007/s12525-012-0111-5

Cody, E., Sharman, R., Rao, R., & Upadhyaya, S. (2008). Security in grid computing: A review and synthesis. *Decision Support Systems,* (44), 749–764.

Coleman, E. (2008). The Surveyability of Long Proofs. *Foundations of Science, 14*(1/2), 27–43.

Commander Twenty-Fourth Air Force. (2013). Cyber professionals in the military and industry—partnering in defense of the nation. *Air & Space Power Journal, 27*, 4–21.

Compliance: still a board-level issue. (2007). *MarketWatch: Global Round-up*, pp. 176-177.

Conti, M., Das, S. K., Bisdikian, C., Kumar, M., Ni, L. M., Passarella, A., & Zambonelli, F. et al. (2012). Looking ahead in Pervasive Computing: Challenges, Opportunities in the era of Cyber Physical Convergence. *Pervasive and Mobile Computing, 8*(1), 2–21. doi:10.1016/j.pmcj.2011.10.001

Conway, G., & Curry, E. (2012). Managing cloud computing: A life cycle approach. In *Proceedings of the 2nd International Conference of Cloud Computing and Services Science*, (pp. 198-207).

Cooper, D. A., & Birman, K. P. (1995). *Preserving privacy in a network of mobile computers*. Paper presented at the Security and Privacy, 1995.

Corwin, J. (2002). *AI Boxing*. Paper presented at the SL4.org. Available at: http://www.sl4.org/archive/0207/4935.html

Coulouris, G., Dollimore, J., & Kindberg, T. (2012). *Distributed systems - Concepts and design* (5th ed.). London: Addison – Wesley.

Cross-Domain Interoperability. (2015). Retrieved from https://www.ncoic.org/cross-domain-interoperability

Dabas, P., & Arya, A. (2013). Grid computing: An introduction. *International Journal of Advanced Research in Computer Science and Software Engineering, 3*(3), 467–470.

Dagorn, N., Bernard, N., & Varrette, S. (2005). Practical authentication in distributed environments. In *Proceedings of the IEEE International Conference on Computer Systems and Information Technology* (vol. 1).

Danezis, G. (2003). *Mix-networks with restricted routes.* Paper presented at the Privacy Enhancing Technologies. doi:10.1007/978-3-540-40956-4_1

Das, R., Purkayastha, B. S., & Das, P. (2011). Security Measures for Black Hole Attack in MANET. *An Approach, 3*(4), 2832–2838.

Davenport, T. (2004). Small banks say Sec. 404 forcing sale. *American Banker, 169*(227), 9–10.

Dawson, M., Omar, M., Abramson, J., & Bessette, D. (2014). The Future of National and International Security on the Internet. *Information Security in Diverse Computing Environments*, 149.

Dawson, M., Wright, J., & Omar, M. (2016). Mobile Devices: The Case for Cyber Security Hardened Systems. In Mobile Computing and Wireless Networks: Concepts, Methodologies, Tools, and Applications (pp. 1103-1123). Hershey, PA: Information Science Reference. doi:10.4018/978-1-4666-8751-6.ch047

Dawson, M. E. Jr, Crespo, M., & Brewster, S. (2013). DoD cyber technology policies to secure automated information systems. *International Journal of Business Continuity and Risk Management, 4*(1), 1–22. doi:10.1504/IJBCRM.2013.053089

Dawson, M., Leonard, B., & Rahim, E. (2015). Advances in Technology Project Management: Review of Open Source Software Integration. In M. Wadhwa & A. Harper (Eds.), *Technology, Innovation, and Enterprise Transformation* (pp. 313–324). Hershey, PA: Business Science Reference; doi:10.4018/978-1-4666-6473-9.ch016

Dawson, M., & Omar, M. (2015). *New Threats and Countermeasures in Digital Crime and Cyber Terrorism.* Hershey, PA: IGI Global; doi:10.4018/978-1-4666-8345-7.ch001

Dawson, M., Omar, M., & Abramson, J. (2015). Understanding the Methods behind Cyber Terrorism. In M. Khosrow-Pour (Ed.), *Encyclopedia of Information Science and Technology* (3rd ed.; pp. 1539–1549). Hershey, PA: Information Science Reference; doi:10.4018/978-1-4666-5888-2.ch147

Dawson, M., Omar, M., Abramson, J., & Bessette, D. (2014). The Future of National and International Security on the Internet. In A. Kayem & C. Meinel (Eds.), *Information Security in Diverse Computing Environments* (pp. 149–178). Hershey, PA: Information Science Reference; doi:10.4018/978-1-4666-6158-5.ch009

Compilation of References

Dehghantanha, A., Udzir, N., & Mahmod, R. (2011). Evaluating User-Centered Privacy Model (UPM) in Pervasive Computing Systems Computational Intelligence in Security for Information Systems. Springer Berlin / Heidelberg.

Dehghantanha, A., Mahmod, R., & Udzir, N. I. (2009). A XML based, User-centered Privacy Model in Pervasive Computing Systems. *International Journal of Computer Science and Network Security, 9*(10), 167–173.

Dellarocas, C. (2001). *The Design of Reliable Trust Management Systems for Electronic Trading Communities*. MIT.

Deltacloud. (2011, Oktober). *About Deltacloud*. Retrieved August 16, 2013, from http://delta-cloud.apache.org/rest-api.html

Deng, L., Zeng, J., & Qu, Y. (2014). *Certificateless Proxy Signature from RSA, 2014*. Academic Press.

Denning, D. (2014). Framework and principles for active cyber defense. *Computers & Security, 40*, 108–113. doi:10.1016/j.cose.2013.11.004

Dennis, A., Jones, R., Kildare, D., & Barclay, C. (2014). A Design Science approach to developing and evaluating a national cybersecurity framework for Jamaica. *The Electronic Journal of Information Systems in Developing Countries, 62*(6), 1–18.

Dhar, S. (2012). From outsourcing to cloud computing: Evolution of IT services. *Management Research Review, 35*(8), 664–675. doi:10.1108/01409171211247677

Dimension Data. (2012). *Cloud Security: Developing a Secure Cloud Approach* (No. CS / DDMS-1072). Retrieved from http://www.dimensiondata.com/

Dingledine, R., Mathewson, N., & Syverson, P. (2004). *Tor: The second-generation onion router*. Naval Research Lab Washington DC.

Dingledine, R., Serjantov, A., & Syverson, P. (2006, June). Blending different latency traffic with alpha-mixing. In *Privacy Enhancing Technologies* (pp. 245–257). Springer Berlin Heidelberg. doi:10.1007/11957454_14

Djenouri, D., & Khelladi, L. (2005). A survey of security issues in mobile ad hoc networks. *IEEE Communications Surveys*. Retrieved from http://www.lsi-usthb.dz/Rapports_pdf/2004/LSIIR-TR0504.pdf

Dombrowski, P., & Demchak, C. (2014). Cyber War, cybered conflict, and the maritime domain. *Naval War College Review, 67*(2), 70.

Drexler, E. (1986). *Engines of Creation*. Anchor Press.

Du, J., Wei, W., Gu, X., & Yu, T. (2009). Toward secure dataflow processing in open distributed systems.*InProceedings of ACM Scalable Trusted Computing Workshop* (pp. 67-72). doi:10.1145/1655108.1655120

Dutta, S., & Bilbao-Osorio, B. (2012). *The Global information technology report 2012: Living in a hyperconnected world*. World Economic Forum.

Edman, M., Sivrikaya, F., & Yener, B. (2007, May). *A Combinatorial Approach to Measuring Anonymity*. ISI.

Elkhodr, M., Shahrestani, S., & Cheung, H. (2012). *A Review of Mobile Location Privacy in the Internet of Things*. Paper presented at the 2012 Tenth International Conference on ICT and Knowledge Engineering, Bangkok, Thailand. doi:10.1109/ICTKE.2012.6408566

Elkhodr, M., Shahrestani, S., & Cheung, H. (2013a). *The Internet of Things: Vision & Challenges*. Paper presented at the IEEE Tencon Spring 2013, Sydney, Australia.

Elkhodr, M., Shahrestani, S., & Cheung, H. (2013b). *Preserving the Privacy of Patient Records in Health Monitoring Systems. In Theory and Practice of Cryptography Solutions for Secure Information Systems* (pp. 499–529). IGI Global. doi:10.4018/978-1-4666-4030-6.ch019

Elkhodr, M., Shahrestani, S., & Cheung, H. (2016a). The Internet of Things: New Interoperability, Management and Security Challenges. *The International Journal of Network Security & Its Applications, 8*(2), 85–102. doi:10.5121/ijnsa.2016.8206

Elkhodr, M., Shahrestani, S., & Cheung, H. (2016b). *Wireless Enabling Technologies for the Internet of Things. In Handbook of Research on Next-Generation High Performance Computing*. Hershey, PA: IGI Global.

Enck, W., Gilbert, P., Chun, B.-G., Cox, L. P., Jung, J., McDaniel, P., & Sheth, A. N. (2010). *TaintDroid: an information-flow tracking system for realtime privacy monitoring on smartphones*. Paper presented at the 9th USENIX conference on Operating systems design and implementation, Vancouver, Canada.

Epstein, R. G. (1997). *Computer Psychologists Command Big Bucks*. Available at http://www.cs.wcupa.edu/~epstein/comppsy.htm

ETSI. (2012). CLOUD; SLAs for Cloud services (Technical Report No. ETSI TR 103 125 V1.1.1 (2012-11)). European Telecommunications Standards Institute.

European Commission. (2014). *Cloud Service Level Agreements Standadisation Guidelines*. Brussels: Author.

Evans, D. (2012). The Internet of Everything. How More Relevant and Valuable Connections. Will Change the World. *Cisco IBSG*, 1-9.

Evans, D. (2012). The internet of everything: How more relevant and valuable connections will change the world. *Cisco IBSG*, 1-9.

Fagoyinbo, J. B. (2013). *The Armed Forces: Instrument of Peace, Strength, Development and Prosperity*. AuthorHouse.

Compilation of References

Fahl, S., Harbach, M., Muders, T., & Smith, M. (2012). Confidentiality as a Service – Usable Security for the Cloud. In *2012 IEEE 11th International Conference on Trust, Security and Privacy in Computing and Communications (TrustCom)* (pp. 153–162). http://doi.org/doi:<ALIGNMENT.qj></ALIGNMENT>10.1109/TrustCom.2012.112

Farouk, A., Abdelhafez, A., & Fouad, M. (2012). Authentication mechanisms in grid computing environment: Comparative study. In *Proceedings of the International Conference on Engineering and Technology* (pp. 10-11). doi:10.1109/ICEngTechnol.2012.6396116

FDIC Law Regulations, Related Acts. (2013). *Uniform Interagency Consumer Compliance Rating System*. FDIC Website. Retrieved from, http://www.fdic.gov/regulations/laws/rules/5000-1700.html

Fernandes, A., Soares, F., Gomes, V., Freire, M., & Inácio, R. (2014). Security issues in cloud environments: A survey. *International Journal of Information Security*, *13*(2), 113–170. doi:10.1007/s10207-013-0208-7

Finances of Tails. (2015). Retrieved from: https://tails.boum.org/doc/about/finances/index.en.html

Firdhous, M., Ghazali, O., & Hassan, S. (2011). Trust Management in Cloud Computing: A Critical Review. *International Journal on Advances in ICT for Emerging Regions*.

Firdhous, M. (2011). Implementation of security in distributed systems – A comparative study. *International Journal of Computer Information Systems*, *2*(2), 1–6.

Fischer, E. A. (2013). *Federal Laws Relating to Cybersecurity: Overview and Discussion of Proposed Revisions*. Congressional Research Service. Retrieved from, http://www.fas.org/sgp/crs/natsec/R42114.pdf

Fitsanakis, J. (2013, June 20). Analysis: PRISM Revelations Harm US Political, Financial Interests. *IntelNews*.

Fitzgerald, J. (2012). Coping with the burdens of Dodd-Frank. *Massachusetts Banker, 2012*(4), 17-20.

Flowers, A., & Zeadally, S. (2014). US policy on active cyber defense. *Journal of Homeland Security and Emergency Management*, *11*(2), 289–308. doi:10.1515/jhsem-2014-0021

Fredette, J., Marom, R., Steiner, K., & Witters, L. (2012). The promise and peril of hyperconnectivity for organizations and societies. *The global information technology report*, 113-119.

Fredrik, H. (2011). *System Integrity for Smartphones: A security evaluation of iOS and BlackBerry OS. (Master)*. Linkoping University.

Friese, I., Hogberg, J., Foll, F. A., Gourmelen, G., Lischka, M., Brennan, J., . . . Lampe, S. (2010). *Bridging IMS and Internet Identity*. Paper presented at the 2010 14th International Conference on Intelligence in Next Generation Networks (ICIN). doi:10.1109/ICIN.2010.5640948

FSF. (2010). *2010 Free Software Awards announced*. Free Software Foundation.

Gartner. (2014, August 11). *Gartner's 2014 Hype Cycle for Emerging Technologies Maps the Journey to Digital Business*. Retrieved February 28, 2016, from http://www.gartner.com/newsroom/id/2819918

Gavrilova, M., & Yampolskiy, R. (2010). *Applying Biometric Principles to Avatar Recognition*. Paper presented at the International Conference on Cyberworlds (CW2010), Singapore.

Gentry, C. (2009). *A Fully Homomorphic Encryption Scheme*. Available at http://crypto.stanford.edu/craig/craig-thesis.pdf

Gheorghe, G., Cigno, R., & Montresor, A. (2011). Security and privacy issues in P2P streaming systems: A Survey. *Peer-to-Peer Networking and Applications*, (4), 75–91.

Gilbert, D. (2015). Hacking Team hacked: Spy tools sold to oppressive regimes Sudan, Bahrain and Kazakhstan. *International Business Times Magazine*.

Gingrich, N., & Kralik, D. W. (2008, November 5). Repeal Sarbanes-Oxley. *The San Francisco Chronicle*. Retrieved from http://www.sfgate.com

Givens, A., & Busch, N. (2013). Integrating federal approaches to post-cyber incident mitigation. *Journal of Homeland Security and Emergency Management*, *10*(1), 1–28. doi:10.1515/jhsem-2012-0001

Glass, D., Davis, C., Mason, J., Gursky, D., Thomas, J., Carr, W., & Levine, D. (2009). Security audits, standards and inspections. In S. Bosworth, M. E. Kabay, & E. Whyne (Eds.), *Computer security handbook* (5th ed.). New York, NY: John Wiley & Sons.

Glotzbach, R., Mordkovich, D., & Radwan, D. (2008). Syndicated RSS feeds for course information distribution. *Journal of Information Technology Education: Research*, *7*(1), 163–183.

Gonzalez-Martínez, J., Bote-Lorenzo, M., Gomez-Sanchez, E., & Cano-Parra, R. (2015). Cloud computing and education: A state-of-the-art survey. *Computers & Education*, *80*, 132–151. doi:10.1016/j.compedu.2014.08.017

Good, I. J. (1966). Speculations Concerning the First Ultraintelligent Machine. *Advances in Computers*, *6*, 31–88. doi:10.1016/S0065-2458(08)60418-0

Goodman, S., Kirk, J., & Kirk, M. (2007). Cyberspace as a medium for terrorists. *Technological Forecasting and Social Change*, *74*(2), 193–210. doi:10.1016/j.techfore.2006.07.007

Goyal, P., Batra, S., & Singh, A. (2010). A Literature Review of Security Attack in Mobile Ad-hoc Networks. *International Journal of Computers and Applications*, *9*(12), 11–15. doi:10.5120/1439-1947

Goyal, P., Parmar, V., & Rishi, R. (2011). MANET: Vulnerabilities, Challenges, Attacks, Application. *IJCEM International Journal of Computational Engineering & Management*, *11*(January), 32–37.

Compilation of References

Greenberg, P. (2012, August 20). *National Conference of State Legislatures*. Retrieved from State Security Breach Notification Laws: http://www.ncsl.org/issues-research/telecom/security-breach-notification-laws.aspx

Greenwald, G., MacAskill, E., Poitras, L., Ackerman, S., & Rushe, D. (2013). Microsoft handed the NSA access to encrypted messages. *The Guardian,* 12.

Greenwald, G. (2014). *No place to hide: Edward Snowden, the NSA, and the US surveillance state*. Macmillan.

Groups team up to improve cybersecurity. (2011). *Journal of Business, 26*(3), B7.

Gubbi, J., Buyya, R., Marusic, S., & Palaniswami, M. (2013). Internet of Things (IoT): A vision, architectural elements, and future directions. *Future Generation Computer Systems, 29*(7), 1645–1660. doi:10.1016/j.future.2013.01.010

Guinard, D. (2011). *A web of things application architecture-Integrating the real-world into the web*. (Doctoral dissertation). ETH Zurich.

Guinard, D., & Trifa, V. (2009, April). Towards the web of things: Web mashups for embedded devices. In *Workshop on Mashups, Enterprise Mashups and Lightweight Composition on the Web (MEM 2009), in proceedings of WWW (International World Wide Web Conferences),*(p. 15).

Guinchard, A. (2011). Between hype and understatement: Reassessing cyber risks as a security strategy. *Journal of Strategic Security, 4*(2), 75–96. doi:10.5038/1944-0472.4.2.5

Gunes, V., Peter, S., Givargis, T., & Vahid, F. (2014). A survey on concepts, applications, and challenges in cyber-physical systems. *Transactions on Internet and Information Systems (Seoul), 8*(12), 4242–4268. doi:10.3837/tiis.2014.12.001

Gupta, M., & Gupta, G. (2013). Security requirements for increasing reliability in Grid Computing. *Journal of Engineering, Computers and Applied Sciences, 2*(9), 6-10.

Gupta, P. (2012). *Metro Interface Improves Windows 8 While Increasing Some Risks*. Retrieved from http://blogs.mcafee.com/mcafee-labs/metro-interface-improves-windows-8-while-increasing-some-risks

Gupta, G., Laxmi, P., & Sharma, S. (2014). A survey on cloud security issues and techniques. *International Journal on Computational Sciences and Applications, 4*(1), 125–132. doi:10.5121/ijcsa.2014.4112

Gurnow, M., (2014, July). Seated Between Pablo Escobar and Mahatma Gandhi: The Sticky Ethics of Anonymity Networks. *Dissident Voice*.

Habib, M. S., Hauke, S., Ries, S., & Habib. (2012). Trust as a facilitator in cloud computing: a survey. *Journal of Cloud Computing: Advances, Systems and Applications*.

313

Habib, S. M., Ries, S., & Muhlhauser, M. (2010). Cloud Computing Landscape and Research Challenges Regarding Trust and Reputation. In *2010 7th International Conference on Ubiquitous Intelligence Computing and 7th International Conference on Autonomic Trusted Computing (UIC/ATC)* (pp. 410 –415). http://doi.org/ doi:10.1109/UIC-ATC.2010.48

Habib, S. M., Ries, S., Mühlhäuser, M., & Varikkattu, P. (2014). Towards a trust management system for cloud computing marketplaces: Using caiq as a trust information source. *Security and Communication Networks*, *7*(11), 2185–2200. doi:10.1002/sec.748

Hagen, W. (2008). *Professional Xen virtualization*. Birmingham, UK: Wrox Press Ltd.

Hall, J. S. (2000). *Ethics for Machines*. Available at: http://autogeny.org/ethics.html

Hall, J. S. (2007, October). Self-Improving AI: An Analysis. *Minds and Machines*, *17*(3), 249–259. doi:10.1007/s11023-007-9065-3

Hanson, R. (2001). Economic Growth Given Machine Intelligence. *Journal of Artificial Intelligence Research*.

Hanson, R. (2008, June). Economics of the Singularity. *IEEE Spectrum*, *45*(6), 45–50. doi:10.1109/MSPEC.2008.4531461

Han, Y., Sun, J., Wang, G., & Li, H. (2010). A cloud-based BPM architecture with user-end distribution of non-compute-intensive activities and sensitive data. *Journal of Computer Science and Technology*, *25*(6), 1157–1167.

Harris, S., & Meyers, M. (2002). *CISSP*. McGraw-Hill/Osborne.

Harris, D. (2003). Privacy rule catches dealers off guard. *Automotive News*, *77*(6039), 24.

Hashizume, K., Rosado, D., Fernndez-Medina, E., & Fernandez, E. (2013). An analysis of security issues for cloud computing. *Journal of Internet Services Applications*, *4*(5), 1–13.

HealthCast 2020: Creating a Sustainable Future. (2005). Retrieved from http://www.pwc.com/il/he/publications/assets/2healthcast_2020.pdf

Hedley, T. P., & Ben-Chorin, O. (2011). Auditing and monitoring activities help uncover fraud and assess control effectiveness. *The CPA Journal*, *81*(6), 68–71.

Hentea, M. (2008). Improving security for SCADA control systems. *Interdisciplinary Journal of Information, Knowledge, and Management*, *3*(1), 73–86.

Hibbard, B. (2005). *The Ethics and Politics of Super-Intelligent Machines*. Available at www.ssec.wisc.edu/~billh/g/SI_ethics_politics.doc

Hightower, J., & Borriello, G. (2001). Location systems for ubiquitous computing. *Computer*, *34*(8), 57–66. doi:10.1109/2.940014

Himral, L., Vig, V., & Chand, N. (2011). Preventing AODV Routing Protocol from Black Hole Attack. *International Journal of Engineering Science and Technology, 3*(5), 3927–3932. doi:10.13140/2.1.2220.3206

Hoehl, M. (2015). *Proposal for standard Cloud Computing Security SLAs – Key Metrics for Safeguarding Confidential Data in the Cloud.* The SANs Institute.

Hoffman, L., Burley, D., & Toregas, C. (2012). Holistically building the cybersecurity workforce. *Security & Privacy, IEEE, 10*(2), 33–39. doi:10.1109/MSP.2011.181

Hoh, B., Gruteser, M., Xiong, H., & Alrabady, A. (2006). Enhancing security and privacy in traffic-monitoring systems. *IEEE Pervasive Computing / IEEE Computer Society [and] IEEE Communications Society, 5*(4), 38–46. doi:10.1109/MPRV.2006.69

Huang, J. & Nicol, D. (2013). Trust mechanisms for cloud computing. *Journal of Cloud Computing: Advances, Systems and Applications.*

Huawei FusionSphere 5.0: Technical White Paper on Virtualization. (2014, September). Huawei Technologies Company Limited.

Hult, F., & Sivanesan, G. (2014). What good cyber resilience looks like. *Journal of Business Continuity & Emergency Planning, 7*(2), 112–125. PMID:24457323

Hu, Y. C., Perrig, A., & Johnson, D. B. (2006). Wormhole attacks in wireless networks. Selected Areas in Communications. *IEEE Journal, 24*(2), 370–380.

Hu, Y.-C., Perrig, A., & Johnson, D. B. (2005). Ariadne: A Secure On-Demand Routing Protocol for Ad Hoc Networks. *Wireless Networks, 11*(1-2), 21–38. doi:10.1007/s11276-004-4744-y

Hwang, K. (2010). *Trusted Cloud Computing with Secure Resources and Data Coloring.* IEEE Computer Society.

Hwang, K., Fox, G., & Dongarra, J. (2010). *Distributed computing: Clusters, grids and clouds.* Morgan Kaufmann, Elsevier, Inc.

Hwang, K., Fox, G., & Dongarra, J. (2012). *Distributed and cloud computing.* Morgan Kaufmann, Elsevier, Inc.

Iasiello, E. (2013). Getting ahead of the threat: Aviation and cyber security. *Aerospace America, 51*(7), 22–25.

Iasiello, E. (2014). A review of "A framework for aviation cybersecurity" -- A decision paper from the American Institute of Aeronautics and Astronautics. *Journal Of Homeland Security & Emergency Management, 11*(1), 95–100. doi:10.1515/jhsem-2013-0076

Idel, M. (1990). *Golem: Jewish Magical and Mystical Traditions on the Artificial Anthropoid.* Albany, NY: SUNY Press.

IEEE Standard Computer Dictionary: A Compilation of IEEE Standard Computer Glossaries. (1991). *IEEE Std 610.* doi:10.1109/IEEESTD.1991.106963

International Telecommunication Union. (2012a). ITU-T recommendation Y.2060: Series Y: Global information infrastructure, internet protocol aspects and next-generation networks: Frameworks and functional architecture models: Overview of the Internet of Things. Geneva: International Telecommunication Union.

International Telecommunication Union. (2012b). ITU-T recommendation Y.2063: Series Y: Global information infrastructure, internet protocol aspects and next-generation networks: Frameworks and functional architecture models: Framework of the Web of Things. Geneva: International Telecommunication Union.

International Telecommunication Union. (2012c). ITU-T recommendation Y.2069: Series Y: Global information infrastructure, internet protocol aspects and next-generation networks: Frameworks and functional architecture models: Terms and definitions for the Internet of Things. Geneva: International Telecommunication Union.

Itani, N., O'Connell, J., & Mason, K. (2015). Towards realizing best-in-class civil aviation strategy scenarios. *Transport Policy*, *43*, 42–54. doi:10.1016/j.tranpol.2015.05.013

ITU. (2012). *ITU-T Y.2060 overview of the internet of things*. ITU.

Jabeur, N., Sahli, N., & Zeadally, S. (2015). Enabling cyber-physical systems with wireless sensor networking technologies, multiagent system paradigm, and natural ecosystems. *Mobile Information Systems*, *501*, 908315.

Jaisankar, N., Saravanan, R., & Swamy, K. D. (2010). A novel security approach for detecting black hole attack in MANET. *Communications in Computer and Information Science*, *70*, 217–223. doi:10.1007/978-3-642-12214-9_36

James, R. (2009, May 11). A brief history of Chinese internet censorship. *Time*.

Janczewski, L., & Colarik, A. (2007). *Cyber Warfare and Cyber Terrorism*. Hershey, PA: IGI Global. doi:10.4018/978-1-59140-991-5

Jarvis, L., Macdonald, S., & Nouri, L. (2014). The cyber terrorism threat: Findings from a survey of researchers. *Studies in Conflict and Terrorism*, *37*(1), 68–90. doi:10.1080/1057610X.2014.853603

jClouds. (2011). *What is jClouds?* Retrieved April 27, 2013, from http://www.jclouds.org/documentation/gettingstarted/what-is-jclouds/

Johnson, L., Levine, A., Smith, R., & Smythe, T. (2009). *The 2009 horizon report: K. Austin, Texas: The New Media Consortium. Cover photograph: "Chapped Lips" by Vox_Efx on Flickr.* Retrieved from http://www.flickr.com/photos/vox_efx/3186014896/

Jonathan, P. J. Y., Fung, C. C., & Wong, K. W. (2009). Devious Chatbots - Interactive Malware with a Plot, Progress in Robotics. Springer Berlin Heidelberg.

Joseph, A., Kathrine, J., & Vijayan, R. (2014). Cloud security mechanisms for data protection: A survey. *International Journal of Multimedia and Ubiquitous Engineering*, *9*(9), 81–90. doi:10.14257/ijmue.2014.9.9.09

Compilation of References

Kaas, S., Rayhawk, S., Salamon, A., & Salamon, P. (2010). *Economic Implications of Software Minds*. Paper presented at the VIII European Conference of Computing and Philosophy (ECAP10).

Kahneman, D., Slovic, P., & Tversky, A. (1982). *Judgement under Uncertainty: Heuristics and Biases*. Cambridge University Press. doi:10.1017/CBO9780511809477

Kannhavong, B., Nakayama, H., Nemoto, Y., Kato, N., & Jamalipour, A. (2007). A survey of routing attacks in mobile ad hoc networks. *IEEE Wireless Communications*, *14*(5), 85–91. doi:10.1109/MWC.2007.4396947

Kanuparthi, A., Karri, R., & Addepalli, S. (2013, November). Hardware and embedded security in the context of internet of things. In *Proceedings of the 2013 ACM Workshop on Security, Privacy & Dependability for Cyber Vehicles*, (pp. 61-64). ACM. doi:10.1145/2517968.2517976

Karajeh, H., Maqableh, M., & Masa'deh, R. (2011). Security of cloud computing environment. In *Proceedings of the 23rd IBIMA Conference on Vision 2020: Sustainable Growth, Economic Development, and Global Competitiveness*.

Katzan, H. Jr. (2010). On the privacy of cloud computing. *International Journal of Management and Information Systems*, *14*(2), 1–12.

Kaur, K., & Rai, A. (2014). A comparative analysis: Grid, cluster and cloud computing. *International Journal of Advanced Research in Computer and Communication Engineering*, *3*(3), 5730–5734.

Kavitha, G., & Sankaranarayanan, V. (2011). Secure selection of multiple resources based on virtual private network for computational grids. *Journal of Computer Science*, *7*(12), 1881–1887. doi:10.3844/jcssp.2011.1881.1887

Kazemi, A. (2014). Review of grid computing security and present a new authentication Method for Improving Security. *International Journal of Advance Foundation and Research in Computer*, *1*(4), 77–89.

Kemmerer, R. A. (2002). *A Practical Approach to Identifying Storage and Timing Channels: Twenty Years Later*. Paper presented at the 18th Annual Computer Security Applications Conference (ACSAC'02), Las Vegas, NV. doi:10.1109/CSAC.2002.1176284

Kemmerer, R. A. (1983, August). Shared Resource Matrix Methodology: An Approach to Identifying Storage and Timing Channels. *ACM Transactions on Computer Systems*, *1*(3), 256–277. doi:10.1145/357369.357374

Kessler, G., & Ramsay, J. (2013). Paradigms for Cybersecurity Education in a Homeland Security Program. *Journal of Homeland Security Education*, 2. Retrieved from http://commons.erau.edu/db-applied-aviation/12

Khalid, G., Ghafoor, A., Irum, M., & Shibli, M. A. (2013). Cloud Based Secure and Privacy Enhanced Authentication & Authorization Protocol. *Procedia Computer Science*, *22*, 680–688. doi:10.1016/j.procs.2013.09.149

Khalil, I., Bagchi, S., & Shroff, N. B. (2005, June). LITEWORP: a lightweight countermeasure for the wormhole attack in multihop wireless networks. In *Proceedings. International Conference on Dependable Systems and Networks, 2005 DSN 2005*, (pp. 612-621). IEEE. doi:10.1109/DSN.2005.58

Khan, M. K., & Malluhi, Q. (2010). *Establishing Trust in Cloud Computing*. IEEE Computer Society.

Khan, M., Xiang, Y., Horng, S., & Chen, H. (2013). Trust, security, and privacy in next-generation wireless sensor networks. *International Journal of Distributed Sensor Networks*, *2013*, 1–2. doi:10.1155/2013/956736

Khanna, A., & Dere, P. U. (2014). *A Review on Intrusion Detection and Security of Wormhole Attacks in MANET*. Academic Press.

Kidder, L. (2012). *Top Challenges Facing Financial Services in 2013*. Bank Systems & Technology. Retrieved from, http://www.banktech.com/management-strategies/top- challenges-facing-financial-services/240144973

Kim, T. H., Kim, D. S., Lee, S. M., & Park, J. S. (2009). Detecting DDoS attacks using dispersible traffic matrix and weighted moving average. *Advances in Information Security and Assurance* (pp. 290-300). Springer Berlin Heidelberg.

Kim, H. (2012). Security and vulnerability of SCADA systems over IP-based wireless sensor networks. *International Journal of Distributed Sensor Networks*, *2012*, 1–10. doi:10.1155/2012/268478

Kim, W., Kim, S. D., Lee, E., & Lee, S. (2009, December). Adoption issues for cloud computing. In *Proceedings of the 7th International Conference on Advances in Mobile Computing and Multimedia* (pp. 2-5). ACM.

Kirk, J. (2012). Pacemaker hack can deliver deadly 830-volt jolt. *Computerworld*, 17.

Klitch, S. (2012, September 17). Commity banks and the JOBS Act. *Idaho Business Review*.

Knowles, W., Prince, D., Hutchison, D., Disso, J., & Jones, K. (2015). A survey of cyber security management in industrial control systems. *International Journal of Critical Infrastructure Protection*, *9*, 52–80. doi:10.1016/j.ijcip.2015.02.002

Ko, R. K., Jagadpramana, P., Mowbray, M., Pearson, S., Kirchberg, M., Liang, Q., & Lee, B. S. (2011). TrustCloud: A framework for accountability and trust in cloud computing. In *2011 IEEE World Congress on Services (SERVICES)*, (pp. 584-588). IEEE. doi:10.1109/SERVICES.2011.91

Koshutanski, H. (2009). A Survey on distributed access control systems for web business processes. *International Journal of Network Security*, *9*(1), 61–69.

Koutrouli, E., & Tsalgatidou, A. (2012). Taxonomy of attacks and defense mechanisms in P2P reputation systems-lessons for reputation system designers. *Computer Science Review*, *6*(6), 47–70. doi:10.1016/j.cosrev.2012.01.002

Compilation of References

Kshetri, N. (2013). Privacy and security issues in cloud computing: The role of institutions and institutional evolution. *Telecommunications Policy*, *37*(4-5), 372–386. doi:10.1016/j.telpol.2012.04.011

Kuada, E. (2013). Trust Management System for Opportunistic Cloud Services. In *2013 IEEE 2nd International Conference on Cloud Networking (CloudNet)* (pp. 33 – 41). San Francisco, CA: IEEE. doi:10.1109/CloudNet.2013.6710555

Kuada, E. (2014). *Opportunistic Cloud Services: A Social Network Approach to Provisioning and Management of Cloud Computing Services for Enterprises*. GlobeEdit. Retrieved from https://www.morebooks.de/gb/bookprice_offer_df165575e272c9927b008d4f5d2a05da0745c426

Kuada, E., Adanu, K., & Olesen, H. (2013). Cloud Computing and Information Technology Resource Cost Management for SMEs. In *Proceedings of IEEE Region 8 Conference EuroCon 2013* (pp. 258 – 265). University of Zagreb, Croatia: IEEE. Retrieved from http://www.eurocon2013.org/index.html

Kumar, M., & Agrawal, N. (2013). Analysis of different security issues and attacks in distributed system: A-review. *International Journal of Advanced Research in Computer Science and Software Engineering*, *3*(4), 232–237.

Kumar, M., & Rishi, R. (2010). Security Aspects in Mobile Ad Hoc Network (MANETs): Technical Review. *International Journal of Computers and Applications*, *12*(2), 37–43. doi:10.5120/1304-1642

Kumar, R., & Charu, S. (2015). Comparison between cloud computing, grid computing, cluster computing and virtualization. *International Journal of Modern Computer Science and Applications*, *3*(1), 42–47.

Kumar, V., & Kumar, R. (2015). An Optimal Authentication Protocol Using Certificateless ID-Based Signature in MANET. Security in Computing and Communications Volume 536 of the series. *Communications in Computer and Information Science*, *536*, 110–121. doi:10.1007/978-3-319-22915-7_11

Kurosawa, S., Nakayama, H., Kato, N., Jamalipour, A., & Nemoto, Y. (2007). Detecting blackhole attack on AODV-based mobile Ad Hoc networks by dynamic learning method. *International Journal of Network Security*, *5*(3), 338–346.

Kurzweil, R. (2005). *The Singularity is Near: When Humans Transcend Biology*. Viking Press.

Lakshmi, K., & Manju Priya, S., Jeevarathinam, A., Rama, K., & Thilagam, K. (2010). Modified AODV protocol against blackhole attacks in MANET. *IACSIT International Journal of Engineering and Technology*, *2*(6), 444–449.

Lampson, B. W. (1973, October). A Note on the Confinement Problem. *Communications of the ACM*, *16*(10), 613–615. doi:10.1145/362375.362389

Larence, E. A. (2007). Critical Infrastructure: Challenges Remain in Protecting Key Sectors: GAO-07-626T. *GAO Reports*, *1*.

Lauinger, T., Pankakoski, V., Balzarotti, D., & Kirda, E. (2010). *Honeybot, your man in the middle for automated social engineering.* Paper presented at the 3rd USENIX conference on Large-scale exploits and emergent threats: botnets, spyware, worms, and more (LEET'10), Berkeley, CA.

Lawrence, D. (2014). *The inside story of Tor, the best Internet anonymity tool the government ever built.* Bloomberg Businessweek.

Lee, H. (2014). *Automated performance attack discovery in distributed system implementations.* (Doctoral dissertation). Purdue University, West Lafayette, IN.

Lenka, S., & Nayak, B. (2014). Enhancing data security in cloud computing using RSA encryption and MD5 algorithm. *International Journal of Computer Science Trends and Technology, 2*(3), 60–64.

Leonhardt, D. (2008, September 28). Washington's invisible hand. *New York Times.* Retrieved from http://www.nytimes.com/2008/09/28/magazine/28wwln-reconsider.html?pagewanted=print&_r=1&

LessWrong. (2012). *Paperclip Maximiser.* Available at: http://wiki.lesswrong.com/wiki/Paperclip_maximizer

Levine, Y. (2014). Almost everyone involved in developing Tor was (or is) funded by the US government. *PandoDally.* Retrieved from: http://www.infowars.com/almost-everyone-involved-in-developing-tor-was-or-is-funded-by-the-us-government/

Lew, M., Corder, T., & Ruck, B. (2015). *Please fasten your seat belts: Managing digital risk to support aviation innovation.* Deloitte Development LLC.

Li, J. (2008). *A Survey of peer-to-peer network security issue.* Retrieved September 1, 2008, from http://www.cse.wustl.edu/~jain/cse571-07/ftp/p2p/index.html

Li, L., Wang, Z., Liu, W., & Wang, Y. (2011). A Certificateless Key Management Scheme in Mobile Ad Hoc Networks. *2011 7th International Conference on Wireless Communications, Networking and Mobile Computing.* http://doi.org/ doi:<ALIGNMENT.qj></ALIGNMENT>10.1109/wicom.2011.6040439

Li, W., & Joshi, A. (2008). *Security Issues in Mobile Ad Hoc Networks-A Survey.* http://doi.org/<ALIGNMENT.qj></ALIGNMENT>10.1007/978-3-642-36169-2_2

Lim, B. (2014). Emerging threats from cyber security in aviation – challenges and mitigation. *Journal of Aviation Management.*

Li, M., & Liu, Y. (2009). Underground coal mine monitoring with wireless sensor networks. *ACM Transactions on Sensor Networks, 5*(2), 10. doi:10.1145/1498915.1498916

Lin, M., Wu, Y., & Wassell, I. (2008). *Wireless sensor network: Water distribution monitoring system.* Paper presented at the Radio and Wireless Symposium. doi:10.1109/RWS.2008.4463607

Compilation of References

Lin, A., & Chen, N. C. (2012). Cloud computing as an innovation: Perception, attitude, and adoption. *International Journal of Information Management*, *32*(6), 533–540. doi:10.1016/j.ijinfomgt.2012.04.001

Lioudakis, G. V., Koutsoloukas, E. A., Dellas, N. L., Tselikas, N., Kapellaki, S., Prezerakos, G. N., & Venieris, I. S. et al. (2007). A middleware architecture for privacy protection. *Computer Networks*, *51*(16), 4679–4696. doi:10.1016/j.comnet.2007.06.010

Lipner, S. B. (1975, November). A Comment on the Confinement Problem. *5th Symposium on Operating Systems Principles, ACM. Operating Systems Review*, *9*(5), 192–196. doi:10.1145/1067629.806537

Liu, C. H., Yang, B., & Liu, T. (2014). Efficient naming, addressing and profile services in Internet-of-Things sensory environments. *Ad Hoc Networks*, *18*(0), 85–101. doi:10.1016/j.adhoc.2013.02.008

Li, W., & Vaughn, R. (2006). Cluster security research involving the modeling of network exploitations using exploitation graphs. In *Proceedings of the 6th IEEE International Symposium on Cluster Computing and the Grid Workshop* (pp. 26-36). doi:10.1109/CCGRID.2006.1630921

Lo, B., Thiemjarus, S., King, R., & Yang, G.-Z. (2005). *Body sensor network-a wireless sensor platform for pervasive healthcare monitoring.* Paper presented at the The 3rd International Conference on Pervasive Computing.

Lomas, N. (2009). *Online gizmos could top 50 billion in 2020.* Retrieved from http://www.businessweek.com/globalbiz/content/jun2009/gb20090629_492027.htm

Loving, W. A. (2007, December 12). *Sarbanes-Oxley and financial reporting: Statement of William A. Loving, Jr. Chief Executive Officer Pendleton Community Bank.* Committee on House Small Business.

Low, K. S., Win, W. N. N., & Er, M. J. (2005). *Wireless sensor networks for industrial environments.* Paper presented at the Computational Intelligence for Modelling, Control and Automation, 2005 and International Conference on Intelligent Agents, Web Technologies and Internet Commerce, International Conference on.

Lu, S., Li, L., Lam, K. Y., & Jia, L. (2009). SAODV: A MANET routing protocol that can withstand black hole attack. *CIS 2009 - 2009 International Conference on Computational Intelligence and Security*. http://doi.org/ doi:<ALIGNMENT.qj></ALIGNMENT>10.1109/CIS.2009.244

Luo, J., Fan, M., & Ye, D. (2008). Black hole attack prevention based on authentication mechanism. *2008 11th IEEE Singapore International Conference on Communication Systems, ICCS 2008,* (pp. 173–177). http://doi.org/ doi:<ALIGNMENT.qj></ALIGNMENT>10.1109/ICCS.2008.4737166

Lu, T., Guo, X., Li, Y., Peng, Y., Zhang, X., Xie, F., & Gao, Y. (2014). Cyber physical security for industrial control systems based on wireless sensor networks. *International Journal of Distributed Sensor Networks*.

MacSweeney, G. (2012). *10 Financial Services Cyber Security Trends for 2013*. Wall Street & Technology. Retrieved from, http://www.wallstreetandtech.com/data-security/10- financial-services-cyber-security-tre/240143809?pgno=1

Madsen, P. (Producer). (2013). *OpenID Connect and its role in Native SSO*. Retrieved from https://www.youtube.com/watch?v=mTZ0bcNphVg

Mahajan, , R., & Singh, D. (2013). Cloud computing issues. *International Journal of Computers and Technology*, *4*(2), 626–630.

Mahmoud, M., Pirovano, A., & Larrieu, N. (2014). Aeronautical communication transition from analog to digital data: A network security survey. *Computer Science Review*, *11*, 1–29. doi:10.1016/j.cosrev.2014.02.001

Malešević, S. (2013). *Future Identities: Changing identities in the UK–the next 10 years*. Academic Press.

Manyika, J., Chui, M., Bughin, J., Dobbs, R., Bisson, P., & Marrs, A. (2013). *Disruptive technologies: Advances that will transform life, business, and the global economy* (Vol. 180). San Francisco, CA: McKinsey Global Institute.

Marble, J., Lawless, W., Mittu, R., Coyne, J., Abramson, M., & Sibley, C. (2015). The Human Factor in Cybersecurity: Robust & Intelligent Defense. In Cyber Warfare (pp. 173-206). Springer International Publishing. doi:10.1007/978-3-319-14039-1_9

Marco, M. (2008, September 17). *Consumerist*. Retrieved from What Types Of Accounts Are FDIC Insured? Are My Investments Safe?: http://consumerist.com/2008/09/17/what-types-of-accounts-are-fdic-insured-are-my-investments-safe/

Marshall, D. (2011, November 2). *Top 10 benefits of server virtualization*. Retrieved from http://www.infoworld.com/article/2621446/server-virtualization/server-virtualization-top-10-benefits-of-server-virtualization.html

Mather, T., Kumaraswamy, S., & Latif, S. (2009). *Cloud security and privacy*. O'Reilly Media.

Mathew, S., & Jose, A. (2012). Securing cloud from attacks based on intrusion detection system. *International Journal of Advanced Research in Computer and Communication Engineering*, *1*(10), 753–759.

McAfee Inc. (2007). *Virtualization and Risk—Key Security Considerations for Your Enterprise Architecture*. McAfee Inc.

McDaniel, E. (2013, July). Securing the information and communications technology global supply chain from exploitation: Developing a strategy for education, training, and awareness. In *Proceedings of the Informing Science and Information Technology Education Conference*.

McKenney, B. (2014, July 1). *Securing the internet of things*. Retrieved from MITRE: http://www.mitre.org/capabilities/cybersecurity/overview/cybersecurity-blog/securing-the-internet-of-things

Compilation of References

Meghdadi, M., Ozdemir, S., & Güler, I. (2011). A survey of wormhole-based attacks and their countermeasures in wireless sensor networks. *IETE Technical Review*, *28*(2), 89–102. doi:10.4103/0256-4602.78089

Mehlman, M., Lin, P., & Abney, K. (2013). *Enhanced Warfighters: Risk, Ethics, and Policy.* Case Legal Studies Research Paper, (2013-2).

Mell, P., & Grance, T. (2011). The NIST definition of cloud computing (draft). *NIST Special Publication*, *800*, 145.

Menn, J. (2015, February 16). *Russian Researchers Expose Breakthrough US Spying Program.* Reuters.

Miorandi, D., Sicari, S., De Pellegrini, F., & Chlamtac, I. (2012). Internet of things: Vision, applications and research challenges. *Ad Hoc Networks*, *10*(7), 1497–1516. doi:10.1016/j.adhoc.2012.02.016

Mishra, N., Yadav, R., & Maheshwari, S. (2014). Security issues in grid computing. *International Journal on Computational Sciences and Applications*, *4*(1), 179–187. doi:10.5121/ijcsa.2014.4118

Mistry, N., Jinwala, D. C., & Zaveri, M. (2010). Improving AODV Protocol against Blackhole Attacks. *International Multiconference of Engineers and Computer Scientists (Imecs 2010).*

Mitrokotsa, A., Rieback, M. R., & Tanenbaum, A. S. (2010). Classifying RFID attacks and defenses. *Information Systems Frontiers*, *12*(5), 491–505. doi:10.1007/s10796-009-9210-z

Modi, C., Patel, D., Borisaniya, B., Patel, A., & Rajarajan, M. (2013). A survey on security issues and solutions at different layers of cloud computing. *The Journal of Supercomputing*, *63*(2), 561–592. doi:10.1007/s11227-012-0831-5

Mon, E. (2011). The privacy-aware access control system using attribute and role based access control in private cloud. In *Proceedings of the 4th IEEE International Conference on Broadband Network and Multimedia Technology (IC-BNMT)* (pp. 447–451). doi:10.1109/ICBNMT.2011.6155974

Moor, J. H. (2006, July/August). The Nature, Importance, and Difficulty of Machine Ethics. *IEEE Intelligent Systems*, *21*(4), 18–21. doi:10.1109/MIS.2006.80

Moskowitz, I. S., & Kang, M. H. (1994). *Covert Channels - Here to Stay?* Paper presented at the Ninth Annual Conference on Safety, Reliability, Fault Tolerance, Concurrency and Real Time, Security, Computer Assurance (COMPASS'94), Gaithersburg, MD.

Murray, A., & Grubesic, T. (2012). Critical infrastructure protection: The vulnerability conundrum. *Telematics and Informatics*, *29*(1), 56–65. doi:10.1016/j.tele.2011.05.001

Myers, C., Foster, S., & Williford, K. (2008). SOX relief for smaller banks. *U.S. Banker*, *118*(3), 64.

Myles, G., Friday, A., & Davies, N. (2003). Preserving privacy in environments with location-based applications. *Pervasive Computing, IEEE*, *2*(1), 56–64. doi:10.1109/MPRV.2003.1186726

Naber, J. D. (2008). Community bank audit's changing role. *Connecticut Banking, 2008*(1), 4-15.

Nadeem, A., & Howarth, M. P. (2013). A survey of manet intrusion detection & prevention approaches for network layer attacks. *IEEE Communications Surveys and Tutorials, 15*(4), 2027–2045. doi:10.1109/SURV.2013.030713.00201

Nafi, K., Kar, T., Hoque, S., & Hashem, M. (2012). A newer user authentication, file encryption and distributed server based cloud computing security architecture. *International Journal of Advanced Computer Science and Applications, 3*(10), 181–186.

Nakamoto, S. (2008). *Bitcoin: A peer-to-peer electronic cash system.* Retrieved from: https://bitcoin.org/bitcoin.pdf

National Cyber Security Centre. (2014). *Cyber Security Assessment Netherland (CSAN4).* Retrieved from https://www.google.co.jp/?gfe_rd=cr&ei=yJbIVZKNEcr98wfK4KioDg&gws_rd=ssl#q=how+to+cite+cyber+security+assessment+netherlands

Neisse, R., Steri, G., Baldini, G., Tragos, E., Fovino, I. N., & Botterman, M. (2014). *Dynamic Context-Aware Scalable and Trust-based IoT Security, Privacy Framework. Chapter in Internet of Things Applications-From Research and Innovation to Market Deployment.* IERC Cluster Book.

Nepal, S., Chen, S., Yao, J., & Thilakanathan, D. (2011). DIaaS: Data Integrity as a Service in the Cloud. In *2011 IEEE International Conference on Cloud Computing (CLOUD)* (pp. 308–315). http://doi.org/ doi:10.1109/CLOUD.2011.35

Neumann, J. V., & Morgenstern, O. (1944). *Theory of Games and Economic Behaivor.* MIT Press.

Nicholson, A., Webber, S., Dyer, S., Patel, T., & Janicke, H. (2012). SCADA security in the light of cyber-warfare. *Computers & Security, 31*(4), 418–436. doi:10.1016/j.cose.2012.02.009

Nielsen, S. C. (2012). Pursuing security in cyberspace: Strategic and organizational challenges. *Orbis, 56*(3), 336–356. doi:10.1016/j.orbis.2012.05.004

Nobles, C. (2015). *Exploring Pilots' Experiences of Integrating Technologically Advanced Aircraft Within General Aviation: A Case Study.* ProQuest. Retrieved from http://search.proquest.com/docview/1658234326

Norton, Q. (2007). *The Next Humans: Body Hacking and Human Enhancement.* O'Reilly Emerging Technology Conference.

Okezie, C. C., Chidiebele, U. C., & Kennedy, O. C. (2012). Cloud computing: A cost effective approach to enterprise web application implementation (A case for cloud ERP web model). *Academic Research International, 3*(1), 432–443.

Omar, M., & Dawson, M. (2013, April). Research in Progress-Defending Android Smartphones from Malware Attacks. In *Advanced Computing and Communication Technologies (ACCT), 2013 Third International Conference on* (pp. 288-292). IEEE. doi:10.1109/ACCT.2013.69

Compilation of References

Omohundro, S. M. (2008). *The Basic AI Drives*. Paper presented at the Proceedings of the First AGI Conference.

Online, C. S. O. (2012). *The security laws, regulations and guidelines directory*. Security Leadership. Retrieved from, http://www.csoonline.com/article/632218/the-security-laws-regulations-and-guidelines-directory

Onyegbula, F., Dawson, M., & Stevens, J. (2011). Understanding the need and importance of the cloud computing environment within the National Institute of Food and Agriculture, an agency of the United States Department of Agriculture. *Journal of Information Systems Technology & Planning, 4*(8), 17–42.

Ord, T., Hillerbrand, R., & Sandberg, A. (2010). Probing the improbable: Methodological challenges for risks with low probabilities and high stakes. *Journal of Risk Research, 13*(2), 191–205. doi:10.1080/13669870903126267

Oster, C. Jr, Strong, J., & Zorn, C. (2013). Analyzing aviation safety: Problems, challenges, opportunities. *Research in Transportation Economics, 43*(1), 148–164. doi:10.1016/j.retrec.2012.12.001

Out-Law.com. (2013). *Data security breaches mainly involve outsourced IT service providers, according to Trustwave report*. Retrieved from, http://www.out- law.com/en/articles/2013/february/data-security-breaches-mainly-involve-outsourced-it- service-providers-according-to-trustwave-report/

Paganini, P. (2014). New powers for the Russian surveillance system SORM-2. *Security Affairs*. Retrieved http://securityaffairs.co/wordpress/27611/digital-id/new-powers-sorm-2.html

Panda G., Shankar G. M. & Kumar A. S. (2012). *Prevention of Black hole Attack in AODVprotocols for Mobile Ad Hoc Network by Key Authentication*. Academic Press.

Paul, Selvi, & Ibrahim. (2011). A Novel Trust Management System for Cloud Computing - IaaS Providers. *Journal of Combinatorial Mathematics and Combinatorial Computing, 79*, 3-22.

Paulsen, C., McDuffie, E., Newhouse, W., & Toth, P. (2012). NICE: Creating a cybersecurity workforce and aware public. *IEEE Security and Privacy, 10*(3), 76–79. doi:10.1109/MSP.2012.73

Pearce, M., Zeadally, S., & Hunt, R. (2013, February). Virtualization: Issues, Security Threats, and Solutions. *ACM Computing Surveys, 45*(2), 39. doi:10.1145/2431211.2431216

Pearson, S. (2012). *Privacy, Security and Trust in Cloud Computing. HP Laboratories, HPL-2012-80R1*. Springer.

Perera, C., Zaslavsky, A., Christen, P., & Georgakopoulos, D. (2014). Context aware computing for the internet of things: A survey. *IEEE Communications Surveys and Tutorials, 16*(1), 414–454. doi:10.1109/SURV.2013.042313.00197

Perkins, C. E., Park, M., & Royer, E. M. (1999). Ad-hoc On-Demand Distance Vector Routing. In *Proceedings of Second IEEE Workshop on Mobile Computing Systems and Applications (WMCSA)*. http://doi.org/ doi:10.1109/MCSA.1999.749281

Pettersen, K., & Bjørnskau, T. (2015). Organizational contradictions between safety and security–Perceived challenges and ways of integrating critical infrastructure protection in civil aviation. *Safety Science*, *71*, 167–177. doi:10.1016/j.ssci.2014.04.018

Pohls, H. C., Angelakis, V., Suppan, S., Fischer, K., Oikonomou, G., Tragos, E. Z., . . . Mouroutis, T. (2014, April). RERUM: Building a reliable IoT upon privacy-and security-enabled smart objects. In Wireless Communications and Networking Conference Workshops (WCNCW), 2014 IEEE (pp. 122-127). IEEE.

Popper, S., Bankes, S., Callaway, R., & DeLaurentis, D. (2004). *System-of-Systems Symposium: Report on a Summer Conversation*. Arlington, VA: Potomac Institute for Policy Studies.

Pourqasem, J., Karimi, S., & Edalatpanah, S. (2014). Comparison of cloud and grid computing. *American Journal of Software Engineering*, *2*(1), 8–12.

Price, J. (2012). *Practical aviation security: predicting and preventing future threats*. Butterworth-Heinemann.

Provos, N., & Honeyman, P. (2003, May-June). Hide and Seek: An Introduction to Steganography. *IEEE Security and Privacy*, *1*(3), 32–44. doi:10.1109/MSECP.2003.1203220

Puttaswamy, K., Zheng, H., & Zhao, B. (2009). Securing structured overlays against identity attacks. *IEEE Transactions on Parallel and Distributed Systems*, *20*(10), 1487–1498. doi:10.1109/TPDS.2008.241

Rabai, L., Jouini, M., Aissa, A., & Mili, A. (2013). A cyber security model in cloud computing environments. *Journal of King Saud University - Computer and Information Sciences, 25*(1), 63-75.

Rahman, M., Ranjan, R., & Buyya, R. (2012). Decentralization in distributed systems: Challenges, technologies, and opportunities. In A. Pathan, M. Pathan, & H. Lee (Eds.), Advancements in Distributed Computing and Internet Technologies: Trends and Issues (pp. 386-399). Information Science Reference, IGI Global. doi:10.4018/978-1-61350-110-8.ch018

Raj, P. N., & Swadas, P. B. (2009). *DPRAODV: A Dynamic Learning System Against Blackhole Attack In AODV Based MANET*. Retrieved from http://cogprints.org/6697/

Ranadivé, V. (2013, February 19). *Hyperconnectivity: The Future is Now*. Retrieved March 21, 2016, from http://www.forbes.com/sites/vivekranadive/2013/02/19/hyperconnectivity-the-future-is-now/#401d45d26b9f

Ranganathan, A., Al-Muhtadi, J., Biehl, J., Ziebart, B., Campbell, R. H., & Bailey, B. (2005). *Towards a pervasive computing benchmark*. Paper presented at the Pervasive Computing and Communications Workshops, 2005. PerCom 2005 Workshops. Third IEEE International Conference on.

Rappaport, Z. H. (2006). Robotics and artificial intelligence: Jewish ethical perspectives. *Acta Neurochirurgica*, *98*, 9–12. PMID:17009695

Compilation of References

Reavis, D. (2012). Information evaporation: The migration of information to cloud computing platforms. *International Journal of Management & Information Systems (Online)*, *16*(4), 291.

Reed, M. G., Syverson, P. F., & Goldschlag, D. M. (1998). Anonymous connections and onion routing. *Selected Areas in Communications. IEEE Journal on*, *16*(4), 482–494.

Ren, K., Samarati, P., Gruteser, M., Ning, P., & Liu, Y. (2014). Guest Editorial Special Issue on Security for IoT: The State of the Art. *Internet of Things Journal, IEEE*, *1*(5), 369–371. doi:10.1109/JIOT.2014.2361608

Richardson, C. (n.d.). Critical Infrastructure Protection. *Alternative Energy CBRN Defense Critical Infrastructure Protection, 13*.

Rivard, S., & Lapointe, L. (2012). Information technology implementers' responses to user resistance: Nature and effects. *Management Information Systems Quarterly*, *36*(3), 897–920.

Roesener, A., Bottolfson, C., & Fernandez, G. (2014). Policy for US cybersecurity. *Air & Space Power Journal*, *29*(5), 38–54.

Roman, R., Najera, P., & Lopez, J. (2011). Securing the Internet of Things. *Computer*, *44*(9), 51–58. doi:10.1109/MC.2011.291

Rong, C., Nguyen, S., & Jaatun, M. (2013). Beyond lightning: A survey on security challenges in cloud computing. *Computers & Electrical Engineering*, *39*(1), 47–54. doi:10.1016/j.compeleceng.2012.04.015

Rotenberg, M. (2011). *President Electronic Privacy Information. Cybersecurity and Data Protection in the Financial Sector. FDCH*. Congressional Testimony.

Rouse, M. (2013, May). *Search Security*. Retrieved from Federal Information Security Management Act (FISMA): http://searchsecurity.techtarget.com/definition/Federal-Information-Security-Management-Act

Rowland, J., Rice, M., & Shenoi, S. (2014). Whither cyberpower? *International Journal of Critical Infrastructure Protection*, *7*(2), 124–137. doi:10.1016/j.ijcip.2014.04.001

Russell, B., (2014, May). Domestic violence survivors turn to Tor to escape abusers. *The Verge*.

Sadashiv, N., & Kumar, S. (2011). Cluster, grid and cloud computing: A detailed comparison. In *Proceedings of the 6th International Conference on Computer Science and Education (ICCSE 2011)*. doi:10.1109/ICCSE.2011.6028683

Saha, S., Chaki, R., & Chaki, N. (2008). A New Reactive Secure Routing Protocol for Mobile Ad-Hoc Networks. *2008 7th Computer Information Systems and Industrial Management Applications*, (pp. 103–108). http://doi.org/<ALIGNMENT.qj></ALIGNMENT>10.1109/CISIM.2008.13

Salim, A., Tiwari, R., & Tripathi, S. (2013). Addressing security challenges in cloud computing. *International Journal of Computer Engineering and Applications*, *2*(2), 1–13.

Sampigethaya, K., Poovendran, R., & Bushnell, L. (2008). Secure operation, control, and maintenance of future e-enabled airplanes. *Proceedings of the IEEE, 96*(12), 1992–2007. doi:10.1109/JPROC.2008.2006123

Sampigethaya, K., Poovendran, R., & Bushnell, L. (2009). A framework for securing future e-enabled aircraft navigation and surveillance. In *AIAA Proceedings* (pp. 1-10). doi:10.2514/6.2009-1820

Sampigethaya, K., Poovendran, R., Shetty, S., Davis, T., & Royalty, C. (2011). Future e-enabled aircraft communications and security: The next 20 years and beyond. *Proceedings of the IEEE, 99*(11), 2040–2055. doi:10.1109/JPROC.2011.2162209

Sandberg, A. (2001). *Friendly Superintelligence*. Available at: http://www.nada.kth.se/~asa/Extro5/Friendly%20Superintelligence.htm

Satyanarayanan, M. (2001). Pervasive computing: Vision and challenges. *Personal Communications, IEEE, 8*(4), 10–17. doi:10.1109/98.943998

Saucer, C. (2009, October 23). Impact of Gramm-Leach-Bliley still debated 10 years later. *BusinessWire*. Retrieved from http://www.reuters.com/article/2009/10/23/idUS205297+23-Oct-2009+BW20091023

Scarborough, M. (2007). Casey-Landry testifies on Sarbanes-Oxley. *Community Banker, 16*(7), 18.

Schelling, T. (1960). *The Strategy of Conflict*. Harvard University Press.

Science, H. y. D. o. C., Eliassen, F., & Veijalainen, J. (1988). *A functional approach to information system interoperability*. Academic Press.

Sehgal, A., Perelman, V., Kuryla, S., & Schonwalder, J. (2012). Management of resource constrained devices in the internet of things. *Communications Magazine, IEEE, 50*(12), 144–149. doi:10.1109/MCOM.2012.6384464

Selamat, Z., & Jaffar, N. (2011). IT acceptance: From perspective of Malaysian bankers. *International Journal of Business and Management, 6*(1), 207–217.

Selvaraja, C., & Anandb, S. (2012). A survey on security issues of reputation management systems for peer-to-peer networks. *Computer Science Review, 6*(6), 145–160. doi:10.1016/j.cosrev.2012.04.001

Semantic interoperability of health information. (2011). Retrieved from http://www.en13606.org/the-ceniso-en13606-standard/semantic-interoperability

Shackelford, S., Proia, A., Martell, B., & Craig, A. (2015). Toward a global cyber security standard of care? Exploring the implications of the 2014 NIST cybersecurity framework on shaping reasonable national and international cybersecurity practices. *Texas International Law Journal*.

Shackelford, S., & Bohm, Z. (2015). *Securing North American critical infrastructure: A comparative case study in cybersecurity regulation. Canada-US Law Journal*.

Shamir, A. (1985). *Identity-Based Cryptosystems and Signature Schemes*. Academic Press.

Compilation of References

Shamir, A. (1979). How to share a secret. *Communications of the ACM, 22*(11), 612–613. doi:10.1145/359168.359176

Shen, L. (2014). The NIST cybersecurity framework: Overview and potential impacts. *Journal of Internet Law, 18*(6), 3–6.

Shulman, C. (2010). *Omohundro's "Basic AI Drives" and Catostrophic Risks.* Available at: singinst.org/upload/ai-resource-drives.pdf.

Siani, P. (2011). Toward accountability in the cloud. *IEEE Internet Computing*, (15): 64–69.

Sicari, S., Rizzardi, A., Grieco, L. A., & Coen-Porisini, A. (2015). Security, privacy and trust in Internet of Things: The road ahead. *Computer Networks, 76*, 146–164. doi:10.1016/j.comnet.2014.11.008

Singh, P. K., & Sharma, G. (2012). An efficient prevention of black hole problem in AODV routing protocol in MANET. *Proc. of the 11th IEEE Int. Conference on Trust, Security and Privacy in Computing and Communications, TrustCom-2012 - 11th IEEE Int. Conference on Ubiquitous Computing and Communications, IUCC-2012*, (pp. 902–906). http://doi.org/ doi:10.1109/ TrustCom.2012.78

Singh, A., Korupolu, M., & Mohapatra, D. (2008). *Server-Storage Virtualization: Integration and Load Balancing in Data Centers.* Austin, TX: IEEE.

Smith, A. (2014). U.S. Spy Scandal Triggers Outrage, Paranoia in Germany. NBC News. August 2, 2014. "Tails report for May, 2014". *Tails.* Retrieved from: https://tails.boum.org/news/ report_2014_05/index.en.html

Snow, G. (2011). *Statement before the House Financial Services Committee Subcommittee on Financial Institutions and Consumer Credit.* Assistant Director, Cyber Division Federal Bureau of Investigation. Retrieved from, http://www.fbi.gov/news/testimony/cyber-security-threats-to-the-financial-sector

Solnik, C. (2012, May 25). Feds let private banks broaden investor base. *Long Island Business Review.*

Srinivasa, K., & Muppalla, A. (2015). *Guide to high performance distributed computing: case studies with hadoop.* Scalding and Spark, Springer International Publishing. doi:10.1007/978-3-319-13497-0

Srinivasan, M. (2012). Building a secure enterprise model for cloud computing environment. *Academy of Information and Management Sciences Journal, 15*(1), 127–133.

Srinivas, V. B., & Umar, S. (2013). Spoofing attacks in wireless sensor networks. International journal of Computer Science. *Engineering and Technology, 3*(6), 201–210.

Stallings, W. (2014). *Cryptography and Network Security: Principles and Practice.* Pearson Education Inc.

Steen, M., Pierre, G., & Voulgaris, S. (2012). Challenges in very large distributed systems. *Journal of Internet Services and Applications*, (3), 59-66.

Steinberg, J. (2014, January 27). *These devices may be spying on you (even in your own home)*. Retrieved from Forbes: http://www.forbes.com/sites/josephsteinberg/2014/01/27/these-devices-may-be-spying-on-you-even-in-your-own-home/#4cc6ef63769e

Stevens, G. (2012). *Data Security Breach Notification Laws*. Congressional Research Service. Retrieved from, http://www.fas.org/sgp/crs/misc/R42475.pdf

Stuhlmuller, R. (2013, December 18). *4 ways network virtualization improves security*. Retrieved from http://www.infoworld.com/article/2609571/networking/4-ways-network-virtualization-improves-security.html

Stults, G. (2004). An overview of Sarbanes-Oxley for the information security professional. *SANS Infosec Reading Room*. Retrieved from http://www.sans.org/reading_room/whitepapers/legal/overview-sarbanes-oxley-information-security-professional_1426

Subashini, S., & Kavitha, V. (2011). A survey on security issues in service delivery models of cloud computing. *Journal of Network and Computer Applications*, *34*(1), 1–11. doi:10.1016/j.jnca.2010.07.006

Sullivan, B., Tabet, S., Bonver, E., Furlong, J., Orrin, S., & Uhley, P. (2013). Practices for Secure Development of Cloud Applications. SAFECode & Cloud Security Alliance.

Sultan, N. (2010). Cloud computing for education: A new dawn? *International Journal of Information Management*, *30*(2), 109–116. doi:10.1016/j.ijinfomgt.2009.09.004

Summers, G. (2004). Data and databases. In *Developing Databases with Access*. Nelson Australia Pty Limited.

Sun, Y., Zhang, J., Xiong, Y., & Zhu, G. (2014). Data security and privacy in cloud computing. *International Journal of Distributed Sensor Networks*, (7): 1–9.

Suo, H., Wan, J., Zou, C., & Liu, J. (2012, March). Security in the internet of things: a review. In *Computer Science and Electronics Engineering (ICCSEE), 2012 International Conference on* (Vol. 3, pp. 648-651). IEEE. doi:10.1109/ICCSEE.2012.373

Suresh, S., & Kannan, M. (2014). A study on system virtualization techniques. *International Journal of Advanced Research in Computer Science and Technology, 2*(1), 134-139.

Surie, D., Laguionie, O., & Pederson, T. (2008). *Wireless sensor networking of everyday objects in a smart home environment*. Paper presented at the Intelligent Sensors, Sensor Networks and Information Processing, 2008. ISSNIP 2008. International Conference on. doi:10.1109/ISSNIP.2008.4761985

Sutton, R., & Barto, A. (1998). *Reinforcement Learning: An Introduction*. Cambridge, MA: MIT Press.

Compilation of References

Tabansky, L. (2011). Critical infrastructure protection against cyber threats. *Military and Strategic Affairs*, *3*(2), 2.

Tamilselvan, L., & Sankaranarayanan, V. (2008). Prevention of co-operative black hole attack in MANET. *Journal of Networks*, *3*(5), 13–20. doi:10.4304/jnw.3.5.13-20

Tan, Y., Ko, R., & Holmes, G. (2013). Security and data accountability in distributed systems: A provenance survey. In *2013 IEEE 10th International Conference on High Performance Computing and Communications & 2013 IEEE International Conference on Embedded and Ubiquitous Computing (HPCC_EUC)* (pp. 1571-1578). doi:10.1109/HPCC.and.EUC.2013.221

Tanenbaum, A., & Steen, M. (2007). *Distributed systems: Principles and Paradigms* (2nd ed.). Pearson Higher Education Inc. Press.

Ten, C. W., Liu, C. C., & Manimaran, G. (2008). Vulnerability assessment of cybersecurity for SCADA systems. Power Systems. *IEEE Transactions on Power Systems*, *23*(4), 1836–1846. doi:10.1109/TPWRS.2008.2002298

Tešić, J. (2005). Metadata practices for consumer photos. *MultiMedia, IEEE*, *12*(3), 86–92. doi:10.1109/MMUL.2005.50

Teslik, L. H. (2008). *The U.S. Financial Regulatory System*. Council on Foreign Relations. Retrieved from, http://www.cfr.org/economic-development/us-financial-regulatory- system/p17417

Thalod, S., & Niwas, R. (2013). Security model for computer network based on cluster computing. *International Journal of Engineering and Computer Science*, *2*(6), 1920–1927.

The Guardian. (2013). *Tor: The king of high-secure, low-latency anonymity*. Tor Project.

The Internet of Things. (2005). Retrieved from http://www.itu.int/osg/spu/publications/internetofthings/

The Roadmap to Secure Control Systems in the Transportation Sector Working Group. (2012). *The Roadmap to Secure Control Systems in the Transportation Sector*. Retrieved from https://ics-cert.us-cert.gov/sites/default/files/ICSJWG-Archive/TransportationRoadmap20120831.pdf

Thierer, A. D. (2015). The internet of things and wearable technology: Addressing privacy and security concerns without derailing innovation. *Adam Thierer, The Internet of Things and Wearable Technology: Addressing Privacy and Security Concerns without Derailing Innovation, 21.*

Thurm, S., & Kane, Y. I. (2010). *Your Apps Are Watching You*. Retrieved from http://online.wsj.com/article/SB10001424052748704368004576027751867039730.html

Tomáš, S., Ivan, K., & Stanislav, S. (2012). Present and potential security threats posed to civil aviation. *Incas Bulletin*, *4*(2), 169–175. doi:10.13111/2066-8201.2012.4.2.17

Tonkens, R. (2009). A Challenge for Machine Ethics. *Minds and Machines*, *19*(3), 421–438. doi:10.1007/s11023-009-9159-1

Tseng, F.-H., Chou, L.-D., & Chao, H.-C. (2011a). A survey of black hole attacks in wireless mobile ad hoc networks. *Human-Centric Computing and Information Sciences*, *1*(1), 4. doi:10.1186/2192-1962-1-4

U.S. Department of Energy (USDOE). (2007). *21 Steps to Improve Cyber Security of SCADA Networks*. Washington, DC: U.S. Department of Energy.

U.S. Department of Transportation. (2014). *Federal Aviation Administration*. Washington, DC: The Economic Impact of Civil Aviation on the U.S. Economy.

U.S. Federal Trade Commission. (2002a). *How to comply with the privacy of consumer financial information rule of the Gramm-Leach-Bliley Act*. Retrieved from http://business.ftc.gov/documents/bus67-how-comply-privacy-consumer-financial-information-rule-gramm-leach-bliley-act

U.S. Federal Trade Commission. (2002b). *Federal Trade Commission*. Retrieved from Federal Trade Commission: http://www.ftc.gov/os/2002/05/67fr36585.pdf

U.S. Federal Trade Commission. (2013). *Privacy*. Retrieved from Gramm-Leach-Bliley Act: http://www.ftc.gov/privacy/glbact/glbsub1.htm

U.S. Government Accountability Office. (2012, April). *Cybersecurity. Threats impact the nation*. (Publication No. GAO-12-666T). Retrieved from GAO Reports Main Page via GPO Access database: http://www.gpoaccess.gov/gaoreports/index.html

U.S. Government Accountability Office. (2015, April). *Air traffic control: FAA needs a more comprehensive approach to address cyber security as agency transitions to NextGen*. (Publication No. GAO-15-370). Retrieved from GAO Reports Main Page via GPO Access database: http://www.gpoaccess.gov/gaoreports/index.html

U.S. Securities and Exchange Commission. (2011). *CF Disclosure Guidance: Topic No. 2, Cybersecurity*. Retrieved from http://www.sec.gov/divisions/corpfin/guidance/cfguidance-topic2.htm

Ularu, E. G., Puican, F. C., Suciu, G., Vulpe, A., & Todoran, G. (2013). Mobile computing and cloud maturity Introducing machine learning for ERP configuration automation. *Informatica Economica*, *17*(1), 40–52. doi:10.12948/issn14531305/17.1.2013.04

Ullah, I., & Rehman, S. (2010). *Analysis of Black Hole attack on MANETs Using different MANET routing protocols*. School of Computing Blekinge Institute of Technology; doi:10.1109/ICUFN.2012.6261716

van der Veer, H., & Wiles, A. (2008). *Achieving technical interoperability*. European Telecommunications Standards Institute.

Vassar, M. (2005). *AI Boxing (dogs and helicopters)*. Paper presented at the SL4.org, Available at: http://sl4.org/archive/0508/11817.html

Veeraraghavan, P., & Limaye, V. (2007). Security Threats in Mobile Ad Hoc Networks. *2007 IEEE International Conference on Telecommunications and Malaysia International Conference on Communications*. Retrieved from http://eprints.whiterose.ac.uk/46064/

Compilation of References

Vinge, V. (March 30-31, 1993). *The Coming Technological Singularity: How to Survive in the Post-human Era*. Paper presented at the Vision 21: Interdisciplinary Science and Engineering in the Era of Cyberspace, Cleveland, OH.

Virtue, T. (2009). U.S. legal and regulatory security issues. In S. Bosworth, M. E. Kabay, & E. Whyne (Eds.), *Computer security handbook* (5th ed.). New York, NY: John Wiley & Sons.

Vitti, P., & Santos, D. (2014). Current issues in cloud computing security and management. In *Proceedings of the JARIA Conference* (pp. 36-42).

VMware Product Guide. (2015). Retrieved March, 2015, from www.vmware.com/files/pdf/vmware-productguide

VMware, Inc. (n.d.). *VMware ThinApp Agentless Application Virtualization Overview* (White Paper No. VMW-WP-THINAPP-APPVIRT-USLET-20120525-WEB). Retrieved from www.vmware.com

VMware. (2007). *VMware Understanding Full Virtualization, Paravirtualization, and Hardware Assist* (White Paper No. WP-028-PRD-01-01). VMware, Inc.

Von Solms, R., & Van Niekerk, J. (2013). From information security to cyber security. *Computers & Security*, *38*, 97–102. doi:10.1016/j.cose.2013.04.004

Vouk, M. A. (2008). Cloud computing-Issues, research and implementations. *Journal of Computing and Information Technology, 4*, 235-246. doi: 10.2498/cit.1001391

Wagner, A., & Arkin, R. C. (2009). *Robot Deception: Recognizing when a Robot Should Deceive*. Paper presented at the IEEE International Symposium on Computational Intelligence in Robotics and Automation (CIRA-09), Daejeon, Korea. doi:10.1109/CIRA.2009.5423160

Wagner, A. R., Arkin, R. C., & Deception, A. D. P. R. C. (2011). Acting Deceptively: Providing Robots with the Capacity for Deception. *International Journal of Social Robotics*, *3*(1), 5–26. doi:10.1007/s12369-010-0073-8

Wang, W. Y. C., Rashid, A., & Chuang, H. (2011). Toward the trend of cloud computing. *Journal of Electronic Commerce Research*, *12*(4), 238–242.

Ward, M. (2015). Warning after security experts hack Tesla car. *BBC News*. Retrieved from: http://www.bbc.com/news/technology-33802344

Watts, J. (2009, June 8). China orders PC makers to install blocking software. *The Guardian*.

Weber, R. H. (2010). Internet of Things-New security and privacy challenges. *Computer Law & Security Report*, *26*(1), 23–30. doi:10.1016/j.clsr.2009.11.008

Weise, E. (2015). IRS Hacked, 100,000 Tax Accounts Breached. *USA Today*. Retrieved from: http://www.usatoday.com/story/tech/2015/05/26/irs-breach-100000-accounts-get-transcript/27980049/

Weissman, C. G. (2015, January 21). *We asked executives about the internet of things and their answers reveal that security remains a huge concern.* Retrieved from Business Insider: http://www.businessinsider.in/We-Asked-Executives-About-The-Internet-Of-Things-And-Their-Answers-Reveal-That-Security-Remains-A-Huge-Concern/articleshow/45959921.cms

Welsh, M., & Mainland, G. (2004). *Programming Sensor Networks Using Abstract Regions.* Paper presented at the NSDI.

Wikipedia. (n.d.). *Interoperability.* Retrieved from https://en.wikipedia.org/wiki/Interoperability

Wittenburg-georg, G. (2003). *A defense against replay attacks on chaumian mixes.* (Bachelor thesis). Retrieved from Google Scholar: http://page.mi.fu-berlin.de/gwitten/papers/wittenburg-03defense.pdf

Wolf, M., Minzlaff, M., & Moser, M. (2014). IT security threats to modern e-enabled aircraft-a cautionary note. *Journal of Aerospace Information Systems, 11*(7), 447–457. doi:10.2514/1.I010156

Wolfram, S. (2002). *A New Kind of Science*: Wolfram Media, Inc.

Wood, A. D., & Stankovic, J. (2002). Denial of service in sensor networks. *Computer, 35*(10), 54–62. doi:10.1109/MC.2002.1039518

Wu, H., Ding, Y., Winer, C., & Yao, L. (2010). Network security for virtual machine in cloud computing. In *Proceedings of the 2010 5th IEEE International Conference on Computer Sciences and Convergence Information Technology (ICCIT)* (pp.18-21). IEEE Computer Society.

Wu, B., Chen, J., Wu, J., & Cardei, M. (2007). A Survey on Attacks and Countermeasures in Mobile Ad hoc Networks. *Wireless/Mobile. Network Security,* 103–135. doi:10.1007/978-0-387-33112-6_5

Xia, F., Yang, L. T., Wang, L., & Vinel, A. (2012). Internet of things. *International Journal of Communication Systems, 25*(9), 1101–1102. doi:10.1002/dac.2417

Xiao, Z., Kathiresshan, N., & Xiao, Y. (2012). A survey of accountability in computer networks and distributed systems. *Security and Communication Network, 9*(4), 290–315. doi:10.1002/sec.574

Xiao, Z., & Xiao, Y. (2013). Security and privacy in cloud computing. *IEEE Communications Surveys and Tutorials, 15*(2), 843–859. doi:10.1109/SURV.2012.060912.00182

Xie, T., & Qin, X. (2008). Security-aware resource allocation for real-time parallel jobs on homogeneous and heterogeneous clusters. *IEEE Transactions on Parallel and Distributed Systems, 19*(5), 682–697. doi:10.1109/TPDS.2007.70776

Xu, X. (2012). From cloud computing to cloud manufacturing. *Robotics and Computer-integrated Manufacturing, 28*(1), 75–86. doi:10.1016/j.rcim.2011.07.002

Yampolskiy, R. V. (2007). *Behavioral Biometrics for Verification and Recognition of AI Programs.* Paper presented at the 20th Annual Computer Science and Engineering Graduate Conference (GradConf2007), Buffalo, NY.

Compilation of References

Yampolskiy, R. V. (2011). AI-Complete CAPTCHAs as Zero Knowledge Proofs of Access to an Artificially Intelligent System. *ISRN Artificial Intelligence, 271878.*

Yampolskiy, R. V. (2011a). *Artificial Intelligence Safety Engineering: Why Machine Ethics is a Wrong Approach.* Paper presented at the Philosophy and Theory of Artificial Intelligence (PT-AI2011), Thessaloniki, Greece.

Yampolskiy, R. V. (2011b). *What to Do with the Singularity Paradox?* Paper presented at the Philosophy and Theory of Artificial Intelligence (PT-AI2011), Thessaloniki, Greece.

Yampolskiy, R. V. (2012). *AI-Complete, AI-Hard, or AI-Easy – Classification of Problems in AI.* Paper presented at the The 23rd Midwest Artificial Intelligence and Cognitive Science Conference, Cincinnati, OH.

Yampolskiy, R. V. (2013). Turing Test as a Defining Feature of AI-Completeness. In Artificial Intelligence, Evolutionary Computation and Metaheuristics - In the footsteps of Alan Turing (pp. 3-17). Springer.

Yampolskiy, R. V. (2015). *Analysis of Types of Self-Improving Software.* Paper presented at the The Eighth Conference on Artificial General Intelligence, Berlin, Germany

Yampolskiy, R. V., & Govindaraju, V. (2007). *Behavioral Biometrics for Recognition and Verification of Game Bots.* Paper presented at the The 8th annual European Game-On Conference on simulation and AI in Computer Games (GAMEON'2007), Bologna, Italy.

Yampolskiy, R. V., & Govindaraju, V. (2008). *Behavioral Biometrics for Verification and Recognition of Malicious Software Agents.* Paper presented at the Sensors, and Command, Control, Communications, and Intelligence (C3I) Technologies for Homeland Security and Homeland Defense VII. SPIE Defense and Security Symposium, Orlando, FL. doi:10.1117/12.773554

Yampolskiy, R. V. (2012a). Leakproofing Singularity - Artificial Intelligence Confinement Problem. *Journal of Consciousness Studies, 19*(1-2), 194–214.

Yampolskiy, R. V. (2012b). Turing Test as a Defining Feature of AI-Completeness. In X.-S. Yang (Ed.), *Artificial Intelligence, Evolutionary Computation and Metaheuristics (AIECM) --In the footsteps of Alan Turing (Turing 2012).* Springer.

Yampolskiy, R. V. (2015). *Artificial Superintelligence: A Futuristic Approach.* Chapman and Hall/CRC.

Yampolskiy, R. V. (2015). *The Space of Possible Mind Designs. In Artificial General Intelligence* (pp. 218–227). Springer. doi:10.1007/978-3-319-21365-1_23

Yampolskiy, R. V., & Fox, J. (2012a). Artificial Intelligence and the Human Mental Model. In A. Eden, J. Moor, J. Soraker, & E. Steinhart (Eds.), *In the Singularity Hypothesis: a Scientific and Philosophical Assessment.* Springer. doi:10.1007/978-3-642-32560-1_7

Yampolskiy, R. V., & Fox, J. (2012b). *Safety Engineering for Artificial General Intelligence.* Topoi. Special Issue on Machine Ethics & the Ethics of Building Intelligent Machines.

Yampolskiy, R. V., & Govindaraju, V. (2007). Computer Security: A Survey of Methods and Systems. *Journal of Computer Science*, *3*(7), 478–486. doi:10.3844/jcssp.2007.478.486

Yang, L., Yu, P., Bailing, W., Yun, Q., Xuefeng, B., & Xinling, Y. (2013). Hash-based RFID mutual authentication protocol. *International Journal of Security & Its Applications*, *7*(3), 183–194.

Yan, Z., Zhang, P., & Vasilakos, A. V. (2014). A survey on trust management for Internet of Things. *Journal of Network and Computer Applications*, *42*, 120–134. doi:10.1016/j.jnca.2014.01.014

Yao, T. (2005). *Adaptive firewalls for the grid*. (Master dissertation). Technical University of Denmark, Denmark.

Yu, A. (2012). Regulatory financial reform: Impact of Dodd-Frank Act on IT compliance. *Rutgers Computer & Technology Law Journal*, *38*(2), 254–276. Retrieved from http://ehis.ebscohost.com.ezproxy.umuc.edu

Yudkowsky, E. S. (2001a). *Creating Friendly AI - The Analysis and Design of Benevolent Goal Architectures*. Available at: http://singinst.org/upload/CFAI.html

Yudkowsky, E. S. (2001b). *General Intelligence and Seed AI - Creating Complete Minds Capable of Open-Ended Self-Improvement*. Available at: http://singinst.org/ourresearch/publications/GISAI/

Yudkowsky, E. S. (2002). *The AI-Box Experiment*. Available at: http://yudkowsky.net/singularity/aibox

Yudkowsky, E. (2008). Artificial Intelligence as a Positive and Negative Factor in Global Risk. In N. Bostrom & M. M. Cirkovic (Eds.), *Global Catastrophic Risks* (pp. 308–345). Oxford, UK: Oxford University Press.

Zapata, M. G. (2002). Secure ad hoc on-demand distance vector routing. *Mobile Computing and Communications Review*, *6*(3), 106. doi:10.1145/581291.581312

Zargar, S., & Tipper, D. (2013). A Survey of defense mechanisms against Distributed Denial of Service (DDoS) flooding attacks. *IEEE Communications Surveys and Tutorials*, *15*(4), 2046–2069. doi:10.1109/SURV.2013.031413.00127

Zeadally & Yu. (2013). Trust Management of Services in Cloud Environments: Obstacles and Solutions. ACM Computing Surveys, 46(1), Article 12.

Zhai, Z., Qiao, Y., & Shao, M. (2012). Analysis on grid security patterns based on PKI. *Advances in Information Sciences and Service Sciences*, *4*(23), 239–248.

Zhang, X., Sekiya, Y., & Wakahara, Y. (2009). Proposal of a method to detect black hole attack in MANET. *2009 International Symposium on Autonomous Decentralized Systems, ISADS 2009*, (pp. 149–154). http://doi.org/ doi:10.1109/ISADS.2009.5207339

Zhang, Z. K., Cho, M. C. Y., & Shieh, S. (2015, April). Emerging Security Threats and Countermeasures in IoT. In *Proceedings of the 10th ACM Symposium on Information, Computer and Communications Security*, (pp. 1-6). ACM. doi:10.1145/2714576.2737091

Compilation of References

Zhao, G., Rong, C., Jaatun, M. G., & Sandnes, F. E. (2012). Reference deployment models for eliminating user concerns on cloud security. *The Journal of Supercomputing, 61*(2), 337–352. doi:10.1007/s11227-010-0460-9

Zhao, L., Sakr, S., Liu, A., & Bouguettaya, A. (2014). *Cloud data management.* Springer International Publishing. doi:10.1007/978-3-319-04765-2

Zhongqiu, J., Shu, Y., & Liangmin, W. (2009). Survivability evaluation of cluster-based wireless sensor network under DoS attacks. In *Proceedings of the 5th International Conference on Wireless Communications, Networking and Mobile Computing, (WiCom '09)* (pp. 1-4).

Zissis, D., & Lekkas, D. (2012). Addressing cloud computing security issues. *Future Generation Computer Systems, 28*(3), 583–592. doi:10.1016/j.future.2010.12.006

Zureich, D., & Graebe, W. (2015). Cybersecurity: The continuing evolution of insurance and ethics. *Defense Counsel Journal, 82*(2), 192.

About the Contributors

Maurice Dawson serves as an Assistant Professor of Information Systems at University of Missouri-St. Louis, former Visiting Assistant Professor (Honorary) of Industrial and Systems Engineering at The University of Tennessee Space Institute, and Fulbright Scholar: Specialist in the Faculty of Computational Mathematics & Informatics at South Ural State University in Chelyabinsk, Russia. Dawson is recognized as an Information Assurance System Architect and Engineer by the U.S. Department of Defense. Research focus area is cyber security, systems security engineering, open source software (OSS), mobile security, and engineering management.

Mohamed Eltayeb is a dependable, conscientious, and enthusiastic engineer who possesses a wealth of comprehensive experience working with complex technologies from the early stages of design through to post-implementation adaptation. His research specializes in the areas of cloud computing, The Internet of Things, cyber security, enterprise information management, software quality assurance, and mobile computing. His research efforts to date have specifically focused on examining the user acceptance of new technologies, and he has conducted detailed and comprehensive analysis of user acceptance in the domain of cloud computing. Dr. Eltayeb is also actively associated with a number of professional organizations, including the Association for Computing Machinery (ACM), CTU Alumni Association, and the International Association of Engineers (IAENG).

Marwan Omar serves an Assistant Professor of Computer Science at the department of computer science and CIS. Prior to joining Academia, Omar worked for Hewlett-Packard as a database developer where he helped build, design, and implement MS SQL database for their software and hardware products in the server industry. Omar is recognized for his information security expertise and knowledge and holds a security + certification from Comptia. Research interests are: cyber security, mobile security, open source software, and cloud computing.

* * *

Stuart Armstrong, Alexander Tamas Fellow in Artificial Intelligence and Machine Learning Stuart Armstrong's research at the Future of Humanity Institute centres on formal decision theory, general existential risk, the risks and possibilities of Artificial Intelligence (AI), assessing expertise and predictions, and anthropic (self-locating) probability. He has been working on several methods of analysing the likelihood of certain outcomes and in making decisions under the resulting uncertainty, as well as specific measures for reducing AI risk. His booklet "Smarter than Us: the rise of machine intelligence" lays out some the challenges in this area, and why it's an important focus. He is also interested in collaborations for these research interests, which he currently doesn't have time to develop on his own. His Oxford D.Phil was in parabolic geometry, calculating the holonomy of projective and conformal Cartan geometries. He later transitioned into computational biochemistry, designing several new ways to rapidly compare putative bioactive molecules for virtual screening of medicinal compounds.

J. Antonio Cárdenas-Haro received his Ph.D. in Computer Science from the Arizona State University (ASU), his Master's in Computer Science was granted by the Ensenada Center for Scientific Research and Higher Education (CICESE), and also he holds a B.S. in Electronic engineering from the Technological Institute of Los Mochis (ITLM). His research interests include parallel and distributed computing, algorithms, network security, cyber security, bioinformatics and applied mathematics. He is currently working as a full time assistant professor at the department of Mathematics and Computer Science of the University of Missouri-St. Louis (UMSL).

Hon Cheung graduated from The University of Western Australia in 1984 with First Class Honours in Electrical Engineering. He received his PhD degree from the same university in 1988. He was a lecturer in the Department of Electronic Engineering, Hong Kong Polytechnic from 1988 to 1990. From 1990 to 1999, he was a lecturer in Computer Engineering at Edith Cowan University, Western Australia. He has been a senior lecturer in Computing at Western Sydney University since 2000. Dr Cheung has research experience in a number of areas, including conventional methods in artificial intelligence, fuzzy sets, artificial neural networks, digital signal processing, image processing, network security and forensics, and communications and networking. In the area of teaching, Dr Cheung has experience in development and delivery of a relative large number of subjects in computer science, electrical and electronic engineering, computer engineering and networking.

Ghada F. El Kabbany is an Associate Professor at Electronics Research Institute, Cairo-Egypt. She received her B. Sc. degree, M. Sc. degree and Ph. D. degree in Electronics and Communications Engineering from Faculty of Engineering, Cairo University, Egypt in 1990, 1994 and 2007 respectively. Her research interests include: High Performance Computing (HPC), computer network security, and image processing.

Mahmoud Elkhodr is with the School of Computing, Engineering and Mathematics at Western Sydney University (Western), Australia. He has been awarded the International Postgraduate Research Scholarship (IPRS) and Australian Postgraduate Award (APA) in 2012-2015. Mahmoud has been awarded the High Achieving Graduate Award in 2011 as well. His research interests include: Internet of Things, e-health, Human Computer-Interactions, Security and Privacy.

Eric Kuada received his PhD degree in Information Technology in 2014 from Aalborg University, Denmark. He received his MSc. degree in Network Services and Systems in 2009 from the Royal Institute of Technology, Sweden. He also received a BSc. degree in Electrical and Electronic Engineering in 2003. He has worked as a lecturer in several universities in Ghana and Denmark. He is currently a lecturer with School of Technology at the Ghana Institute of Management and Public Administration.

Rakesh Kumar is an Associate Professor in the Department of Computer Science Engineering at MMM University of Technology, Gorakhpur (U.P), India. He received his B. Tech Degree in 1990 from MMM Engineering College, Gorakhpur and M.E from SGS Institute of Technology and Science, Indore in 1994. He did his Ph.D. from Indian Institute of Technology, Roorkee, India in 2011. Before joining MMM Engineering College, he worked in HBTI Kanpur and BIET Jhansi. Currently, he is a principal investigator of a major research project sanctioned from University Grant Commission, New Delhi, India. Dr. Kumar has supervised a large number of M. Tech Dissertations and guiding several Ph.D. students. He has published a large number of various research papers in international and national journals and conferences of high repute. He is a life member of CSI, ISTE and also a Fellow of IETE and I.E (India). His main interests lie in mobile ad hoc network, MANET- Internet integration, Sensor network, Network Security, QoS Provisioning and performance evaluation.

Vimal Kumar is a research scholar in the Department of Computer Science Engineering at Madan Mohan Malaviya University of Technology, Gorakhpur (U.P), India. He obtained his B.Tech degree in 2007 from Uttar Pradesh Technicial University, Lucknow. He received his M.Tech degree in Information Security from Motilal Nehru National Institute of Technology, Allahabad. His research interests lie in Mobile Ad hoc Network, Network Security and Network Forensics.

Derek Mohammed is an associate professor who teaches undergraduate and graduate courses in Cybersecurity at Saint Leo University in Florida. Prior to joining academia, he worked extensively in both the public and private sectors to improve the security of their critical information systems. His research focuses on IT Auditing, Security Compliance, and Network Security.

Van Nguyen is an assistant professor of Computer Science at Saint Leo University, Florida. He obtained his Ph.D. from the Center for Advanced Computer Studies at the University of Louisiana at Lafayette, where he participated in a multi-million dollar project (UCoMS) funded by the Department of Energy. His research areas are in computer wireless networks, performance evaluation, protocol design, and data mining. He also specializes in computer security and computer management. His vision of a future computer world is that there would be one massive computer consisting of all the computing devices in the world to collaboratively solve any problem presented to it.

Calvin Nobles is from Mount Vernon, GA and is currently serving in the United States Navy. Dr. Nobles earned a B.S. in Management, a Masters in Aeronautical Science, a Masters in Military Operational Art and Strategy, a Masters of Business Administration, and Ph.D. in Business Administration. Dr. Nobles' professional works consist of leadership, directing, and project management in aviation, cryptology, operations, and military planning areas of expertise. He is a commercial rated pilot and general aviation enthusiast. Dr. Nobles is committed to improving general aviation safety; hence, the reason for this book. His research focus areas are: technology implementation, technological discontinuities, disruptive innovations, and the adverse implications cause by the continuous integration of new technologies into general aviation. Dr. Nobles is a Life Member of the Omega Psi Phi Fraternity Incorporated.

Mohamed Rasslan is an Assistant Professor at Electronics Research Institute, Cairo, Egypt. He received the B.Sc., M.Sc., degrees from Cairo University and Ain Shams University, Cairo, Egypt, in 1999 and 2006 respectively, and his his Ph.D. from Concordia University, Canada 2010. His research interests include: Cryptology, Digital Forensics, and Networks Security.

Seyed Shahrestani completed his PhD degree in Electrical and Information Engineering at the University of Sydney. He joined Western Sydney University (Western) in 1999, where he is currently a Senior Lecturer. He is also the head of the Networking, Security and Cloud Research (NSCR) group at Western. His main teaching and research interests include: computer networking, IoT, wireless networking, management and security of networked systems, analysis, control and management of complex systems, artificial intelligence applications, and ehealth. He is also highly active in higher degree research (PhD) training supervision.

Roman V. Yampolskiy is a Tenured Associate Professor in the department of Computer Engineering and Computer Science at the Speed School of Engineering, University of Louisville. He is the founding and current director of the Cyber Security Lab and an author of many books including Artificial Superintelligence: a Futuristic Approach. During his tenure at UofL, Dr. Yampolskiy has been recognized as: Distinguished Teaching Professor, Professor of the Year, Faculty Favorite, Top 4 Faculty, Leader in Engineering Education, Top 10 of Online College Professor of the Year, and Outstanding Early Career in Education award winner among many other honors and distinctions. Yampolskiy is a Senior member of IEEE and AGI; Member of Kentucky Academy of Science, and Research Advisor for MIRI and Associate of GCRI. Roman Yampolskiy holds a PhD degree from the Department of Computer Science and Engineering at the University at Buffalo. He was a recipient of a four year NSF (National Science Foundation) IGERT (Integrative Graduate Education and Research Traineeship) fellowship. Before beginning his doctoral studies Dr. Yampolskiy received a BS/MS (High Honors) combined degree in Computer Science from Rochester Institute of Technology, NY, USA. After completing his PhD dissertation Dr. Yampolskiy held a position of an Affiliate Academic at the Center for Advanced Spatial Analysis, University of London, College of London. He had previously conducted research at the Laboratory for Applied Computing (currently known as Center for Advancing the Study of Infrastructure) at the Rochester Institute of Technology and at the Center for Unified Biometrics and Sensors at the University at Buffalo. Dr. Yampolskiy is an alumnus of Singularity University (GSP2012) and a Visiting Fellow of the Singularity Institute (Machine Intelligence Research Institute). Dr. Yampolskiy's main areas of interest are AI Safety, Artificial Intelligence, Behavioral Biometrics, Cybersecurity, Digital Forensics, Games, Genetic Algorithms, and Pattern Recognition. Dr. Yampolskiy is an author of over 100 publications including multiple journal articles and books. His research has been cited by 1000+ scientists and profiled in popular magazines both American and foreign (New Scientist, Poker Magazine, Science World Magazine), dozens of websites (BBC, MSNBC, Yahoo! News), on radio (German National Radio, Swedish National Radio, Alex Jones Show) and TV. Dr. Yampolskiy's research has been featured 250+ times in numerous media reports in 22 languages.

Index

Become an IRMA Member

Members of the **Information Resources Management Association (IRMA)** understand the importance of community within their field of study. The Information Resources Management Association is an ideal venue through which professionals, students, and academicians can convene and share the latest industry innovations and scholarly research that is changing the field of information science and technology. Become a member today and enjoy the benefits of membership as well as the opportunity to collaborate and network with fellow experts in the field.

IRMA Membership Benefits:

- **One FREE Journal Subscription**

- **30% Off Additional Journal Subscriptions**

- **20% Off Book Purchases**

- Updates on the latest events and research on Information Resources Management through the IRMA-L listserv.

- Updates on new open access and downloadable content added to Research IRM.

- A copy of the Information Technology Management Newsletter twice a year.

- A certificate of membership.

IRMA Membership $195

Scan code to visit irma-international.org and begin by selecting your free journal subscription.

Membership is good for one full year.